HOLLYWOOD
SCREENWRITING
DIRECTORY

FALL/WINTER • VOLUME 3

D1572884

BURBANK, CALIFORNIA

Printed and bound in the United States of America.

Published by F+W Media, Inc.
3510 West Magnolia Boulevard
Burbank, California 91505
www.fwmedia.com

Disclaimer

Every reasonable effort has been made to ensure the accuracy of the information contained in the Hollywood Screenwriting Directory. F+W Media, Inc. cannot be held responsible for any inaccuracies, or the misrepresentation of those listed in the Hollywood Screenwriting Directory.

Updates/Change Listing

Please submit corrections and updates to corrections@screenwritingdirectory.com

Print ISBN 13: 978-1-59963-777-8
Print ISBN 10: 1-59963-777-4
ePub ISBN 13: 978-1-59963-783-9
ePub ISBN 10: 1-59963-783-9
PDF ISBN 13: 978-1-59963-780-8
PDF ISBN 10: 1-59963-780-4

Contents

How to Use the Hollywood Screenwriting Directory

Dear Fellow Screenwriter,

Congratulations! You've made an investment in your screenwriting career that's sure to reap significant benefits. And that's because what you have in your hands is the resource everyone's talking about: *The Hollywood Screenwriting Directory* is the must-have reference guide that takes the mystery out of the script submission process, and literally puts the contact information of the Industry's top players right at your fingertips. Many of our loyal readers have secured representation and found script-selling success using it. And now, it's your turn.

This Fall/Winter edition brings you current contact information for more than 2,500 Industry insiders, along with updates on hundreds of our listings. Plus, *The Hollywood Screenwriting Directory* is now available online! Visit ScreenwritingDirectory.com. Updates and additions are made daily. **Enter code HSDV3P for a free 90-day subscription**.

The HSD is a very specialized directory created by The Writers Store based on our extensive experience serving the screenwriting community since 1982. It contains a range of people to contact regarding your script, from ambitious upstarts to established studio execs, along with management companies who package production deals and independent financiers/ distributors with a production wing. For each listing, you'll find the kind of useable information you need: Street and email addresses, whether or not they accept unsolicited material, and how they prefer to receive submissions.

While having access to this data is crucial, just as essential is an understanding of the right way to use it. These insiders are flooded with submissions daily. Any indication of incorrect format or other amateur flubs in the first few pages will quickly send your script to the trash.

We can't emphasize enough how important it is that your submission is polished and professional before you send it out for consideration. Screenwriting software makes producing an Industry-standard screenplay simple and straightforward. Programs like Final Draft and Movie Magic Screenwriter put your words into proper format as you type, letting you focus on a well-told story rather than the chore of margins and spacing. In these pages, we've also included a guide to proper screenplay format, along with sample title and first pages to help you send out a professional script.

Besides a properly packaged submission, it's also wise to know your audience before you send out any materials. If your script is an action thriller with a strong female lead, don't send it to Philip Seymour Hoffman's production company. Actors establish their own companies so that they're not reliant on studios for roles. Pad an actor's vanity (and his pipeline) by submitting materials catered specifically to him.

You may find that a good number of companies do not want unsolicited submissions. It's not that they're not open to new ideas; they're not open to liability. A script is property, and with it, come ramifications if not handled properly. If you choose to disregard "no unsolicited submissions," sending your script with a submission release form gives it a better chance of getting read. Consult with an entertainment attorney to draft an appropriate form, or consult a guide like *Clearance and Copyright* by Michael C. Donaldson, which has submission release form templates. It's also prudent to protect your work. We recommend registering your script with the WGA (Writers Guild of America, West) or the ProtectRite registration service.

A benefit of the digital age is that the same companies that are not open to receiving unsolicited submissions will gladly accept a query letter by email. Take advantage of this opportunity. Craft a well-written and dynamic query letter email that sells you and your script. We have included a sample query, and some tips and guidelines on how to write great query letters.

While Hollywood is a creative town it is, above all, professional. Do a service to yourself and the potential buyer by being courteous. If you choose to follow up by phone, don't be demanding and frustrated. These people are overworked and do not owe you anything. It's okay to follow up, but be sure to do so with respect. And if you pique a buyer's interest and she asks for a treatment, you must be ready to send off this vital selling tool at once! That's why we've also included a handy guide to writing treatments in this volume.

While it may oftentimes feel like the opposite, The Entertainment Industry *is* looking for new writers and fresh material. BUT (and this is important) they're also looking for those aspiring scribes to take the time to workshop their scripts with an experienced professional and get them to a marketable level. The Writers Store can help you get ready for the big leagues through our slate of screenwriting courses, personalized coaching and Development Notes service, which works in a format that mirrors the same process occurring in the studio ranks.

Hollywood is the pinnacle of competition and ambition. But that's not to say that dreams can't happen—they can, and they do. By keeping to these professional guidelines and working on your craft daily, you can find the kind of screenwriting success you seek.

Wishing you the best of luck,

Jesse Douma
Editor

What is a Screenplay?

In the most basic terms, a screenplay is a 90-120 page document written in Courier 12pt font on 8 ½" x 11" bright white three-hole punched paper. Wondering why Courier font is used? It's a timing issue. One formatted script page in Courier font equals roughly one minute of screen time. That's why the average page count of a screenplay should come in between 90 and 120 pages. Comedies tend to be on the shorter side (90 pages, or 1 ½ hours) while Dramas run longer (120 pages, or 2 hours).

A screenplay can be an original piece, or based on a true story or previously written piece, like a novel, stage play or newspaper article. At its heart, a screenplay is a blueprint for the film it will one day become. Professionals on the set including the producer, director, set designer and actors all translate the screenwriter's vision using their individual talents. Since the creation of a film is ultimately a collaborative art, the screenwriter must be aware of each person's role and as such, the script should reflect the writer's knowledge.

For example, it's crucial to remember that film is primarily a visual medium. As a screenwriter, you must show what's happening in a story, rather than tell. A 2-page inner monologue may work well for a novel, but is the kiss of death in a script. The very nature of screenwriting is based on how to show a story on a screen, and pivotal moments can be conveyed through something as simple as a look on an actor's face. Let's take a look at what a screenplay's structure looks like.

The First Page of a Screenplay

Screenwriting software makes producing an Industry-standard script simple and straightforward. While screenplay formatting software such as Final Draft, Movie Magic Screenwriter, Movie Outline, Montage and Scriptly for the iPad frees you from having to learn the nitty-gritty of margins and indents, it's good to have a grasp of the general spacing standards.

The top, bottom and right margins of a screenplay are 1". The left margin is 1.5". The extra half-inch of white space to the left of a script page allows for binding with brads, yet still imparts a feeling of vertical balance of the text on the page. The entire document should be single-spaced.

Screenplay Elements

Following is a list of items that make up the screenplay format, along with indenting information. Again, screenplay software will automatically format all these elements, but a screenwriter must have a working knowledge of the definitions to know when to use each one.

Ⓐ Fade In

The very first item on the first page should be the words FADE IN:.

Ⓑ Page Numbers

The first page is never numbered. Subsequent page numbers appear in the upper right hand corner, 0.5" from the top of the page, flush right to the margin.

Ⓒ Mores and Continueds

Use mores and continueds between pages to indicate the same character is still speaking.

Ⓓ Scene Heading

Indent: Left: 0.0" Right: 0.0" Width: 6.0"

A scene heading is a one-line description of the location and time of day of a scene, also known as a "slugline." It should always be in CAPS. Example: EXT. WRITERS STORE - DAY reveals that the action takes place outside The Writers Store during the daytime.

Ⓔ Subheader

Indent: Left: 0.0" Right: 0.0" Width: 6.0"

When a new scene heading is not necessary, but some distinction needs to be made in the action, you can use a subheader. But be sure to use these sparingly, as a script full of subheaders is generally frowned upon. A good example is when there are a series of quick cuts between two locations, you would use the term INTERCUT and the scene locations.

Ⓕ Action

Indent: Left: 0.0" Right: 0.0" Width: 6.0"

The narrative description of the events of a scene, written in the present tense. Also less commonly known as direction, visual exposition, blackstuff, description or scene direction. Remember—only things that can be seen and heard should be included in the action.

Sample Screenplay Page

(A) FADE IN:

(D) EXT. WRITERS STORE - DAY

(F) In the heart of West Los Angeles, a boutique shop's large OPEN sign glows like a beacon.

(M) DISSOLVE TO:

INT. WRITERS STORE - SALES FLOOR - DAY

Writers browse the many scripts in the screenplay section.

(G) ANTHONY, Canadian-Italian Story Specialist extraordinaire, 30s and not getting any younger, ambles over.

(H) ANTHONY
(I) Hey, how's everyone doin' here?

A WRITING ENTHUSIAST, 45, reads the first page of "The Aviator" by John Logan.

                    ENTHUSIAST
          Can John Logan write a killer first
          page or what?

                    ANTHONY
          You, sir, are a gentleman of
          refined taste. John Logan is my
          non-Canadian idol.

The phone RINGS. Anthony goes to--

(E) THE SALES COUNTER

And answers the phone.

                    ANTHONY (CONT'D)
          Writers Store, Anthony speaking.

                    VOICE
(J)   (over phone)
          Do you have Chinatown in stock?

I/E LUXURIOUS MALIBU MANSION - DAY

A FIGURE roams his estate, cell phone pressed to his ear.

                    ANTHONY (O.S.)
          'Course we have Chinatown!
          Robert Towne's masterpeice is
          arguably the Great American
          Screenplay...
                    (MORE) **(C)**

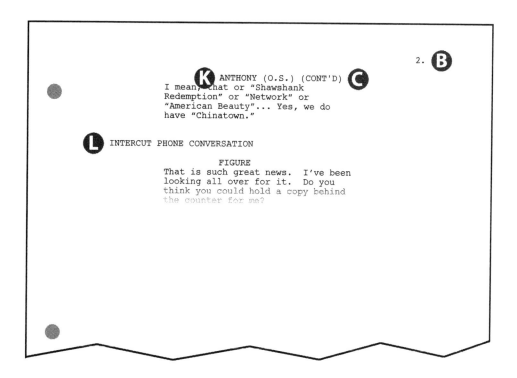

Character

Indent: Left: 2.0" Right: 0.0" Width: 4.0"

When a character is introduced, his name should be capitalized within the action. For example: The door opens and in walks LIAM, a thirty-something hipster with attitude to spare.

A character's name is CAPPED and always listed above his lines of dialogue. Minor characters may be listed without names, for example TAXI DRIVER or CUSTOMER.

Dialogue

Indent: Left: 1.0" Right: 1.5" Width: 3.5"

Lines of speech for each character. Dialogue format is used anytime a character is heard speaking, even for off-screen and voice-overs.

Parenthetical

Indent: Left: 1.5" Right: 2.0" Width: 2.5"

A parenthetical is direction for the character, that is either attitude or action-oriented. Parentheticals are used very rarely, and only if absolutely necessary. Why? First, if you need to use a parenthetical to convey what's going on with your dialogue, then it probably needs a good re-write. Second, it's the director's job to instruct an actor, and everyone knows not to encroach on the director's turf!

Ⓚ Extension

Placed after the character's name, in parentheses

An abbreviated technical note placed after the character's name to indicate how the voice will be heard onscreen, for example, if the character is speaking as a voice-over, it would appear as `LIAM (V.O.)`.

Ⓛ Intercut

Intercuts are instructions for a series of quick cuts between two scene locations.

Ⓜ Transition

Indent: Left: 4.0" Right: 0.0" Width: 2.0"

Transitions are film editing instructions, and generally only appear in a shooting script. Transition verbiage includes:

```
CUT TO:
DISSOLVE TO:
SMASH CUT:
QUICK CUT:
FADE TO:
```

As a spec script writer, you should avoid using a transition unless there is no other way to indicate a story element. For example, you might need to use `DISSOLVE TO:` to indicate that a large amount of time has passed.

Shot

Indent: Left: 0.0" Right: 0.0" Width: 6.0"

A shot tells the reader the focal point within a scene has changed. Like a transition, there's rarely a time when a spec screenwriter should insert shot directions. Examples of Shots:

```
ANGLE ON --
EXTREME CLOSE UP --
LIAM'S POV --
```

Spec Script vs. Shooting Script

A "spec script" literally means that you are writing a screenplay on speculation. That is, no one is paying you to write the script. You are penning it in hopes of selling the script to a buyer. Spec scripts should stick stringently to established screenwriting rules. Once a script is purchased, it becomes a shooting script, also called a production script. This is a version of the screenplay created for film production. It will include technical instructions, like film editing notes, shots, cuts and the like. All the scenes are numbered, and revisions are marked with a color-coded system. This is done so that the production assistants and director can then arrange the order in which the scenes will be shot for the most efficient use of stage, cast, and location resources.

A spec script should never contain the elements of shooting script. The biggest mistake any new screenwriter can make is to submit a script full of production language, including camera angles and editing transitions.

It can be very difficult to resist putting this type of language in your script. After all, it's your story and you see it in a very specific way. However, facts are facts. If you want to direct your script, then try to go the independent filmmaker route. But if you want to sell your script, then stick to the accepted spec screenplay format.

Script Presentaction and Binding

Just like the format of a script, there are very specific rules for binding and presenting your script. The first page is the title page, which should also be written in Courier 12pt font. No graphics, no fancy pictures, only the title of your script, with "written by" and your name in the center of the page. In the lower left-hand or right-hand corner, enter your contact information.

In the lower left-hand or right-hand corner you can put Registered, WGA or a copyright notification, though this is generally not a requirement.

Sample Screenplay Title Page

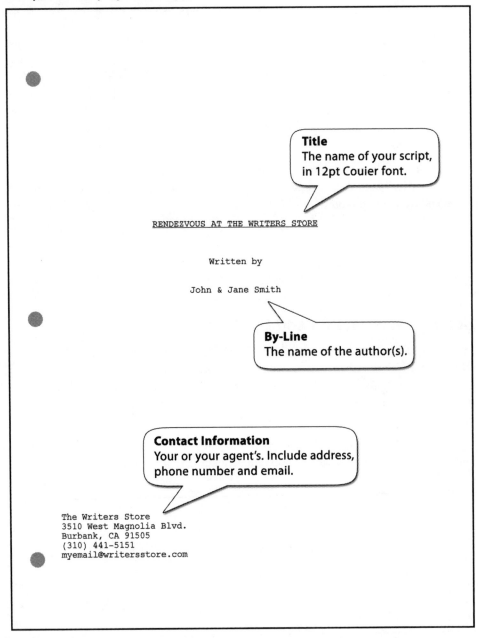

Title
The name of your script, in 12pt Couier font.

RENDEZVOUS AT THE WRITERS STORE

Written by

John & Jane Smith

By-Line
The name of the author(s).

Contact Information
Your or your agent's. Include address, phone number and email.

The Writers Store
3510 West Magnolia Blvd.
Burbank, CA 91505
(310) 441-5151
myemail@writersstore.com

Query Letters

A query is a one-page, single-spaced letter that quickly tells who you are, what the work is, and why the work is appropriate for the market in question. Just as queries are used as the first means of contact for pitching magazine articles and novels, they work just the same for scripts.

A well-written query is broken down into three parts.

Part I: Your Reason for Contacting/Script Details

Before even looking at the few sentences describing your story, a producer wants to see two other things:

1. **What is it?** State the title, genre, and whether it's a full-length script or a shorter one.
2. **Why are you contacting this market/person in particular?** There are thousands of individuals who receive scripts. Why have you chosen this person to review the material? Is it because you met them in person and they requested to see your work? Have they represented writers similar to yourself? Did you read that they were actively looking for zombie comedies? Spelling out your reason upfront shows that you've done your research, and that you're a professional.

Part II: The Elevator Pitch

If you wrote the first paragraph correctly, you've got their attention, so pitch away. Explain what your story is in about 3-6 sentences. The point here is to intrigue and pique only. Don't get into nitty-gritty details of any kind. Hesitate using a whole lot of character names or backstory. Don't say how it ends or who dies during the climax or that the hero's father betrays him in Act II. Introduce us to the main character and his situation, then get to the key part of the pitch: the conflict.

Try to include tidbits here and there that make your story unique. If it's about a cop nearing retirement, that's nothing new. But if the story is about a retiring cop considering a sex change operation in his bid to completely start over, while the police union is threatening to take away his pension should he do this, then you've got something different that readers may want to see.

Sample Query Letter

(A) **John. Q. Writer**
123 Main St.
Writerville, USA
(212) 555-1234
johnqwriter@email.com

Agent
JQA & Associates
678 Hollywood St.
Hollywood, CA 90210

(B) Dear Mr./Ms (Last Name):

(C) My name is John Q. Writer and we crossed paths at the Screenwriters World Conference in Los Angeles in October 2012. After hearing the pitch for my feature-length thriller, October Surprise, you requested that I submit a query, synopsis and the first 10 pages of the script. All requested materials are enclosed. This is an exclusive submission, as you requested.

(D) U.S. Senator Michael Hargrove is breaking ranks with his own political party to endorse another candidate for President of the United States. At the National Convention, he's treated like a rock star V.I.P. -- that is, until, he's abducted by a fringe political group and given a grim ultimatum: Use your speech on live TV to sabotage and derail the presidential campaign you're now supporting, or your family back home will not live though the night.

(E) The script was co-written with my scriptwriting partner, Joe Aloysius. I am a produced playwright and award-winning journalist. Thank you for considering October Surprise. I will be happy to sign any release forms that you request. May I send the rest of the screenplay?

Best,
John Q. Writer

Part III: The Wrap Up

Your pitch is complete. The last paragraph is where you get to talk about yourself and your accomplishments. If the script has won any awards or been a finalist in a prominent competition, this is the place to say so. Mention your writing credentials and experience. Obviously, any paid screenwriting experience is most valuable, but feel free to include other tidbits such as if you're a magazine freelancer or a published novelist.

Sometimes, there won't be much to say at the end of a query letter because the writer has no credits, no contacts and nothing to brag about. As your mother would tell you: If you don't have anything nice to say, don't say anything at all. Keep the last section brief if you must, rather than going on and on about being an "active blogger" or having one poem published in your college literary magazine.

Following some information about yourself, it's time to wrap up the query and propose sending more material. A simple way to do this is by saying "The script is complete. May I send you the treatment and full screenplay?"

Here are the elements of a query letter in the example on the facing page:

A Include all of your contact information—including phone and e-mail—as centered information at the top.

B Use proper greetings and last names.

C Include a reason for contacting the reader.

D Try and keep the pitch to one paragraph.

E Regarding your credentials, be concise and honest.

Treatments and Log Lines

Introduction to the Treatment

Nobody reads a full script in Hollywood anymore. Execs don't want to put in the time to read a 90-page comedy script, much less a 180-page epic. They want to know if the goods are there before they invest their precious time, and this is where the treatment comes in. Think of it as reading the back cover of a book before you invest in buying it. You'd never just pay for a book without knowing what type of story to expect. So it is with the movie industry. The treatment is the essential selling tool that can make or break your script.

What is a Treatment

A treatment is a short document written in prose form and in the present tense that emphasizes, with vivid description, the major elements of a screenplay.

That's a very broad definition, to be sure. And while the main purpose of a treatment is as a selling tool, there are variations of the definition to consider.

1. A treatment could be your first attempt toward selling your screenplay to a producer, your first try at getting someone to pay you to write the script.
2. A treatment could be a sales tool for a script that you've already written—a shorter, prose version of the screenplay's story for producers to read, to pique their interest in your project and entice them to read your screenplay.
3. A treatment could describe how you intend to attack a rewrite, either of your own script or of another writer's script. Often when a producer hires a writer to do a rewrite, they'll ask for a treatment first.
4. A treatment could be the first step toward writing your screenplay—it could be one of the first steps toward getting your story down on paper. Maybe you don't have time to write the screenplay yet—a treatment can help cement the story in your mind (and on paper) so that you can work on it later.

Why Write a Treatment?

Ultimately, the best reason to write a treatment is that the process of writing your treatment can help you write a better script. It can be easier to find and solve structural challenges, plot incongruities, lapses in logic, etc. in the prose treatment format than it is to find and solve those challenges in the screenplay format.

Writing a screenplay is a step-by-step process, and some steps are more involved than others. Writing a treatment is a very achievable step in the screenwriting process, and taking that step from beginning to end can be a rewarding boost for your writing ego.

Writing a treatment helps give tangible shape to your story, and makes sharing your story with others simpler and more precise. If you can share your story with others, you can get feedback, which may open up more channels in your brain and help your story to grow. The treatment format is much easier to read and comprehend for people who aren't familiar with the screenplay format.

You might not be ready to write your complete screenplay yet—you might not have time, you might not be fully committed to the idea. Writing a treatment is a good stopgap measure, so that an idea doesn't just exist as an idea—it may exist as something you can sell, share with a collaborator, or simply file away for a rainy day.

When is a Treatment Used

A treatment is usually used when you begin the process of selling your script. When you pitch your script to a producer and he shows interest in your script, he will most likely ask you to send over the treatment. This way, he can review the story and see if he is interested in reading the full script.

Think of the treatment as your business card—the thing you leave behind after you've pitched your story.

You may have heard of writers who sell a script based only a treatment. Yes, this happens, but this happens only for established writers with a track record of produced scripts. They have proven to Hollywood that they can write a blockbuster script, so buyers know that if they like the treatment, they will most likely love the script.

The treatment can also be used as an outline for the writer before he begins his script. It's smart to either outline or summarize a script before you begin writing. If you can complete the story in a smaller form, you know that you'll be able to sustain it in the longer script format. Architects don't erect a building without first designing a blueprint and then creating a model of the structure. The outline is your blueprint and the treatment is your model.

Treatment vs. Synopsis, Coverage, Beat Sheet and Outline

The term treatment is thrown around loosely in Hollywood, and you can be sure that you'll hear a different definition each time you ask. Some buyers will request a treatment when they really want a synopsis, an outline or a beat sheet. So what are the definitions of the other items?

Synopsis

A Synopsis is a brief description of a story's plot or a straightforward presentation of the scenes and events in a story. It is not a selling tool, but rather a summation of the story, and is typically no more than 2 pages long. It's generally used by professional script readers when writing coverage on a script.

Coverage

Coverage is the name of the document generated by the buyer's in house script readers. The main purpose of this document is to assess the commercial viability of the script. The reader supplies the buyer with the basic identifying information of the script, a synopsis, their comments on the script and a rating chart on all of the elements of the script, including characters, dialogue, action, setting, and commercial appeal. The reader then rates the script "pass" (no, thanks. Don't call us, cause we're certainly not gonna call you) "consider" (maybe someone we know can rewrite this puppy into something marketable) or "recommend" (this is the script that will move me from script reader hell to producing heaven!).

Beat Sheet

A Beat Sheet lists the sequence of major events that takes place in a script. It shows what will happen to the main character, and the order in which the events will occur. It can be anywhere from a short paragraph to three pages. Each beat is described in only 1-2 sentences.

Here is an extremely short example from "Die Hard."

1. New York Detective John McClane flies to Los Angeles to reconcile with his wife Holly at her company Christmas party.
2. When he arrives at Holly's high-rise office building, they argue and Holly leaves McClane alone in her executive bathroom.
3. From the bathroom, McClane hears terrorists, lead by Hans Gruber, break in and take over the building.
4. McClane witnesses the murder of Takagi, the CEO of the company, by Gruber and decides to take action.
5. McClane kills the brother of the lead henchman, Karl, and many other terrorists. He greatly angers Hans and Karl in the process.
6. McClane battles the terrorists with the help of a lone police officer.
7. The other police are against McClane and he feels alone in his fight. The police approach fails, so McClane is totally alone.
8. McClane fights Karl, kills him and prepares to go save Holly from Gruber.
9. Seemingly outnumbered, McClane appears to give up.
10. Using his New York wits, McClane kills Gruber and saves Holly.

Outline

An outline is a list of the scenes that make up a screenplay, from FADE IN to FADE OUT. Every writer has a different method of outlining—some are very detailed, while some list only a sentence or even just a word for each scene.

A good way to start a screenplay is to write a beat sheet, an outline and then a treatment. If you work out the story problems with these three tools, you will find that writing the actual script is a breeze.

Why Do I Need a Treatment

Besides being an important selling tool, a treatment allows you to see if your idea can sustain a feature-length film. Many writers take an idea straight to screenplay form, and then find 30 pages in that there is not enough story to continue the script. In this short summary form, you will also be able to identify any weaknesses in your plot, theme and characters.

It is much easier to find and solve these challenges in the prose treatment form than it is to locate them in the screenplay format.

How Long Should It Be?

Sadly, there is no cut and dry length for a treatment. Generally, treatments vary in length from 1-25 pages.

A general rule—the more power the executive holds, the shorter the treatment you should send them. It is recommended to have a few different versions of your treatment. Besides a lengthy summary of the story, have a quick one pager on hand.

What Is the Format?

Your treatment should be written in prose form, and in 12 point Courier font. In essence, the treatment looks like a short story. There should be one line of space between each paragraph, and no indenting.

DON'T insert dialogue, slug lines, or anything else in screenplay format.

DO use standard punctuation for dialogue.

However, be careful not to rely on much dialogue in your treatment in order to effectively tell the story in 10 pages or less. A few carefully chosen thematic lines will suffice. For instance, the treatment for "Forrest Gump" would likely use the line, "Life is like a box of chocolates. You never know what you're gonna get," because it is used throughout the script as a thematic tag line.

What Should I Aspire to Do with the Treatment?

The treatment should not look, sound or read like an outline, a beat sheet or a screenplay. The essence of the story and the characters should be evoked through exhilarating language and imagery. It should sound like an excited moviegoer recanting the details of a film he just saw that was thought provoking, exhilarating and made him feel like he just had to share all the details with his friends. The prose you use in a treatment should be different than the narrative lines of a screenplay.

The beginning of the treatment has to grab the reader and not let go until the very end. Your reader should be able to see the script play out on the silver screen in front of his or her very eyes. After reading the treatment, the reader should be on fire to get this script to her boss, pronto!

The Log Line

A Log Line is a one sentence description of your film. It's really that simple. You've seen log lines, even if you're not aware of it. In essence, TV Guide descriptions of films are log lines. A log line may describe the following elements:

- Genre—comedy, drama, thriller, love story, etc.
- Setting—time and place, locale, other pertinent information
- Plot—the main narrative thrust of the story
- Character—the lead character or group of characters
- Theme—the main subject of the movie

A log line need not contain the following elements:

- Character names (unless the characters are historical figures)
- Back story
- Qualitative judgments—"A hilarious story..." "A fascinating tale..."
- Comparisons to other films—"It's 'Jaws' meets 'Mary Poppins'..."

Here are a few examples of log lines for well-known films. See if you can guess the film being described (the answers are right below, so don't cheat!):

1. A throwback to the serial adventure films of the 1930s, this film is the story of a heroic archeologist who races against the Nazis to find a powerful artifact that can change the course of history.
2. Set at a small American college in the early 1960s, this broad comedy follows a fraternity full of misfits through a year of parties, mishaps and food fights.
3. An illiterate boy looks to become a contestant on the Hindi version of "Who Wants to be A Millionaire" in order to re-establish contact with the girl he loves, who is an ardent fan of the show.

4. A man decides to change his life by saying 'yes' to everything that comes his way. On his journey, he wins $45,000, meets a hypnotic dog, obtains a nursing degree, travels the globe, and finds romance.

5. A behind-the-scenes view of the 2000 presidential election and the scandal that ensued in the weeks following.

Get the idea? The log line is designed to describe and to tease, like a line of advertising copy for your film. It has to be accurate, it can't be misleading. It's the first sentence a producer or executive is going to read, and you've got to make sure it isn't the last. Make it count.

By the way, the log lines above are for:

1. "Raiders of the Lost Ark"
2. "Animal House"
3. "Slumdog Millionaire"
4. "Yes Man"
5. "Recount"

Why Is the Log Line Important in a Treatment?

The log line is the first sentence an executive will ever read from your hand. It's also the shorthand that executives will use to discuss your project with each other. If a junior executive reads your treatment and likes it, she'll need to tell her boss about the project in order to move it to the next step (probably a meeting between you and the boss).

The boss will ask the junior executive "What's it about?" The junior executive will respond with your log line, if you've written it well and accurately. You are helping to provide the junior executive with the tools she needs to help move your project forward. If you don't provide a log line at the beginning of your treatment, you rely on the junior executive's ability to digest your treatment and come up with a good log line of her own. Even in a collaborative art form like filmmaking, it's never a good idea to leave a job undone for someone else to do if you are more capable of doing it yourself. And who knows your story better than you do? Write a great log line for your treatment, and you'll know that your treatment is being discussed in your own words.

Who Is the Log Line For

The log line is for the buyer: the executive, the producer, the agent. By writing a log line for your treatment, you are helping them to process your material more efficiently. Getting a movie made is a sales process, a constant, revolving door sales process. You sell your work to an agent, who then sells your work to a producer, who then sells it to a director, who then sells it to actors and key crew members.

Once the movie is made, the sales process starts all over again, as the producer has to sell the movie to distributors and marketing executives, who have to sell the film to theater owners who have to sell the film to audiences. A good log line can ride the film all the way from start to finish, helping to sell it at each step.

Should the Log Line Refer to Other Movies?

No. It used to be popular to write log lines that were entirely film references. This practice became so prevalent that it became a cliché, and should be avoided if at all possible. Nothing says "schlock" as quickly as a "Die Hard" reference—the classic action movie reference that every movie strived for in the early 1990s. "Speed" was called "Die Hard" on a bus. "Passenger 57" was called "Die Hard" on a plane. Descriptive as these log lines may be, they read as lazy writing, and if your writing isn't even original in the log line, who will be interested in reading your treatment or your script? Avoid hucksterism, overselling and hype. It's a turnoff.

How Long Should the Log Line Be

Your log line should be one sentence long. Pare it down to its essence, and don't let your sentence become a run-on. Try it out loud, see if it works. You don't have to follow every twist and turn of the plot in your log line, you only have to convey the flavor of the script. One sentence will do it.

What Is the Difference Between the Log Line and the Theme?

Your log line is a sales tool that is a teaser and an invitation to read your script. The theme may be contained in the log line, but not necessarily. Theme is the real answer to "What is your script about?" and Theme need not be confined to a one sentence answer. Theme is often related to the discovery that your main character makes during the course of the film. For instance, in "Raiders of the Lost Ark," Indiana Jones discovers that people are actually more important to him than historical artifacts. In "Animal House," the Deltas discover that the camaraderie that they've discovered in their fraternity is the real lasting value of their college experience, not their class work or their social status on campus.

In Closing

You've spent months or years (or even decades) on your script, and so it may be frustrating to jump through the hoops of the submission process—but it's important. Don't give readers an excuse to ignore your work. You must craft a killer query, treatment and log line before the script gets its big shot. Compose them well, and you're on your way to selling that screenplay.

The Directory

100% ENTERTAINMENT

201 N Irving Blvd
Los Angeles, CA 90004
Phone: 323-461-6360
Fax: 323-871-8203

Email: 100percent@iname.com
Home Page: 100percent.com
IMDb: imdb.com/company/co0077804

Accepts query letter from unproduced, unrepresented writers via email. Project types include TV. Preferred genres include Drama, Non-Fiction, and Science Fiction. Established in 1998.

Stanley Isaacs

President
Phone: 323-461-6360
Email: sisaacs100@mac.com
IMDb: imdb.com/name/nm0410570

100% TERRYCLOTH

421 Waterview St
Los Angeles, CA 90293
Phone: 310-823-3432
Fax: 310-861-9093

Email: contact@terencemichael.com
Home Page: terencemichael.com
IMDb: imdb.com/company/co0194989
Facebook: facebook.com/pages/100-Percent-Terry-Cloth-Inc/147268518656038

Accepts query letter from unproduced, unrepresented writers via email. Project types include TV. Preferred genres include Comedy and Reality.

Terence Michael

Producer
Phone: 310-823-3432
Email: tm@terencemichael.com

Erik Adams

Development

1019 ENTERTAINMENT

1680 N Vine St, Suite 600
Hollywood, CA 90028
Phone: 323-645-6840
Fax: 323-645-6841

Email: info@1019ent.com
Home Page: 1019ent.com
IMDb: imdb.com/company/co0263748
Facebook: facebook.com/pages/1019-Entertainment/339985172752485

Accepts query letter from unproduced, unrepresented writers via email. Project types include TV. Preferred genres include Comedy, Drama, and Non-Fiction.

Terry Botwick

Principal
Phone: 323-645-6840
Email: terry@1019ent.com
IMDb: imdb.com/company/co0263748

Ralph Winter

Principal
Phone: 323-645-6840
Email: ralph@1019ent.com
IMDb: imdb.com/name/nm0003515

10X10 ENTERTAINMENT

1640 S Sepulveda Blvd, Suite 450
Los Angeles, CA 90025
Phone: 310-575-1235
Fax: 310-575-1237

IMDb: imdb.com/company/co0112253
Facebook: facebook.com/pages/10x10-Entertainment/114948301852714

Accepts query letter from unproduced, unrepresented writers. Project types include TV. Preferred genres include Comedy, Drama, and Non-Fiction.

Ken Mok

Producer/Founder
Phone: 310-575-1235
IMDb: imdb.com/name/nm0596298

Brad Austin

Director of Development
Phone: 310-575-1235
IMDb: imdb.com/name/nm4114614

1821 PICTURES

10900 Wilshire Blvd, Suite 1400
Los Angeles, CA 90024
Phone: 310-860-1121
Fax: 310-860-1123

Email: asst@1821pictures.com
Home Page: 1821pictures.com
IMDb: imdb.com/company/co0237259
Facebook: facebook.com/1821Pictures

Accepts query letter from unproduced, unrepresented writers via email. Project types include TV. Preferred genres include Animation, Comedy, Drama, and Non-Fiction. Established in 2005.

Paris Kasidokostas-Latsis
Principal
Phone: 310-860-1121
Email: asst@1821pictures.com
IMDb: imdb.com/company/co0237259

Terry Douglas
Principal
Phone: 310-860-1121
Email: asst@1821pictures.com
IMDb: imdb.com/name/nm0234806

Billy Piché
Director of Development
Phone: 310-860-1121
Email: asst@1821pictures.com
IMDb: imdb.com/name/nm5046038

19 ENTERTAINMENT, LTD

8560 W Sunset Blvd, 9th Floor
West Hollywood, CA 90069
Phone: 310-777-1940
Fax: 310-777-1949

Email: contact@19.co.uk
Home Page: 19.co.uk
IMDb: imdb.com/company/co0085773
Facebook: facebook.com/19EntertainmentLtd

Does not accept any unsolicited material. Project types include TV. Preferred genres include Animation, Comedy, and Drama.

Iain Pirie
President US
Phone: 310-777-1940
IMDb: imdb.com/name/nm2227040

21 LAPS ENTERTAINMENT

c/o Twentieth Century Fox
10201 W Pico Blvd

Building 41, Suite 400
Los Angeles, CA 90064
Phone: 310-369-7170
Fax: 310-969-0443

IMDb: imdb.com/company/co0158853
Facebook: facebook.com/pages/21-Laps-Entertainment/185829081580687

Does not accept any unsolicited material. Project types include Feature Films and TV. Preferred genres include Action, Comedy, and Drama.

Dan Levine
President of Production
IMDb: imdb.com/name/nm0505782

Shawn Levy
Principal
Phone: 310-369-4466
IMDb: imdb.com/name/nm0506613

Billy Rosenberg
Senior Vice President Development
Phone: 310-369-7170
IMDb: imdb.com/name/nm1192785

Will Rack
Director of Development
Phone: 310-369-7170
IMDb: imdb.com/name/nm5211280

25/7 PRODUCTIONS

10999 Riverside Dr, Suite 100
North Hollywood, CA 91602
Phone: 818-432-2800
Fax: 818-432-2810

Email: info@257productions.com
Home Page: 257productions.com
IMDb: imdb.com/company/co0200336

Accepts query letter from unproduced, unrepresented writers. Project types include TV. Preferred genres include Animation, Comedy, Drama, and Non-Fiction. Established in 2003.

David Broome
President
Phone: 818-432-2800
IMDb: imdb.com/company/co0200336

26 FILMS

8748 Holloway Dr
Los Angeles, CA, 90069
Phone: 310-205-9922
Fax: 310-206-9926

Email: asst@26films.com
Home Page: 26films.com

Accepts query letter from unproduced, unrepresented writers via email.

Nathalie Marciano
Principal
Phone: 310-205-9922
Email: asst@26films.com
IMDb: imdb.com/name/nm0545695

Elena Brooks
Director of Development
Phone: 310-205-9922
Email: asst@26films.com
IMDb: imdb.com/name/nm4542983

2929 PRODUCTIONS

1437 Seventh St, Suite 250
Santa Monica, CA 90401
Phone: 310-309-5200
Fax: 310-309-5716

Home Page: 2929entertainment.com

Accepts query letter from unproduced, unrepresented writers. Preferred genres include Action, Drama, and Non-Fiction.

Todd Wagner
Principal
Phone: 310-309-5200
Email: todd@2929entertainment.com
IMDb: imdb.com/company/co0005596

Shay Weiner
Creative Executive
Phone: 310-309-5200
Email: sweiner@2929ent.com
IMDb: imdb.com/name/nm1674317

2S FILMS

10390 Santa Monica Blvd
Suite 210
Los Angeles, CA 90025
Phone: 310-789-5450
Fax: 310-789-3060

Email: info@2sfilms.com
Home Page: 2sfilms.com
IMDb: imdb.com/company/co0238996

Does not accept any unsolicited material. Project types include Feature Films. Preferred genres include Comedy and Romance. Established in 2007.

Molly Smith
Partner/Producer
Phone: 310-789-5450
Email: info@2sfilms.com
IMDb: imdb.com/company/co0238996

Allison Rayne
Vice President of Development
Phone: 310-789-5450
Email: info@2sfilms.com
IMDb: imdb.com/name/nm2588349

2WAYTRAFFIC - A SONY PICTURES ENTERTAINMENT COMPANY

Middenweg 1
PO Box 297
Hilversum 1217 HS
The Netherlands
Phone: +31(0)357508000
Fax: +31(0)357508020

Email: info@2waytraffic.com
Home Page: 2waytraffic.com
IMDb: imdb.com/company/co0211160

Accepts query letter from unproduced, unrepresented writers. Project types include Feature Films and TV. Established in 2004.

3311 PRODUCTIONS

8938 Keith
West Hollywood, CA 90069
Phone: 323-319-5060
Fax: 323-306-5534

Email: info@3311productions.com
Home Page: 3311productions.com

Accepts query letter from produced or represented writers. Project types include Feature Films. Preferred genres include Comedy and Drama.

Ross Jacobson
Executive/Producer
IMDb: imdb.com/name/nm2278951

Mark Roberts
Executive
IMDb: imdb.com/name/nm4224736

Eddie Vaisman
Executive/Producer
IMDb: imdb.com/name/nm4224744

34TH STREET FILMS

8200 Wilshire Blvd, Suite 300
Beverly Hills, CA 90211
Phone: 323-315-7963
Fax: 323-315-7117

Does not accept any unsolicited material. Project types include Feature Films. Preferred genres include Action, Comedy, Family, and Romance.

Matt Moore
Executive Vice President
Phone: 323-315-7963
IMDb: imdb.com/name/nm0601597

Poppy Hanks
Senior Vice President (Production & Development)
Phone: 323-315-7963

Amber Rasberry
Director of Development
Phone: 323-315-7963
IMDb: imdb.com/name/nm2248393

360 PICTURES

301 N Canon Dr, Suite 207
Beverly Hills, CA 90210
Phone: 310-205-9900
Fax: 310-205-9909

IMDb: imdb.com/company/co0157610

Does not accept any unsolicited material. Preferred genres include Comedy, Science Fiction, and Thriller.

Frank Mancuso
President
Phone: 310-205-9900
IMDb: imdb.com/name/nm0541548

Jennifer Nieves
Vice President (Development)
Phone: 310-205-9900
IMDb: imdb.com/name/nm2707034

3 ARTS ENTERTAINMENT, INC.

9460 Wilshire Blvd 7th Floor
Beverly Hills, CA 90212
Phone: 310-888-3200
Fax: 310-888-3210

49 W 27th St 5th Floor
New York, NY 10001
Phone: 212-213-4245

Home Page: 3arts.com
IMDb: imdb.com/company/co0070636

Accepts query letter from unproduced, unrepresented writers. Project types include Feature Films and TV. Preferred genres include Comedy and Drama. Established in 1992.

Howard Klein
Partner/Talent Manager
Phone: 310-888-3200
Email: hklein@3arts.com
IMDb: imdb.com/name/nm2232433

Erwin Stoff
Partner/Talent Manager
Phone: 310-888-3200
Email: estoff@3arts.com
IMDb: imdb.com/name/nm0831098

3 BALL PRODUCTIONS

3650 Redondo Beach Ave
Redondo Beach, CA 90278
Phone: 424-236-7500
Fax: 424-236-7501

Email: 3ball.reception@eyeworks.tv
Home Page: 3ballproductions.com
IMDb: imdb.com/company/co0100000

Accepts query letter from unproduced, unrepresented writers via email. Project types include TV. Preferred genres include Drama.

J.D. Roth
CEO
Phone: 424-236-7500
IMDb: imdb.com/name/nm0744870

Brandt Pinvidic
Executive Vice President Development
Phone: 424-236-7500
IMDb: imdb.com/name/nm1803480

40 ACRES & A MULE FILMWORKS, INC.

75 S Elliot Place
Brooklyn, NY 11217
Phone: 718-624-3703
Fax: 718-624-2008

Home Page: 40acres.com
IMDb: imdb.com/company/co0029134

Does not accept any unsolicited material. Project types include TV. Preferred genres include Action, Comedy, Drama, and Non-Fiction.

Spike Lee
Chairman
Phone: 718-624-3703
IMDb: imdb.com/name/nm0000490

44 BLUE PRODUCTIONS, INC.

4040 Vineland Ave, Suite 105
Studio City, CA 11217
Phone: 818-760-4442
Fax: 818-760-1509

Email: reception@44blue.com
Home Page: 44blue.com
IMDb: imdb.com/company/co0012712

Does not accept any unsolicited material. Project types include TV. Preferred genres include Comedy, Drama, and Non-Fiction.

Rasha Drachkovitch
Co-Founder
Phone: 818-760-4442
Email: reception@44blue.com
IMDb: imdb.com/name/nm0236624

Stephanie Drachkovitch
Co-Founder
Phone: 818-760-4442
Email: reception@44blue.com
IMDb: imdb.com/name/nm1729517

495 PRODUCTIONS

4222 Burbank Blvd, 2nd Floor
Burbank, CA 91505
Phone: 818-840-2750
Fax: 818-840-7083

Email: info@495productions.com
Home Page: 495productions.com
IMDb: imdb.com/company/co0192481

Does not accept any unsolicited material. Project types include TV. Preferred genres include Comedy, Drama, Non-Fiction, and Reality.

SallyAnn Salsano
President
Phone: 818-840-2750
Email: info@495productions.com
IMDb: imdb.com/name/nm1133163

Stephanie Lydecker
Head of Development
Phone: 818-840-2750
Email: info@495productions.com
IMDb: imdb.com/name/nm1738248

4TH ROW FILMS

27 W 20th St, Suite 1006
New York, NY 10011
Phone: 212-974-0082
Fax: 212-627-3090

Email: info@4throwfilms.com
Home Page: 4throwfilms.com
IMDb: imdb.com/company/co0117932

Does not accept any unsolicited material. Project types include TV. Preferred genres include Comedy, Drama, and Non-Fiction.

Douglas Tirola
President / Producer
Phone: 212-974-0082
Email: info@4throwfilms.com
IMDb: imdb.com/name/nm0864263

Susan Bedusa
Vice President, Development
Phone: 212-974-0082
Email: info@4throwfilms.com
IMDb: imdb.com/name/nm1513256

51 MINDS ENTERTAINMENT

6565 Sunset Blvd, Suite 301
Los Angeles, CA 90028
Phone: 323-466-9200
Fax: 323-466-9202

Email: info@51minds.com
Home Page: 51minds.com
IMDb: imdb.com/company/co0166565

Accepts query letter from unproduced, unrepresented writers via email. Project types include TV. Preferred genres include Comedy, Drama, and Reality.

Mark Cronin
Executive Producer
Phone: 323-466-9200
Email: info@51minds.com
IMDb: imdb.com/name/nm0188782

Nicole Elliott
Executive, Development
Phone: 323-466-9200
Email: info@51minds.com
IMDb: imdb.com/name/nm1627222

David Caplan
Vice President, Development
Phone: 323-466-9200
Email: info@51minds.com
IMDb: imdb.com/name/nm4933376

59TH STREET FILMS

101 Destiny Dr
Lafayette, LA 70506
Phone: 337-280-9370

Email: 59thstreetfilms@gmail.com

Accepts scripts from unproduced, unrepresented writers. Project types include TV. Preferred genres include Comedy and Drama.

Sarah Agor
Producer
IMDb: imdb.com/name/nm2706070

Jennifer Jarrett
Producer
IMDb: imdb.com/name/nm1838264

Nicholas Scott
Producer & Writer
IMDb: imdb.com/name/nm4641966

Steve Sirkis
Producer & Director
IMDb: imdb.com/name/nm2401659

Alfred Rubin Thompson
Producer
IMDb: imdb.com/name/nm0867022

5IVE SMOOTH STONES PRODUCTIONS

8500 Wilshire Blvd, Suite #527
Beverly Hills, CA 90211

Home Page: 5ivesmoothstones.com

Accepts query letter from unproduced, unrepresented writers via email. Project types include Feature Films. Preferred genres include Comedy and Family.

Terry Crews
Actor/CEO
IMDb: imdb.com/name/nm0187719

Robert Wise
President Scripted Development

72ND STREET PRODUCTIONS

1041 N Formosa Ave
West Hollywood, CA 90046
Phone: 323-850-3139
Fax: 323-850-3179

Email: contact@72ndstreetproductions.com
Home Page: 72ndstreetproductions.com
IMDb: imdb.com/company/co0180596

Accepts query letter from unproduced, unrepresented writers via email. Project types include Feature Films, TV, and Commercials. Preferred genres include Drama.

Steven Krieger
President - Executive
Phone: 323-850-3139
Email: skrieger@72ndstreetproductions.com
IMDb: imdb.com/name/nm2544844

Tim Harms
Producer
Phone: 323-850-3139
Email: tharms@72ndstreetproductions.com
IMDb: imdb.com/name/nm0363608

Lee Krieger
President - Executive
Phone: 323-850-3139
Email: lkrieger@72ndstreetproductions.com
IMDb: imdb.com/name/nm1767218

72 PRODUCTIONS

8332 Melrose Ave, 2nd Floor
West Hollywood, CA 90069
Phone: 310-278-1221
Fax: 310-278-1224

Home Page: 72productions.com
IMDb: imdb.com/company/co0196483

Accepts query letter from unproduced, unrepresented writers. Preferred genres include Science Fiction and Thriller.

Jennifer Chaiken
Producer
Phone: 310-278-1221
IMDb: imdb.com/name/nm0149671

Sebastian Dungan
Producer
Phone: 310-278-1221
IMDb: imdb.com/name/nm0242253

777 GROUP

1015 Gayley Ave, Suite 1128
Los Angeles, CA 90024
Phone: 312-834-7770

Email: info@the777group.com
Home Page: the777group.com
IMDb: imdb.com/company/co0133127

Accepts query letter from unproduced, unrepresented writers via email. Project types include TV. Preferred genres include Animation, Comedy, Drama, and Non-Fiction.

Marcello Robinson
CEO/President
Phone: 312-834-7770
Email: info@the777group.com
IMDb: imdb.com/name/nm0732883

7ATE9 ENTERTAINMENT

740 N. La Brea Ave
Los Angeles, CA 90038
Phone: 323-936-6789
Fax: 323-937-6713

Email: info@7ate9.com
Home Page: 7ate9.com
IMDb: imdb.com/company/co0171281

Does not accept any unsolicited material. Project types include TV.

Artur Spigel
Creative Director
IMDb: imdb.com/name/nm1742493

8:38 PRODUCTIONS

10390 Santa Monica Blvd, Suite 200
Los Angeles, CA 90064
Phone: 310-789-3056
Fax: 310-789-3077

IMDb: imdb.com/company/co0252672

Does not accept any unsolicited material. Preferred genres include Family and Romance.

Kira Davis
Producer
Phone: 310-789-3056
IMDb: imdb.com/name/nm0204987

8790 PICTURES, INC.

11400 W Olympic Blvd, Suite 590
Los Angeles, CA 90064
Phone: 310-471-9983
Fax: 310-471-6366

Email: 8790pictures@gmail.com
IMDb: imdb.com/company/co0159892

Accepts query letter from unproduced, unrepresented writers via email. Project types include Feature Films and TV. Preferred genres include Action, Animation, Comedy, Drama, and Romance.

Joan Singleton

Writer/Producer
Phone: 310-471-9983
Email: 8790pictures@gmail.com
IMDb: imdb.com/name/nm0802306

Ralph Singleton

Writer/Producer
Phone: 310-471-9983
Email: 8790pictures@gmail.com
IMDb: imdb.com/name/nm0802326

8TH WONDER ENTERTAINMENT

7961 W 3rd St
Los Angeles, CA 90048
Phone: 323-549-3456
Fax: 323-549-9475

Email: info@8thwonderent.com
Home Page: 8thwonderent.com
IMDb: imdb.com/company/co0226729

Accepts query letter from unproduced, unrepresented writers via email.

Michael McQuarn

CEO/President
Phone: 323-860-0319
Email: mcq@8thwonderent.com

David Luong

Director of Development
Phone: 323-860-0319
Email: info@8thwonderent.com

900 FILMS

1611A South Melrose Dr, #362
Vista, CA 92081
Phone: 760-477-2470
Fax: 760-477-2478

Email: asst@900films.com
Home Page: 900films.com
IMDb: imdb.com/company/co0086829

Accepts query letter from unproduced, unrepresented writers via email. Project types include Feature Films, TV, and Commercials. Preferred genres include Non-Fiction and Reality.

Krista Parkinson

VP of Development
Phone: 760-477-2470
Email: irene@900films.com
IMDb: imdb.com/name/nm2221276

9.14 PICTURES

1804 Chestnut St, Suite 2
Philadelphia, PA 19103
Phone: 215-238-0707
Fax: 215-238-0663

Email: info@914pictures.com
Home Page: 914pictures.com
IMDb: imdb.com/company/co0145535

Accepts query letter from unproduced, unrepresented writers via email. Established in 2002.

Don Argott

Owner/Producer
Phone: 215-238-0707 ext. 12#
Email: info@914pictures.com
IMDb: imdb.com/name/nm0034531

Sheena Joyce

Owner
Phone: 215-238-0707 ext. 11#
Email: info@914pictures.com
IMDb: imdb.com/name/nm1852224

AARDMAN ANIMATIONS

Gas Ferry Rd
Bristol BS1 6UN
United Kingdom
Phone: +44 117-984-8485
Fax: +44 117-984-8486

Email: mail@aardman.com
Home Page: aardman.com
IMDb: imdb.com/company/co0103531

Does not accept any unsolicited material. Preferred genres include Animation.

Alicia Gold

Head of Development, Features
Phone: +44 117-984-8485
Email: mail@aardman.com
IMDb: imdb.com/name/nm1664759imdb.com/name/nm4211100

ABANDON PICTURES, INC.

711 Route 302
Pine Bush, NY 12566
Phone: 845-361-9317
Fax: 845-361-9150

Email: info@abandoninteractive.com
Home Page: abandoninteractive.com
IMDb: imdb.com/company/co0025591

Does not accept any unsolicited material.

Karen Lauder

President & CEO
Phone: 845-361-9317
Email: info@abandoninteractive.com
IMDb: imdb.com/name/nm0490746

ABBY LOU ENTERTAINMENT

1411 Edgehill Pl.
Pasadena, CA 91103
Phone: 626-795-7334
Fax: 626-795-4013

Email: ale@full-moon.com

Accepts query letter from produced or represented writers. Project types include Feature Films.

George Le Fave

President
IMDb: imdb.com/name/nm2247957

Cheryl Pestor

Executive VP
IMDb: imdb.com/name/nm2453743

ABC STUDIOS

500 S Buena Vista St
Burbank, CA 91505
Phone: 818-460-7777

Does not accept any unsolicited material. Project types include TV and Commercials. Preferred genres include Comedy and Drama.

Gary French

Senior Vice President of Production
IMDb: imdb.com/name/nm2380686

Brenda Kyle

Vice President of Production
IMDb: imdb.com/name/nm0477368

Robert Sertner

Executive Producer
Email: bobsertner@gmail.com
IMDb: imdb.com/name/nm0785750

Patrick Moran

Head of Creative Development
IMDb: imdb.com/name/nm3988896

ABERRATION FILMS

1425 N Crescent Heights Blvd, #203
West Hollywood, CA 90046
Phone: 323-656-1830

Email: aberrationfilms@yahoo.com
Home Page: aberrationfilms.com
IMDb: imdb.com/company/co0164476

Accepts query letter from unproduced, unrepresented writers. Project types include Feature Films. Preferred genres include Drama.

Susan Dynner

Director / Producer
Phone: 323-656-1830
Email: aberrationfilms@yahoo.com
IMDb: imdb.com/name/nm1309839

ACAPPELLA PICTURES

8271 Melrose Ave, Suite 101
Los Angeles, CA 90046
Phone: 323-782-8200
Fax: 323-782-8210

Email: charmaine@acappellapictures.com
Home Page: acappellapictures.com
IMDb: imdb.com/company/co0055414

Accepts query letter from unproduced, unrepresented writers via email.

Charles Evans

President
Phone: 323-782-8200
Email: charmaine@acappellapictures.com
IMDb: imdb.com/name/nm0262509

Charmaine Parcero

Executive Development / Production
Phone: 323-782-8200
Email: charmaine@acappellapictures.com
IMDb: imdb.com/name/nm0661019

ACCELERATED ENTERTAINMENT LLC

10201 W Pico Blvd, Building 6
Los Angeles, CA 90064

Email: cleestorm@acceleratedent.com
Home Page: acceleratedent.com
IMDb: imdb.com/company/co0208920

Accepts query letter from unproduced, unrepresented writers via email. Project types include Feature Films. Preferred genres include Drama and Non-Fiction.

Jason Perr

Partner/Executive Producer
Email: jperr@acceleratedent.com
IMDb: imdb.com/name/nm1280790

Christina Storm

Partner/Producer
Email: cleestorm@acceleratedent.com
IMDb: imdb.com/name/nm0497028

Allison Calleri

Partner/Producer
Email: acalleri@acceleratedent.com
IMDb: imdb.com/name/nm1819857

A.C. LYLES PRODUCTIONS, INC.

5555 Melrose Ave, Hart Building 409
Hollywood, CA 90038-3197
Phone: 323-956-5819

IMDb: imdb.com/company/co0074718

Accepts query letter from unproduced, unrepresented writers via email.

A.C. Lyles

Producer
Phone: 323-956-5819
Email: ac_lyles@paramount.com
IMDb: imdb.com/name/nm0528121

ACT III PRODUCTIONS

100 N Crescent Dr, Suite 250
Beverly Hills, CA 90210
Phone: 310-385-4111
Fax: 310-385-4148

Home Page: normanlear.com/act_iii.html
IMDb: imdb.com/company/co0030401

Accepts query letter from unproduced, unrepresented writers.

Norman Lear

Chairman/CEO
Phone: 310-385-4111
Email: normanl@actiii.com
IMDb: imdb.com/name/nm0005131

Brent Miller

VP of Development
Phone: 310-385-4111
IMDb: imdb.com/name/nm1226252

ACTUAL REALITY PICTURES

Phone: 310-202-1272
Fax: 310-202-1502

Email: questions@arp.tv
Home Page: actualreality.tv
IMDb: imdb.com/company/co0004087

Does not accept any unsolicited material.

R.J. Cutler

President
Phone: 310-202-1272
IMDb: imdb.com/name/nm0191712

ADAM FIELDS PRODUCTIONS

8899 Beverly Blvd, Suite 821
West Hollywood, CA 90048

Phone: 310-859-9300
Fax: 310-859-4795

IMDb: imdb.com/company/co0064962

Accepts query letter from unproduced, unrepresented writers.

Adam Fields
President
Phone: 310-859-9300
IMDb: imdb.com/name/nm0276178

ADELSTEIN PRODUCTIONS

144 S Beverly Dr, Suite 500
Beverly Hills, CA 90212
Phone: 310-860-5502

Does not accept any unsolicited material.

Marty Adelstein
Producer
Phone: 310-270-4570
IMDb: imdb.com/name/nm1374351

AD HOMINEM ENTERPRISES

506 Santa Monica Blvd, Suite 400
Santa Monica, CA 90401
Phone: 310-394-1444
Fax: 310-394-5401

IMDb: imdb.com/company/co0171502

Does not accept any unsolicited material. Project types include Feature Films.

Alexander Payne
Partner
Phone: 310-394-1444
IMDb: imdb.com/name/nm0668247
Assistant: Anna Musso

Jim Burke
Partner
Phone: 310-394-1444
Email: jwb@adhominem.us
IMDb: imdb.com/name/nm0121724
Assistant: Adam Wagner

Evan Endicott
Director of Development
Phone: 310-394-1444
IMDb: imdb.com/name/nm1529002

ADULT SWIM

1065 Williams St NW
Atlanta, GA 30309
Phone: 404-827-1500

Home Page: adultswim.com
IMDb: imdb.com/company/co0153115

Does not accept any unsolicited material.

Keith Crofford
Vice-President Production
IMDb: imdb.com/name/nm0188443

AEGIS FILM GROUP

7510 Sunset Blvd
Ste 275
Los Angeles, CA 90046
Phone: 323-848-7977
Fax: 323-650-9954

Email: info@aegisfilmgroup.com
Home Page: aegisfilmgroup.com

Project types include Feature Films. Preferred genres include Documentary.

Arianna Eisenberg
Owner
Phone: 323-848-7977
IMDb: imdb.com/name/nm1985255

Steve Shultz
Executive Producer
Phone: 323-848-7977
IMDb: imdb.com/name/nm0795789

AEI - ATCHITY ENTERTAINMENT INTERNATIONAL, INC.

9601 Wilshire Blvd, #1202
Beverly Hills, CA 90210
Phone: 323-932-0407
Fax: 323-932-0321

Email: submissions@aeionline.com
Home Page: aeionline.com
IMDb: wwwimdb.com/company/co0010944

Accepts query letter from unproduced, unrepresented writers.

Jennifer Pope
Submissions Coordinator
Phone: 323-932-0407
Email: jp@aeionline.com
IMDb: imdb.com/name/nm1026413

A&E NETWORK

235 E 45th St
New York, NY 10017
Phone: 212-210-1400
Fax: 212-210-9755

Email: feedback@aetv.com
Home Page: aetv.com
IMDb: imdb.com/company/co0056790

Does not accept any unsolicited material.

Thomas Moody
Senior Vice-President Programming, Planning & Acquisitions
Phone: 212-210-1400
Email: feedback@aetv.com
IMDb: imdb.com/name/nm1664759

AFTER DARK FILMS

8967 Sunset Blvd
West Hollywood, CA 90069
Phone: 310-270-4260
Fax: 310-270-4262

Email: info@afterdarkfilms.com
Home Page: afterdarkfilms.com
IMDb: imdb.com/company/co0166161

Does not accept any unsolicited material. Preferred genres include Horror.

Stephanie Caleb
Executive Vice-President Acquisitions & Creative Affairs
Phone: 310-270-4260
Email: info@afterdarkfilms.com
IMDb: imdb.com/name/nm2554487

AGAMEMNON FILMS, INC.

650 N Bronson Ave, Suite B225
Los Angeles, CA 90004
Phone: 323-960-4066
Fax: 323-960-4067

Home Page: agamemnon.com
IMDb: imdb.com/company/co0004137

Accepts query letter from unproduced, unrepresented writers via email. Project types include TV. Preferred genres include Action, Drama, Family, Non-Fiction, Reality, and Thriller.

Fraser Heston
President, CEO and Co-Founder
IMDb: imdb.com/name/nm0381699
Assistant: Heather Thomas

Alex Butler
Senior Partner and Producer
Phone: 323-960-4066
IMDb: imdb.com/name/nm0124808

AGGREGATE FILMS

100 Universal City Plaza
Bungalow 414
Universal City, CA 91608
Phone: 818-777-8180

Does not accept any unsolicited material. Project types include Feature Films. Preferred genres include Comedy and Family.

Jason Bateman
Principal
IMDb: imdb.com/name/nm0000867

Jim Garavente
President
IMDb: imdb.com/name/nm4814574

AGILITY STUDIOS

11928 1/2 Ventura Blvd
Studio City, CA 91604
Phone: 310-314-1440
Fax: 310-496-3292

Email: info@agilitystudios.com
Home Page: agilitystudios.com
IMDb: imdb.com/company/co0293230

Accepts query letter from unproduced, unrepresented writers via email. Established in 2008.

Scott Ehrlich
CEO
Phone: 310-314-1440
Email: info@agilitystudios.com
IMDb: imdb.com/name/nm3796990

AHIMSA FILMS

6671 Sunset Blvd, Suite 1593
Los Angeles, CA 90028
Phone: 323-464-8500
Fax: 323-464-8535

IMDb: imdb.com/company/co0202538

Accepts query letter from unproduced, unrepresented writers.

Rebecca Yeldham
President
Phone: 323-464-8500
IMDb: imdb.com/name/nm0947344

AHIMSA MEDIA

8060 Colonial Dr, Suite 204
Richmond, BC V7C 4V1
Canada
Phone: 604-785-3602

Email: info@ahimsamedia.com
Home Page: ahimsamedia.com
IMDb: imdb.com/company/co0222513
Facebook: facebook.com/ahimsamedia

Accepts query letter from unproduced, unrepresented writers via email. Project types include Commercials.

Erica Hargreave
President/Head of Creative and Interactive
Phone: 604-785-3602
Email: info@ahimsamedia.com
IMDb: imdb.com/name/nm2988128

AIRMONT PICTURES

344 Mesa Rd
Santa Monica, CA 90402
Phone: 310-985-3896

IMDb: imdb.com/company/co0176167

Accepts query letter from unproduced, unrepresented writers.

Matthew Gannon
Producer
Phone: 310-985-3896
IMDb: imdb.com/name/nm0304478

AKIL PRODUCTIONS

Phone: 212-608-2000

Email: info@akilproductions.com
Home Page: akilproductions.com

Project types include TV. Preferred genres include Drama.

Salim Akil
Principal
IMDb: imdb.com/name/nm0015328

Mara Akil
Executive Producer
IMDb: imdb.com/name/nm0015327

ALAN BARNETTE PRODUCTIONS

100 Universal City Plaza
Building 2352, Suite 101
Universal City, CA 91608
Phone: 818-733-0993
Fax: 818-733-3172

Email: dabarnette@aol.com
IMDb: imdb.com/company/co0056462

Does not accept any unsolicited material.

Alan Barnette
Executive Producer
Phone: 818-733-0993
Email: dabarnette@aol.com
IMDb: imdb.com/name/nm0056002

ALAN DAVID MANAGEMENT

8840 Wilshire Blvd,
Suite 200
Beverly Hills, CA 90211
Phone: 310-358-3155
Fax: 310-358-3256

Email: ad@adgmp.com
IMDb: imdb.com/company/co0097077

Does not accept any unsolicited material.

Alan David
President
Phone: 310-358-3155
Email: ad@adgmp.com
IMDb: imdb.com/name/nm2220960

ALAN SACKS PRODUCTIONS

11684 Ventura Blvd, Suite 809
Studio City, CA 91604
Phone: 818-752-6999
Fax: 818-752-6985

Email: asacks@pacbell.net
IMDb: imdb.com/company/co0013945

Does not accept any unsolicited material.

Alan Sacks
Executive Producer
Phone: 818-752-6999
Email: asacks@pacbell.net
IMDb: imdb.com/name/nm0755286

ALCHEMY ENTERTAINMENT

7024 Melrose Ave, Suite 420
Los Angeles, CA 90038
Phone: 323-937-6100
Fax: 323-937-6102

IMDb: imdb.com/company/co0094892

Does not accept any unsolicited material.

Jason Barrett
Manager/Producer
Phone: 323-937-6100
IMDb: imdb.com/name/nm2249074

ALCON ENTERTAINMENT, LLC

10390 Santa Monica Blvd, Suite 250
Los Angeles, CA 90025
Phone: 310-789-3040
Fax: 310-789-3060

Email: info@alconent.com
Home Page: alconent.com
IMDb: imdb.com/company/co0054452

Does not accept any unsolicited material. Project types include Feature Films.

Broderick Johnson
Co-Founder/Co-CEO
Phone: 310-789-3040
Email: info@alconent.com
IMDb: imdb.com/name/nm0424663

Steven Wegner
Executive Vice President, Development
Phone: 310-789-3040
Email: info@alconent.com
IMDb: imdb.com/name/nm1176853

Carl Rogers
Director, Development
Phone: 310-789-3040
Email: info@alconent.com
IMDb: imdb.com/name/nm0736770

ALDAMISA ENTERTAINMENT

15760 Ventura Blvd.
Suite 1450
Encino, CA 91436
Phone: 818-753-2442
Fax: 818-753-2310

Email: sales@aldamisa.com
Home Page: aldamisa.com

Accepts query letter from produced or represented writers. Project types include Feature Films. Preferred genres include Action, Comedy, Crime, Drama, Fantasy, Horror, Romance, and Thriller.

Sergei Bespalov
Co-Chairman
IMDb: imdb.com/name/nm3703488
Assistant: Michelle Faraji

Marina Bespalov
Co-Chairman
IMDb: imdb.com/name/nm4208519
Assistant: Kirby Lodin

Jere Hausfater
COO

Michael Kupisk
Head of Development
IMDb: imdb.com/name/nm3161790
Assistant: Josh Baker

James D. Brubaker
President
IMDb: imdb.com/name/nm0115384

Russell Gray
Producer
IMDb: imdb.com/name/nm0336925

ALEXANDER/ENRIGHT & ASSOCIATES

201 Wilshire, Blvd, 3rd Floor
Santa Monica, CA 90401
Phone: 310-458-3003
Fax: 310-393-7238

IMDb: imdb.com/company/co0048897

Accepts query letter from unproduced, unrepresented
writers.

Les Alexander
Executive Producer
Phone: 310-458-3003
IMDb: imdb.com/name/nm0018573

ALEXANDER/MITCHELL PRODUCTIONS

201 Wilshire Blvd Third Floor
Santa Monica, CA 90401
Phone: 310-458-3003
Fax: 310-393-7238

IMDb: imdb.com/company/co0241249

Accepts query letter from unproduced, unrepresented
writers via email. Project types include Feature Films
and TV. Preferred genres include Drama.

Les Alexander
Principal (Executive Producer)
IMDb: imdb.com/name/nm0018573

Jonathan Mitchell
Principal
IMDb: imdb.com/name/nm2927057

ALEX ROSE PRODUCTIONS, INC.

8291 Presson Place
Los Angeles, CA 90069
Phone: 323-654-8662
Fax: 323-654-0196

IMDb: imdb.com/company/co0177705

Accepts query letter from unproduced, unrepresented
writers.

Alexandra Rose
President/Writer/Producer
Phone: 323-654-8662
IMDb: imdb.com/name/nm0741228

ALIANZA FILMS INTERNATIONAL LTD.

11941 Weddington St, Suite #106
Studio City, CA 91607
Phone: 310-933-6250
Fax: 310-388-0874

Email: shari@alianzafilms.com
Home Page: alianzafilms.com
IMDb: imdb.com/company/co0022267

Accepts query letter from unproduced, unrepresented
writers. Established in 1984.

Shari Hamrick
Executive
Phone: 310-933-6250
Email: shari@alianzafilms.com
IMDb: imdb.com/name/nm0359089

A-LINE PICTURES

2231 Broadway #19
New York, NY 10024
Phone: 212-496-9496
Fax: 212-496-9497

Email: info@a-linepictures.com
Home Page: a-linepictures.com
IMDb: imdb.com/company/co0156447

Does not accept any unsolicited material. Established
in 2005.

Caroline Baron
Producer
Phone: 212-496-9496
Email: info@a-linepictures.com
IMDb: imdb.com/name/nm0056205

ALLAN MCKEOWN PRESENTS

1534 17th St, #102
Santa Monica, CA 90404
Phone: 310-264-2474
Fax: 310-264-4663

Email: info@ampresents.tv
Home Page: ampresents.tv
IMDb: imdb.com/company/co0206885

Accepts query letter from unproduced, unrepresented writers via email. Established in 2007.

Allan McKeown
CEO/Producer
Phone: 310-264-2474
Email: info@ampresents.tv
IMDb: imdb.com/name/nm0571647

ALLENTOWN PRODUCTIONS

100 Universal City Plaza
Building 2372B, Suite 114
Universal City, CA 91608
Phone: 818-733-1002
Fax: 818-866-4181

Email: writetous@allentownproductions.com
Home Page: allentownproductions.com
IMDb: imdb.com/company/co0122945

Does not accept any unsolicited material. Preferred genres include Non-Fiction. Established in 1994.

James Moll
Founder/Producer/Director
Phone: 818-733-1002
Email: writetous@allentownproductions.com
IMDb: imdb.com/name/nm0002224

Chris W. King
Director of Development
Phone: 818-733-1002
Email: writetous@allentownproductions.com
IMDb: imdb.com/name/nm1648242

ALLIANCE FILMS

45 Kings St East Suite 300
Toronto, ON, Canada, M5C2Y7
Phone: 416-309-4200
Fax: 416-309-4290

Email: info@alliancefilms.com
Home Page: alliancefilms.com

Does not accept any unsolicited material. Project types include Feature Films. Preferred genres include Action, Comedy, Crime, Drama, Fantasy, Horror, Romance, Science Fiction, and Thriller.

Xavier Marchand
President
IMDb: imdb.com/name/nm0545421

Mark Slone
Executive Vice President
IMDb: imdb.com/name/nm1093545

Laurie May
Executive Vice President

ALLOY ENTERTAINMENT

6300 Wilshire Blvd, Suite 2150
Los Angeles, CA 90048
Phone: 323-801-1373
Fax: 323-801-1355

Email: LAassistant@alloyentertainment.com
Home Page: alloyentertainment.com
IMDb: imdb.com/company/co0142434

Accepts query letter from unproduced, unrepresented writers via email.

Bob Levy
Executive Vice-President of Film
Phone: 323-801-1373
Email: LAassistant@alloyentertainment.com
IMDb: imdb.com/name/nm2145920

ALOE ENTERTAINMENT

433 N Camden Dr, Suite 600
Beverly Hills, CA 90210
Phone: 310-288-1886
Fax: 310-288-1801

Email: info@aloeentertainment.com
Home Page: aloeentertainment.com
IMDb: imdb.com/company/co0261920

Does not accept any unsolicited material. Established in 1999.

Mary Aloe
Producer/President
Phone: 310-288-1886
Email: info@aloeentertainment.com
IMDb: imdb.com/name/nm0022053

AL ROKER PRODUCTIONS

250 W 57th St, Suite 1525
New York, NY 10019
Phone: 212-757-8500
Fax: 212-757-8513

Email: info@alroker.com
Home Page: alrokerproductions.com
IMDb: imdb.com/company/co0095131

Does not accept any unsolicited material. Project types include Feature Films. Established in 1994.

Al Roker
CEO
Phone: 212-757-8500
Email: info@alroker.com
IMDb: imdb.com/name/nm0737963

Tracie Brennan
VP Operations
Phone: 212-757-8500
Email: info@alroker.com
IMDb: imdb.com/name/nm2200420

ALTA LOMA ENTERTAINMENT

2706 Media Center Dr
Los Angeles, CA 90065-1733
Phone: 323-276-4211
Fax: 323-276-4500

Home Page: alta-loma.com
IMDb: imdb.com/company/co0008514

Does not accept any unsolicited material.

Richard Rosenzweig
Executive Producer
Phone: 323-276-4211
IMDb: imdb.com/name/nm0742866

Jason Burns
SVP of Development
Phone: 323-276-4211
IMDb: imdb.com/name/nm2135146

J.W. Starrett
Director of Development
Phone: 323-276-4211
IMDb: imdb.com/name/nm2852786

ALTURAS FILMS

2403 Main St
Santa Monica, CA 90405
Phone: 310-401-6200
Fax: 310-401-6129

Email: info@alturasfilms.com
Home Page: alturasfilms.com
IMDb: imdb.com/company/co0169508

Does not accept any unsolicited material. Established in 2004.

Marshall Rawlings
Owner/Producer
Phone: 310-401-6200
Email: reception@alturasfilms.com
IMDb: imdb.com/name/nm1987844

A-MARK ENTERTAINMENT

233 Wilshire Blvd, Suite 200
Santa Monica, CA 90401
Phone: 310-255-0900

Email: info@amarkentertainment.com
Home Page: amarkentertainment.com
IMDb: imdb.com/company/co0135086

Does not accept any unsolicited material. Established in 2004.

Bruce McNall
Co-Chair
Phone: 310-255-0900
Email: info@amarkentertainment.com
IMDb: imdb.com/name/nm1557652

AMBASSADOR ENTERTAINMENT

P. O. Box 1522
Pacific Palisades, CA 90272
Phone: 310-862-5200
Fax: 310-496-3140

Email: aspeval@ambassadortv.com
Home Page: ambassadortv.com
IMDb: imdb.com/company/co0175998

Does not accept any unsolicited material. Established in 1999.

Albert Spevak
President
Phone: 310-862-5200
Email: aspeval@ambassadortv.com
IMDb: imdb.com/name/nm0818411

AMBER ENTERTAINMENT

21 Ganton St, 4th Floor
London
United Kingdom
W1F 98N
Phone: +44 207-292-7170

6030 Wilshire Blvd
Suite 300
Los Angeles, CA 90036
Phone: 310-242-6445

Email: info@amberentertainment.com
Home Page: amberentertainment.com
IMDb: imdb.com/company/co0266476

Does not accept any unsolicited material. Project types include Feature Films. Preferred genres include Crime, Drama, Fantasy, Horror, and Thriller. Established in 2010.

Lawrence Elman
Executive Producer
IMDb: imdb.com/name/nm3793846

Ileen Maisel
Executive
Phone: +44 207-292-7170
Email: info@amberentertainment.com
IMDb: imdb.com/name/nm0537884

AMBLIN ENTERTAINMENT

100 Universal Plaza
Bldg 477
Universal City, CA 91608
Phone: 818-733-7000
Fax: 818-509-1433

Does not accept any unsolicited material. Project types include Feature Films. Preferred genres include Action, Comedy, Drama, Fantasy, and Science Fiction.

Steven Spielberg
Owner
Phone: 818-733-7000
IMDb: imdb.com/name/nm0000229

AMBUSH ENTERTAINMENT

7364-1/2 Melrose Ave
Los Angeles, CA 90046
Phone: 323-951-9197
Fax: 323-951-9998

Email: info@ambushentertainment.com
Home Page: ambushentertainment.com
IMDb: imdb.com/company/co0091524

Accepts scripts from produced or represented writers. Established in 2000.

Miranda Bailey
Partner/Producer
Phone: 323-951-9197
Email: 323-951-9998
IMDb: imdb.com/name/nm0047419

AMERICAN MOVING PICTURES

108 W 2nd St.
Suite 1012
Los Angeles, CA 90012

Home Page: americanmovingpictures.com

Accepts query letter from unproduced, unrepresented writers via email. Project types include Feature Films. Preferred genres include Comedy and Drama.

Matt D'Elia
Co-Founder
Email: matt@americanmovingpictures.com
IMDb: imdb.com/name/nm2532035

Julian King
Co-Founder
Email: julian@americanmovingpictures.com
IMDb: imdb.com/name/nm2398047

AMERICAN WORK INC.

7030 Delongpre
Los Angeles, CA 90028
Phone: 323-668-1100
Fax: 323-668-1133

IMDb: imdb.com/company/co0167015

Accepts query letter from unproduced, unrepresented writers. Preferred genres include Comedy.

Scot Armstrong
Writer/Director/Producer
IMDb: imdb.com/name/nm0035905

AMERICAN WORLD PICTURES

21700 Oxnard St, Suite 1770
Woodland Hills, CA 91367
Phone: 818-340-9004
Fax: 818-340-9011

Email: info@americanworldpictures.com
Home Page: americanworldpictures.com
IMDb: imdb.com/company/co0054536

Accepts scripts from unproduced, unrepresented writers. Project types include Feature Films. Preferred genres include Action, Comedy, Drama, Family, Horror, Romance, and Thriller.

Mark Lester
President/CEO
Phone: 818-340-9004
Email: mark@americanworldpictures.com
IMDb: imdb.com/name/nm0504495

Dana Dubovsky
President of Production
Phone: 818-340-9004
Email: dana@americanworldpictures.com
IMDb: imdb.com/name/nm0239541

Dee Camp
Vice-President of Acquisitions
Phone: 818-340-9004
Email: dee@americanworldpictures.com
IMDb: imdb.com/name/nm3036636

AMERICAN ZOETROPE

916 Kearny St Sentinel Building
San Francisco, CA 94133
Phone: 415-788-7500
Fax: 415-989-7910

1641 N Ivar Ave
Los Angeles, CA 90028

Email: contests@zoetrope.com
Home Page: zoetrope.com
IMDb: imdb.com/company/co0020958

Accepts scripts from unproduced, unrepresented writers. Preferred genres include Action, Crime, Non-Fiction, and Thriller. Established in 1972.

Francis Coppola
Emeritus
Phone: 415-788-7500
IMDb: imdb.com/name/nm0000338

Michael Zakin
VP, Production & Acquisitions
Phone: 323-460-4420
IMDb: imdb.com/name/nm2943902

AMY ROBINSON PRODUCTIONS

101 Broadway, Suite 405
Brooklyn, NY 11211
Phone: 718-599-2202
Fax: 718-408-9553

Email: arobinsonprod@aol.com
IMDb: imdb.com/company/co0055694

Accepts query letter from unproduced, unrepresented writers via email.

Amy Robinson
Producer
Phone: 718-599-2202
Email: arobinsonprod@aol.com
IMDb: imdb.com/name/nm0732364

Gabrielle Cran
Director of Development
Phone: 718-599-2202
Email: arobinsonprod@aol.com
IMDb: imdb.com/name/nm1660887

ANCHOR BAY FILMS

9242 Beverly Blvd Suite 201
Beverly Hills, CA 90210
Phone: 424-204-4166

Email: questions@anchorbayent.com
Home Page: anchorbayent.com

Accepts query letter from unproduced, unrepresented writers. Preferred genres include Crime, Horror, and Thriller. Established in 1997.

Bill Clark
President
Phone: 424-204-4166
IMDb: imdb.com/name/nm0163694

ANDREA SIMON ENTERTAINMENT

4230 Woodman Ave.
Sherman Oaks, CA 91423
Phone: 818-380-1901
Fax: 818-380-1932

Email: asimon@andreasimonent.com
IMDb: imdb.com/company/co0102747

Accepts query letter from unproduced, unrepresented writers. Project types include Feature Films and TV. Preferred genres include Comedy and Drama.

Andrea Simon
Principal / Producer
Email: asimon@andreasimonent.com
IMDb: imdb.com/name/nm2231084

Anna Henry
Director of Development
IMDb: imdb.com/name/nm1326063

ANDREW LAUREN PRODUCTIONS

36 E 23rd St, Suite 6F
New York, NY 10010
Phone: 212-475-1600
Fax: 212-529-1095

Email: asst@andrewlaurenproductions.com
Home Page: andrewlaurenproductions.com
IMDb: imdb.com/company/co0032488

Accepts scripts from unproduced, unrepresented writers. Project types include Feature Films and TV. Preferred genres include Drama.

Andrew Lauren
Chairman & CEO
Phone: 212-475-1600
Email: asst@andrewlaurenproductions.com
IMDb: imdb.com/name/nm0491054

Dave Platt
Creative Executive
Phone: 212-475-1600
Email: asst@andrewlaurenproductions.com
IMDb: imdb.com/name/nm5255879

ANGELWORLD ENTERTAINMENT LTD.

New Bridge House
30-34 New Bridge St
London
EC4 V6BJ

6 Triq Ta Fuq Il Widien
Mellieha
Malta

Email: asst@angelworldentertainment.com
Home Page: angelworldentertainment.com

Accepts query letter from unproduced, unrepresented writers via email. Project types include Feature Films. Established in 2007.

Darby Angel
CEO/Producer
Email: chris@angelworldentertainment.com
IMDb: imdb.com/name/nm3786007
Assistant: Christopher Tisa

John Michaels
Head Production/Executive Producer

Max Mai
Development Associate
Email: max@angelworldentertainment.com
IMDb: imdb.com/name/nm4221777

ANIMUS FILMS

914 Hauser Blvd
Los Angeles, CA 90036
Phone: 323-988-5557
Fax: 323-571-3361

Email: info@animusfilms.com
Home Page: animusfilms.com
IMDb: imdb.com/company/co0092860

Accepts query letter from unproduced, unrepresented writers. Preferred genres include Non-Fiction and Thriller. Established in 2003.

Jim Young
Producer
Phone: 323-988-5557
Email: info@animusfilms.com
IMDb: imdb.com/name/nm1209063

ANNAPURNA PICTURES

Phone: 310-724-5678
Fax: 310-724-8111

Home Page: annapurnapics.com
IMDb: imdb.com/company/co0323215

Does not accept any unsolicited material. Project types include Feature Films and TV. Preferred genres include Action, Comedy, Crime, Drama, Non-Fiction, and Thriller.

David Distenfeld
Development Executive
IMDb: imdb.com/name/nm3367048

Megan Ellison
Producer
IMDb: imdb.com/name/nm2691892

ANNE CARLUCCI PRODUCTIONS

9200 Sunset Blvd
Penthouse 20
Los Angeles, CA 90069
Phone: 310-550-9545
Fax: 310-550-8471

Email: acprod@sbcglobal.net
IMDb: imdb.com/company/co0094863

Accepts query letter from unproduced, unrepresented writers. Preferred genres include Non-Fiction.

Anne Carlucci
Executive Producer
Phone: 310-913-5626
Email: acprod@sbcglobal.net
IMDb: imdb.com/name/nm0138243

AN OLIVE BRANCH PRODUCTIONS, INC.

9100 Wilshire Blvd, Suite 616
East Tower
Beverly Hills, CA 90212
Phone: 310-860-6088
Fax: 310-362-8922

Email: info@anolivebranchmedia.com
Home Page: anolivebranchmedia.com
IMDb: imdb.com/company/co0055694imdb.com/company/co0308344

Accepts scripts from produced or represented writers. Project types include Feature Films. Preferred genres include Drama.

Cybill Lui
Principal/Producer
Phone: 310-860-6088
Email: info@AnOlivBranchmedia.com
IMDb: imdb.com/name/nm3359236

George Zakk
Principal/Producer
Phone: 310-860-6088
Email: info@AnOlivBranchmedia.com
IMDb: imdb.com/name/nm0952327

ANOMALY ENTERTAINMENT

10990 Wilshire Blvd
Eighth Floor
Los Angeles, CA 90024

Project types include Feature Films and TV. Preferred genres include Documentary, Drama, Non-Fiction, and Period.

Stephen J. Rivele
President & CEO
IMDb: imdb.com/name/nm0729151

Christopher Wilkinson
Principal
IMDb: imdb.com/name/nm0929349

ANONYMOUS CONTENT

3532 Hayden Ave
Culver City, CA 90232
Phone: 310-558-3667
Fax: 310-558-4212

Email: filmtv@anonymouscontcnt.com
Home Page: anonymouscontent.com

Accepts query letter from unproduced, unrepresented writers via email. Project types include Feature Films, TV, and Commercials. Preferred genres include Action, Comedy, Crime, Drama, Family, Non-Fiction, and Thriller. Established in 1999.

Steve Golin
CEO

Matt DeRoss
Vice-President, Features
Phone: 310-558-3667
Email: mattd@anonymouscontent.com
IMDb: imdb.com/name/nm2249185

Emmeline Yang
Director of Development
Phone: 310-558-3667
IMDb: imdb.com/name/nm2534779

ANTIDOTE FILMS

PO Box 150566
Brooklyn, NY 11215-0566
Phone: 646-486-4344

Email: info@antidotefilms.com
Home Page: antidotefilms.com

Does not accept any unsolicited material. Project types include Feature Films. Preferred genres include Documentary. Established in 2000.

Jeffrey Levy-Hinte
President
Phone: 646-486-4344 x301
Email: jeff@antidotefilms.com
IMDb: imdb.com/name/nm0506664

Takeo Hori
Vice President
Phone: 646-486-4344 x300
IMDb: imdb.com/name/nm0394659

Gerry Kim
Director of Operation

James Debbs
Supervisor
Phone: 646-486-4344 x305
IMDb: imdb.com/namc/nm0999455

APATOW PRODUCTIONS

11788 W Pico Blvd
Los Angeles, CA 90064
Phone: 310-943-4400
Fax: 310-479-0750

IMDb: imdb.com/company/co0073081

Does not accept any unsolicited material. Project types include Feature Films and TV. Preferred genres include Action, Comedy, Documentary, Drama, and Romance. Established in 2000.

Judd Apatow
Writer, Director, Producer, President
IMDb: imdb.com/name/nm0031976
Assistant: Amanda Glaze, Rob Turbovsky, Michael Lewen

APERTURE ENTERTAINMENT

7620 Lexington Ave
West Hollywood, CA 90046
Phone: 323-848-4069

Email: agasst@aperture-ent.com
IMDb: imdb.com/company/co0265611

Accepts scripts from unproduced, unrepresented writers. Project types include Feature Films and TV. Preferred genres include Action, Fantasy, Horror, Science Fiction, and Thriller. Established in 2009.

Adam Goldworm
Manager/Producer
Phone: 323-848-4069
Email: adam@aperture-ent.com
IMDb: imdb.com/name/nm0326411
Assistant: David Okubo

APPIAN WAY

9255 Sunset Blvd
West Hollywood, CA 90069
Phone: 310-300-1390
Fax: 310-300-1388

Does not accept any unsolicited material. Project types include Feature Films. Preferred genres include Crime, Detective, Drama, Non-Fiction, and Thriller.

Leonardo DiCaprio
CEO
IMDb: imdb.com/name/nm0000138

Jennifer Davisson Killoran
Head of Production
IMDb: imdb.com/name/nm2248832

John Ridley
Vice President of Production
IMDb: imdb.com/name/nm4244643

Alex Mace
Executive
IMDb: imdb.com/name/nm2858852

Nathaniel Posey
Executive

Aaron Criswell
Development
IMDb: imdb.com/name/nm2082839

Madison Ainley
Assistant

APPLE AND HONEY FILM CORP

9190 W Olympic Blvd, Suite 363
Beverly Hills, CA 90212
Phone: 310-556-5639
Fax: 310-556-1295

Email: quarrel@pacbell.net
IMDb: imdb.com/company/co0069050

Accepts query letter from unproduced, unrepresented writers via email.

David Brandes
Writer, Producer, Director
Phone: 310-556-5639
Email: quarrel@pacbell.net
IMDb: imdb.com/name/nm0104617

APPLESEED ENTERTAINMENT

7715 Sunset Blvd
Ste 101
Hollywood, CA 90046
Phone: 818-718-6000
Fax: 818-556-5610

Email: queries@appleseedent.com
Home Page: appleseedent.com
IMDb: imdb.com/company/co0176039

Does not accept any unsolicited material. Project types include Feature Films. Preferred genres include Comedy, Drama, and Family.

Ben Moses
Executive
Email: ben@appleseedent.com
IMDb: imdb.com/name/nm0608558

Lynne Moses
Executive
Email: lynne@appleseedent.com
IMDb: imdb.com/name/nm1030988

Katherine Lotze
Assistant
Email: katherine@appleseedent.com

ARC LIGHT FILMS

8447 Wilshire Blvd, Suite 101
Beverly Hills, CA 90211
Phone: 310-777-8855
Fax: 310-777-8882

Email: info@arclightfilms.com
Home Page: arclightfilms.com

Accepts query letter from unproduced, unrepresented writers via email. Project types include Feature Films.

Mike Gabrawy
Vice-President Creative
Phone: 310-475-2330
Email: info@arclightfilms.com
IMDb: imdb.com/name/nm0300166

Gary Hamilton
Managing Director
Phone: 310-528-5888
Email: gary@arclightfilms.com
IMDb: imdb.com/name/nm0357861

ARENAS ENTERTAINMENT

3375 Barham Blvd
Los Angeles, CA 90068
Phone: 323-785-5555
Fax: 323-785-5560

Email: general@arenasgroup.com
Home Page: arenasgroup.com
IMDb: imdb.com/company/co0051527

Does not accept any unsolicited material. Project types include Feature Films. Established in 1988.

Santiago Pozo
CEO
IMDb: imdb.com/name/nm0694815

ARGONAUT PICTURES

Phone: 310-359-8481

Home Page: argonautpictures.com

Accepts query letter from unproduced, unrepresented writers. Project types include Feature Films. Preferred genres include Drama.

Scott Bloom
Owner
IMDb: imdb.com/name/nm0089231

Giovanni Agnelli
Owner
IMDb: imdb.com/name/nm1278301

Paul Marashlian
Senior VP Development
Email: Paul@argonautpictures.com
IMDb: imdb.com/name/nm2281671

Karim Mashouf
Owner
IMDb: imdb.com/name/nm3196690

Manny Mashouf
Owner
IMDb: imdb.com/name/nm3196705

Carter Hall
Executive Assistant
Email: carter@argonautpictures.com
IMDb: imdb.com/name/nm3050292

ARIESCOPE PICTURES

10750 Cumpston St
North Hollywood, CA 91601

Email: info@ariescope.com
Home Page: ariescope.com

Accepts query letter from unproduced, unrepresented writers. Project types include Feature Films and TV. Preferred genres include Comedy, Crime, Drama, Fantasy, Horror, Romance, and Thriller.

Will Barratt
Principal
IMDb: .imdb.com/name/nm1701139

Cory Neal
Principal
IMDb: imdb.com/name/nm1425628

Adam Green
Principal
IMDb: imdb.com/name/nm1697112

ARS NOVA

511 W 54th St
New York, NY 10019
Phone: 212-586-4200
Fax: 212-489-1908

Email: info@arsnovaent.com
Home Page: arsnovaent.com
IMDb: imdb.com/company/co0176042

Accepts scripts from unproduced, unrepresented writers. Preferred genres include Action, Comedy, Fantasy, Myth, and Science Fiction.

Jon Steingart
Producer
Phone: 212-586-4200
Email: japfelbaum@arsnovaent.com
IMDb: imdb.com/name/nm0826050

Jillian Apfelbaum
Producer
Phone: 212-586-4200
Email: japfelbaum@arsnovaent.com
IMDb: imdb.com/name/nm2249752

ARTFIRE FILMS

740 N. La Brea Ave.
Hollywood, CA 90038
Phone: 323-937-7188
Fax: 323-937-6713

Email: contact@artfirefilms.com
Home Page: artfirefilms.com
IMDb: imdb.com/company/co0188290

Does not accept any unsolicited material. Project types include Feature Films. Preferred genres include Action, Comedy, Crime, Documentary, Drama, Horror, Period, Romance, and Science Fiction. Established in 2007.

Arthur Spigel
Principal
IMDb: imdb.com/name/nm1742493

Dan Fireman
Principal
IMDb: imdb.com/name/nm2379207

Jennah Dirksen
Creative Executive
IMDb: imdb.com/name/nm3302694

Ara Katz
Producer
IMDb: imdb.com/name/nm1433420

Andy Spellman
Executive Producer

ARTICLE 19 FILMS

247 Centre St, Suite 7W
New York, NY 10013
Phone: 212-777-1987
Fax: 212-777-2585

Email: article19films@gmail.com
Home Page: article19films.com
IMDb: imdb.com/company/co0164965

Accepts query letter from unproduced, unrepresented writers. Preferred genres include Non-Fiction.

Filippo Bozotti
Producer-Executive
Phone: 212-777-1987
Email: article19films@gmail.com
IMDb: imdb.com/name/nm1828075

ARTISTS PRODUCTION GROUP (APG)

9348 Civic Center Dr, 2nd Floor
Beverly Hills, CA 90210
Phone: 310-300-2400
Fax: 310-300-2424

IMDb: imdb.com/company/co0024601

Accepts scripts from produced or represented writers.

Chris George
Creative Executive
Phone: 310-300-2400
IMDb: imdb.com/name/nm0313383

ARTISTS PUBLIC DOMAIN

225 W 13th St
New York, NY 10011

Email: info@artistspublicdomain.com
Home Page: artistspublicdomain.com

Accepts query letter from unproduced, unrepresented writers. Project types include Feature Films. Preferred genres include Comedy, Drama, Family, Non-Fiction, Romance, Sociocultural, and Thriller.

Andrew Adair
Head of Production
IMDb: imdb.com/name/nm4253715

Hunter Gray
Producer
IMDb: imdb.com/name/nm0336683

Alex Orlovsky
Producer
IMDb: imdb.com/name/nm0650164

A. SMITH & COMPANY PRODUCTIONS

9911 W Pico Blvd, Suite 250
Los Angeles, CA 90035
Phone: 310-432-4800
Fax: 310-551-3085

Email: info@asmithco.com
Home Page: asmithco.com
IMDb: imdb.com/company/co0095150

Accepts query letter from unproduced, unrepresented writers via email.

Arthur Smith

CEO
Phone: 310-432-4800
Email: info@asmithco.com
IMDb: wwwimdb.com/name/nm0807368

Christmas Rini

VP, Development
Phone: 310-432-4800
Email: info@asmithco.com
IMDb: imdb.com/name/nm2859471

ASYLUM ENTERTAINMENT

15301 Ventura Blvd
Suite 400 Building B
Sherman Oaks, CA 91403
Phone: 310-696-4401
Fax: 310-696-4891

Email: info@asylument.com
Home Page: asylument.com

Accepts scripts from unproduced, unrepresented writers. Project types include TV. Preferred genres include Action, Crime, Drama, Fantasy, Horror, Non-Fiction, Science Fiction, and Thriller.

Marielle Skouras

Director of Development
Phone: 310-696-4401
Email: info@asylument.com
IMDb: imdb.com/name/nm4413245

ATLAS ENTERTAINMENT (PRODUCTION BRANCH OF MOSAIC)

9200 Sunset Blvd, 10th Floor
Los Angeles, CA 90069
Phone: 310-786-8900
Fax: 310-777-2185

IMDb: imdb.com/company/co0028338

Does not accept any unsolicited material. Project types include Feature Films and TV.

Alex Gartner

Producer
Phone: 310-786-8105
IMDb: imdb.com/name/nm0308672

Jake Kurily

Vice President (Motion Pictures & Television)
Phone: 310-786-8974
IMDb: imdb.com/name/nm2464228

Andy Horwitz

Vice President (Motion Pictures & Television)
Phone: 310-786-4948
IMDb: imdb.com/name/nm2191045

ATLAS MEDIA CORPORATION

242 W 36th St, 11th Floor
New York, NY, 10018
Phone: 212-714-0222
Fax: 212-714-0240

Email: info@atlasmediacorp.com
Home Page: atlasmediacorp.com
IMDb: imdb.com/company/co0280783

Accepts query letter from produced or represented writers. Preferred genres include Non-Fiction.

Glen Freyer

Sr. Vice-President Development
Phone: 212-714-0222
Email: info@atlasmediacorp.com
IMDb: imdb.com/name/nm0294662

Andrew Jacobs

Director Of Development
Phone: 212-714-0222
Email: info@atlasmediacorp.com

ATMOSPHERE ENTERTAINMENT MM, LLC

4751 Wilshire, Blvd, 3rd Floor
Los Angeles, CA, 90010
Phone: 323-549-4350
Fax: 323-549-9832

IMDb: imdb.com/company/co0014103

Accepts scripts from produced or represented writers. Preferred genres include Fantasy, Horror, and Thriller.

David Hopwood
SVP, Film & TV Development
Phone: 323-549-4350
IMDb: imdb.com/name/nm2055027

AUTOMATIC PICTURES

5225 Wilshire Blvd
Suite 525
Los Angeles, CA 90036
Phone: 323-935-1800
Fax: 323-935-8040

Email: automaticstudio@mail.com
Home Page: automaticpictures.net

Accepts query letter from unproduced, unrepresented writers via email. Project types include Video Games. Preferred genres include Fantasy.

Frank Beddor
Principal
IMDb: imdb.com/name/nm0065980
Assistant: Bo Liebman

Nate Barlow
VP of New Media
Email: nate@automaticpictures.net
IMDb: imdb.com/name/nm0055269

Liz Cavalier
Creative Executive
IMDb: imdb.com/name/nm2248983

AUTOMATIK ENTERTAINMENT

8322 Beverly Blvd, Suite 303C
Los Angeles, CA 90048
Phone: 323-677-2486
Fax: 323-657-5354

Email: info@imglobalfilm.com
Home Page: imglobalfilm.com
IMDb: imdb.com/company/co0323227

Does not accept any unsolicited material. Project types include Feature Films and TV. Preferred genres include Action, Comedy, Fantasy, and Thriller.

Brian Kavanaugh-Jones
President-Producer
Phone: 323-677-2486
Email: office@automatikent.com
IMDb: imdb.com/name/nm2271939
Assistant: Alex Saks

Bailey Conway
Vice President, Production and Development
Phone: 323-677-2486
Email: office@automatikent.com
IMDb: imdb.com/name/nm2811848

BAD HAT HARRY

10201 W Pico Blvd
Building 50
Los Angeles, CA 90064
Phone: 310-369-2080

Email: reception@badhatharry.com
Home Page: badhatharry.com
IMDb: imdb.com/company/co0057712

Accepts scripts from produced or represented writers. Project types include TV. Preferred genres include Action, Drama, Fantasy, Myth, Science Fiction, and Thriller.

Bryan Singer
Chief Executive Officer
Phone: 310-369-2080
IMDb: imdb.com/name/nm0001741

Mark Berliner
Vice President (Development)
Phone: 310-369-2080
IMDb: imdb.com/name/nm2249392

BAD ROBOT

1221 Olympic Blvd
Santa Monica, CA 90404
Phone: 310-664-3456
Fax: 310-664-3457

Home Page: badrobot.com
IMDb: wwwimdb.com/company/co0021593

Does not accept any unsolicited material. Project types include Feature Films and TV. Preferred genres include Action, Drama, Fantasy, and Science Fiction.

J.J. Abrams
Chairman (Chief Executive Officer)
Phone: 310-664-3456
IMDb: imdb.com/name/nm0009190
Assistant: Morgan Dameron

Bryan Burk
Partner, Executive Vice President
IMDb: imdb.com/name/nm1333357
Assistant: Max Taylor

Kathy Lingg
Head of Television
IMDb: imdb.com/name/nm2489727
Assistant: Matthew Owens

David Baronoff
Executive (New Media, Film & Television
IMDb: imdb.com/name/nm2343623

Jonathan Cohen
Executive
Assistant: Veronica Baker

Kevin Jarzynski
Executive
IMDb: imdb.com/name/nm1704653
Assistant: Veronica Baker

Lindsey Paulson Weber
Head of Film
IMDb: imdb.com/name/nm1439829
Assistant: Corrine Aquino

Athena Wickham
Executive of Television
IMDb: imdb.com/name/nm2204043
Assistant: Casey Haver

BALDWIN ENTERTAINMENT GROUP, LTD.

3000 W Olympic Blvd Suite 2510
Santa Monica, CA
Phone: 310-243-6634

Email: info@baldwinent.com
Home Page: baldwinent.com
IMDb: imdb.com/company/co0057712mdb.com/
company/co0145519

Does not accept any unsolicited material. Project types
include Feature Films. Preferred genres include Action,

Comedy, Drama, Non-Fiction, and Romance.
Established in 2009.

Howard Baldwin
Producer/President
Phone: 310-243-6634
IMDb: imdb.com/name/nm0049920

Karen Baldwin
Senior Vice-President
Phone: 310-243-6634
IMDb: imdb.com/name/nm0049945

Ryan Wuerfel
Creative Executive
Phone: 310-243-6634
Email: ryan@baldwinent.com
IMDb: imdb.com/name/nm3601274

BALLYHOO, INC.

6738 Wedgewood Place
Los Angeles, CA 90068
Phone: 323-874-3396

Accepts scripts from unproduced, unrepresented
writers. Project types include Feature Films. Preferred
genres include Action and Comedy.

Michael Besman
Producer
Phone: 323-874-3396
IMDb: imdb.com/name/nm0078698

BALTIMORE PICTURES

8306 Wilshire Blvd
PMB 1012
Beverly Hills, CA 90211
Phone: 310-234-8988

Home Page: levinson.com/index_bsc.htm
IMDb: imdb.com/company/co0038108

Does not accept any unsolicited material. Project types
include Feature Films. Preferred genres include
Comedy, Crime, Drama, Romance, Science Fiction,
and Thriller.

Barry Levinson
Principal (Director/Producer/Writer)
IMDb: imdb.com/name/nm0001469

Jason Sosnoff
Director Of Development
IMDb: imdb.com/name/nm0815369

BANDITO BROTHERS

3115 S La Cienega Blvd.
Los Angeles, CA 90016
Phone: 310-559-5404
Fax: 310-559-5230

Email: info@banditobrothers.com
Home Page: banditiobrothers.com

Project types include Feature Films. Preferred genres include Action, Comedy, Drama, Fantasy, Science Fiction, and Thriller.

Mike McCoy
CEO & Creative Director
IMDb: imdb.com/name/nm0566788

Scott Waugh
Founder
IMDb: imdb.com/name/nm0915304

Max Leitman
COO
IMDb: imdb.com/name/nm2649648

Jay Pollak
Managing Director & Executive Producer

Suzanne Hargrove
Managing Director
IMDb: imdb.com/name/nm2597628

Jacob Rosenberg
Chief Technology Officer
IMDb: imdb.com/name/nm0742230

BARNSTORM FILMS

73 Market St
Venice, CA 90291
Phone: 310-396-5937
Fax: 310-450-4988

Email: tbtb@comcast.net
IMDb: imdb.com/company/co0044065

Accepts query letter from unproduced, unrepresented writers.

Tony Bill
Producer/Director
Phone: 310-396-5937
Email: tbtb@comcast.net
IMDb: imdb.com/name/nm0082300

BARNSTORM PICTURES LLC

8524 Fontana St
Downey, CA 90241

IMDb: imdb.com/company/co0221137

Does not accept any unsolicited material. Project types include Feature Films.

Justin Lin
Producer/Director
IMDb: imdb.com/name/nm0510912

Elaine Chin
Producer
IMDb: imdb.com/name/nm1227183

BARRY FILMS

4081 Redwood Ave
Los Angeles, CA 90066
Phone: 310-871-3392

Email: mail@barryfilms.com
Home Page: barryfilms.com
IMDb: imdb.com/company/co0075789

Accepts query letter from unproduced, unrepresented writers via email. Project types include Feature Films. Preferred genres include Action, Animation, Detective, Fantasy, and Romance.

Benito Mueller
Producer
Phone: 310-871-3392
Email: benito@barryfilms.com
IMDb: imdb.com/name/nm1762339

BASRA ENTERTAINMENT

68-444 Perez Rd, Suite O
Cathedral City, CA 92234
Phone: 760-324-9855
Fax: 760-324-9035

Email: info@basraentertainment.com
Home Page: basraentertainment.com
IMDb: imdb.com/company/co0092056

Accepts query letter from unproduced, unrepresented writers. Established in 2002.

Daniela Ryan
Producer
Phone: 760-324-9855
Email: daniela@basraentertainment.com
IMDb: imdb.com/name/nm0752491

BAUER MARTINEZ STUDIOS

601 Cleveland St, Suite 501
Clearwater, FL 33755
Phone: 727-210-1408
Fax: 727-210-1470

Email: cindy@bauermartinez.com
Home Page: bauermartinez.com
IMDb: imdb.com/company/co0025891

Accepts query letter from unproduced, unrepresented writers.

Phillipe Martinez
Producer/CEO
Phone: 727-210-1408
Email: cindy@cinepropictures.com
IMDb: imdb.com/name/nm0553662

BAY FILMS

631 Colorado Ave
Santa Monica, CA 90401
Phone: 310-319-6565
Fax: 310-319-6570

Does not accept any unsolicited material. Project types include Feature Films. Preferred genres include Action, Comedy, Drama, Fantasy, Science Fiction, and Thriller.

Michael Bay
CEO
IMDb: imdb.com/name/nm0000881
Assistant: Talley Singer

Matthew Cohan
Vice President of Development
IMDb: www,imdb.com/name/nm0169134

Michael Kase
VP of Production
IMDb: imdb.com/name/nm0440476

BAYONNE ENTERTAINMENT

6560 W Sunset Blvd Ninth Floor
West Hollywood, CA 90069
Phone: 310-777-1940
Fax: 310-889-9323

Email: assistant@bayonne-ent.com

Accepts query letter from produced or represented writers. Project types include TV. Preferred genres include Comedy, Drama, Fantasy, and Science Fiction.

Rob Lee
President
IMDb: imdb.com/name/nm0498098

BAZELEVS PRODUCTION

Pudovkina St
6/1
Moscow 119285
Russia
Phone: +7 495-223-04-00

Email: film@bazelevs.ru
Home Page: bazelevs.ru
IMDb: imdb.com/company/co0042742

Does not accept any unsolicited material. Project types include Feature Films.

Timur Bekmambetov
CEO/Director/Producer
Phone: +7 495-223-04-00
Email: film@bazelevs.ru
IMDb: imdb.com/name/nm0067457

BBC FILMS

Room 6023
BBC Television Centre
Wood Ln, London W12 7RJ
UK
Phone: +44 20-8576-7265
Fax: +44 20-8576-7268

Home Page: bbc.co.uk/bbcfilms
IMDb: imdb.com/company/co0103694

Accepts scripts from unproduced, unrepresented writers. Project types include Feature Films and TV. Preferred genres include Action, Comedy, Crime, Detective, Drama, Fantasy, Horror, Myth, Non-Fiction, Romance, Science Fiction, and Thriller.

Joe Oppenheimer
Development
Phone: +44 20-8576-7265
IMDb: imdb.com/name/nm0649189

Jamie Laurenson
Development
Phone: +44 20-8576-7265
IMDb: imdb.com/name/nm0491191

BCDF PICTURES

P.O. Box 849
Kerhonkson, NY 12446
Phone: 212-945-8618
Fax: 917-591-7589

Email: submissions@bcdfpictures.com
Email: info@bcdfpictures.com
Home Page: bcdfpictures.com

Accepts query letter from unproduced, unrepresented writers via email. Project types include Feature Films. Preferred genres include Comedy, Crime, Drama, Family, Romance, and Thriller.

Paul Prokop
Executive Producer
IMDb: imdb.com/name/nm2373782

Brice Dal Farra
Principal
IMDb: imdb.com/name/nm3894454

Claude Dal Farra
Principal
IMDb: imdb.com/name/nm3894387

Lauren Munsch
Producer
IMDb: imdb.com/name/nm3907323

BEACON PICTURES

2900 Olympic Blvd
2nd Floor
Santa Monica, CA 90404

Phone: 310-260-7000
Fax: 310-260-7096

Email: contactus@beaconpictures.com
Home Page: beaconpictures.com

Does not accept any unsolicited material. Project types include Feature Films and TV. Preferred genres include Action, Comedy, Crime, Detective, Drama, Family, Fantasy, Romance, Science Fiction, and Thriller. Established in 1990.

Armyan Berstein
Chairman
IMDb: imdb.com/name/nm0077000

Suzann Ellis
President
Email: sellis@beaconpictures.com
IMDb: imdb.com/name/nm0255104

Rudy Langlais
Producer

Mark Pennell
Producer
Email: mpennell@beaconpictures.com
IMDb: imdb.com/name/nm0672075

Peter Almond
Producer

Glenn Klekowski
Beacon TV
IMDb: imdb.com/name/nm0459192

Joeanna Sayler
Beacon TV

Jeffrey Crooks
Director of Special Projects
IMDb: imdb.com/name/nm3715349

BEE HOLDER PRODUCTIONS

Phone: 310-860-1005
Fax: 310-860-1007

Email: asst@beeholder.com

Accepts query letter from unproduced, unrepresented writers. Project types include Feature Films. Preferred genres include Comedy, Crime, Detective, Documentary, Drama, and Thriller.

John Hill
Assistant
IMDb: imdb.com/name/nm4787026

Michelle Jones
Executive
IMDb: imdb.com/name/nm4786947

Steven Lee Jones
President
IMDb: imdb.com/name/nm2831867

Dan Fugardi
Director of Development
Email: dan@beeholder.com
IMDb: imdb.com/name/nm2809882

Chad Hively
Assistant
Email: chad@beeholder.com
IMDb: imdb.com/name/nm3510973

BEFORE THE DOOR PICTURES

1138 Hyperion Ave
Los Angeles, CA 90029
Phone: 323-644-5525
Fax: 323-644-5528

Email: staff@beforethedoor.com
Home Page: beforethedoor.com
IMDb: imdb.com/company/co0271126

Does not accept any unsolicited material. Project types include Feature Films, TV, and Commercials. Preferred genres include Action, Comedy, Crime, Drama, Science Fiction, and Thriller.

Zachary Quinto
Partner / Producer
IMDb: imdb.com/name/nm0704270

Corey Moosa
Partner / Producer
IMDb: imdb.com/name/nm0602161

Neal Dodson
Partner / Producer
IMDb: imdb.com/name/nm0230306

Sean Akers
Development / Web
IMDb: imdb.com/name/nm3577109

BELISARIUS PRODUCTIONS

1901 Ave of the Stars Second Floor
Los Angeles, CA 90067
Phone: 310-461-1361
Fax: 310-461-1362

Does not accept any unsolicited material. Project types include TV. Preferred genres include Crime, Detective, Drama, and Thriller.

Donald Bellisario
Executive Producer
IMDb: imdb.com/name/nm0069074

David Bellisario
Producer
IMDb: imdb.com/name/nm0069072

John C. Kelley
Co-Executive Producer
IMDb: imdb.com/name/nm0445931

Chas Floyd Johnson
Co-Executive Producer
IMDb: imdb.com/name/nm0424759

Mark Horowitz
Co-Executive Producer
IMDb: imdb.com/name/nm0395317

Shane Brennan
Producer
IMDb: imdb.com/name/nm0107402

BELLADONNA PRODUCTIONS

164 W 25th St 9th Floor
New York, NY 10001
Phone: 212-807-0108
Fax: 212-807-6263

Email: mail@belladonna.bz
Home Page: belladonna.bz
IMDb: imdb.com/company/co0003224
Facebook: facebook.com/belladonnaproductions

Accepts query letter from unproduced, unrepresented writers. Preferred genres include Comedy, Non-Fiction, and Thriller. Established in 1994.

René Bastian
Owner/Producer
Phone: 212-807-0108
Email: mail@belladonna.bz
IMDb: imdb.com/name/nm0060459

BELLWETHER PICTURES

Accepts query letter from unproduced, unrepresented writers via email. Project types include Feature Films and Commercials. Preferred genres include Action, Comedy, Drama, and Science Fiction. Established in 2011.

Joss Whedon
Writer/Producer/Co-Founder
IMDb: imdb.com/name/nm0923736

Kai Cole
Producer/Co-Founder
IMDb: imdb.com/name/nm4740874

BENAROYA PICTURES

8383 Wilshire Blvd
Suite 310
Beverly Hills, CA 90212
USA
Phone: 323-883-0056
Fax: 866-220-5520

Email: general@benaroyapics.com
Home Page: benaroyapics.com
IMDb: imdb.com/company/co0232586

Accepts query letter from unproduced, unrepresented writers via email. Project types include Feature Films. Preferred genres include Drama. Established in 2006.

Michael Benaroya
Founder-CEO
Phone: 323-883-0056
IMDb: imdb.com/name/nm2918260

Joe Jenckes
Head of Production
Phone: 323-883-0056
Email: joel@benaroyapics.com
IMDb: imdb.com/name/nm3765270

Clayton Young
Business Development
Phone: 323-883-0056
Email: clay@benaroyapics.com
IMDb: imdb.com/name/nm4464240

BENDERSPINK

5870 W Jefferson Blvd, Studio E
Los Angeles, CA 90016
Phone: 323-904-1800
Fax: 323-297-2442

Email: info@benderspink.com
Home Page: benderspink.com
IMDb: imdb.com/company/co0044439

Does not accept any unsolicited material. Project types include TV. Preferred genres include Action, Comedy, Crime, Detective, Drama, Fantasy, Horror, Myth, Non-Fiction, Romance, Science Fiction, and Thriller.

Chris Bender
Founder
Phone: 323-904-1800
Email: info@benderspink.com
IMDb: imdb.com/name/nm0818940

J.C. Spink
Founder
Phone: 323-904-1800
Email: info@benderspink.com
IMDb: imdb.com/name/nm0818940

BERK LANE ENTERTAINMENT

9595 Wilshire Blvd, Suitee 900
Beverly Hills, CA 90212
Phone: 310-300-8410

Email: info@berklane.com
IMDb: wwwimdb.com/company/co0183891

Does not accept any unsolicited material. Preferred genres include Action, Comedy, and Crime.

Jason Berk
Co-Chairman
Phone: 310-300-8410
Email: info@berklane.com
IMDb: imdb.com/name/nm1357809

Matt Lane
Co-Chairman
Phone: 310-300-8410
Email: info@berklane.com
IMDb: imdb.com/name/nm2325262

BERLANTI TELEVISION

500 S Buena Vista St
Old Animation Building, 2B-5
Burbank, CA 91521
Phone: 818-560-4536
Fax: 818-560-3931

IMDb: imdb.com/company/co0192672

Accepts query letter from unproduced, unrepresented writers. Project types include TV. Preferred genres include Drama.

Greg Berlanti
Writer-Producer-Director
IMDb: imdb.com/name/nm0075528

BERMANBRAUN

2900 W Olympic Blvd, 3rd Floor
Sanata Monica, CA, 90404
Phone: 310-255-7272
Fax: 310-255-7058

Email: info@bermanbraun.com
Home Page: bermanbraun.com
IMDb: imdb.com/company/co0199425

Does not accept any unsolicited material.

Chris Cowan
Executive, Head of Unscripted Television
Phone: 310-255-7272
Email: info@bermanbraun.com
IMDb: imdb.com/name/nm0184544

Andrew Mittman
Executive, Head of Feature Film
Phone: 310-255-7272
Email: info@bermanbraun.com
IMDb: imdb.com/name/nm3879410

BERNERO PRODUCTIONS

500 S. Buena Vista St, Suite 2D-4
Burbank, CA 91521
Phone: 818-560-1442

Email: info@berneroproductions.com
Home Page: berneroproductions.com
IMDb: imdb.com/company/co0281008

Accepts query letter from unproduced, unrepresented writers via email.

Bob Kim
Producer
IMDb: imdb.com/name/nm2344755

BETH GROSSBARD PRODUCTIONS

5168 Otis Ave
Tarzana, CA 91356
Phone: 818-758-2500
Fax: 818-705-7366

Email: bgpix@sbcglobal.net
IMDb: imdb.com/company/co0037144

Accepts query letter from produced or represented writers. Project types include TV. Preferred genres include Comedy and Drama.

Beth Grossbard
Executive Producer
Email: bgpix@sbcglobal.net
IMDb: imdb.com/name/nm0343526

BET NETWORKS

One BET Plaza
1235 W St NE
Washington, DC 20018-1211
Phone: 202-608-2000
Fax: 206-608-2631

Home Page: bet.com
IMDb: imdb.com/company/co0176390

Does not accept any unsolicited material. Project types include Feature Films and TV. Preferred genres include Comedy, Documentary, and Drama.

Rickey Austyn Biggers
Director of Development
Phone: 310-481-3741
Email: austyn.biggers@bet.net
IMDb: imdb.com/name/nm2056137

Robyn Lattaker-Johnson
Sr. VP - Development, Original Programming
IMDb: imdb.com/name/nm0426464

BIG FOOT ENTERTAINMENT INC.

1214 Abbot Kinney Blvd
Los Angeles, CA 90291
Phone: 310-593-4646

Email: info@bigfoot.com
Home Page: bigfoot.com
IMDb: imdb.com/company/co0261687

Accepts query letter from unproduced, unrepresented writers via email. Project types include Feature Films and TV. Preferred genres include Action, Animation, Drama, Fantasy, Myth, Science Fiction, and Thriller. Established in 2004.

Ashley Jordan
CEO
Email: ashley@bigfootcorp.com
IMDb: imdb.com/name/nm1248442

BIG TALK PRODUCTIONS

26 Nassau St
London
W1W 7AQ
Phone: +44 (0) 20-7255-1131
Fax: +44 (0) 20-7255-1132

Email: info@bigtalkproductions.com
Home Page: bigtalkproductions.com

Does not accept any unsolicited material. Project types include TV. Preferred genres include Action, Comedy, Crime, Drama, and Science Fiction.

Rachael Prior
Head of Development - Fim
Phone: +44 (0) 20-7255-1131
Email: info@bigtalkproductions.com
IMDb: imdb.com/name/nm0975099

BIRCH TREE ENTERTAINMENT INC.

10620 Southern Highlands Parkway
Suite 110-418
Las Vegas, NV 89141
Phone: 702-858-2782
Fax: 702-583-7928

Email: sales@birchtreefilms.com
Home Page: birchtreeentertainment.com
IMDb: imdb.com/company/co0114722

Accepts scripts from produced or represented writers. Project types include Feature Films. Preferred genres include Action.

Art Birzneck
President/CEO
Phone: 702-858-2782
Email: sales@birchtreefilms.com
IMDb: imdb.com/name/nm1010723

BISCAYNE PICTURES

500 S Buena Vista St
Animation Building
Burbank, CA 91521-1802
Phone: 310-777-2007

Email: info@biscaynepictures.com
Home Page: biscaynepictures.com
IMDb: imdb.com/company/co0152645

Does not accept any unsolicited material. Project types include Feature Films and TV. Preferred genres include Action, Crime, Drama, and Thriller.

Jeff Silver
President-Producer
Phone: 310-777-2007
Email: info@biscaynepictures.com
IMDb: imdb.com/name/nm0798711
Assistant: Matthew Bradley

BIX PIX ENTERTAINMENT

3511 W Burbank Blvd
Burbank, CA 91505
Phone: 818-953-7474
Fax: 818-953-9948

Email: info@bixpix.com
Home Page: bixpix.com
IMDb: imdb.com/company/co0187260

Accepts query letter from unproduced, unrepresented writers. Preferred genres include Fantasy. Established in 1998.

Kelli Bixler

Founder/President/Executive Producer
Phone: 818-953-7474
Email: info@bixpix.com
IMDb: imdb.com/name/nm1064778

BLACK BEAR PICTURES

185 Franklin St
4th Floor
New York, NY 10013
Phone: 212-931-5714
Fax: 212-966-3311

Email: info@blackbearpictures.com
Home Page: blackbearpictures.com

Accepts query letter from unproduced, unrepresented writers. Project types include Feature Films. Preferred genres include Comedy, Drama, and Romance. Established in 2011.

Teddy Schwarzman

Co-Founder/Principal
IMDb: imdb.com/name/nm3267061

Ben Stillman

Creative Executive
IMDb: imdb.com/name/nm4212466

Amanda Greenblatt

Executive Assistant
IMDb: imdb.com/name/nm1716375

BLACKLIGHT TRANSMEDIA

9465 Wilshire Blvd
Beverly Hills, CA 90212
Phone: 310-858-2196

Email: info@blacklighttransmedia.com
Home Page: blacklighttransmedia.com
IMDb: imdb.com/company/co0333337

Accepts scripts from produced or represented writers. Project types include Feature Films.

Zak Kadison

Founder/CEO
Phone: 310-858-2196
Email: info@blacklighttransmedia.com
IMDb: imdb.com/name/nm1780162

Justin Catron

Creative Executive
Phone: 310-858-2196
Email: info@blacklighttransmedia.com
IMDb: imdb.com/name/nm2031037

BLACK SHEEP ENTERTAINMENT

11271 Ventura Blvd, #447
Studio City, CA 91604
Phone: 310-424-5085
Fax: 310-424-7117

Email: info@blacksheept.com
IMDb: imdb.com/company/co0029807

Accepts query letter from unproduced, unrepresented writers. Established in 2009.

Steven Feder

Owner/Writer/Producer/Director
Phone: 310-424-5085
Email: steven@blacksheepent.com
IMDb: imdb.com/name/nm027009

BLEIBERG ENTERTAINMENT

225 S Clark Dr
Beverly Hills, CA 90211
Phone: 310-273-0003
Fax: 310-273-0007

Email: info@bleibergent.com
Home Page: bleibergent.com
IMDb: imdb.com/company/co0165151

Accepts query letter from unproduced, unrepresented writers via email. Project types include Feature Films and TV.

Ehud Bleiberg

CEO/Founder
Phone: 310-273-0003
Email: ehud@bleibergent.com
IMDb: imdb.com/name/nm0088173

Nicholas Donnermeyer
Vice-President Acquisitions & Development
Phone: 310-273-0003
Email: nick@bleibergent.com
IMDb: imdb.com/name/nm2223730

BLIND WINK PRODUCTIONS

8 Mills Place 2nd Floor
Pasadena, CA 91105
Phone: 626-600-4100

Email: info@blindwink.com
Home Page: blindwink.com

Does not accept any unsolicited material. Project types include Feature Films. Preferred genres include Action, Comedy, Crime, Drama, Family, Fantasy, Science Fiction, and Thriller.

Gore Verbinski
Principal
IMDb: imdb.com/name/nm0893659

Nils Peyron
Executive Vice President
IMDb: imdb.com/name/nm3741163

Will Stahl
Senior Vice President of Gaming Development

Jonathan Krauss
Head of Film Production & Development
IMDb: imdb.com/name/nm0470310

Josh Pincus
Director of Development

James Ward Byrkit
Creative & Story
IMDb: imdb.com/name/nm0126096

BLONDIE GIRL PRODUCTIONS

1040 N Las Palmas
Building 40
Los Angeles, CA 90038
Phone: 323-860-8610
Fax: 323-860-8601

Email: jessica@blondiegirlprod.com
Home Page: blondiegirlproductions.com
IMDb: imdb.com/company/co0261290

Does not accept any unsolicited material. Project types include TV.

Ashley Tisdale
Principal
IMDb: imdb.com/name/nm0864308

Jennifer Tisdale
Coordinator (Development & Production)
IMDb: imdb.com/name/nm1056279

Jessica Rhodes
Producing Partner
IMDb: imdb.com/name/nm1224043

BLUEGRASS FILMS

100 Universal City Plaza
Bungalow 4171
Universal City, CA 91608
Phone: 818-777-3200
Fax: 818-777-0020

IMDb: imdb.com/company/co0376117

Does not accept any unsolicited material. Project types include Feature Films and TV. Preferred genres include Action, Crime, Drama, Fantasy, Romance, Science Fiction, and Thriller.

Scott Stuber
Producer
IMDb: imdb.com/name/nm0835959

Michael Clear
Creative Executive
IMDb: imdb.com/name/nm2752795

Nicholas Nesbitt
Creative Executive
IMDb: imdb.com/name/nm1704779

BLUEPRINT PICTURES

43-45 Charlotte St
London W1T 1RS
United Kingdom
Phone: +44 0207-580-6915
Fax: +44 0207-580-6934

Email: asst@blueprintpictures.com

Does not accept any unsolicited material. Established in 2004.

Graham Broadbent

Producer
Phone: +44 0207-580-6915
Email: asst@blueprintpictures.com
IMDb: imdb.com/name/nm0110357

BLUE SKY STUDIOS

One American Ln
Greenwich, CT 06831
Phone: 203-992-6000
Fax: 203-992-6001

Email: info@blueskystudios.com
Home Page: blueskystudios.com
IMDb: imdb.com/company/co0047265

Does not accept any unsolicited material. Project types include Feature Films. Established in 1997.

Chris Wedge

Vice-President
IMDb: imdb.com/name/nm0917188

Lisa Fragner

Head (Feature Development)
IMDb: imdb.com/name/nm0289591

BLUMHOUSE PRODUCTIONS

5555 Melrose Ave
Lucy Bungalow 103
Los Angeles, CA 90038
Phone: 323-956-4480

IMDb: imdb.com/company/co0098315

Accepts query letter from unproduced, unrepresented writers. Preferred genres include Action, Horror, and Thriller. Established in 2000.

Jason Blum

Producer
IMDb: imdb.com/name/nm0089658

Jessica Hall

Director Of Development
IMDb: imdb.com/name/nm4148859

BOBKER/KRUGAR FILMS

1416 N La Brea Ave
Hollywood, CA 90028

Phone: 323-469-1440
Fax: 323-802-1597

IMDb: imdb.com/company/co0163148

Accepts query letter from unproduced, unrepresented writers.

Daniel Bobker

Producer
IMDb: imdb.com/name/nm0090394

Ehren Kruger

Writer / Producer
IMDb: imdb.com/name/nm0472567

BOGNER ENTERTAINMENT

269 S Beverly Dr, Suite 8
Beverly Hills, CA 90212
Phone: 310-553-0300

Email: info.beitv@gmail.com
Home Page: bognerentertainment.com
IMDb: imdb.com/company/co0068550

Accepts scripts from unproduced, unrepresented writers. Preferred genres include Horror and Thriller. Established in 2000.

Oliver Bogner

Vice-President Development & Casting
Email: oliverbogner@gmail.com
IMDb: imdb.com/name/nm3331124

Jonathan Bogner

President
Email: jsbogner@aol.com
IMDb: imdb.com/name/nm0091845

BOKU FILMS

1438 N Gower St
Box 87
Hollywood, CA 90028
Phone: 323-860-7710
Fax: 323-860-7706

IMDb: imdb.com/company/co0047458

Does not accept any unsolicited material. Project types include TV. Preferred genres include Drama and Thriller.

Alan Poul
Producer/Director
IMDb: imdb.com/name/nm0693561

BOLD FILMS

6464 Sunset Blvd, Suite 800
Los Angeles, CA 90028
Phone: 323-769-8900
Fax: 323-769-8954

Email: info@boldfilms.com
Home Page: boldfilms.com
IMDb: imdb.com/company/co0135575

Does not accept any unsolicited material. Project types include Feature Films and TV. Preferred genres include Action, Fantasy, Horror, and Thriller.

Jon Oakes
Vice-President of Development
IMDb: imdb.com/name/nm1198333

Garrick Dion
Senior Vice-President of Development
IMDb: imdb.com/name/nm1887182

Stephanie Wilcox
Creative Executive
IMDb: imdb.com/name/nm3432545

BONA FIDE PRODUCTIONS

8899 Beverly Blvd, Suite 804
Los Angeles, CA 90048
Phone: 310-273-6782
Fax: 310-273-7821

IMDb: imdb.com/company/co0063938

Accepts query letter from unproduced, unrepresented writers. Project types include Feature Films. Established in 1993.

Albert Berger
Producer
IMDb: imdb.com/name/nm0074100

Ken Furer
Director of Development
IMDb: imdb.com/name/nm1738727

BORDERLINE FILMS

545 8th Ave
11th Floor
New York, NY 10018

Email: contact@blfilm.com
Home Page: blfilm.com

Does not accept any unsolicited material. Project types include Feature Films. Preferred genres include Crime, Detective, Drama, and Thriller.

Josh Mond
Principal
IMDb: imdb.com/name/nm1317614

Sean Durkin
Principal
IMDb: imdb.com/name/nm1699934

Antonio Campos
Principal
IMDb: imdb.com/name/nm1290515

BOSS MEDIA

9440 Santa Monica Blvd, Suite 400
Beverly Hills, CA 90210
Phone: 310-205-9900
Fax: 310-205-9909

IMDb: imdb.com/company/co0341936

Does not accept any unsolicited material.

Frank Mancuso
President
IMDb: imdb.com/name/nm0541548

Jennifer NIeves Gordon
Vice President (Development)
IMDb: imdb.com/name/nm2707034

BOXING CAT PRODUCTIONS

11500 Hart St
North Hollywood, CA 91605
Phone: 818-765-4870
Fax: 818-765-4975

IMDb: imdb.com/company/co0080834

Accepts query letter from unproduced, unrepresented writers via email. Project types include Feature Films and TV. Preferred genres include Comedy and Family.

Tim Allen
Actor/Producer
IMDb: imdb.com/name/nm0000741

BOY WONDER PRODUCTIONS

68 Jay St, Suite 423
Brooklyn, NY 11201
Phone: 347-632-2961
Fax: 347-332-6953

Email: info@boywonderproductions.net
Home Page: boywonderproductions.net
IMDb: imdb.com/company/co0255525

Accepts query letter from unproduced, unrepresented writers via email. Project types include TV. Preferred genres include Comedy, Drama, and Non-Fiction. Established in 2006.

Michael Morrisesy
President/Producer
IMDb: imdb.com/name/nm3155184

BOZ PRODUCTIONS

429 Santa Monica Blvd, Suite 710
Santa Monica, CA 90401
Phone: 323-876-3232

Email: bozenga@sbcglobal.net
Home Page: bozproductions.com
IMDb: imdb.com/company/co0068487

Accepts query letter from unproduced, unrepresented writers.

Bo Zenga
Writer/Director/Producer
Email: bozenga@sbcglobal.net
IMDb: imdb.com/name/nm0954848

BRANDED FILMS

4000 Warner Blvd
Building 139, Suite 107
Burbank, CA 91522
Phone: 818-954-7969

Email: info@branded-films.com
Home Page: branded-films.com
IMDb: imdb.com/company/co0347637

Does not accept any unsolicited material. Project types include Feature Films and TV. Preferred genres include Comedy. Established in 2011.

Russell Brand
Founder/Actor/Producer
IMDb: imdb.com/name/nm1258970
Assistant: Lee Sacks

Nik Linnen
Partner-Producer
IMDb: imdb.com/name/nm3800556

Beau Bauman
President
Email: beau@branded-films.com
IMDb: imdb.com/name/nm0062149

BRANDMAN PRODUCTIONS

2062 N Vine St, Suite 5
Los Angeles, CA 90068
Phone: 323-463-3224
Fax: 323-463-0852

IMDb: imdb.com/company/co0082006

Accepts query letter from unproduced, unrepresented writers.

Michael Bradman
President/Producer
IMDb: imdb.com/name/nm0104701

BRIGHTLIGHT PICTURES

The Bridge Studios
2400 Boundary Rd
Burnaby, BC V5M 3Z3
Canada
Phone: 604-628-3000
Fax: 604-628-3001

Email: info@brightlightpictures.com
Home Page: brightlightpictures.com
IMDb: imdb.com/company/co0065717

Does not accept any unsolicited material. Project types include Feature Films and TV. Preferred genres include Comedy and Drama. Established in 2001.

Stephen Hegyes
Co-Chairman/Producer
IMDb: imdb.com/name/nm0373812

Shawn Williamson
Co-Chairman/Producer
IMDb: imdb.com/name/nm0932144

Rebecca Nield
Creative Executive
IMDb: imdb.com/name/nm2422059

Kyle McCachen
Creative Executive
IMDb: imdb.com/name/nm5131630

BROKEN CAMERA PRODUCTIONS

San Antonio, TX
Phone: 210-454-8103

Email: info@brokencameraproductions.com
Home Page: brokencameraproductions.com

Accepts query letter from unproduced, unrepresented writers via email. Project types include Feature Films. Preferred genres include Comedy, Drama, and Thriller.

Matthew Garth
Producer
Phone: 210-454-8103
Email: matthew@brokencameraproductions.com
IMDb: imdb.com/name/nm2123288

David Y. Duncan
Producer
Phone: 210-884-5234
Email: dave@brokencameraproductions.com
IMDb: imdb.com/name/nm2839229

Lynette C. Aleman
Producer
Phone: 210-317-4647
Email: lynette@brokencameraproductions.com
IMDb: imdb.com/name/nm4074593

BROOKLYN FILMS

3815 Hughes Ave.
Culver City, CA 90232
Phone: 310-841-4300
Fax: 310-204-3464

IMDb: imdb.com/company/co0088618

Accepts query letter from unproduced, unrepresented writers. Project types include Feature Films and TV. Preferred genres include Crime and Drama.

Jon Avnet
Director / Producer
IMDb: imdb.com/name/nm0000816

Marsha Oglesby
Producer
IMDb: mdb.com/name/nm0644749

BRUCE COHEN PRODUCTIONS

8292 Hollywood Blvd
Los Angeles, CA 90069
Phone: 323-650-4567
Fax: 323-843-9534

Does not accept any unsolicited material. Project types include TV. Preferred genres include Drama.

Bruce Cohen
Principal
IMDb: imdb.com/name/nm0169260

Jessica Leventhal
Creative Executive
IMDb: imdb.com/name/nm4202199

BUCKAROO ENTERTAINMENT

10202 W Washington Blvd
David Lean Bldg, Suite 100
Culver City, CA 90232
Phone: 310-244-4646

Does not accept any unsolicited material. Project types include Feature Films. Preferred genres include Crime, Detective, Fantasy, Horror, and Thriller.

Sam Raimi
Partner
IMDb: imdb.com/name/nm0000600

Joshua Donen
Partner
IMDb: imdb.com/name/nm0232433

Ryan Carroll
Executive
IMDb: imdb.com/name/nm1498070

BUENA VISTA HOME ENTERTAINMENT

500 S. Buena Vista St.
Burbank, CA 91521-6369
USA
Phone: 818-560-1000

Home Page: bvhe.com
IMDb: imdb.com/company/co0049546

Does not accept any unsolicited material. Project types include Feature Films, Short Films, and TV. Preferred genres include Action, Animation, Comedy, Crime, Documentary, Drama, Family, Fantasy, Horror, Non-Fiction, Romance, Science Fiction, and Thriller. Established in 1952.

BUENA VISTA PICTURES

500 S Buena Vista St
Burbank, CA 91521
Phone: 818-560-1000

Home Page: disney.com
IMDb: imdb.com/company/co0044279

Does not accept any unsolicited material. Project types include Feature Films, Short Films, and TV. Preferred genres include Action, Animation, Comedy, Crime, Documentary, Drama, Family, Fantasy, Horror, Non-Fiction, Romance, Science Fiction, and Thriller. Established in 1932.

Nadia Aleyd
Casting
IMDb: imdb.com/name/nm0019022

Louanne Brickhouse
IMDb: imdb.com/name/nm1749168

Kristin Burr
Executive Vice President
IMDb: imdb.com/name/nm0123013

Jeanne Hobson
Senior Vice President of Domestic Sale and Distribution
IMDb: imdb.com/name/nm2653496

John Lasseter
Chief Creative Officer, Disney Animation
IMDb: imdb.com/name/nm0005124

Cherise McVicar
Senior Vice President of National Promotions and Mobile Marketing
IMDb: imdb.com/name/nm2660270

Todd Murata
Executive
IMDb: imdb.com/name/nm0613611

BUENA VISTA TELEVISION

500 S Buena Vista St
Burbank, CA 91521
Phone: 818-460-6552
Fax: 818-460-5296

Email: bvtv.webmaster@disney.com
Home Page: disneyabc.tv
IMDb: imdb.com/company/co0078478

Does not accept any unsolicited material. Project types include Feature Films and TV. Preferred genres include Action, Animation, Comedy, Crime, Documentary, Drama, Family, Fantasy, Non-Fiction, Romance, Science Fiction, and Thriller. Established in 1957.

BUNIM-MURRAY PRODUCTIONS

6007 Sepulveda Blvd
Van Nuys, CA 91411
Phone: 818-756-5100
Fax: 818-756-5140

Email: bmp@bunim-murray.com
Home Page: bunim-murray.com

Does not accept any unsolicited material. Project types include TV. Preferred genres include Documentary and Reality.

Jonathan Murray
Chairman
IMDb: imdb.com/name/nm0615086

Gil Goldschein
President
IMDb: imdb.com/name/nm2251455

Scott Freeman
EVP of Current Programming & Development
IMDb: imdb.com/name/nm1321720

Jeff Jenkins
EVP of Entertainment & Programming
IMDb: imdb.com/name/nm0420870

Erin Cristall
SVP of Development
IMDb: imdb.com/name/nm0188058

John Greco
Vice President of Production

Cara Goldberg
Production Executive

BURLEIGH FILMWORKS

22287 Mulholland Highway, Suite 129
Calabasas, CA 91302
Phone: 818-224-4686
Fax: 818-223-9089

IMDb: imdb.com/company/co0176271

Accepts query letter from unproduced, unrepresented writers.

Steve Burleigh
Producer
Email: steve.burleigh@burleighfilmworks.com
IMDb: imdb.com/name/nm0122114

BURNSIDE ENTERTAINMENT INC.

2424 N Ontario St
Burbank, CA 91504
Phone: 818-565-5986

Email: mail@burnsideentertainment.com
Home Page: burnsideentertainment.com
IMDb: imdb.com/company/co0180518

Accepts query letter from unproduced, unrepresented writers.

Glen Trotiner
Producer/Partner
IMDb: imdb.com/name/nm0873641

CALIBER MEDIA COMPANY

5670 Wilshire Blvd.
Ste 1600

Los Angeles, CA 90036
Phone: 310-786-9210

Home Page: calibermediaco.com
IMDb: imdb.com/company/co0228420

Accepts query letter from unproduced, unrepresented writers. Project types include Feature Films. Preferred genres include Action, Crime, Drama, Family, Horror, Sociocultural, and Thriller. Established in 2008.

Jack Heller
Principal
IMDb: imdb.com/name/nm2597331

Dallas Sonnier
Principal
IMDb: imdb.com/name/nm2447772

Morgan White
Director of Production and Development
IMDb: imdb.com/name/nm4765803

CALLAHAN FILMWORKS

3800 Barham Blvd
Suite 500
Los Angeles, CA 90068
Phone: 323-878-0645
Fax: 323-878-0649

Does not accept any unsolicited material. Project types include Feature Films and TV. Preferred genres include Action, Comedy, Crime, Drama, Family, Fantasy, and Romance.

Peter Segal
Partner
IMDb: imdb.com/name/nm0781842

Michael Ewing
Partner
IMDb: imdb.com/name/nm0263989

Chris Osbrink
Creative Executive
IMDb: imdb.com/name/nm1644713

Omar El-Hajoui
Executive Assistant
IMDb: imdb.com/name/nm5389420

CAMELOT ENTERTAINMENT GROUP

10 Universal City Plaza NBC/Universal Building Floor 20
Universal City, CA 91608
Phone: 818-308-8858
Fax: 818-308-8848

Email: submissions@camelotfilms.com
Home Page: camelotent.com/index.php
IMDb: imdb.com/company/co0006731

Accepts scripts from unproduced, unrepresented writers. Project types include Feature Films and TV. Preferred genres include Action, Animation, Comedy, Drama, Family, Horror, Non-Fiction, Romance, Science Fiction, and Thriller.

Robert Atwell
Chairman
IMDb: imdb.com/name/nm0041164

Steven Istock
Partner
IMDb: imdb.com/name/nm1916408

Jessica Kelly
President of Distribution

CAMELOT PICTURES

9255 Sunset Blvd, Suite 711
Los Angeles, CA 90069
Phone: 310-288-3000
Fax: 310-288-3054

IMDb: imdb.com/company/co0084122

Accepts query letter from unproduced, unrepresented writers via email. Project types include Feature Films. Preferred genres include Comedy, Drama, and Family.

Gary Gilbert
President
IMDb: imdb.com/name/nm1344784

Jordan Horowitz
Vice-President, Production and Development
IMDb: imdb.com/name/nm0395302

CANADIAN BROADCASTING COMPANY

181 Queen St
Ottawa, ON, Canada, K1P 1K9
Phone: 613-288-6000

Email: liaison@cbc.ca
Home Page: cbc.ca
IMDb: imdb.com/company/co0045850

Does not accept any unsolicited material. Project types include Feature Films and TV. Preferred genres include Action, Animation, Comedy, Crime, Documentary, Drama, Family, Non-Fiction, and Period. Established in 2007.

David Ridgen
Producer
IMDb: imdb.com/name/nm3236527

Hebert Lacroix
President
IMDb: imdb.com/name/nm4522750

Suzanne Colvin-Goulding
Head of Physical Production for TV Arts & Entertainment, CBC English Television
IMDb: imdb.com/name/nm0003681

Scott McEwen
Head of Drama Development
IMDb: imdb.com/name/nm1469582

Kim Wilson
Head of Creative CBC Children's Programming

Anton Leo
Head of Comedy
IMDb: imdb.com/name/nm2502480

Jennifer Stewart
Director of Acquisitions and Development
IMDb: imdb.com/name/nm4219237

Jenny Hacker
Executive of Creative/Comedy
IMDb: imdb.com/name/nm4236429

Trevor Walton
Head (Co-Productions)
IMDb: imdb.com/name/nm4280633

CAPACITY PICTURES

PO Box 96143
Las Vegas, NV 89193
Phone: 310-247-8534

Email: capacitypictures@gmail.com
IMDb: imdb.com/company/co0192878

Does not accept any unsolicited material. Project types include Feature Films. Preferred genres include Comedy, Crime, Drama, Horror, and Thriller. Established in 2008.

Rich Heller
Executive
IMDb: imdb.com/name/nm0375378

Wayne Allen Rice
Executive
IMDb: imdb.com/name/nm0723573

CAPITAL ARTS ENTERTAINMENT

23315 Clift on Plaza
Valencia, CA 91354
Phone: 818-343-8950
Fax: 818-343-8962

Email: info@capitalarts.com
Home Page: capitalarts.com
IMDb: imdb.com/company/co0009722

Accepts query letter from unproduced, unrepresented writers via email. Preferred genres include Action, Comedy, Horror, and Thriller. Established in 1995.

Mike Elliot
Partner/Producer
IMDb: imdb.com/name/nm0254291

CAPTIVATE ENTERTAINMENT

100 Universal City Plaza
Bungalow 4111
Universal City, CA 91608
Phone: 818-777-6711
Fax: 818-733-4303

IMDb: imdb.com/company/co0263292

Does not accept any unsolicited material. Project types include Feature Films and TV. Preferred genres include Action, Comedy, Drama, Fantasy, Myth, Romance, Science Fiction, and Thriller.

Jeffrey Weiner
Chairman/CEO
IMDb: imdb.com/name/nm1788648

Ben Smith
Producer
IMDb: imdb.com/name/nm3328356

Tony Shaw
Creative Executive
Email: tony.shaw@univfilms.com
IMDb: imdb.com/name/nm4130192

CARNIVAL FILMS

3rd Fl
55 New Oxford St
London WC1A 1BS
Phone: +44 0203 618 6600
Fax: +44 023 618 8900

Email: info@carnivalfilms.co.uk
Home Page: carnivalfilms.co.uk

Does not accept any unsolicited material. Project types include TV. Preferred genres include Documentary, Drama, and Thriller.

Henrietta Colvin
Head of Development
IMDb: imdb.com/name/nm2188710

Kimberly Hikaka
Production Executive
IMDb: imdb.com/name/nm2529465

Sam Symons
Development Executive
IMDb: imdb.com/name/nm1599585

Steven Williams
Development Executive
IMDb: imdb.com/name/nm1034831

CASEY SILVER PRODUCTIONS

506 Santa Monica Blvd, Suite 322
Santa Monica, CA 90401
Phone: 310-566-3750
Fax: 310-566-3751

IMDb: imdb.com/company/co0058884

Does not accept any unsolicited material. Project types include Feature Films. Preferred genres include Action, Comedy, Drama, Family, and Thriller.

Casey Silver
Chairman
Email: casey@caseysilver.com
IMDb: imdb.com/name/nm0798661

Matthew Reynolds
Creative Executive
Email: matthew@caseysilver.com
IMDb: imdb.com/name/nm2303863

CASTLE ROCK ENTERTAINMENT

335 N Maple Dr, Suite 350
Beverly Hills, CA 90210-3867
Phone: 310-285-2300
Fax: 310-285-2345

IMDb: imdb.com/company/co0040620

Accepts scripts from produced or represented writers.

Rob Reiner
Director/Producer/Writer
Email: rob.reiner@castle-rock.com
IMDb: imdb.com/name/nm0001661

Andrew Scheinman
Producer/Director
Email: andres.scheinman@castle-rock.com
IMDb: imdb.com/name/nm0770650

CATAPULT FILMS

832 Third St, Suite 303
Santa Monica, CA 90403-1155
Phone: 310-395-1470
Fax: 310-401-0122

IMDb: imdb.com/company/co0100754

Accepts scripts from produced or represented writers.

Lisa Josefsberg
Producer
IMDb: imdb.com/name/nm2248853

CBS FILMS

11800 Wilshire Blvd
Los Angeles, CA 90025
Phone: 310-575-7700

Home Page: cbsfilms.com

Does not accept any unsolicited material. Project types include Feature Films. Preferred genres include Action, Drama, Fantasy, Romance, and Science Fiction.

Maria Faillace
Senior Vice President of Production
IMDb: imdb.com/name/nm1299267

Mark Ross
Vice President of Production
IMDb: imdb.com/name/nm0743653

Wolfgang Hammer
Co-President
IMDb: imdb.com/name/nm1424985

Terry Press
Co-President
IMDb: imdb.com/name/nm1437110

CECCHI GORI PICTURES

5555 Melrose Ave
Bob Hope 203
Los Angeles, CA 90038
Phone: 323-956-5954
Fax: 323-862-2254

Email: info@cgglobalmedia.com
Home Page: cecchigoripictures.com

Project types include Feature Films. Preferred genres include Drama, Family, Horror, Romance, and Thriller.

Niels Juul
CEO
IMDb: imdb.com/name/nm3887220

Alex Shub
VP of Business & Legal Affairs

Jennifer Parker
Development
IMDb: imdb.com/name/nm4487725

Andy Scott
Art Director
IMDb: imdb.com/name/nm4866101

Dana Galinsky
Development Coordinator
IMDb: imdb.com/name/nm1919300

CELADOR FILMS

39 Long Acre
London, WC2E 9LG
United Kingdom
Phone: +44 20-7845-6800
Fax: +44 20-7845-6801

Home Page: celador.co.uk
IMDb: imdb.com/company/co0152921

Accepts scripts from produced or represented writers.
Established in 1989.

Paul Smith
Chairman/Executive Producer
Email: psmith@celador.co.uk
IMDb: imdb.com/name/nm0809531

CENTROPOLIS ENTERTAINMENT

1445 N Stanley
3rd Floor
Los Angeles, CA 90046
Phone: 323-850-1212
Fax: 323-850-1201

Email: info@centropolis.com
Home Page: centropolis.com
IMDb: imdb.com/company/co0050111

Accepts scripts from produced or represented writers.
Preferred genres include Action, Fantasy, Myth, Non-Fiction, and Romance. Established in 1985.

Roland Emmerich
Partner/Producer
IMDb: imdb.com/name/nm0000386

Ute Emmerich
Partner/Producer
IMDb: imdb.com/name/nm0256498

CHAIKEN FILMS

802 Potrero Ave
San Francisco, CA 94110
Phone: 415-826-7880
Fax: 415-826-7882

Email: info@chaikenfilms.com
Home Page: chaikenfilms.com
IMDb: imdb.com/company/co0064208

Accepts query letter from unproduced, unrepresented writers. Preferred genres include Non-Fiction. Established in 1998.

Jennifer Chaiken
Producer
Email: jen@chaikenfilms.com
IMDb: imdb.com/name/nm0149671

CHARTOFF PRODUCTIONS

1250 Sixth St, Suite 101
Santa Monica, CA 90401
Phone: 310-319-1960
Fax: 310-319-3469

Email: hendeechartoff@cs.com
IMDb: imdb.com/company/co0094865

Accepts scripts from produced or represented writers.
Established in 1986.

Robert Chartoff
CEO/Producer
IMDb: imdb.com/name/nm0153590

CHERNIN ENTERTAINMENT

1733 Ocean Ave, Suite 300
Santa Monica, CA 90401
Phone: 310-899-1205

Home Page: cherninent.com
IMDb: imdb.com/company/co0286257

Accepts scripts from produced or represented writers.
Project types include Feature Films and TV. Preferred genres include Action, Comedy, and Drama. Established in 2009.

Peter Chernin
Principle
IMDb: imdb.com/name/nm1858656

Dylan Dark
Email: dc@cherninent.com
IMDb: imdb.com/name/nm1249995

Jenno Topping
Executive Vice-President
Email: jt@cherninent.com
IMDb: imdb.com/name/nm0867768

Katherine Pope
President (Television)
Email: kp@cherninent.com
IMDb: imdb.com/name/nm0691142

Jesse Henderson
Director of Development
Email: jh@cherninent.com

Pavun Shetty
Director of Television
Email: ps@cherninent.com

Ivana Schechter-Garcia
Creative Executive

CHERRY SKY FILMS

2100 Sawtelle Blvd.,
Suite 101
Los Angeles, CA 90025
Phone: 310-479-8001
Fax: 310-479-8815

Email: contact@cherryskyfilms.com
Home Page: cherryskyfilms.com

Does not accept any unsolicited material. Project types include Feature Films. Preferred genres include Comedy, Drama, Family, and Romance. Established in 2001.

Joan Huang
Producer
IMDb: imdb.com/name/nm0399009

Jeffrey Gou
Producer
IMDb: imdb.com/name/nm2370188

CHESTNUT RIDGE PRODUCTIONS

8899 Beverly Blvd, Suite 800
Los Angeles, CA
Phone: 310-285-7011

IMDb: imdb.com/company/co0273538

Does not accept any unsolicited material. Established in 2009.

Paula Wagner
Owner/Producer
IMDb: imdb.com/name/nm0906048

CHEYENNE ENTERPRISES LLC

406 Wilshire Blvd
Santa Monica, CA 90401
Phone: 310-455-5000
Fax: 310-688-8000

IMDb: imdb.com/company/co0041195

Accepts scripts from produced or represented writers. Established in 2000.

Arnold Rifkin
President/Producer
IMDb: imdb.com/name/nm0726476

Joshua Rowley
Director of Development
IMDb: imdb.com/name/nm2282373

CHICAGOFILMS

253 W 72nd St
Suite 1108
New York, NY 10023
USA
Phone: 212-721-7700
Fax: 212-721-7701

IMDb: imdb.com/company/co0012485

Accepts scripts from produced or represented writers.

Bob Balaban
Actor/Producer
IMDb: imdb.com/name/nm0000837

CHICKFLICKS

8861 St Ives Dr
Los Angeles, CA 90069
Phone: 310-854-7210

Email: info@chickflicksinc.com
Home Page: chickflicksinc.com
IMDb: imdb.com/company/co0156986

Accepts scripts from produced or represented writers.
Preferred genres include Comedy, Fantasy, Myth,
Non-Fiction, and Romance.

Sara Risher
Producer (Managing Partner)
Phone: 310-854-7210
Email: sara@chickflicksinc.com
IMDb: imdb.com/name/nm0728260

Stephanie Austin
Producer (Managing Partner)
Phone: 310-854-7210
Email: stephanie@chickflicksinc.com
IMDb: imdb.com/name/nm0042520

CHOCKSTONE PICTURES

22355 Carbon Mesa Rd
Malibu, CA 90265
Phone: 310-456-2945

Email: steves@chockstonepictures.com
Home Page: chockstonepictures.com
IMDb: imdb.com/company/co0192912
Facebook: facebook.com/chockstonepictures?fref=ts

Accepts query letter from unproduced, unrepresented
writers via email. Project types include Feature Films.
Established in 2004.

Steve Schwartz
President
Email: steves@chockstonepictures.com
IMDb: imdb.com/name/nm0777455

Paula Mae Schwartz
CEO
Email: paulamae@chockstonepictures.com
IMDb: imdb.com/name/nm2445382

Roger Schwartz
Development Executive
Phone: 310-600-6840
Email: rogers@chockstonepictures.com
IMDb: imdb.com/name/nm0970118

CHOTZEN/JENNER PRODUCTIONS

4178 Dixie Canyon Ave.
Sherman Oaks, CA 91423
Phone: 323-465-9877
Fax: 323-460-6451

IMDb: imdb.com/company/co0176334

Accepts scripts from produced or represented writers.
Project types include TV. Preferred genres include
Comedy and Drama. Established in 1990.

Yvonne Chotzen
Producer/Partner
IMDb: imdb.com/name/nm0159278

William Jenner
Producer/Partner
IMDb: imdb.com/name/nm0421076

CHRIS/ROSE PRODUCTIONS

3131 Torreyson Place
Los Angeles, CA 90046
Phone: 323-851-8772
Fax: 323-851-0662

IMDb: imdb.com/company/co0040069

Accepts scripts from produced or represented writers.
Project types include TV. Preferred genres include
Comedy, Drama, and Non-Fiction.

Robert Christiansen
Executive Producer
Phone: 310-781-0833
IMDb: imdb.com/name/nm0160222

CHUBBCO FILM CO.

373 N Kenter Ave
Los Angeles, CA 90049
Phone: 310-729-5858
Fax: 310-933-1704

Email: chubbco@gmail.com
IMDb: imdb.com/company/co0026094

Does not accept any unsolicited material. Preferred genres include Action, Crime, and Non-Fiction.

Caldecot Chubb
Producer
Email: chubbco@gmail.com
IMDb: imdb.com/name/nm0160941

CHUCK FRIES PRODUCTIONS

9903 Santa Monica Blvd, Suite 870
Beverly Hills, CA 90212
Phone: 310-203-9520
Fax: 310-203-9519

IMDb: imdb.com/company/co0040068

Accepts scripts from produced or represented writers. Preferred genres include Crime and Detective.

Charles Fries
Chairman/President/CEO
IMDb: imdb.com/name/nm0295594

CINDY COWAN ENTERTAINMENT, INC.

8265 W Sunset Blvd, Suite 205
Los Angeles, CA 90046
Phone: 323-822-1082
Fax: 323-822-1086

Email: info@cowanent.com
Home Page: cowanent.com
IMDb: imdb.com/company/co0094925

Accepts scripts from produced or represented writers. Established in 1999.

Cindy Cowan
President
IMDb: imdb.com/name/nm0184546

CINEMA EPHOCH

10 Universal City Plaza, 20th Floor
Universal City, CA 91608
Phone: 818-753-2345

Email: acquisitions@cinemaepoch.com
Home Page: cinemaepoch.com
IMDb: imdb.com/company/co0028810

Accepts query letter from unproduced, unrepresented writers. Preferred genres include Action, Comedy, Crime, Detective, Horror, Myth, Non-Fiction, and Thriller. Established in 2001.

Gregory Hatanaka
President/Distributor/Producer
IMDb: imdb.com/name/nm0368693

CINEMAGIC ENTERTAINMENT

9229 Sunset Blvd, Suite 610
West Hollywood, CA 90069
Phone: 310-385-9322
Fax: 310-385-9347

Home Page: cinemagicent.com
IMDb: imdb.com/company/co0183883

Accepts query letter from unproduced, unrepresented writers. Preferred genres include Action, Crime, Detective, Fantasy, Horror, Myth, Science Fiction, and Thriller.

Lee Cohn
Vice-President, Development
IMDb: imdb.com/name/nm2325144

CINEMA LIBRE STUDIO

8328 De Soto Ave
Canoga Park, CA 91304
Phone: 818-349-8822
Fax: 818-349-9922

Email: project@CinemaLibreStudio.com
Home Page: CinemaLibreStudio.com
IMDb: imdb.com/company/co0132224

Accepts query letter from unproduced, unrepresented writers. Established in 2003.

Philippe Diaz
Producer/Owner
IMDb: imdb.com/name/nm0225034

CINE MOSAIC

130 W 25th St, 12th Floor
New York, NY 10001
Phone: 212-625-3797
Fax: 212-625-3571

Email: info@cinemosaic.net
Home Page: cinemosaic.net
IMDb: imdb.com/company/co0124029

Accepts scripts from produced or represented writers. Project types include TV. Preferred genres include Action, Drama, and Non-Fiction. Established in 2002.

Lydia Pilcher
Independent Producer/Founder
IMDb: imdb.com/name/nm0212990

CINESON ENTERTAINMENT

4519 Varna Ave.
Sherman Oaks, CA 91423
Phone: 818-501-8246
Fax: 818-501-3647

Email: cineson@cineson.com
Home Page: cineson.com
IMDb: imdb.com/company/co0127539

Does not accept any unsolicited material. Project types include Feature Films and TV. Preferred genres include Comedy, Crime, Drama, Non-Fiction, Period, Romance, and Thriller. Established in 1999.

Andy Garcia
Producer / Director
IMDb: imdb.com/name/nm0000412

CINETELE FILMS

8255 Sunset Blvd
Los Angeles, CA 90046
Phone: 323-654-4000
Fax: 323-650-6400

Email: info@cinetelfilms.com
Home Page: cinetelfilms.com
IMDb: imdb.com/company/co0017447

Does not accept any unsolicited material. Project types include TV. Preferred genres include Crime, Drama, Horror, and Thriller. Established in 1985.

Paul Hertzberg
President/CEO
IMDb: imdb.com/name/nm0078473

CINEVILLE

3400 Airport Ave
Santa Monica, CA 90405
Phone: 310-397-7150
Fax: 310-397-7155

Email: info@cineville.com
Home Page: cineville.com
IMDb: imdb.com/company/co0063993

Accepts query letter from unproduced, unrepresented writers. Preferred genres include Comedy, Non-Fiction, and Romance. Established in 1990.

Carl Colpaert
President
IMDb: imdb.com/name/nm0173207

CIRCLE OF CONFUSION

8931 Ellis Ave
Los Angeles, CA 90034
Phone: 310-691-7000
Fax: 310-691-7099

Email: queries@circleofconfusion.com
Home Page: circleofconfusion.com
IMDb: imdb.com/company/co0090153

Accepts query letter from unproduced, unrepresented writers. Project types include TV. Preferred genres include Action, Comedy, Crime, Detective, Drama, Fantasy, Horror, Myth, Non-Fiction, Romance, Science Fiction, and Thriller.

Stephen Emery
Executive Vice-President Production and Development
Email: stephen@circleofconfusion.com
IMDb: imdb.com/name/nm1765323

CITY ENTERTAINMENT

266 1/2 S Rexford Dr
Beverly Hills, CA 90212
Phone: 310-273-3101
Fax: 310-273-3676

IMDb: imdb.com/company/co0093881

Does not accept any unsolicited material.

Joshua Maurer
President/Producer
IMDb: imdb.com/name/nm0561027

CLARITY PICTURES LLC.

1107 Fair Oaks Ave
Ste 155
South Pasadena, CA 91030
USA
Phone: 310-226-7046
Fax: 310-388-5846

Email: info@claritypictures.net
Home Page: claritypictures.net
IMDb: imdb.com/company/co0151012

Does not accept any unsolicited material. Project types include Feature Films and TV. Preferred genres include Comedy, Documentary, and Horror. Established in 2004.

David Basulto
President, Producer
IMDb: imdb.com/name/nm0060617

Loren Basulto
Vice President of Production
IMDb: imdb.com/name/nm1457923

CLASS 5 FILMS

200 Park Ave South, 8th Floor
New York, NY 10003
Phone: 917-414-9404

IMDb: imdb.com/company/co0113781

Accepts query letter from unproduced, unrepresented writers.

Edward Norton
Producer/Actor/Director/Writer
IMDb: imdb.com/name/nm0001570

CLEAR PICTURES ENTERTAINMENT

12400 Ventura Blvd, Suite 306
Studio City, CA 91604
Phone: 818-980-5460
Fax: 818-980-4716

Email: clearpicturesinc@aol.com
IMDb: imdb.com/company/co0171732

Accepts query letter from unproduced, unrepresented writers via email. Project types include Feature Films and TV. Preferred genres include Drama and Non-Fiction. Established in 2009.

Elizabeth Fowler
Principle
IMDb: imdb.com/name/nm2085583

CLEARVIEW PRODUCTIONS

1180 S Beverly Dr, Suite 700
Los Angeles, CA 90035
Phone: 310-271-7698
Fax: 310-278-9978

Does not accept any unsolicited material.

Albert Ruddy
Producer
IMDb: imdb.com/name/nm0748665

CLIFFORD WERBER PRODUCTIONS

232 S Beverly Dr, Suite 224
Beverly Hills, CA 90212
Phone: 310-288-0900
Fax: 310-288-0600

IMDb: imdb.com/company/co0097249

Accepts query letter from produced or represented writers.

Clifford Werber
Producer
IMDb: imdb.com/name/nm0921222

CLOSED ON MONDAYS ENTERTAINMENT

3800 Barham Blvd Suite 100
Los Angeles, CA 90068
Phone: 818-526-6707

IMDb: imdb.com/company/co0186526

Does not accept any unsolicited material. Established in 2003.

Joe Nozemack
Prodocer/Co-founder
IMDb: imdb.com/name/nm1060496

CLOUD EIGHT FILMS

39 Long Acre
London WC2E 9LG
United Kingdom
Phone: +44 20-7845-6877

IMDb: imdb.com/company/co0265704

Accepts scripts from produced or represented writers.
Established in 2009.

Christian Colson
Chairman/Producer
Phone: +44 20 7845 6988
IMDb: imdb.com/name/nm1384503

CODEBLACK ENTERTAINMENT

111 Universal Hollywood Dr, Suite 2260
Universal City, CA 91608
Phone: 818-286-8600
Fax: 818-286-8649

Email: info@codeblackentertainment.com
Home Page: codeblackentertainment.com
IMDb: imdb.com/company/co0172361

Does not accept any unsolicited material. Established
in 2005.

Jeff Clanagan
CEO
IMDb: imdb.com/name/nm0163335

CODE ENTERTAINMENT

9229 Sunset Blvd, Suite 615
Los Angeles, CA 90069
Phone: 310-772-0008
Fax: 310-772-0006

Email: contact@codeentertainment.com
Home Page: codeentertainment.com
IMDb: imdb.com/company/co0143069

Accepts scripts from produced or represented writers.
Established in 2005.

Bart Rosenblatt
Producer
Phone: 310-772-0008 ext. 3
IMDb: imdb.com/name/nm0742386

COLLEEN CAMP PRODUCTIONS

6464 Sunset Blvd, Suite 800
Los Angeles, CA 90028
Phone: 323-463-1434
Fax: 323-463-4379

Email: asst@ccprods.com
IMDb: imdb.com/company/co0092983

Accepts query letter from unproduced, unrepresented
writers.

Colleen Camp
Producer
IMDb: imdb.com/name/nm0131974

COLOR FORCE

1524 Cloverfield Blvd, Suite C
Santa Monica, CA 90404
Phone: 310-828-0641
Fax: 310-828-0672

IMDb: imdb.com/company/co0212151

Accepts query letter from unproduced, unrepresented
writers. Preferred genres include Action and Comedy.
Established in 2007.

Nina Jacobson
Producer
Email: nina.jacobson@colorforce.com
IMDb: imdb.com/name/nm1749221

COLOSSAL ENTERTAINMENT

PO Box 461010
Los Angeles, CA 90046
Phone: 323-656-6647

Email: clsslent@aol.com
IMDb: imdb.com/company/co0176684

Accepts query letter from unproduced, unrepresented
writers.

Kelly Rowan
Producer
IMDb: imdb.com/name/nm0746414

Graham Ludlow
Producer / Writer
IMDb: imdb.com/name/nm0524905

COLUMBIA PICTURES

10202 W Washington Blvd Thalberg Building
Culver City, CA 90232
Phone: 310-244-4000
Fax: 310-244-2626

Home Page: spe.sony.com
IMDb: imdb.com/company/co0071509

Does not accept any unsolicited material. Project types include Feature Films. Preferred genres include Action, Animation, Comedy, Crime, Drama, Family, Fantasy, Horror, Non-Fiction, Period, Romance, Science Fiction, and Thriller. Established in 1939.

Amy Pascal
Chairman
IMDb: imdb.com/name/nm1166871

Doug Belgrad
President
IMDb: imdb.com/name/nm1000411

Hannah Minghella
President of Production
IMDb: imdb.com/name/nm1098742
Assistant: Mahsa Moayeri
mahsa_moayeri@spe.sony.com

Elizabeth Cantillon
Executive Vice President of Production
IMDb: imdb.com/name/nm0134578
Assistant: Katherine Spada
katherine_spada@spe.sony.com

Samuel C. Dickerman
Executive Vice President of Production
IMDb: imdb.com/name/nm0225385

Andrea Giannetti
Executive Vice President of Production
IMDb: imdb.com/name/nm1602150

Pete Corral
Senior Vice President of the Production Administration
IMDb: imdb.com/name/nm0180707

DeVon Franklin
Senior Vice President of Production
IMDb: imdb.com/name/nm2035952

Andy Given
Senior Vice President of the Production Administration
IMDb: imdb.com/name/nm0321429

Jonathan Kadin
Senior Vice President of Production
IMDb: imdb.com/name/nm2142367
Assistant: Ashley Johnson
ashley_johnson@spe.sony.com

Rachel O'Connor
Senior Vice President of Production
IMDb: imdb.com/name/nm1471418

Lauren Abrahams
Vice President of Production
IMDb: imdb.com/name/nm1036268

Debra Bergman
Vice President of the Production Administration
IMDb: imdb.com/name/nm2984630

Adam Moos
Vice President of the Production Administration
IMDb: imdb.com/name/nm0602149

Foster Driver
Creative Executive
IMDb: imdb.com/name/nm5372839

Eric Fineman
Creative Executive
IMDb: imdb.com/name/nm2349857

COMEDY ARTS STUDIOS

2500 Broadway
Santa Monica, CA 90404
Phone: 310-382-3677
Fax: 310-382-3170

IMDb: imdb.com/company/co0220109

Accepts query letter from unproduced, unrepresented writers. Project types include TV. Preferred genres include Comedy and Drama.

Stu Smiley
Owner/Executive Producer
IMDb: imdb.com/name/nm0806979

COMPLETION FILMS

60 E 42nd St, Suite 4600
New York, NY 10165
Phone: 718-693-2057
Fax: 888-693-4133

Email: info@completionfilms.com
Home Page: completionfilms.com
IMDb: imdb.com/company/co0175660

Accepts query letter from unproduced, unrepresented writers. Preferred genres include Non-Fiction.

Kisha Imani Cameron
President
IMDb: imdb.com/name/nm0131650

CONCEPT ENTERTAINMENT

334 1/2 N Sierra Bonita Ave
Los Angeles, CA 90036
Phone: 323-937-5700
Fax: 323-937-5720

Email: enquiries@conceptentertainment.biz
Home Page: conceptentertainment.biz
IMDb: .imdb.com/company/co0096670

Accepts query letter from unproduced, unrepresented writers. Project types include TV. Preferred genres include Action, Comedy, Crime, Detective, Drama, Fantasy, Horror, Myth, Non-Fiction, Romance, Science Fiction, and Thriller.

David Faigenblum
Producer/Manager
IMDb: imdb.com/name/nm1584960

CONSTANTIN FILM

9200 W Sunset Blvd, Suite 800
West Hollywood, CA 90069
Phone: 310-247-0300
Fax: 310-247-0305

Feilitzschstr. 6
Munich, Bavaria D-80802
Germany
Phone: +49-89-44-44-60-0
Fax: +49-89-44-44-60-666

Email: zentrale@constantin-film.de
IMDb: imdb.com/company/co0002257
Home Page: constantin-film.de
Facebook: facebook.com/constantinfilm

Accepts query letter from produced or represented writers. Project types include Feature Films and TV. Preferred genres include Action, Crime, and Thriller. Established in 1950.

Stefan Wood
Development
Email: stefan.wood@constatin-film.de
IMDb: imdb.com/name/nm0940008

Robert Kultzer
Executive
Phone: 310-247-0300 ext. 3
Email: robert.kultzer@constantin-film.de
IMDb: imdb.com/name/nm0474709

Fred Kogel
CEO
Email: elisabeth.kasch@constantin-film.de
IMDb: imdb.com/name/nm1827684
Assistant: Elisabeth Kasch

Friedrich Wildfeuer
Head of TV Production
Email: zentrale@constantin-film.de
IMDb: imdb.com/name/nm0928662

Herman Weigel
Executive Producer
Email: hermanweigel@constantin.film.de
IMDb: imdb.com/name/nm0917833

CONTENT MEDIA CORPORATION PLC

225 Arizona Ave, Suite #250
Santa Monica, CA 90401
Phone: 310-576-1059
Fax: 310-576-1859

Email: jcassistant@contentmediacorp.com
Home Page: contentmediacorp.com
IMDb: imdb.com/company/co0366223

Accepts query letter from unproduced, unrepresented writers.

Jamie Carmichael
President, Film Division
Email: jamie.carmichael@contentmediacorp.com
IMDb: imdb.com/name/nm0138430

CONTRAFILM

1531 N Cahuenga Blvd
Los Angeles, CA 90028
Phone: 323-467-8787
Fax: 323-467-7730

Accepts query letter from unproduced, unrepresented writers. Project types include Feature Films. Preferred genres include Drama, Horror, and Thriller.

Tripp Vinson
Producer
IMDb: imdb.com/name/nm1246087
Assistant: Tara Farney

Alexandra Church
Creative Executive
IMDb: imdb.com/name/nm0161344

Tucker Williams
Creative Executive
IMDb: imdb.com/name/nm2606099

CONUNDRUM ENTERTAINMENT

325 Wilshire Blvd, Suite 201
Santa Monica, CA 90401
Phone: 310-319-2800
Fax: 310-319-2808

IMDb: imdb.com/company/co0030016

Accepts scripts from produced or represented writers. Preferred genres include Comedy.

Peter Farrelly
Executive
IMDb: imdb.com/name/nm0268380

Bobby Farrelly
Executive
IMDb: imdb.com/name/nm0268370

COOPER'S TOWN PRODUCTIONS

302A West 12th St, Suite 214
New York, NY 10014
Phone: 212-255-7566
Fax: 212-255-0211

Email: info@copperstownproductions.com
Home Page: copperstownproductions.com
IMDb: imdb.com/company/co0132168

Accepts query letter from unproduced, unrepresented writers. Project types include Feature Films. Preferred genres include Non-Fiction.

Phillip Hoffman
Partner
IMDb: imdb.com/name/nm0000450

Sara Murphy
Head, Development (Executive)
IMDb: imdb.com/name/nm2072976

COQUETTE PRODUCTIONS

8105 W Third St
Los Angeles, CA 90048
Phone: 323-801-1000
Fax: 323-801-1001

Does not accept any unsolicited material. Project types include TV. Preferred genres include Comedy, Crime, Drama, and Romance.

David Arquette
Principal
IMDb: imdb.com/name/nm0000274

Courtney Cox
Principal
IMDb: imdb.com/name/nm0001073

Thea Mann
Head of Development
IMDb: imdb.com/name/nm0542996

Jeff Bowland
Executive
IMDb: imdb.com/name/nm0101188

CORNER STORE ENTERTAINMENT

9615 Brighton Way
Ste 201

Beverly Hills, CA 90210
Phone: 310-276-6400
Fax: 310-276-6410

Home Page: cornerstore-ent.com

Does not accept any unsolicited material. Project types include Feature Films. Preferred genres include Comedy, Drama, and Romance.

Matthew Weaver
Principal
IMDb: imdb.com/name/nm2822461

Scott Prisand
Principal
IMDb: imdb.com/name/nm1964055

CRAVE FILMS

3312 Sunset Blvd
Los Angeles, CA 90026
Phone: 323-669-9000
Fax: 323-669-9002

Home Page: cravefilms.com
IMDb: imdb.com/company/co0146364

Does not accept any unsolicited material. Project types include Feature Films. Preferred genres include Drama.

David Ayer
Writer/Director/Producer
Email: david@cravefilms.com
IMDb: imdb.com/name/nm0043742

Alex Ott
Vice-President, Productions
Email: alex@cravefilms.com
IMDb: imdb.com/name/nm1944773

CREANSPEAK PRODUCTIONS LLC

120 S El Camino Dr
Beverly Hills, CA 90212
Phone: 310-273-8217

Email: info@creanspeak.com
IMDb: imdb.com/company/co0097231

Accepts query letter from unproduced, unrepresented writers via email. Project types include Feature Films, TV, and Commercials. Preferred genres include

Action, Comedy, Drama, Family, Non-Fiction, and Reality.

Kelly Crean
Founder/Executive
Phone: 310-273-8217
Email: info@creanspeak.com
IMDb: imdb.com/name/nm1047631

Jon Freis
Vice-President/Executive
Phone: 310-273-8217
Email: info@creanspeak.com
IMDb: imdb.com/name/nm2045371

CRESCENDO PRODUCTIONS

252 N Larchmont Blvd, Suite 200
Los Angeles, CA 90004
Phone: 323-465-2222
Fax: 323-464-3750

IMDb: ww.imdb.com/company/co0025116

Accepts query letter from unproduced, unrepresented writers. Project types include Feature Films and TV. Preferred genres include Non-Fiction and Reality.

Don Cheadle
Actor/Executive
Phone: 323-465-2222
IMDb: imdb.com/name/nm0000332

CREST ANIMATION PRODUCTIONS

333 N Glenoaks Blvd, Suite 300
Burbank, CA 91502
Phone: 818-846-0166
Fax: 818-846-6074

Email: info@crestcgi.com
Home Page: crestcgi.com
IMDb: imdb.com/company/co0218880

Accepts query letter from unproduced, unrepresented writers via email. Project types include Feature Films. Preferred genres include Animation.

Richard Rich
President/Writer
Phone: 818-846-0166
Email: info@crestcgi.com
IMDb: imdb.com/name/nm0723704

Gregory Kasunich
Production Coordinator/Manager
Phone: 818-846-0166
Email: gkasunich@crestcgi.com
IMDb: imdb.com/name/nm3215310

CRIME SCENE PICTURES

3450 Cahuenga Blvd W, Suite 701
Los Angeles, CA 90068
Phone: 323-963-5136
Fax: 323-963-5137

Email: info@crimescenepictures.net
Home Page: crimescenepictures.net
IMDb: imdb.com/company/co0326645

Does not accept any unsolicited material. Project types include Feature Films. Established in 2010.

Adam Ripp
Writer/Producer/Director
IMDb: imdb.com/name/nm0728063

Brett Hedblom
Director of Development
IMDb: imdb.com/name/nm3916261

Jennifer Marmor
Creative Executive
IMDb: imdb.com/name/nm4420063

CRISPY FILMS

2812 Santa Monica Blvd
Ste 205
Santa Monica, CA 90404
Phone: 310-453-4545

Email: crispyfilms@gmail.com

Does not accept any unsolicited material. Project types include Feature Films. Preferred genres include Comedy, Drama, and Romance.

Jonathan Schwartz
Producer
Phone: 310-453-4545
IMDb: imdb.com/name/nm2009933

Andrea Sperling
Producer
Phone: 310-453-4545
IMDb: imdb.com/name/nm0818304

CROSS CREEK PICTURES

9220 W Sunset Blvd, Suite 100
West Hollywood, CA 90069
Phone: 310-248-4061
Fax: 310-248-4068

Email: info@crosscreekpictures.com
Home Page: crosscreekpictures.com
IMDb: imdb.com/company/co0285648

Accepts query letter from unproduced, unrepresented writers via email. Project types include Feature Films and TV. Preferred genres include Drama.

Brian Oliver
President
Email: brian@crosscreekpicture.com
IMDb: imdb.com/name/nm1003922

John Shepherd
Creative Executive
Phone: 310-248-4061
Email: info@crosscreekpicture.com
IMDb: imdb.com/name/nm3005173

Stephanie Hall
Development
Email: stephanie@crosscreekpicture.com
IMDb: imdb.com/name/nm24206

CROSSROADS FILMS

1722 Whitley Ave
Los Angeles, CA 90028
Phone: 310-659-6220
Fax: 310-659-3105

Home Page: crossroadsfilms.com
IMDb: imdb.com/company/co0061179

Accepts query letter from unproduced, unrepresented writers. Project types include Feature Films, TV, and Commercials. Preferred genres include Comedy, Crime, Drama, Romance, and Thriller.

Camille Taylor
Producer/Partner
Phone: 310-659-6220
IMDb: imdb.com/name/nm0852088

CRUCIAL FILMS

2220 Colorado Ave, 5th Floor
Santa Monica, CA 90404
Phone: 310-865-8249
Fax: 310-865-7068

Email: crucialfilms.asst@gmail.com
IMDb: imdb.com/company/co0049027

Does not accept any unsolicited material. Project types include Feature Films and TV. Preferred genres include Action, Comedy, Crime, Drama, Fantasy, Horror, Romance, and Thriller.

Daniel Schnider
Head of Production & Development/Producer
Phone: 310-865-8249
Email: crucialfilms.asst@gmail.com
IMDb: imdb.com/name/nm3045845

CRYSTAL LAKE ENTERTAINMENT, INC.

4420 Hayvenhurst Ave
Encino, CA 91436
Phone: 818-995-1585
Fax: 818-995-1677

Email: sscfilms@earthlink.net
IMDb: imdb.com/company/co0067362

Accepts query letter from unproduced, unrepresented writers via email. Project types include Feature Films and TV. Preferred genres include Horror, Science Fiction, and Thriller.

Sean Cunningham
Producer/Director/Writer
Phone: 818-995-1585
Email: sscfilms@earthlink.net
IMDb: imdb.com/name/nm0192446

Geoff Garrett
Creative Executive/Producer/Production Manager/
Cinematographer
Phone: 818-995-1585
Email: sscfilms@earthlink.net
IMDb: imdb.com/name/nm0308117

CRYSTAL SKY PICTURES, LLC

10203 Santa Monica Blvd, 5th Floor
Los Angeles, CA 90067
Phone: 310-843-0223
Fax: 310-553-9895

Email: info@crystalsky.com
Home Page: crystalsky.com
IMDb: imdb.com/company/co0004724

Accepts query letter from unproduced, unrepresented writers via email. Project types include Feature Films. Preferred genres include Action, Comedy, Crime, Drama, Family, Fantasy, Horror, Science Fiction, and Thriller.

Steven Paul
Executive/CEO
Phone: 310-843-0223
Email: info@crystalsky.com
IMDb: imdb.com/name/nm0666999

Eric Breiman
Executive/Producer/Production Manager/Actor
Phone: 310-843-0223
Email: info@crystalsky.com

Florent Gaglio
Executive
Phone: 310-843-0223
Email: info@crystalsky.com
IMDb: imdb.com/name/nm2904382

CUBE VISION

9000 W Sunset Blvd
West Hollywood, CA 90069
Phone: 310-461-3490
Fax: 310-461-3491

Home Page: icecube.com
IMDb: imdb.com/company/co0044714

Accepts query letter from unproduced, unrepresented writers. Project types include Feature Films and TV. Preferred genres include Action, Animation, Comedy, Crime, Drama, Family, Non-Fiction, Reality, Romance, and Thriller.

Ice Cube

Owner/Partner
Phone: 310-461-3495
IMDb: imdb.com/name/nm0001084
Assistant: Nancy Leiviska

Matt Alvarez

Partner
Phone: 310-461-3490
IMDb: imdb.com/name/nm0023297
Assistant: Lawtisha Fletcher

CURB ENTERTAINMENT

3907 W Alameda Ave
Burbank, CA 91505
Phone: 818-843-8580
Fax: 818-566-1719

Email: info@curbentertainment.com
Home Page: curbentertainment.com
IMDb: mdb.com/company/co0089886

Accepts query letter from unproduced, unrepresented writers via email. Project types include Feature Films and TV. Preferred genres include Animation, Comedy, Crime, Drama, Family, Horror, Romance, Science Fiction, and Thriller. Established in 1984.

Carole Nemoy

President/Executive Producer
Phone: 818-843-8580
Email: ccurb@curb.com
IMDb: imdb.com/name/nm0626002

Mona Kirton

Director/Head, Distribution Services
Phone: 818-843-8580
Email: mkirton@curb.com
IMDb: imdb.com/name/nm1310398

Christy Peterson

Acquisitions
Phone: 818-843-8580
Email: cpeterson@curb.com

CYAN PICTURES

410 Park Ave, 15th Floor
New York, NY 10022
Phone: 212-274-1085

Email: info@cyanpictures.com
IMDb: imdb.com/company/co0080910

Accepts query letter from unproduced, unrepresented writers via email. Project types include Feature Films and TV. Preferred genres include Comedy, Crime, Drama, Horror, Non-Fiction, Reality, Romance, Science Fiction, and Thriller.

Joshua Newman

CEO
Phone: 212-274-1085
Email: newman@cyanpictures.com
IMDb: imdb.com/name/nm1243333

Alexander Burns

CFO
Phone: 212-274-1085
Email: info@cyanpictures.com

Wes Schrader

Vice-President of Distribution
Phone: 212-274-1085
Email: schrader@cyanpictures.com

CYPRESS FILMS, INC.

630 Ninth Ave, Suite 415
New York, NY 10036
Phone: 212-262-3900
Fax: 212-262-3925

Home Page: cypressfilms.com
IMDb: imdb.com/company/co0044830

Accepts query letter from unproduced, unrepresented writers via email. Project types include Feature Films. Preferred genres include Comedy, Drama, Family, Romance, and Science Fiction.

Joseph Pierson

President/Director/Producer
Phone: 212-262-3900
Email: joseph@cypressfilms.com
IMDb: imdb.com/name/nm0682777

Jon Glascoe

Co-Founder/Executive Producer/Writer
Phone: 212-262-3900
Email: jglascoe@cypressfilms.com
IMDb: imdb.com/name/nm0321797

Jessica Forsythe
Submissions Director
Email: jforsythe@cypressfilms.com

CYPRESS POINT PRODUCTIONS

3000 Olympic Blvd
Santa Monica, CA 90404
Phone: 310-315-4787
Fax: 310-315-4785

Email: cppfilms@earthlink.net
IMDb: imdb.com/company/co0038030

Accepts query letter from unproduced, unrepresented writers via email. Project types include TV. Preferred genres include Action, Comedy, Crime, Drama, Family, Non-Fiction, Romance, Science Fiction, and Thriller.

Gerald Abrams
Chairman
Phone: 310-315-4787
Email: cppfilms@earthlink.net
IMDb: imdb.com/name/nm0009181

Michael Waldron
Director, Development
Phone: 310-315-4787
Email: cppfilms@earthlink.net
IMDb: imdb.com/name/nm1707236

DAKOTA PICTURES

4133 Lankershim Blvd
North Hollywood, CA 91602
Phone: 818-760-0099
Fax: 818-760-1070

Email: info@dakotafilms.com
Home Page: dakotafilms.com

Does not accept any unsolicited material. Project types include Feature Films and TV. Preferred genres include Action, Animation, Comedy, Crime, Drama, Family, Fantasy, Non-Fiction, Reality, and Thriller.

Troy Miller
Founder/Director/Producer
Phone: 818-760-0099
Email: info@dakotafilms.com
IMDb: imdb.com/name/nm0003474

A.J. DiAntonio
Producer/Production Executive
Phone: 818-760-0099
Email: info@dakotafilms.com
IMDb: imdb.com/name/nm1472504

Matt Magielnicki
Producer/Development Executive
Phone: 818-760-0099
Email: info@dakotafilms.com
IMDb: imdb.com/name/nm2616148

DANIEL L. PAULSON PRODUCTIONS

9056 Santa Monica Blvd, Suite 203A
West Hollywood, CA 90069
Phone: 310-278-9747
Fax: 310-278-3751

Email: dlpprods@sbcglobal.net

Does not accept any unsolicited material. Project types include Feature Films and TV. Preferred genres include Action, Comedy, Crime, Detective, Drama, Family, Non-Fiction, Reality, Romance, and Thriller.

Daniel Paulson
President/Executive
Phone: 310-278-9747
Email: dlpprods@sbcglobal.net
IMDb: imdb.com/name/nm0667340

Steve Kennedy
Director/Adminstration
Phone: 310-278-9747
Email: dlpprods@sbcglobal.net
IMDb: imdb.com/name/nm0448346

DANIEL OSTROFF PRODUCTIONS

2046 N Hillhurst Ave. #120
Los Angeles, CA 90027
Phone: 323-284-8824

Email: oteamthe@gmail.com
IMDb: imdb.com/company/co0138101

Accepts query letter from unproduced, unrepresented writers. Project types include Feature Films and TV. Preferred genres include Comedy, Detective, Non-Fiction, and Reality.

Daniel Ostroff

Producer
Phone: 323-284-8824
Email: oteamthe@gmail.com
IMDb: imdb.com/name/nm0652491

DANIEL PETRIE JR. & COMPANY

18034 Ventura Blvd, Suite 445
Encino, CA 91316
Phone: 818-708-1602
Fax: 818-774-0345

IMDb: imdb.com/company/co0120842

Accepts query letter from unproduced, unrepresented writers. Project types include Feature Films and TV. Preferred genres include Action, Comedy, Crime, Detective, Drama, Horror, Romance, Science Fiction, and Thriller.

Daniel Petrie,

Director/Writer/Producer
Phone: 818-708-1602
IMDb: imdb.com/name/nm0677943

Rick Dugdale

Vice-President/Executive/Producer/Production Manager
Phone: 818-708-1602
IMDb: imdb.com/name/nm1067987

DANIEL SLADEK ENTERTAINMENT CORPORATION

8306 Wilshire Blvd, Suite 510
Beverly Hills, CA 90211
Phone: 323-934-9268
Fax: 323-934-7362

Email: danielsladek@mac.com
Home Page: danielsladek.com

Does not accept any unsolicited material. Project types include Feature Films and TV. Preferred genres include Action, Comedy, Crime, Drama, Fantasy, Horror, Non-Fiction, Reality, Romance, Science Fiction, and Thriller. Established in 1998.

Daniel Sladek

President/Producer
Phone: 323-934-9268
Email: danielsladek@mac.com
IMDb: imdb.com/name/nm0805202

DANJAQ

2400 Broadway
Ste 310
Santa Monica, CA 90404
Phone: 310-449-3185

Does not accept any unsolicited material. Project types include Feature Films. Preferred genres include Action.

Barbara Broccoli

Vice President of Development & Production
IMDb: imdb.com/name/nm0110483

David Pope

CEO
Phone: 310-449-3185
IMDb: imdb.com/name/nm0691102

Michael Wilson

President
Phone: 310-449-3185
IMDb: imdb.com/name/nm0933865

DAN LUPOVITZ PRODUCTIONS

936 Alandele Ave
Los Angeles, CA 90036
Phone: 323-930-0769
Fax: 310-385-0196

Email: dlupovitz@aol.com

Accepts query letter from unproduced, unrepresented writers via email. Project types include Feature Films and TV. Preferred genres include Comedy, Drama, and Romance.

Dan Lupovitz

Executive/Producer
Phone: 323-930-0769
Email: dlupovitz@aol.com
IMDb: imdb.com/name/nm0526991

Randy Albelda

Development
Phone: 323-930-0769

DAN WINGUTOW PRODUCTIONS

534 Laguardia Pl., Suite 3
New York, NY 10012
Phone: 212-477-1328
Fax: 212-254-6902

Accepts query letter from unproduced, unrepresented writers. Project types include Feature Films and TV. Preferred genres include Comedy, Crime, Drama, Fantasy, Horror, Romance, Science Fiction, and Thriller.

Dan Wigutow
Executive Producer
Phone: 212-477-1328
IMDb: imdb.com/name/nm0927887

Caroline Moore
Co-Producer
Phone: 212-477-1328
IMDb: imdb.com/name/nm0601006

DARIUS FILMS INCORPORATED

1020 Cole Ave, Suite 4363
Los Angeles, CA 90038
Phone: 310-728-1342
Fax: 310-494-0575

Email: info@dariusfilms.com
Home Page: dariusfilms.com
IMDb: imdb.com/company/co0133523

Accepts query letter from produced or represented writers. Project types include Feature Films and TV. Preferred genres include Comedy, Crime, Detective, Drama, Fantasy, Non-Fiction, Romance, Science Fiction, and Thriller.

Nicholas Tabarrok
President/Actor/Producer
Phone: 310-728-1342
Email: info@dariusfilms.com
IMDb: imdb.com/name/nm0002431

Daniel Baruela
Development
Phone: 310-728-1342
Email: info@dariusfilms.com
IMDb: imdb.com/name/nm3758990

DARK CASTLE ENTERTAINMENT

1601 Main St
Venice, CA 90291
Phone: 310-566-6100
Fax: 310-566-6188

Accepts query letter from produced or represented writers. Project types include Feature Films. Preferred genres include Action, Crime, Drama, Horror, and Thriller. Established in 1999.

Joel Silver
Partner
IMDb: imdb.com/name/nm0005428

Steve Richards
Co-President
IMDb: imdb.com/name/nm0724345

Andrew Rona
Co-President
IMDb: imdb.com/name/nm0739868
Assistant: Dash Boam

DARK HORSE ENTERTAINMENT

8425 W 3rd St, Suite 400
Los Angeles, CA 90048
Phone: 323-655-3600
Fax: 323-655-2430

Home Page: dhentertainment.com
IMDb: imdb.com/company/co0020061

Does not accept any unsolicited material. Project types include Feature Films. Preferred genres include Action, Animation, Comedy, Crime, Drama, Family, Fantasy, Horror, Non-Fiction, Romance, Science Fiction, and Thriller.

Mike Richardson
President/Producer
Phone: 323-655-3600
Email: miker@darkhorse.com
IMDb: imdb.com/name/nm0724700
Assistant: Pete Cacioppo

Keith Goldberg
Senior Vice-President Production
Phone: 323-655-3600
Email: keithg@darkhorse.com
IMDb: imdb.com/name/nm1378991

DARKO ENTERTAINMENT

1041 N Formosa Ave,
West Hollywood, CA 90046
Phone: 323-850-2480
Fax: 323-850-2481

Email: info@darko.com
Home Page: darko.com
IMDb: imdb.com/company/co0118694

Does not accept any unsolicited material. Project types
include Feature Films and TV. Preferred genres
include Fantasy, Horror, and Thriller.

Jeff Cullota

Vice President (Production and Development)
IMDb: imdb.com/name/nm2261214

DARK SKY FILMS

16101 S 108th Ave
Orland Park, IL 60467
Phone: 800-323-0442

Email: info@darkskyfilms.com
Home Page: darkskyfilms.com

Does not accept any unsolicited material. Project types
include Feature Films. Preferred genres include Horror
and Thriller.

Malik Ali

Executive
IMDb: imdb.com/name/nm0019446

Greg Newman

Executive
IMDb: imdb.com/name/nm0628103

Todd Wieneke

Producer
IMDb: imdb.com/name/nm2663562

DARKWOODS PRODUCTIONS

301 E Colorado Blvd, Suite 705
Pasadena, CA 91101
Phone: 323-454-4580
Fax: 323-454-4581

IMDb: imdb.com/company/co0029398

Does not accept any unsolicited material. Project types
include Feature Films. Preferred genres include
Comedy, Crime, Drama, Fantasy, Horror, Non-
Fiction, Romance, Science Fiction, and Thriller.

Frank Darobont

Partner/Director/Writer/Producer
Phone: 323-454-4582
IMDb: imdb.com/name/nm0001104
Assistant: Alex Whit

Denise Huth

Vice-President, Production
Phone: 323-454-4580
IMDb: imdb.com/name/nm1040337

DARREN STAR PRODUCTIONS

9200 Sunset Blvd, Suite 430
Los Angeles, CA 90069
Phone: 310-274-2145
Fax: 310-274-1455

Email: d.star.prodco@gmail.com
IMDb: imdb.com/company/co0020963

Accepts query letter from unproduced, unrepresented
writers. Project types include Feature Films and TV.
Preferred genres include Comedy, Crime, Drama,
Non-Fiction, and Romance.

Darren Star

Creator/Executive Producer/Writer
Phone: 310-274-2145
IMDb: imdb.com/name/nm0823015

Charles Pugliese

Vice-President Production and Development
Phone: 310-274-2145
IMDb: imdb.com/name/nm1551399

DAVE BELL ASSOCIATES

3211 Cahuenga Blvd West
Los Angeles, CA 90068
Phone: 323-851-7801
Fax: 323-851-9349

Email: dbamovies@aol.com
IMDb: imdb.com/company/co0033679

Accepts query letter from unproduced, unrepresented
writers via email. Project types include Feature Films
and TV. Preferred genres include Drama, Family,

Horror, Non-Fiction, Reality, Romance, and Science Fiction.

Ted Weiant
Director, Motion Pictures
Phone: 323-851-7801
Email: dbamovies@aol.com
IMDb: imdb.com/name/nm1059707

Dave Bell
President
Phone: 323-851-7801
Email: dbamovies@aol.com
IMDb: imdb.com/name/nm1037012

Fred Putman
Director, TV
Phone: 323-851-7801
IMDb: imdb.com/name/nm1729656

DAVID EICK PRODUCTIONS

100 Universal City Plaza
Universal City, CA 91608
Phone: 818-501-0146
Fax: 818-733-2522

IMDb: imdb.com/company/co0176813

Accepts query letter from unproduced, unrepresented writers. Project types include TV. Preferred genres include Action, Drama, Science Fiction, and Thriller.

David Eick
President
Phone: 818-501-0146
IMDb: imdb.com/name/nm0251594

DAVIS ENTERTAINMENT

10201 W Pico Blvd
31-301
Los Angeles, CA 90064
Phone: 310-556-3550
Fax: 310-556-3688

IMDb: imdb.com/company/co0022730

Accepts scripts from produced or represented writers.

John Davis
Executive/Chairman/Founder
IMDb: imdb.com/name/nm0204862

John Fox
President of Production
IMDb: imdb.com/name/nm2470810

DEED FILMS

Phone: 419-685-4842

Email: sdonely@deedfilms.com
Home Page: deedfilms.com
IMDb: imdb.com/company/co0323092

Accepts query letter from unproduced, unrepresented writers via email. Project types include Feature Films. Preferred genres include Comedy and Crime. Established in 2008.

Scott Donley
President
IMDb: imdb.com/name/nm4238094

DEERJEN FILMS

222 W 23rd St
New York, NY 10011

Home Page: deerjen.com

Accepts query letter from produced or represented writers. Project types include Feature Films. Preferred genres include Comedy, Drama, Period, Romance, and Thriller.

Jen Gatien
Producer
Email: jen@deerjen.com
IMDb: imdb.com/name/nm0309684

DEFIANCE ENTERTAINMENT

6605 Hollywood Blvd, Suite 100
Los Angeles, CA 91401
Phone: 323-393-0132

Email: info@defiance-ent.com
Home Page: defiance-ent.com
IMDb: imdb.com/company/co0236811

Accepts query letter from unproduced, unrepresented writers via email. Project types include Feature Films, TV, and Commercials. Preferred genres include Action, Comedy, Crime, Drama, Fantasy, Horror,

Myth, Science Fiction, and Thriller. Established in 2006.

Brian Keathley
President/CEO
Email: brian@defiance-ent.com
IMDb: imdb.com/name/nm0444080

Clare Kramer
COO
Email: clare@defiance-ent.com
IMDb: imdb.com/name/nm0004456

DE LINE PICTURES

4000 Warner Blvd Building 66, Room 147
Burbank, CA 91522
Phone: 818-954-5200
Fax: 818-954-5430

IMDb: imdb.com/company/co0033149

Does not accept any unsolicited material. Project types include Feature Films. Preferred genres include Action, Animation, Comedy, Crime, Drama, Family, Fantasy, Period, Romance, Science Fiction, and Thriller. Established in 2001.

Donald De Line
President
IMDb: imdb.com/name/nm0209773
Assistant: Matt Gamboa matt@delinepictures.com

Jacob Robinson
Vice President of Development
IMDb: imdb.com/name/nm1563784

Ally Israelson
Story Editor

DELVE FILMS

20727 High Desert Ct
Suite 4+5
Bend, OR 97701
Phone: 424-703-3583

Email: info@delvefilms.com
Home Page: delvefilms.com

Accepts query letter from produced or represented writers. Project types include Feature Films. Preferred genres include Comedy, Documentary, Drama, Fantasy, Romance, and Thriller.

Isaac Testerman
President
Email: isaac@delvefilms.com
IMDb: imdb.com/name/nm4107099

Nate Salciccioli
Vice President
Phone: 541-788-6139
Email: nate@delvefilms.com
IMDb: imdb.com/name/nm4244606

DEMAREST FILMS

100 N Crescent Dr
Suite 350
Beverly Hills, CA 90210
Phone: 310-385-4310

Does not accept any unsolicited material. Project types include Feature Films and TV. Preferred genres include Comedy, Crime, Drama, Fantasy, and Thriller.

Sam Englebardt
Principal
IMDb: mdb.com/name/nm1583132
Assistant: Linda Goetz

William D. Johnso
Principal
IMDb: imdb.com/name/nm4207924

Michael Lambert
Principal
IMDb: imdb.com/name/nm2236003

Brian Flanagan
Vice President

DEPTH OF FIELD

1724 Whitley Ave
Los Angeles, CA 90028
Phone: 323-466-6500
Fax: 323-466-6501

IMDb: imdb.com/company/co0113177

Accepts scripts from produced or represented writers. Project types include Feature Films.

Chris Weitz
Ower
IMDb: imdb.com/name/nm0919363

Andrew Miano
Executive Producer
IMDb: imdb.com/name/nm0583948

DESERT WIND FILMS

13603 Marina Pointe Dr
Ste D529
Marina Del Rey, CA 90292
Phone: 661-200-3509
Fax: 310-499-5254

Email: media@desertwindfilms.com
Home Page: desertwindfilms.com

Accepts query letter from unproduced, unrepresented writers. Project types include Feature Films.

T.J. Amato
President
IMDb: imdb.com/name/nm2125600

Josh Mills
CEO & Managing Director
IMDb: imdb.com/name/nm1836231

Danny Amato
Production Coordinator
IMDb: imdb.com/name/nm3824734

Steven Camp
CFO
IMDb: imdb.com/name/nm3823972

Jeffrey James Ward
Associate Producer
IMDb: imdb.com/name/nm3823932

DESTINY PICTURES

Email: destiny@destinypictures.biz
Home Page: destinypictures.biz
IMDb: imdb.com/company/co0176808
Facebook: facebook.com/pages/Destiny-Pictures/185479521464859

Does not accept any unsolicited material. Preferred genres include Drama, Non-Fiction, and Thriller.

Mark Castaldo
Founder
IMDb: imdb.com/name/nm0144431

Christine Redlin
Executive Producer

DI BONAVENTURA PICTURES

5555 Melrose Ave
DeMille Building, 2nd Floor
Los Angeles, CA 90038
Phone: 323-956-5454
Fax: 323-862-2288

Does not accept any unsolicited material. Project types include Feature Films. Preferred genres include Action, Fantasy, Science Fiction, and Thriller.

Lorenzo di Bonaventura
President/Producer
IMDb: imdb.com/name/nm0225146

Erik Howsam
Senior Vice-President Production
IMDb: imdb.com/name/nm1857184

David Ready
VP (Executive)
IMDb: imdb.com/name/nm2819401

Mark Vahradian
President of Production
(Executive)http://www.imdb.com/name/nm1680607/
IMDb: imdb.com/name/nm1680607

DI BONAVENTURA PICTURES TELEVISION

500 S Buena Vista St Animation Building, Suite 3F-3
Burbank, CA 91521

IMDb: imdb.com/company/co0341152

Does not accept any unsolicited material. Project types include TV. Preferred genres include Drama, Science Fiction, and Thriller. Established in 2011.

Lorenzo di Bonaventura
Partner
IMDb: imdb.com/name/nm0225146
Assistant: Elizabeth Kiernan

Dan McDermott
Partner
IMDb: imdb.com/name/nm1908145

DIFFERENT DUCK FILMS

18 Wardell Ave.,
Rumson, NJ 07760

Email: DifferentDuckFilms@hotmail.com

Does not accept any unsolicited material. Project types
include Feature Films. Preferred genres include
Comedy, Drama, Family, Fantasy, and Thriller.

Rob Margolies
Principal
IMDb: imdb.com/name/nm1827689

DIMENSION FILMS

345 Hudson St
13th Fl
New York, NY 10014
Phone: 646-862-3400

Home Page: weinsteinco.com

Does not accept any unsolicited material. Project types
include Feature Films. Preferred genres include Action,
Comedy, Horror, Science Fiction, and Thriller.

Bob Weinstein
Co-Chairman
IMDb: imdb.com/name/nm0918424

Jeff Maynard
Post Production
IMDb: imdb.com/name/nm0963230

Andrew Kramer
President
IMDb: imdb.com/name/nm2985328

Matthew Signer
Production & Creative Affairs
IMDb: imdb.com/name/nm1529449

DINO DE LAURENTIIS COMPANY

100 Universal City Plaza Bungalow 5195
Universal City, CA 91608

Phone: 818-777-2111
Fax: 818-886-5566

Email: ddlcoffice@ddlc.net
Home Page: ddlc.net

Does not accept any unsolicited material. Project types
include Feature Films and TV. Preferred genres
include Action, Crime, Detective, Drama, Horror,
Romance, Science Fiction, and Thriller.

Martha De Laurentiis
President
IMDb: imdb.com/name/nm0776646

Lorenzo De Maio
President of Production
IMDb: imdb.com/name/nm1298951

Stuart Boros
Executive of Business Affairs
IMDb: imdb.com/name/nm0097214

Bobby Gonzales
Assistant
IMDb: imdb.com/name/nm5260285

Meryl Pestano
Assistant
IMDb: imdb.com/name/nm2535378

DINOVI PICTURES

720 Wilshire Blvd, Suite 300
Santa Monica, CA 90401
Phone: 310-458-7200
Fax: 310-458-7211

IMDb: imdb.com/company/co0062957

Accepts scripts from produced or represented writers.
Project types include Feature Films. Preferred genres
include Drama and Romance. Established in 1993.

Denise DiNovi
Chief Executive Officer
IMDb: imdb.com/name/nm0224145
Assistant: Maureen Poon Fear

Alison Greenspan
President
IMDb: imdb.com/name/nm1327019
Assistant: Rebecca Rajkowski

DMG ENTERTAINMENT

644 N Cherokee Ave
Melrose Gate
Los Angeles, CA 90004
Phone: 310-275-3750
Fax: 310-275-3770

Email: info@dmg-entertainment.com
Home Page: h2f-entertainment.com

Accepts query letter from unproduced, unrepresented writers. Project types include Feature Films and TV. Preferred genres include Action, Comedy, Drama, Horror, Romance, Science Fiction, and Thriller.

Chris Cowles
Producer
IMDb: imdb.com/name/nm1038319

Brian McCurly
Assistant

DNA FILMS

10 Amwell St
London EC1R 1UQ
Phone: +44 020-7843-4410
Fax: +44 020-7843-4411

Email: info@dnafilms.com
Home Page: dnafilms.com

Does not accept any unsolicited material. Project types include Feature Films. Preferred genres include Comedy, Crime, Drama, Horror, Romance, and Thriller. Established in 1999.

Andrew Macdonald
Partner
Phone: +44 020 7843 4410
IMDb: imdb.com/name/nm0531602

Allon Reich
Partner
Phone: +44 020 7843 4410
IMDb: imdb.com/name/nm0716924

DOBRE FILMS

Phone: 310-926-6439

Email: dobrefilms@dobrefilms.com
Home Page: dobrefilms.com

Accepts scripts from unproduced, unrepresented writers. Project types include Feature Films and TV. Preferred genres include Action, Comedy, Crime, Detective, Drama, Fantasy, Horror, Myth, Romance, and Science Fiction.

Christopher D'Elia
CEO Director/Producer
Phone: 310-926-6439
Email: cdelia@dobrefilms.com
IMDb: imdb.com/name/nm3179988

Michael Klein
President - Producer/Manager
Phone: 323-510-0818
Email: mklein@dobrefilms.com
IMDb: imdb.com/name/nm3180840

DONNER'S COMPANY

9465 Wilshire Blvd., Suite 420
Beverly Hills, CA 90212
Phone: 310-777-4600
Fax: 310-777-4610

IMDb: imdb.com/company/co0001946

Does not accept any unsolicited material. Project types include Feature Films. Preferred genres include Action, Comedy, Drama, Family, Fantasy, Period, and Science Fiction.

Richard Donner
Producer
IMDb: imdb.com/name/nm0001149

Lauren Shuler Donner
Producer
IMDb: imdb.com/name/nm0795682

DOUBLE FEATURE FILMS

9320 Wilshire Blvd #200
Beverly Hills, CA 90212
Phone: 310-887-1100

Email: dffproducerdesk@gmail.com

Does not accept any unsolicited material. Project types include Feature Films. Preferred genres include Action, Comedy, Drama, Fantasy, Myth, and Thriller. Established in 2005.

Michael Shamberg
Co-Chair/Partner
IMDb: imdb.com/name/nm0787834

Stacey Sher
Co-Chari/Partner
IMDb: imdb.com/name/nm0792049

Ameet Shukla
Creative Executive
IMDb: imdb.com/name/nm2627415

Carla Santos Shamberg
EVP / Partner
IMDb: imdb.com/name/nm0534411

Taylor Latham
VP Development
IMDb: imdb.com/name/nm2281897

DOUBLE NICKEL ENTERTAINMENT

234 W 138th St
New York, NY 10030
Phone: 646-435-4390
Fax: 212-694-6205

Email: admin@doublenickelentertainment.com
Home Page: doublenickelentertainment.com

Accepts query letter from unproduced, unrepresented
writers via email. Project types include Feature Films.
Preferred genres include Drama.

Jenette Kahn
Partner/Producer
IMDb: imdb.com/name/nm1986495

Adam Richman
Partner/Producer
IMDb: imdb.com/name/nm0725013

Adam Callan
Creative Executive
IMDb: imdb.com/name/nm2565555

D. PETRIE PRODUCTIONS, INC.

13201 Haney Place
Los Angeles, CA 90049
Phone: 310-394-2608
Fax: 310-395-8530

Email: dgpetrie@aol.com

Accepts query letter from unproduced, unrepresented
writers via email. Project types include TV. Preferred
genres include Drama.

Dorothea Petrie
Owner/Executive Producer
Phone: 310-394-2608
Email: dgpetrie@aol.com
IMDb: imdb.com/name/nm0677955
Assistant: John Cockrell

June Petrie
Producer/Co-Producer
Phone: 310-394-2608
IMDb: imdb.com/name/nm0677968

DRAFTHOUSE FILMS

320 E 6th St
Austin, TX 78701
Phone: 512-476-1320

Email: info@drafthousefilms.com
Home Page: drafthousefilms.com
IMDb: imdb.com/company/co0313579
Facebook: facebook.com/drafthousefilms

Does not accept any unsolicited material. Project types
include Feature Films. Preferred genres include Action,
Comedy, Documentary, Drama, and Thriller.

Tim League
CEO
IMDb: imdb.com/name/nm1382506

James Emanuel Shapiro
COO
IMDb: imdb.com/name/nm4874938

Evan Husney
Creative Director
IMDb: imdb.com/name/nm3432889

DREAMBRIDGE FILMS

207 W 25th St
6th Floor
New York, NY 10001
Phone: 323-927-1907

Home Page: dreambridgefilms.com
IMDb: imdb.com/company/co0248660

Accepts query letter from unproduced, unrepresented writers. Project types include Feature Films. Preferred genres include Comedy, Drama, and Family.

Todd J. Labarowski
President
Email: todd27@mac.com
IMDb: imdb.com/name/nm1132640

DREAMWORKS

100 Universal City Plaza
Universal City, CA 91608
Phone: 818-733-7000

Email: info@dreamworksstudios.com
Home Page: dreamworksstudios.com
IMDb: imdb.com/company/co0252576

Does not accept any unsolicited material. Project types include Feature Films and TV. Preferred genres include Action, Comedy, Crime, Drama, Fantasy, Period, Romance, Science Fiction, and Thriller.

Steven Spielberg
Chairman
IMDb: imdb.com/name/nm0000229

Andrea McCall
Senior Vice President (Story Department)
Email: andrea_mccall@dreamworksstudios.com

Mia Maniscalco
Creative Executive
Email: mia_maniscalco@dreamworksstudios.com
IMDb: imdb.com/name/nm4103271

Holly Bario
President
Email: info@wif.org
IMDb: imdb.com/name/nm2302370

Andrea McCall
Senior Vice President (Story Development)
Email: andrea_mccall@dreamworksstudios.com
IMDb: imdb.com/name/nm2569503

Chloe Dan
Vice President (Production)
Email: Chloe_Dan@DreamworksStudios.com
IMDb: imdb.com/name/nm2676603

DREAMWORKS ANIMATION

1000 Flower St
Glendale, CA 91201
Phone: 818-695-5000
Fax: 818-695-3510

Home Page: dreamworksanimation.com
IMDb: imdb.com/company/co0129164

Does not accept any unsolicited material. Project types include Feature Films, Short Films, TV, and Video Games. Preferred genres include Action, Animation, Comedy, Documentary, Family, Fantasy, Horror, and Science Fiction. Established in 2004.

Jeffrey Katzenberg
Chief Executive Officer
IMDb: imdb.com/name/nm0005076

Bill Damaschke
Chief Creative Officer
IMDb: imdb.com/name/nm0198632

Nancy Bernsein
Head of Global Production
IMDb: imdb.com/name/nm0077110

Gregg Taylor
Head of Development
Assistant: Diana Theobald
Diana.Theobald@dreamworks.com

Kyle Arthur Jefferson
Director
IMDb: imdb.com/name/nm2200868

Tom McGrath
Director (Producer)
IMDb: imdb.com/name/nm0569891

Jeffrey Wike
Director of Research and Development
IMDb: imdb.com/name/nm5204969

Chris Kuser
Senior Executive of Development
IMDb: imdb.com/name/nm1936914
Assistant: Beth Cannon

Damon Ross
Senior Executive of Development
IMDb: imdb.com/name/nm1842613

Ben Cawood
Creative Executive
IMDb: imdb.com/name/nm1374730

Diane Ikermiyashiro
Creative Executive
IMDb: imdb.com/name/nm2155308

Amie Karp
Creative Executive of Development
IMDb: imdb.com/name/nm2047897
Assistant: Peter Cacioppo
peter.cacioppo@dreamworks.com

Karen Foster
Development Executive
IMDb: imdb.com/name/nm2259946

Suzanne Buirgy
Production Executive
IMDb: imdb.com/name/nm1330174

Jill Hopper
Production Executive
IMDb: imdb.com/name/nm0394411

Jane Hartwell
Executive of Production
IMDb: imdb.com/name/nm0367286

DUNE ENTERTAINMENT

2121 Ave of the Stars
Suite 2570
Los Angeles, CA 90067
Phone: 310-432-2288

Does not accept any unsolicited material. Project types include Feature Films. Preferred genres include Action, Comedy, Drama, Fantasy, Horror, Romance, Science Fiction, and Thriller.

Greg Coote
Chief Creative Officer

Wendy Weller
Senior Vice President
IMDb: imdb.com/name/nm2956152

Larry Bernstein
Chief Financial Officer
IMDb: imdb.com/name/nm2955628

DUPLASS BROTHERS PRODUCTIONS

902 E Fifth St
Austin, TX 78702

Email: info@duplassbrothers.com
Home Page: duplassbrothers.com

Accepts query letter from unproduced, unrepresented writers via email. Project types include Feature Films. Preferred genres include Comedy, Drama, Horror, and Thriller.

Jay Duplass
Producer
IMDb: imdb.com/name/nm0243231

Mark Duplass
Producer
IMDb: imdb.com/name/nm0243233

Stephanie Langhoff
Producer
IMDb: imdb.com/name/nm1293297

EALING STUDIOS

Ealing Studios
Ealing Green
London, England W5 5EP
Phone: +44-0-20-8567-6655
Fax: +44-0-20-8758-8658

Email: info@ealingstudios.com
Home Page: ealingstudios.com

Does not accept any unsolicited material. Project types include Feature Films and TV. Preferred genres include Comedy, Documentary, Drama, Family, Romance, and Thriller.

Barnaby Thompson
Head of Studio
IMDb: imdb.com/name/nm0859877

James Spring
Managing Director
IMDb: imdb.com/name/nm2020191

Sophie Meyer
Head of Development
IMDb: mdb.com/name/nm1623306

Nic Martin
Development Executive

ECHO BRIDGE ENTERTAINMENT

8383 Wilshire Blvd, Suite 530
Beverly Hills, CA 90211
Phone: 323-658-7900
Fax: 323-658-7922

Email: info@ebellc.com
Home Page: echobridgeentertainment.com

Does not accept any unsolicited material. Project types include Feature Films. Preferred genres include Action, Detective, Drama, Fantasy, Horror, Romance, Science Fiction, and Thriller.

Leonard Shapiro
Executive (Acquisitions)
Email: lshapiro@ebellc.com
IMDb: imdb.com/name/nm0788558

Bobby Rock
Head (Acquisitions)
Email: brock@echobridgehe.com
IMDb: imdb.com/name/nm0734148

ECHO FILMS

c/o Allen Keshishian/Brillstein Entertainment
Partners
9150 Wilshire Blvd, Suite 350
Beverly Hills, CA 90212
Phone: 323-935-2909

Does not accept any unsolicited material. Project types include Feature Films. Preferred genres include Comedy, Drama, and Romance.

Jennifer Aniston
Producer

Kristin Hahn
Producer

ECHO LAKE PRODUCTIONS

421 S Beverly Dr,
8th Floor
Beverly Hills, CA 90212
Phone: 310-789-4790
Fax: 310-789-4791

Email: contact@echolakeproductions.com
Home Page: echolakeproductions.com

Does not accept any unsolicited material. Project types include Feature Films and TV. Preferred genres include Drama, Non-Fiction, Reality, and Thriller.

Douglas Mankoff
President
IMDb: imdb.com/name/nm0542551

Andrew Spaulding
President of Production
IMDb: imdb.com/name/nm1051748

Ida Diffley
Director of Development
IMDb: imdb.com/name/nm3000066

Jessica Staman
VP of Development
IMDb: imdb.com/name/nm1698445

James Smith
Executive Assistant

ECLECTIC PICTURES

7119 Sunset Blvd, Suite 375
Los Angeles, CA 90046
Phone: 323-656-7555
Fax: 323-848-7761

Email: info@eclecticpictures.com
Home Page: eclecticpictures.com

Accepts query letter from unproduced, unrepresented writers via email. Project types include Feature Films.

Benjamin Scott
Head of Development and Production
Email: benjamin@eclecticpictures.com
IMDb: imdb.com/name/nm2623559

John Yarincik
Development
Email: john@eclecticpictures.com
IMDb: imdb.com/name/nm2432490

Patrick Muldoon
Production/Development
Phone: 323 656 7555
IMDb: imdb.com/name/nm0005258

EDEN ROCK MEDIA, INC.

1416 N LaBrea Ave
Hollywood, CA 90028
Phone: 323-802-1718
Fax: 323-802-1832

Email: taugsberger@edenrockmedia.com
Home Page: edenrockmedia.com

Does not accept any unsolicited material. Project types include Feature Films, TV, and Commercials. Preferred genres include Crime, Drama, Family, Non-Fiction, Science Fiction, and Thriller.

Thomas Ausberger
Producer
IMDb: imdb.com/name/nm0041835

EDMONDS ENTERTAINMENT

1635 N Cahuenga Blvd, 6th Floor
Los Angeles, CA 90028
Phone: 323-860-1550
Fax: 323-860-1537

Home Page: edmondsent.com/site/main.html

Accepts scripts from produced or represented writers. Project types include Feature Films and TV. Preferred genres include Drama, Family, Non-Fiction, Reality, and Romance.

Sheila Ducksworth
Sr. Vice-President, TV & Film

Tracey Edmonds
President/CEO
IMDb: imdb.com/name/nm0249525
Assistant: Amy Ficken

Kenneth Edmonds
IMDb: imdb.com/name/nm0004892

EDWARD R. PRESSMAN FILM CORPORATION

1639 11th St, Suite 251
Santa Monica, CA 90404
Phone: 310-450-9692
Fax: 310-450-9705

Home Page: pressman.com/default.asp.html

Does not accept any unsolicited material. Project types include Feature Films. Preferred genres include Action, Comedy, Drama, Fantasy, Myth, and Thriller. Established in 1969.

Edward Pressman
CEO/Chairman
IMDb: imdb.com/name/nm0696299
Assistant: Danielle Halagarda

Jon Katz
COO/Business & Legal Affairs
IMDb: imdb.com/name/nm1853997

Sarah Ramey
Head, Development & Creative Affairs
Phone: 212-489-3333
IMDb: imdb.com/name/nm2269975

EDWARD SAXON PRODUCTIONS

1526 14th St #105
Santa Monica, CA 90404
Phone: 310-893-0903

Email: esaxon@saxonproductions.net
Home Page: saxonproductions.net

Accepts query letter from unproduced, unrepresented writers via email. Project types include Feature Films and TV. Preferred genres include Action, Drama, Family, Non-Fiction, and Romance.

Ed Saxon
Producer
IMDb: imdb.com/name/nm0768324

EFISH ENTERTAINMENT, INC.

4236 Arch St, Suite 407
Studio City, CA 91604
Phone: 818-509-9377

Email: info@efishentertainment.com
Home Page: efishentertainment.com

Accepts query letter from unproduced, unrepresented writers via email. Project types include Feature Films. Preferred genres include Action, Crime, Horror, and Science Fiction. Established in 2009.

Brianna Johnson
Email: briannaasst@efishentertainment.com
IMDb: imdb.com/name/nm3776636

Eric Fischer
CEO/Producer
Email: ericasst@efishentertainment.com
IMDb: imdb.com/name/nm2737789
Assistant: Tatjana Bluchel

Mike Williams
Development
Email: mikeasst@efishentertainment.com
IMDb: imdb.com/name/nm3552724

Tom Reilly
CFO
IMDb: imdb.com/name/nm3948044

EGO FILM ARTS

80 Niagara St
Toronto, ON M5V 1C5
Phone: 416-703-2137

Email: questions@egofilmarts.com
Home Page: egofilmarts.com

Does not accept any unsolicited material. Project types include Feature Films and TV. Preferred genres include Action, Comedy, Crime, Documentary, Drama, Horror, Romance, and Thriller.

Atom Egoyan
Founder
IMDb: imdb.com/name/nm0000382

EIGHTH SQUARE ENTERTAINMENT

606 N Larchmont Blvd, Suite 307
Los Angeles, CA 90004
Phone: 323-469-1003
Fax: 323-469-1516

Does not accept any unsolicited material. Project types include Feature Films, TV, and Theater. Preferred genres include Comedy, Crime, Drama, and Thriller.

Jeff Melnick
Producer
IMDb: imdb.com/name/nm0578179

Janette Jensen
Producer
Email: jjnomiddlename@yahoo.com
IMDb: imdb.com/name/nm1130073

ELECTRIC CITY ENTERTAINMENT

8409 Santa Monica Blvd
West Hollywood, CA 90069
Phone: 323-654-7800
Fax: 323-654-7808

Home Page: electriccityent.com

Accepts query letter from unproduced, unrepresented writers via email. Project types include Feature Films. Preferred genres include Comedy, Drama, and Romance. Established in 2012.

Lynette Howell
Producer/Partner
IMDb: imdb.com/name/nm1987578
Assistant: Jess Engel

Jamie Patricof
Producer/Partner
IMDb: imdb.com/name/nm1364232
Assistant: Jack Hart

Katie McNeill
Vice President of Production
IMDb: imdb.com/name/nm3336352

Crystal Powell
Vice President of Production
IMDb: imdb.com/name/nm2476235

ELECTRIC DYNAMITE

1741 Ivar Ave
Los Angeles, CA 90028
Phone: 323-790-8040
Fax: 818-733-2651

Home Page: electricdynamite.com
IMDb: imdb.com/company/co0190357

Accepts query letter from unproduced, unrepresented writers. Project types include Feature Films, TV, and Commercials. Preferred genres include Comedy, Fantasy, and Science Fiction.

Jack Black
Principal
Phone: 323-790-8000
IMDb: imdb.com/name/nm0085312

Priyanka Mattoo
Development
IMDb: imdb.com/name/nm3339192

ELECTRIC ENTERTAINMENT

940 N Highland Ave, Suite A
Los Angeles, CA 90038
Phone: 323-817-1300
Fax: 323-467-7155

Home Page: electric-entertainment.com

Does not accept any unsolicited material. Project types include Feature Films, TV, and Commercials. Preferred genres include Action, Animation, Comedy, Drama, Non-Fiction, Reality, Science Fiction, and Thriller.

Dean Devlin
President
IMDb: imdb.com/name/nm0002041
Assistant: Chase Friedman

Rachel Olschan
Partner/Producer
IMDb: imdb.com/name/nm1272673

Marc Roskin
VP Development
IMDb: imdb.com/name/nm0743059

ELECTRIC FARM ENTERTAINMENT

3000 Olympic Blvd
Building 3, Suite 1366
Santa Monica, CA 90404
Phone: 310-264-4199
Fax: 310-264-4196

Email: contact@electricfarment.com
Home Page: ef-ent.com

Accepts query letter from unproduced, unrepresented writers via email. Project types include Feature Films, TV, and Commercials. Preferred genres include Action, Drama, Fantasy, and Science Fiction.

Stan Rogow
Principal/Executive Producer
Assistant: Allison Lurie

Brent Friedman
Principal/Executive Producer

ELECTRIC SHEPHERD PRODUCTIONS

8306 Wilshire Blvd, #2016
Beverly Hills, CA 90211
Phone: 310-433-5282
Fax: 323-315-7170

Email: admin@electricshepherdproductions.com
Home Page: electricshepherdproductions.com

Accepts query letter from unproduced, unrepresented writers via email. Project types include Feature Films, TV, and Commercials. Preferred genres include Action, Drama, Fantasy, Myth, Science Fiction, and Thriller.

Kalen Egan
Development Associate

Isa Dick Hackett
CEO/President
IMDb: imdb.com/name/nm2357313

Laura Leslie
Co-Owner

ELEMENT PICTURES

21 Mespil Rd
Dublin 4
Ireland
Phone: 353-1-618-5032
Fax: 353-1-664-3737

Email: info@elementpictures.ie
Home Page: elementpictures.ie

Accepts query letter from unproduced, unrepresented writers. Project types include Feature Films and TV. Preferred genres include Action, Comedy, Documentary, Drama, Horror, and Science Fiction.

Ed Guiney
Company Director
IMDb: imdb.com/name/nm0347384

Andrew Lowe
Company Director
IMDb: imdb.com/name/nm1103466

Lee Magiday
Producer
IMDb: imdb.com/name/nm3717662

Emma Norton
Head of Development
IMDb: imdb.com/name/nm4499999

Gillian Clarke
Development Executive Television

Danny Takhar
Development Executive

ELEPHANT EYE FILMS

89 Fifth Ave
Ste 306
New York, NY 10003
Phone: 212-488-8877
Fax: 212-488-8878

Email: info@elephanteyefilms.com
Home Page: elephanteyefilms.com

Does not accept any unsolicited material. Project types include Feature Films. Preferred genres include Action, Comedy, Drama, Fantasy, and Non-Fiction.

Kim Jose
Principal
Email: Kim@elephanteyefilms.com

Dave Robinson
Principal
Email: Dave@elephanteyefilms.com

Toni Branson
Production/Development Executive
Email: Toni@elephanteyefilms.com

ELEVATE ENTERTAINMENT

1925 Century Park East, Suite 2320
Los Angeles, CA 90067
Phone: 310-788-3490
Fax: 323-848-9867

Email: info@elevate-ent.com
Home Page: elevate-ent.com

Accepts query letter from unproduced, unrepresented writers via email. Project types include Feature Films and TV. Preferred genres include Action, Animation, Comedy, Crime, Drama, Family, Fantasy, Non-Fiction, Romance, and Science Fiction.

Alex Cole
President/Manager
Phone: 310-557-0100
Email: acole@elevate-ent.com
IMDb: imdb.com/name/nm2251162
Assistant: Stephen Hale

Jenny M. Wood
Manager/Producer
Phone: 323-951-9310
Email: jwood@elevate-ent.com

ELIXIR FILMS

8033 W Sunset Blvd, Suite 867
West Hollywood, CA 90046
Phone: 323-848-9867
Fax: 323-848-5945

Email: info@elixirfilms.com
Home Page: elixirfilms.com

Does not accept any unsolicited material. Project types include Feature Films. Preferred genres include Drama and Family.

David Alexanian
Producer

Alexis Alexanian
Producer
Assistant: Joe Brinkman

ELKINS ENTERTAINMENT

8306 Wilshire Blvd
PMB 3643
Beverly Hills, CA 90211
Phone: 323-932-0400
Fax: 323-932-6400

Email: info@elkinsent.com
Home Page: elkinsent.com

Accepts query letter from unproduced, unrepresented writers via email. Project types include Feature Films and TV. Preferred genres include Comedy, Drama, Non-Fiction, Reality, and Romance.

Hillard Elkins
President/Producer/Manager

Sandi Love
Vice-President/Manager

EMBASSY ROW LLC

325 Hudson St
Ste 601
New York, NY 10013
Phone: 212 507 9700
Fax: 212 507 9701

Email: info@embassyrow.com
Home Page: embassyrow.com

Does not accept any unsolicited material. Project types include Feature Films, TV, and Commercials. Preferred genres include Action, Comedy, Drama, Fantasy, Non-Fiction, Reality, and Science Fiction.

Michael Davies
President, Production

Tammy Johnson
Sr. Vice-President, Production/General Manager

EMBER ENTERTAINMENT GROUP

11718 Barrington Court, Suite 116
Los Angeles, CA 90049
Phone: 310-230-9759
Fax: 310-589-4850

Email: eeg.bronson@verizon.net

Accepts query letter from unproduced, unrepresented writers via email. Project types include Feature Films and TV. Preferred genres include Action, Comedy, Drama, Fantasy, and Science Fiction.

T.S. Goldberg
President, Physical Production

J.A. Keller
Finance

Lindsay Dunlap
Producer
IMDb: imdb.com/name/nm0242397

Randall Frakes
President
IMDb: imdb.com/name/nm0289696

EMERALD CITY PRODUCTIONS, INC.

c/o Stankevich-Gochman
9777 Wilshire Blvd, Suite 550
Beverly Hills, CA 90212
Phone: 310-859-8825
Fax: 310-859-8830

Does not accept any unsolicited material. Project types include Feature Films. Preferred genres include Drama, Fantasy, and Science Fiction.

Barrie M. Osborne
Producer
IMDb: imdb.com/name/nm0651614

EM MEDIA

Antenna Media Centre
Beck St
Nottingham
NG1 1EQ
Phone: +44-115-993-23-33

Email: info@em-media.org.uk
Home Page: em-media.org.uk

Accepts query letter from unproduced, unrepresented writers. Project types include Feature Films. Preferred genres include Comedy, Drama, and Romance. Established in 2002.

Debbie Williams
CEO
Phone: 0115-993-2333
Email: Debbie.Williams@em-media.org.uk
IMDb: imdb.com/name/nm3527737

Suzanne Alizart
Head of Content Creation
Email: Suzanne.Alizart@em-media.org
IMDb: imdb.com/name/nm2355251

Anna Seifert-Speck
Development Executive
IMDb: imdb.com/name/nm3527106

John Tobin
Head of Market Development
IMDb: imdb.com/name/nm3527690

ENDEMOL ENTERTAINMENT

9255 W Sunset Blvd
Suite 1100
Los Angeles, CA 90069
Phone: 310-860-9914
Fax: 310-860-0073

Home Page: endemolusa.tv

Accepts query letter from produced or represented writers. Project types include TV. Preferred genres include Comedy, Drama, and Reality.

Michael Weinberg
VP of Development

David Goldberg
Chairman
IMDb: imdb.com/name/nm2499880

Aaron Bilgrad
SVP of Development

Caroline Baumgard
SVP of Development
IMDb: imdb.com/name/nm0062313

Rob Day
SVP of Production
IMDb: imdb.com/name/nm1691117

Jeremy Gold
Head of Scripted Division
IMDb: imdb.com/name/nm0325005

Noah Beery
VP of Production

Dave Hamilton
VP of Development

Sean Loughlin
Executive Development & Producer

Chris Dickie
Coordinator of Development

ENDGAME ENTERTAINMENT

9100 Wilshire Blvd, Suite 100W
Beverly Hills, CA 90212
Phone: 310-432-7300
Fax: 310-432-7301

Email: reception@endgameent.com
Home Page: endgameent.com

Does not accept any unsolicited material. Project types include Feature Films, TV, and Theater. Preferred genres include Action, Animation, Comedy, Crime, Detective, Drama, Non-Fiction, Reality, Romance, Science Fiction, and Thriller.

Adam Del Deo
Sr. Vice-President, Production
IMDb: imdb.com/name/nm0215534

Lucas Smith
Sr. Vice-President, Development
IMDb: imdb.com/name/nm0809156

James Stern
Chairmen & CEO
IMDb: imdb.com/name/nm0827726

Julie Goldstein
President (Production)
IMDb: imdb.com/name/nm0326252

ENERGY ENTERTAINMENT

9348 Civic Center Dr
Mezzanine Level
Beverly Hills, CA 90210
Phone: 310-746-4872

Email: info@energyentertainment.net
Home Page: energyentertainment.net

Does not accept any unsolicited material. Project types include Feature Films. Preferred genres include Comedy, Drama, Fantasy, Horror, Non-Fiction, Science Fiction, and Thriller. Established in 2001.

Angelina Chen
Manager

Brooklyn Weaver
Owner/Manager
IMDb: imdb.com/name/nm0915819
Assistant: David Binns

Derrick Eppich
Producer

Michelle Arenal
Assistant

ENTERTAINMENT ONE GROUP

9465 Wilshire Blvd, Suite 500
Los Angeles, CA 90212
Phone: 310-407-0960

Email: eonetv@entonegroup.com
Home Page: entonegroup.com

Does not accept any unsolicited material. Project types include Feature Films, TV, and Commercials. Preferred genres include Animation, Comedy, Drama, Family, Horror, Non-Fiction, Reality, Romance, and Thriller.

Swin Chang
Director of Development (Kids Television)

Michael Rosenberg
Executive Vice President (U.S. Scripted Television)

Jeff Hevert
Vice President (Current Programming and Development, Reality)

Armand Leo
Vice President (Production)

Adam Blumberg
Director of Development

ENTITLED ENTERTAINMENT

2038 Redcliff St
Los Angeles, CA 90039
Phone: 323-469-9000
Fax: 323-660-5292

Home Page: entitledentertainment.com/index.html

Does not accept any unsolicited material. Project types include Feature Films, TV, and Theater. Preferred genres include Comedy, Crime, Drama, Family, and Non-Fiction.

James Burke
Partner
IMDb: imdb.com/name/nm0121711

Scott Disharoon
Partner
IMDb: imdb.com/name/nm0228318

ENVISION MEDIA ARTS

5555 Melrose Ave
Building 221, Suite 110
Los Angeles, CA 90038
Phone: 323-956-9687
Fax: 323-862-2205

Email: info@envisionma.com
Home Page: envisionma.com

Accepts query letter from unproduced, unrepresented writers via email. Project types include Feature Films and TV. Preferred genres include Action, Comedy, Drama, Family, Fantasy, Myth, and Romance. Established in 2002.

Lee Nelson
CEO
Email: lnelson@envisionma.com
IMDb: imdb.com/name/nm0625540

David Buelow
President of Film & TV
Email: dbuelow@envisionma.com
IMDb: imdb.com/name/nm2149164

David Tish
Director of Development
Email: dtish@envisionma.com
IMDb: imdb.com/name/nm2953843

EPIC LEVEL ENTERTAINMENT, LTD.

7095 Hollywood Blvd #688
Hollywood, CA 91604
Phone: 818-752-6800
Fax: 818-752-6814

Email: info@epiclevel.com
Home Page: epiclevel.com

Accepts query letter from unproduced, unrepresented writers via email. Project types include Feature Films, TV, and Commercials. Preferred genres include Action, Animation, Fantasy, Horror, Myth, Non-Fiction, Reality, Science Fiction, and Thriller.

Cindi Rice
Producer

Paige Barnett
Associate Producer

John Rosenblum
Producer
Email: jfr@jfr.com
IMDb: jfr.com

EPIGRAM ENTERTAINMENT

3745 Longview Valley Rd
Sherman Oaks, CA 91423
Phone: 818-461-8937
Fax: 818-461-8919

Email: epigrament@sbcglobal.net

Accepts query letter from unproduced, unrepresented writers via email. Project types include Feature Films, TV, and Commercials. Preferred genres include Comedy, Drama, and Romance.

Val McLeroy
Partner

Ellen Baskin
Vice-President, Development

EPIPHANY PICTURES, INC.

10625 Esther Ave
Los Angeles, CA 90064
Phone: 310-815-1266
Fax: 310-815-1269

Email: submissions@epiphanypictures.com
Home Page: epiphanypictures.com

Accepts query letter from unproduced, unrepresented writers via email. Project types include Feature Films, TV, and Commercials. Preferred genres include Action, Animation, Comedy, Drama, Family, Fantasy, Myth, Non-Fiction, Reality, Romance, Science Fiction, Sociocultural, and Thriller.

Scott Frank
Producer/Director
Email: scott@epiphanypictures.com

Dan Halperin
Producer/Director
Phone: 310-452-0242
Email: dan@epiphanypictures.com

Joey DePaolo
Director of Development

EQUILIBRIUM ENTERTAINMENT

1259 S. Orange Grove Ave.
Los Angeles, CA 90019
Phone: 323-939-3555
Fax: 323-939-7523

Email: info@eq-ent.com
Home Page: eq-ent.com
IMDb: imdb.com/company/co0232623

Accepts query letter from unproduced, unrepresented writers. Project types include Feature Films. Preferred genres include Action and Comedy.

Demian Lichtenstein
President & CEO
IMDb: imdb.com/company/co0232623

ESCAPE ARTISTS

10202 W Washington Blvd
Astaire Building, 3rd Floor
Culver City, CA 90232
Phone: 310-244-8833
Fax: 310-204-2151

Email: info@escapeartistsent.com
Home Page: escapeartistsent.com

Does not accept any unsolicited material. Project types include Feature Films and TV. Preferred genres include Action, Comedy, Drama, Fantasy, Myth, Reality, Romance, and Science Fiction.

Todd Black
Partner/Producer
Email: todd_black@spe.sony.com
IMDb: imdb.com/name/nm0085542

Jason Blumenthal
Partner/Producer
Email: jason_blumenthal@spe.sony.com
IMDb: imdb.com/name/nm0089820

Steve Tisch
Partner/Producer
Email: steve_tisch@spe.sony.com

E-SQUARED

531A North Hollywood Way
Suite 237

Burbank, CA 91505
Phone: 818-760-1901

Email: info@e2-esquared.com
Home Page: e2-esquared.com
IMDb: imdb.com/company/co0109424

Accepts query letter from unproduced, unrepresented writers.

Chris Emerson
Producer / Manager
Email: esquaredasst@sbcglobal.net
IMDb: imdb.com/name/nm0256193

EVENSTAR FILMS

Phone: 212-219-2020
Fax: 212-219-2323

Email: info@evenstarfilms.com
Home Page: evenstarfilms.com

Does not accept any unsolicited material. Project types include Feature Films. Preferred genres include Drama.

Elizabeth Cuthrell
Producer
IMDb: imdb.com/name/nm0193876

David Urrutia
Producer
IMDb: imdb.com/name/nm0882102

Jeremy Bloom
Artistic Executive

Steven Rinehart
Creative Consultant

EVERYMAN PICTURES

Santa Monica
1512 16th St Suite 3
Santa Monica, CA 90404
Phone: 310-460-7080
Fax: 310-460-7081

Does not accept any unsolicited material. Project types include Feature Films and TV. Preferred genres include Comedy and Drama.

Jay Roach
Director/Chairman/CEO
Email: jay.roach@fox.com
IMDb: imdb.com/name/nm0005366

Jennifer Perini
President (Development)
Assistant: Kristopher Fogel and Lauren Downey

EXCLUSIVE MEDIA

9100 Wilshire Blvd,
Suite 401 East,
Beverly Hills,
Phone: 310-300-9000
Fax: 310-300-9001

Email: info@exclusivemedia.com
Home Page: exclusivemedia.com

Accepts query letter from produced or represented writers. Project types include Feature Films. Preferred genres include Action, Comedy, Crime, Documentary, Drama, Fantasy, Horror, Romance, and Thriller.

Nigel Sinclair
CEO/Co-Chairman
Email: nigelsinclair@spitfirepix.com
IMDb: imdb.com/name/nm0801691
Assistant: Patricia Scott

Guy East
Co-Chairman
Email: geast@exclusivemedia.com
IMDb: imdb.com/name/nm0247524

Glenn Zipper
Head of Documentary Features
Email: info@zipperbrothersfilms.com
IMDb: imdb.com/name/nm3581772

Shira Rockowitz
Director of Development & Production
IMDb: imdb.com/name/nm2798185

Jennifer Ruper
Creative Executive
IMDb: imdb.com/name/nm1536288

Kim Heinemann
Executive Assistant

EXILE ENTERTAINMENT

732 El Medio Ave.
Pacific Palisades, CA 90272
Phone: 310-573-1523
Fax: 310-573-0109

Email: exile_ent@yahoo.com
IMDb: imdb.com/company/co0063047

Accepts query letter from unproduced, unrepresented writers. Project types include Feature Films. Preferred genres include Comedy, Drama, and Horror.

Gary Ungar
Principal
IMDb: imdb.com/name/nm1316083

EXODUS FILM GROUP

1211 Electric Ave
Venice, CA 90291
Phone: 310-684-3155

Email: info@exodusfilmgroup.com
Home Page: exodusfilmgroup.com
IMDb: imdb.com/company/co0080906

Does not accept any unsolicited material. Project types include Feature Films. Preferred genres include Animation, Comedy, and Family.

Max Howard
Producer
Email: max@exodusfilmgroup.com
IMDb: imdb.com/name/nm0397492

EYE ON THE BALL FILMS

PO Box 46877
Los Angeles, CA 90046
Phone: 323-935-0634
Fax: 323-935-4188

IMDb: imdb.com/company/co0102936

Accepts query letter from unproduced, unrepresented writers. Project types include Feature Films. Preferred genres include Comedy.

Yareli Arizmendi
Producer
Email: arauarizmendi@aol.com
IMDb: imdb.com/name/nm0034976

Sergio Arau
Producer
Email: keepyoureye@aol.com
IMDb: imdb.com/name/nm0033190

FACE PRODUCTIONS

335 N Maple Dr, Suite 135
Beverly Hills, CA 90210
Phone: 310-205-2746
Fax: 310-285-2386

Does not accept any unsolicited material. Project types include Feature Films. Preferred genres include Action, Comedy, and Drama.

Billy Crystal
Actor/Writer/Producer
IMDb: imdb.com/name/nm0000345
Assistant: Kia Hellman

Samantha Sprecher
Vice President (Development)
IMDb: imdb.com/name/nm0819616
Assistant: Kia Hellman

FAKE EMPIRE FEATURES

5555 Melrose Ave
Marx Brothers Building #207
Hollywood, CA 90038
Phone: 323-956-8766

Accepts scripts from produced or represented writers. Project types include Feature Films. Preferred genres include Comedy, Drama, and Family.

Jay Marcus
Creative Executive
IMDb: imdb.com/name/nm1682408

Lisbeth Rowinski
Vice President (Feature Film)
IMDb: imdb.com/name/nm2925164
Assistant: Ritu Moondra

FAKE EMPIRE TELEVISION

400 Warner Blvd
Building 138, Room 1101
Burbank, CA 91522
Phone: 818-954-2420

Home Page: fakeempire.com/about

Accepts scripts from produced or represented writers. Project types include TV. Preferred genres include Comedy, Drama, and Family.

Josh Schwatz
Founder/Producer/Writer/Director
IMDb: imdb.com/name/nm0777300

Leonard Goldstein
Head, Television
IMDb: imdb.com/name/nm2325264
Assistant: Brittany Sever

Stephanie Savage
Founder/Producer/Writer/Director
IMDb: imdb.com/name/nm1335634

Stephanie Savage
Founder/Producer/Writer/Director
IMDb: imdb.com/name/nm1335634
Assistant: Kendall Sand

FALCONER PICTURES

100 Wilshire Blvd. Suite 400
Santa Monica, CA 90401
Phone: 310-452-3350
Fax: 310-388-5910

Home Page: http://www.falconerpictures.com
IMDb: imdb.com/company/co0395531

Does not accept any unsolicited material. Project types include Feature Films. Preferred genres include Action, Comedy, Crime, Drama, and Thriller.

Douglas Falconer
CEO
Email: doug@falconerpictures.com
IMDb: imdb.com/name/nm0266000

Sam Saab
Partner
IMDb: imdb.com/name/nm5668114

FARRELL PAURA PRODUCTIONS

11150 Santa Monica Blvd, Suite 450
Los Angeles, CA 90025
Phone: 310-477-7776
Fax: 310-477-7710

Accepts query letter from unproduced, unrepresented writers via email. Project types include Feature Films. Preferred genres include Comedy, Crime, Drama, and Thriller.

Catherine Paura
CEO

Wayne Kline
Vice-President

Joseph Farrell
Executive

FASTBACK PICTURES

Phone: 323-469-5719

Email: info@fastbackpictures.com
Home Page: fastbackpictures.com
IMDb: imdb.com/company/co0151624

Accepts query letter from unproduced, unrepresented writers. Project types include Feature Films. Preferred genres include Drama and Thriller.

Pascal Franchot
Producer
Phone: 323-717-5569
Email: pascal@fastbackpictures.com
IMDb: imdb.com/name/nm0289994

FASTNET FILMS

1st Fl
75-76 Camden St Lower
Dublin 2
Ireland
Phone: +353 1 478 9566
Fax: +353 1 478 9567

Email: enquiries@fastnetfilms.com
Home Page: fastnetfilms.com

Does not accept any unsolicited material. Project types include Feature Films. Preferred genres include Documentary, Drama, and Reality.

Megan Everett
Head of Development
IMDb: imdb.com/name/nm3210746

Ian Jackson
Head of Development
IMDb: imdb.com/name/nm4127212

Aoife McGonigal
Junior Producer
IMDb: imdb.com/name/nm3502464

FEDORA ENTERTAINMENT

11846 Ventura Blvd
Suite 140
Studio City, CA 91604
Phone: 818-508-5310

Email: peterca975@aol.com

Project types include TV. Preferred genres include Comedy and Drama.

Peter Tolan
Producer
IMDb: imdb.com/name/nm0865847

Michael Wimer
Producer
IMDb: imdb.com/name/nm1057590

Marla A. White
VP of Development
Email: marlaw825@me.com
IMDb: imdb.com/name/nm0925187

FILM 360

9111 Wilshire Blvd
Beverly Hills, CA 90210
Phone: 310-272-7000

IMDb: imdb.com/company/co0192833

Does not accept any unsolicited material. Project types include Feature Films. Preferred genres include Action, Comedy, Crime, Drama, Family, Fantasy, Period, Science Fiction, and Thriller. Established in 2009.

Ben Forkner
Producer
IMDb: imdb.com/name/nm2447927

Eric Kranzler
Producer
IMDb: imdb.com/name/nm1023394

Daniel Rappaport
Producer
IMDb: imdb.com/name/nm0710883

Scott Lambert
Producer
IMDb: imdb.com/name/nm0483300

FILM 44

1526 Cloverfield Blvd
Santa Monica, CA 90404
Phone: 310-586-4949
Fax: 310-586-4959

Email: info@film44.com
IMDb: imdb.com/company/co0152188

Does not accept any unsolicited material. Project types include Feature Films and TV. Preferred genres include Action, Drama, Fantasy, Myth, Science Fiction, and Thriller.

Peter Berg
Partner
IMDb: imdb.com/name/nm0000916

Rebecca Hobbs
SVP of Television
IMDb: imdb.com/name/nm1778008

Braden Aftergood
SVP of Features
IMDb: imdb.com/name/nm2302240

FILMCOLONY

4751 Wilshire Blvd Third Floor Los Angeles, CA 90010
Phone: 323-549-4343
Fax: 323-549-9824

Email: info@filmcolony.com
Home Page: filmcolony.com
IMDb: imdb.com/company/co0159642

Does not accept any unsolicited material. Project types include Feature Films and TV. Preferred genres include Comedy, Crime, Drama, Family, Fantasy, Romance, and Thriller. Established in 1998.

Richard Gladstein
President
IMDb: imdb.com/name/nm0321621

Anand Shah
Vice President
IMDb: imdb.com/name/nm4337795

Melanie Donkers
Director of Development
IMDb: imdb.com/name/nm1410650

FILMDISTRICT

1540 2nd St Suite 200
Santa Monica, CA 90401
Phone: 310-315-1722
Fax: 310-315-1723

Email: info@filmdistrict.com
Home Page: filmdistrict.com
IMDb: imdb.com/company/co0314851

Does not accept any unsolicited material. Project types include Feature Films. Preferred genres include Action, Crime, Drama, Fantasy, Horror, Romance, and Thriller. Established in 2010.

Tim Headington
Partner
IMDb: imdb.com/name/nm2593874

Graham King
Partner
IMDb: imdb.com/name/nm0454752

Josie Liang
Coordinator of Acquisitions
IMDb: imdb.com/name/nm4169347

Josh Peters
Coordinator of Acquisitions
IMDb: imdb.com/name/nm5444016

Peter Schlessel
Chief Executive Officer
IMDb: imdb.com/name/nm0772283
Assistant: Jessica Freenborn

Lia Buman
Executive Vice President of Acquisitions and Operations
IMDb: imdb.com/name/nm2513975
Assistant: Patrick Reese

FILM GARDEN ENTERTAINMENT

6727 Odessa Ave
Van Nuys, CA 91406
Phone: 818-783-3456
Fax: 818-752-8186

Home Page: filmgarden.tv
IMDb: imdb.com/company/co0011492

Project types include TV. Preferred genres include Non-Fiction, Period, and Reality.

Chris Deaux
VP of Development
IMDb: imdb.com/name/nm1614981

FILM HARVEST

750 Lillian Way, Suite 6
LA, CA 90038
Phone: 310-926-4131
Fax: 323-481-8499

Email: info@filmharvest.com
Home Page: filmharvest.com

Does not accept any unsolicited material. Project types include Feature Films. Preferred genres include Action, Documentary, Drama, Horror, Non-Fiction, Science Fiction, and Thriller. Established in 2009.

Joseph McKelheer
Executive Producer
Email: joe@filmharvest.com
IMDb: imdb.com/name/nm1559624

Eben Kostbar
Producer
Email: eben@filmharvest.com
IMDb: imdb.com/name/nm1670295

Elana Kostbar
Assistant
Email: info@filmharvest.com
IMDb: imdb.com/name/nm3657939

FILMNATION ENTERTAINMENT

345 N Maple Dr, Suite 202
Beverly Hills, CA 90210
Phone: 310-859-0088
Fax: 310-859-0089

Home Page: wearefilmnation.com

Accepts query letter from unproduced, unrepresented writers. Project types include Feature Films. Preferred genres include Action, Crime, Drama, Fantasy, Horror, and Thriller. Established in 2008.

Glen Basner
Founder/CEO
Email: gbasner@wearefilmnation.com
IMDb: imdb.com/name/nm0059984

Patrick Chu
Director of Development
Email: pchu@wearefilmnation.com
IMDb: imdb.com/name/nm1776958

FILM SCIENCE

201 Lavaca St Suite 502
Austin, TX 78701
Phone: 917-501-5197

Email: info@filmscience.com
Home Page: filmscience.com

Accepts query letter from unproduced, unrepresented writers. Project types include Feature Films. Preferred genres include Comedy, Drama, and Family.

Anish Savjani
Executive
Email: anish@filmscience.com
IMDb: imdb.com/name/nm1507013

FILMSMITH PRODUCTIONS

3400 Airport Dr
Bldg D
Santa Monica, CA 90405
Phone: 310-260-8866
Fax: 310-397-7155

Email: filmsmith@mac.com
IMDb: imdb.com/company/co0017423

Accepts query letter from unproduced, unrepresented writers. Project types include Feature Films and TV. Preferred genres include Comedy, Crime, Drama, and Thriller.

Zachary Matz
Producer
IMDb: imdb.com/name/nm0560693

FIRST RUN FEATURES

The Film Center Building, 630 Ninth Ave, Suite 1213
New York City, NY 10036
Phone: 212-243-0600
Fax: 212-989-7649

Email: info@firstrunfeatures.com
Home Page: firstrunfeatures.com
IMDb: imdb.com/company/co0002318

Does not accept any unsolicited material. Project types include Feature Films and Short Films. Preferred genres include Comedy, Drama, Fantasy, Romance, and Thriller. Established in 1979.

Seymour Wishman
President
IMDb: imdb.com/name/nm0936544

Marc Mauceri
Vice President
IMDb: imdb.com/name/nm1439609

FIVE BY EIGHT PRODUCTIONS

4312 Clarissa Ave
Los Angeles, CA 90027
Phone: 917-658-7545

Home Page: fivebyeight.com

Accepts query letter from unproduced, unrepresented writers via email. Project types include Feature Films and TV. Preferred genres include Drama. Established in 2006.

Michael Connors
Email: mike@fivebyeight.com
IMDb: imdb.com/name/nm2155421

Sean Mullen
Email: sean@fivebyeight.com
IMDb: imdb.com/name/nm2013693

FIVE SMOOTH STONE PRODUCTIONS

106 Oakland Hills Court
Duluth, GA 30097
Phone: 770-476-7171

Home Page: 5ivesmoothstones.com

Does not accept any unsolicited material. Project types include Feature Films. Preferred genres include Action, Drama, and Non-Fiction.

Rick Middlemas
Partner

Morgan Middlemas
Partner

FLASHPOINT ENTERTAINMENT

9150 Wilshire Blvd, Suite 247
Beverly Hills, CA 90212
Phone: 310-205-6300

Email: info@flashpointentertainment.com
Home Page: flashpointent.com

Does not accept any unsolicited material. Project types include Feature Films. Preferred genres include Drama and Romance.

Andrew Tennenbaum
Manager/Producer
IMDb: imdb.com/name/nm0990025

Tom Johnson
Director/Development
Phone: 310-205-6300
IMDb: imdb.com/name/nm1927361

Laura Roman-Rockhold
Assistant
Phone: 310-205-6300
Email: info@flashpointent.com
IMDb: imdb.com/name/nm4099178

FLAVOR UNIT ENTERTAINMENT

119 Washington Ave, Suite 400
Miami Beach, FL 33139
Phone: 201-333-4883
Fax: 973-556-1770

Email: info@flavorunitentertainment.com
Home Page: flavorentertainment.com

Accepts query letter from unproduced, unrepresented writers via email. Project types include Feature Films and TV. Preferred genres include Comedy, Drama, Family, and Romance.

Queen Latifah
CEO
Phone: 201-333-4883
IMDb: imdb.com/name/nm0001451

Otis Best
Producer/General Manager
Phone: 201-333-4883
IMDb: imdb.com/name/nm1454006

Shakim Compere
CEO
Phone: 201-333-4883
IMDb: imdb.com/name/nm1406277
Assistant: Mark Jean

FLOREN SHIEH PRODUCTIONS

20 W 22nd St
Ste 415
New York, NY 10010
Phone: 212-898-0890

Email: katherine@florenshieh.com
IMDb: imdb.com/company/co0287709

Accepts query letter from unproduced, unrepresented writers. Project types include Feature Films. Preferred genres include Drama.

Clay Floren
Producer
IMDb: imdb.com/name/nm2850202

Aimee Shieh
Producer
IMDb: imdb.com/name/nm1848263

FLOWER FILMS INC.

7360 Santa Monica Blvd
West Hollywood, CA 90046
Phone: 323-876-7400
Fax: 323-876-7401

Accepts scripts from produced or represented writers. Project types include Feature Films and TV. Preferred genres include Comedy, Drama, Family, Fantasy, Romance, and Thriller. Established in 1995.

Drew Barrymore
Partner
IMDb: imdb.com/name/nm0000106

Chris Miller
Vice-President/Producer
IMDb: imdb.com/name/nm0588091
Assistant: Steven Acosta

Ember Truesdell
Vice-President Development
Email: ember@flowerfilms.com
IMDb: imdb.com/name/nm1456092

FOCUS FEATURES

100 Universal City Plaza Building 9128
Universal City, CA 91608
Phone: 818-777-7373

Email: press@filminfocus.com
Home Page: focusfeatures.com
IMDb: imdb.com/company/co0042399

Does not accept any unsolicited material. Project types include Feature Films and TV. Preferred genres include Action, Animation, Comedy, Crime, Documentary, Drama, Fantasy, Horror, Non-Fiction, Romance, and Thriller. Established in 1975.

James Schamus
Chief Executive Officer
IMDb: imdb.com/name/nm0770005

Jeb Brody
President of Production
IMDb: imdb.com/name/nm1330162
Assistant: Rebecca Arzoian

Andrew Karpen
President of Focus Features & Focus Features International
IMDb: imdb.com/name/nm2537917

Peter Kujawski
Executive Vice President of Film Acquisitions
IMDb: imdb.com/name/nm1081654

Josh McLaughlin
Senior Vice President of Production
IMDb: imdb.com/name/nm2249958

Christopher Koop
Director of Production and Development
IMDb: imdb.com/name/nm3096137

FORENSIC FILMS

1 Worth St, 2nd Floor
New York, NY 10013
Phone: 212-966-1110
Fax: (212) 966-1125

Email: forensicfilms@gmail.com

Accepts query letter from unproduced, unrepresented writers via email. Project types include Feature Films. Preferred genres include Comedy, Crime, Drama, Romance, and Thriller.

Scott Macauley
Producer
IMDb: imdb.com/name/nm0531337

Robin O'Hara
Producer
IMDb: imdb.com/name/nm0641327

FORESIGHT UNLIMITED

2934 1/2 Beverly Glen Circle, Suite 900
Bel Air, CA 90077
Phone: 310-275-5222
Fax: 310-275-5202

Email: info@foresight-unltd.com
Home Page: foresight-unltd.com

Accepts query letter from unproduced, unrepresented writers via email. Project types include Feature Films. Preferred genres include Action, Comedy, Crime, Drama, Romance, Science Fiction, and Thriller.

Mark Damon
CEO
IMDb: imdb.com/name/nm0198941

Tamara Birkemoe
President (Chief Operating Officer)
IMDb: imdb.com/name/nm1736077

Scott Collette
Director (Development & Distribution)

FOREST PARK PICTURES

11210 Briarcliff Ln
Studio City, CA 91604-4277
Phone: 323-654-2735
Fax: 323-654-2735

Accepts query letter from unproduced, unrepresented writers. Project types include Feature Films. Preferred genres include Drama, Horror, and Thriller. Established in 2002.

Hayden Christensen
Partner
Phone: 323-848-2942 ext. 265
IMDb: imdb.com/name/nm0159789

Tove Christensen
Partner
Phone: 323-848-2942 ext. 265
IMDb: imdb.com/name/nm0159922

FORGET ME NOT PRODUCTIONS

New York

Email: info@4getmenotproductions.com
Home Page: 4getmenotproductions.com

Accepts query letter from unproduced, unrepresented writers via email. Project types include Feature Films. Preferred genres include Drama.

Jennifer Gargano
President/CEO/Producer
Email: jennifergargano@4getmenotproductions.com
IMDb: imdb.com/name/nm2470854

Harry Azano
Producer
Email: harryazano@gmail.com

FORTIS FILMS

8581 Santa Monica Blvd, Suite 1
West Hollywood, CA 90069
Phone: 310-659-4533
Fax: 310-659-4373

Accepts query letter from unproduced, unrepresented writers. Project types include Feature Films and TV. Preferred genres include Comedy, Drama, and Romance.

Sandra Bullock
Partner
Phone: 310-659-4533
IMDb: imdb.com/name/nm0000113

Maggie Biggar
Partner
Phone: 310-659-4533
IMDb: imdb.com/name/nm0081772

Bryan Moore
Office Manager

FORTRESS FEATURES

2727 Main St Suite E
Santa Monica, CA 90405
Phone: 323-467-4700
Fax: (310) 275-2214

Home Page: fortressfeatures.com

Does not accept any unsolicited material. Project types include Feature Films. Preferred genres include Action, Comedy, Crime, Drama, Horror, and Thriller. Established in 2004.

Brett Forbes
Partner
IMDb: imdb.com/name/nm1771405

Patrick Rizzotti
Partner
IMDb: imdb.com/name/nm0729948

Bonnie Forbes
Producer/Development
IMDb: imdb.com/name/nm1424832

FORWARD ENTERTAINMENT

9255 Sunset Blvd, Suite 805
West Hollywood, CA 90069
Phone: 310-278-6700
Fax: 310-278-6770

Accepts query letter from unproduced, unrepresented writers via email. Project types include Feature Films and TV. Preferred genres include Non-Fiction.

Connie Tavel
Partner
Email: ctavel@forward-ent.com
IMDb: imdb.com/name/nm0851679

Vera Mihailovich
Partner
Email: vmihailovich@forward-ent.com
IMDb: imdb.com/name/nm2250568

Adrienne Sandoval
Executive Assistant
Email: asandoval@forward-ent.com
IMDb: imdb.com/name/nm2302898

FORWARD PASS

12233 W Olympic Blvd
Ste 340
Los Angeles, CA 90064
Phone: 310-207-7378
Fax: 310-207-3426

IMDb: imdb.com/company/co0035930

Does not accept any unsolicited material. Project types include Feature Films. Preferred genres include Crime, Detective, Drama, Non-Fiction, Period, Sociocultural, and Thriller.

Michael Mann
Writer / Producter / Director
IMDb: imdb.com/name/nm0000520

FOURBOYS FILMS

4000 Warner Blvd
Burbank, CA 91522
Phone: 818-954-4378
Fax: 818-954-5359

Email: info@fourboysfilms.com
Home Page: fourboysfilms.com

Does not accept any unsolicited material. Project types include Feature Films and TV. Preferred genres include Animation, Comedy, and Drama.

David Hunt
Partner
IMDb: imdb.com/name/nm0402408

A.J. Morewitz
President
Phone: 818-954-4378
IMDb: imdb.com/name/nm1031450

Patricia Heaton
Partner
IMDb: imdb.com/name/nm0005004

FOX 2000 PICTURES

10201 W Pico Blvd
Building 7B
Los Angeles, CA 90035
Phone: 310-369-2000
Fax: 310-369-4258

Home Page: fox.com

Does not accept any unsolicited material. Preferred genres include Action, Animation, Comedy, Crime, Drama, Family, Fantasy, Horror, Myth, Romance, Science Fiction, and Thriller. Established in 1996.

Elizabeth Gabler
President, Production
Email: elizabeth.gabler@fox.com
IMDb: imdb.com/name/nm1992894

Riley Kathryn Ellis
Executive
Email: riley.ellis@fox.com

FOX DIGITAL STUDIOS

10201 W Pico Blvd
Los Angeles, CA 90035
Phone: 310-369-1000

Email: david.brooks@fox.com

Accepts query letter from produced or represented writers. Project types include Feature Films and TV. Preferred genres include Comedy, Crime, Drama, Horror, and Thriller.

David Worthen Brooks
Creative Director
IMDb: imdb.com/name/nm3652161

FOX INTERNATIONAL PRODUCTIONS

10201 W Pico Blvd
Los Angeles, CA 90035
Phone: 310-369-1000

Home Page: foxinternational.com

Does not accept any unsolicited material. Preferred genres include Action, Crime, Drama, Family, Romance, and Thriller. Established in 2008.

Sanford Panitch
President
Phone: 310-369-1000
Email: sanford.panitch@fox.com
IMDb: imdb.com/name/nm0659529

Anna Kokourina
Vice President (Production)
IMDb: imdb.com/name/nm3916463

Marco Mehlitz
Head (Development)
IMDb: imdb.com/name/nm0576438

FOX SEARCHLIGHT PICTURES

10201 W Pico Blvd
Building 38
Los Angeles, CA 90035
Phone: 310-369-1000
Fax: 310-369-2359

Home Page: foxsearchlight.com

Does not accept any unsolicited material. Preferred genres include Action, Comedy, Crime, Drama, Family, Fantasy, Horror, Romance, and Thriller. Established in 1994.

Stephen Gilula
Co-President
Phone: 310-369-1000
Email: stephen.gilula@fox.com
IMDb: imdb.com/name/nm2322989

FREDERATOR STUDIOS

2829 N. Glenoaks Blvd., Ste. 203 Burbank CA 91504
Phone: 818-848-3932

Email: hey@frederator.com
Home Page: frederator.com

Accepts query letter from unproduced, unrepresented writers via email. Project types include Short Films and TV. Preferred genres include Animation, Comedy, and Family. Established in 1998.

Fred Selbert
President-Producer
Phone: 646-274-4601
Email: fred@frederator.com
IMDb: imdb.com/name/nm0782288
Assistant: Zoe Barton - zoe@frederator.com

Eric Homan
Vice-President, Development
Email: eric@frederator.com
IMDb: imdb.com/name/nm2302704

FREDERIC GOLCHAN PRODUCTIONS

c/o Radar Pictures
10900 Wilshire Blvd, 14th Floor
Los Angeles, CA 90024
Phone: 310-208-8525
Fax: 310-208-1764

Email: fgfilm@aol.com

Does not accept any unsolicited material. Preferred genres include Action, Comedy, Crime, Drama, and Thriller.

Frederic Golchan
President-Producer
Email: asstgolchan@gmail.com
IMDb: imdb.com/name/nm0324907
Assistant: Gaillaume Chiasoda

FRED KUENERT PRODUCTIONS

1601 Hilts Ave. #2
Los Angeles, CA 90024
Phone: 310-470-3363
Fax: 310-470-0060

Accepts query letter from unproduced, unrepresented writers via email. Project types include Feature Films. Preferred genres include Action, Fantasy, Horror, Science Fiction, and Thriller.

Fred Kuenert
Email: fkuehnert@earthlink.net
IMDb: imdb.com/name/nm0473896

Sandra Chouinard
Partner

FREEDOM FILMS

15300 Ventura Blvd. #508
Sherman Oaks, CA 91403
Phone: 818-906-2339
Fax: 818-906-2342

Email: info@freedomfilmsllc.com
Home Page: freedomfilms.com

Does not accept any unsolicited material. Project types include Feature Films. Preferred genres include Action, Crime, Drama, Family, Horror, and Thriller.

Brain Presley
CEO
IMDb: imdb.com/name/nm0696169

Carissa Buffel-Matusow
COO & Producer

Kevin J Matusow
COO & Producer

Scott Robinson
Head of Production
IMDb: imdb.com/name/nm1558904

Warren Davis
Head of Development

Alexandria Klipstein
Creative Executive
IMDb: imdb.com/name/nm2317077

FRELAINE

8383 Wilshire Blvd
5th Fl
Beverly Hills, CA 90211
Phone: 323-848-9729
Fax: 323-848-7219

IMDb: imdb.com/company/co0176000

Accepts query letter from unproduced, unrepresented writers. Project types include Feature Films. Preferred genres include Action, Fantasy, Period, and Thriller.

James Jacks
Executive
IMDb: imdb.com/name/nm0413208

FRESH & SMOKED

Studio City
10700 Ventura Blvd. Ste. 2D
Studio City, CA 91604
Phone: 818-505-1311
Fax: 818-301-2135

Email: bdtd@freshandsmoked.com
Home Page: freshandsmoked.com

Accepts scripts from unproduced, unrepresented writers. Project types include Feature Films, TV, and Commercials. Preferred genres include Action, Animation, Comedy, Crime, Detective, Drama, Family, Fantasy, Horror, Myth, Non-Fiction, Reality, Romance, Science Fiction, and Thriller.

Monika Gosch
Producer
Email: monika@freshandsmoked.com
IMDb: imdb.com/name/nm2815838

Jeremy Gosch
Director
Email: jeremy@freshandsmoked.com
IMDb: imdb.com/name/nm0331443

Angela McIntyre
Internal Development
Email: angela@freshandsmoked.com

FRIED FILMS

100 N Crescent Dr, Suite 350
Beverly Hills, CA 90210
Phone: 310-694-8150
Fax: 310-861-5454

Accepts query letter from unproduced, unrepresented writers. Project types include Feature Films and TV. Preferred genres include Action, Comedy, Crime, Detective, Drama, Family, Romance, and Thriller. Established in 1990.

Robert Fried
Producer
IMDb: imdb.com/name/nm0294975

Tyrrell Shaffner
Development Executive
Phone: 424-210-3607
IMDb: imdb.com/name/nm1656222

FRIENDLY FILMS

100 N Crescent Dr, Suite 350
Beverly Hills, CA 90210
Phone: 310-432-1818
Fax: 310-432-1801

Email: info@friendly-films.com
Home Page: friendly-films.com

Accepts query letter from unproduced, unrepresented writers. Project types include Feature Films. Preferred genres include Comedy, Crime, Drama, Family, and Science Fiction. Established in 2006.

David Friendly
Founder, Producer
Phone: 310-432-1800
IMDb: imdb.com/name/nm0295560

FRONT STREET PICTURES

1950 Franklin St
Vancouver, BC V5L 1R2
Canada
Phone: 604-257-4720
Fax: 604-257-4739

Email: info@frontstreetpictures.com
Home Page: frontstreetpictures.com
IMDb: imdb.com/company/co0149567

Accepts query letter from unproduced, unrepresented writers. Project types include Feature Films and TV. Preferred genres include Action, Comedy, Crime, Drama, Fantasy, and Thriller.

Harvey Kahn
Producer
Email: harvey@frontstreetpictures.com
IMDb: imdb.com/name/nm0434838

FR PRODUCTIONS

2980 Beverly Glenn Cir., Suite 200
Los Angeles, CA 90077

Phone: 310-470-9212
Fax: 310-470-4905

Accepts query letter from unproduced, unrepresented writers via email. Project types include Feature Films. Preferred genres include Comedy, Crime, Drama, Family, Romance, and Thriller.

Fred Roos
Producer/President
Email: frprod@earthlink.net
IMDb: imdb.com/name/nm0740407

FULLER FILMS

P.O. BOX 976
Venice, CA 90294
Phone: 310-717-8842

Does not accept any unsolicited material. Project types include Feature Films. Preferred genres include Comedy, Crime, and Drama.

Paul De Souza
Producer
Email: gopics@verizon.net
IMDb: imdb.com/name/nm0996278

Henry Beean
Writer/Director/Producer
IMDb: imdb.com/name/nm0063785

FUN LITTLE MOVIES

2227 W Olive Ave
Burbank, CA 91506
Phone: 323-467-6868

Email: Contact@funlittlemovies.com
Home Page: funlittlemovies.com
IMDb: imdb.com/company/co0161105

Accepts query letter from unproduced, unrepresented writers. Project types include TV. Preferred genres include Animation and Comedy.

Frank Chindamo
President
Email: frank@funlittlemovies.com
IMDb: imdb.com/name/nm0157828

FURST FILMS

8954 W Pico Blvd
2nd Floor
Los Angeles, CA 90035
Phone: 310-278-6468
Fax: 310-278-7401

Email: info@furstfilms.com
Home Page: furstfilms.com

Accepts query letter from unproduced, unrepresented writers via email. Project types include Feature Films and TV. Preferred genres include Action, Crime, Detective, Drama, Horror, Non-Fiction, Reality, and Thriller.

Bryan Furst
Principal/Producer
IMDb: imdb.com/name/nm1227576

Jan-Willem van der Vaart
Creative Executive

Meredith Ditlow
Manager, Creative Affairs
Email: meredith@furstfilms.com
IMDb: imdb.com/name/nm1902828

FURTHUR FILMS

100 Universal City Plaza
Building 5174
Universal City, CA 91608
Phone: 818-777-6700
Fax: 818-866-1278

Accepts query letter from unproduced, unrepresented writers. Project types include Feature Films. Preferred genres include Comedy, Crime, Drama, Romance, and Thriller.

Michael Douglas
Producer
IMDb: imdb.com/name/nm0000140

Andy Ziskin
Development

FUSEFRAME

2332 Cotner Ave, Suite 200
Los Angeles, CA 90064
Phone: 424-208-1765

Does not accept any unsolicited material. Project types include Feature Films. Preferred genres include Horror and Thriller. Established in 2011.

Marcus Chait
Director of Film and New Media
IMDb: imdb.com/name/nm1483939

Eva Konstantopoulos
Book to Screen Coordinator
IMDb: imdb.com/name/nm2192285

FUSION FILMS

2355 Westwood Blvd, Suite 117
Los Angeles, CA 90064
Phone: 310-441-1496

Email: info@fusionfilms.net
Home Page: fusionfilms.net

Accepts query letter from unproduced, unrepresented writers. Project types include Feature Films and TV. Preferred genres include Action, Animation, Comedy, Crime, Drama, Fantasy, Horror, and Thriller.

John Baldecchi
Co-CEO, Producer
IMDb: imdb.com/name/nm0049689

Jay Judah
Creative Executive

FUZZY DOOR PRODUCTIONS

5700 Wilshire Blvd
Suite 325
Los Angeles, CA 90036
Phone: 323-857-8826
Fax: 323-857-8945

Does not accept any unsolicited material. Project types include Feature Films and TV. Preferred genres include Animation, Comedy, and Family.

Seth MacFarlane
President
IMDb: imdb.com/name/nm0532235

GAETA/ROSENZWEIG FILMS

150 Ocean Park Blvd #322
Santa Monica, CA 90405-3572
Phone: 310-399-7101

Accepts query letter from unproduced, unrepresented writers. Project types include Feature Films and TV. Preferred genres include Comedy, Crime, Drama, Horror, and Thriller.

Alison R. Rosenzweig
Partner
IMDb: imdb.com/name/nm0742851

Michael J. Gaeta
Partner
IMDb: imdb.com/name/nm1357812

GALATEE FILMS

19 Ave de Messine
Paris, France 75008
Phone: +33 1 44 29 21 40
Fax: +33 1 44 29 25 90

Accepts query letter from unproduced, unrepresented writers via email. Project types include Feature Films. Preferred genres include Drama, Non-Fiction, and Romance.

Jacques Perrin
Producer/CEO
IMDb: imdb.com/name/nm0674742

Nicolas Mauvernay
Producer
IMDb: imdb.com/name/nm1241814

Christophe Barratier
Producer
IMDb: imdb.com/name/nm0056725

GALLANT ENTERTAINMENT

16161 Ventura Blvd, Suite 664
Encino, CA 91436
Phone: 818-905-9848
Fax: 818-906-9965

Email: mog@gallantentertainment.com
Home Page: gallantentertainment.com

Accepts query letter from unproduced, unrepresented writers via email. Project types include Feature Films, TV, and Commercials. Preferred genres include Drama, Family, Non-Fiction, Reality, Romance, and Thriller. Established in 1992.

Michael Gallant
President/Producer
IMDb: imdb.com/name/nm0302572

K.R. Gallant
Operations
Email: krg@gallantentertainment.com

GARY HOFFMAN PRODUCTIONS

3931 Puerco Canyon Rd
Malibu, CA 90265
Phone: 310-456-1830
Fax: 310-456-8866

Email: garyhofprods@charter.net

Accepts query letter from unproduced, unrepresented writers via email. Project types include Feature Films and TV. Preferred genres include Action, Comedy, Crime, Drama, Romance, and Thriller.

Gary Hoffman
Producer/President
IMDb: imdb.com/name/nm0388888

Ann Ryan
Development

GARY SANCHEZ PRODUCTIONS

729 Seward St
2nd Fl
Los Angeles, CA 90038
USA
Phone: 323-465-4600
Fax: 323-465-0782

Email: gary@garysanchezprods.com
Home Page: garysanchezprods.com

Does not accept any unsolicited material. Project types include Feature Films and TV. Preferred genres include Comedy.

Will Ferrell
Founder/Executive Producer/Actor
IMDb: imdb.com/name/nm0002071

GENEXT FILMS

5610 Soto St
Huntington Park, CA 90255

Email: contact@genextfilms.com
Home Page: genextfilms.com

Accepts query letter from unproduced, unrepresented writers via email. Project types include Feature Films and TV. Preferred genres include Comedy.

Carlos Salas
CEO/Producer
IMDb: imdb.com/name/nm2972624
Assistant: Kathy Snyder

Rossana Salas
CFO/Producer
IMDb: imdb.com/name/nm2970664

GENREBEND PRODUCTIONS, INC.

233 Wilshire Blvd, Suite 400
Santa Monica, CA 90401
Phone: 310-860-0878
Fax: 310-917-1065

Email: genrebend@elvis.com

Accepts query letter from unproduced, unrepresented writers via email. Project types include Feature Films and TV. Preferred genres include Comedy and Drama.

David Nutter
President/Director
IMDb: imdb.com/name/nm0638354

Tom Lavagnino
Vice-President Creative Affairs, Writer
IMDb: imdb.com/name/nm0491706

GEORGE LITTO PRODUCTIONS, INC.

339 N Orange Dr
Los Angeles, CA 90036
Phone: 323-936-6350
Fax: 323-936-6762

Accepts query letter from unproduced, unrepresented writers. Project types include Feature Films. Preferred genres include Action, Comedy, Crime, Drama, Non-Fiction, and Romance. Established in 1997.

George Litto
CEO/Owner
IMDb: imdb.com/name/nm0514788

Linda Lee
Executive Assistant

GERARD BUTLER ALAN SIEGEL ENTERTAINMENT/ EVIL TWINS

345 N Maple Dr
Beverly Hills, CA 90210
Phone: 310-278-8400

Does not accept any unsolicited material. Project types include Feature Films. Preferred genres include Comedy, Drama, and Thriller.

Gerard Butler
Producer/Actor
IMDb: imdb.com/name/nm0124930

Danielle Robinson
Director of Development

Alan Siegel
Executive

GERBER PICTURES

4000 Warner Blvd
Building 138, Suite 1202
Burbank, CA 91522
Phone: 818-954-3046
Fax: 818-954-3706

Does not accept any unsolicited material. Project types include Feature Films and TV. Preferred genres include Action, Animation, Comedy, Drama, Family, and Romance.

Carrie Gillogly
Creative Executive
IMDb: imdb.com/name/nm2235655

Bill Gerber
President
IMDb: imdb.com/name/nm0314088
Assistant: James Leffler

GHOST HOUSE PICTURES

315 S Beverly Dr, Suite 216
Beverly Hills, CA 90212
Phone: 310-785-3900
Fax: 310-785-9176

Email: info@ghosthousepictures.com
Home Page: ghosthousepictures.com

Does not accept any unsolicited material. Project types
include Feature Films and TV. Preferred genres
include Comedy, Drama, Horror, and Thriller.

Sam Raimi
Director/Executive Producer
IMDb: imdb.com/name/nm0000600

Aaron Lam
Executive
IMDb: imdb.com/name/nm1725478

GIGANTIC PICTURES

New York
207 W 25th St Suite 504
New York, NY 10001
Phone: (212) 925-5075
Fax: (212) 925-5061

Email: info@giganticpictures.com
Home Page: giganticpictures.com

Accepts query letter from produced or represented
writers. Project types include Feature Films and TV.
Preferred genres include Comedy, Drama, Non-
Fiction, and Romance.

Edward Bates
Producer
IMDb: imdb.com/name/nm0060901

Brian Devine
Founder
IMDb: imdb.com/name/nm0222601

GIL ADLER PRODUCTIONS

c/o Peter Franciosa's office/United Talent
Agency
9560 Wilshire Blvd, Suite 500
Beverly Hills, CA 90212

Does not accept any unsolicited material. Project types
include Feature Films, TV, and Commercials.
Preferred genres include Action, Horror, Non-Fiction,
Reality, and Thriller.

Gil Adler
Producer
IMDb: imdb.com/name/nm0012155
Assistant: Ryan Lough

GILBERT FILMS

8409 Santa Monica Blvd
West Hollywood, CA 90069
Phone: 323-650-6800
Fax: 323-650-6810

Email: info@gilbertfilms.com
Home Page: gilbertfilms.com

Does not accept any unsolicited material. Project types
include Feature Films. Preferred genres include
Comedy, Drama, and Romance.

Gary Gilbert
CEO/President
IMDb: imdb.com/name/nm1344784

Shauna Bogetz
Director of Development
IMDb: imdb.com/name/nm2868191

Katie Slovon
Assistant
IMDb: imdb.com/name/nm4244578

GIL NETTER PRODUCTIONS

1645 Abbot Kinney Blvd, Suite 320
Venice, CA 90291
Phone: (310) 394-1644
Fax: (310) 899-6722

Does not accept any unsolicited material. Project types
include Feature Films. Preferred genres include Action,
Comedy, Drama, Family, and Romance.

Gil Netter
Producer
IMDb: imdb.com/name/nm0626696
Assistant: Jennifer Ho

Tom Carstens
Development Executive

Charles Thompson

GIRLS CLUB ENTERTAINMENT

30 Sir Francis Drake Blvd
PO Box 437
Ross, CA 94957
Phone: (415) 233-4060
Fax: (415) 233-4082

Email: info@girlsclubentertainment.com
Home Page: girlsclubentertainment.com

Does not accept any unsolicited material. Project types include Feature Films and TV. Preferred genres include Comedy, Crime, Drama, Non-Fiction, Reality, and Romance.

Jennifer Siebel
Founder
IMDb: imdb.com/name/nm1308076

GITLIN PRODUCTIONS

1310 Montana Ave Second Floor
Santa Monica, CA 90403
Phone: (310) 209-8443
Fax: (310) 728-1749

Email: gitlinproduction@aol.com

Accepts query letter from unproduced, unrepresented writers via email. Project types include Feature Films and TV. Preferred genres include Action, Comedy, Drama, Non-Fiction, and Reality.

Mimi Gitlin
President/Producer
IMDb: imdb.com/name/nm0689316

Richard Gitlin

GITTES, INC.

Los Angeles
16615 Park Ln Place
Los Angeles, CA 90049
Phone: (310) 472-2689

Accepts query letter from unproduced, unrepresented writers. Project types include Feature Films. Preferred genres include Comedy and Drama.

Harry Gittes
Producer
Email: harry_gittes@spe.sony.com
IMDb: imdb.com/name/nm0321228

Edward Wang
Director of Development
Phone: 310-244-4334
Email: edward_wang@spe.sony.com
IMDb: imdb.com/name/nm0910882

GK FILMS

1540 2nd St, Suite 200
Santa Monica, CA 90401
Phone: 310-315-1722
Fax: 310-315-1723

Email: contact@gk-films.com
Home Page: gk-films.com

Does not accept any unsolicited material. Project types include Feature Films and TV. Preferred genres include Action, Animation, Comedy, Crime, Drama, Family, Fantasy, Non-Fiction, Romance, Science Fiction, and Thriller. Established in 2007.

Graham King
CEO
IMDb: imdb.com/name/nm0454752
Assistant: Leah Williams, Michelle Reed

David Crocket
Creative Executive

GLASS EYE PIX

18 Bridge St.
#2G
Brooklyn, NY 11201
Phone: 718-643-6911

Email: feedback@glasseyepix.com
Home Page: glasseyepix.com

Accepts query letter from unproduced, unrepresented writers via email. Preferred genres include Crime, Drama, Horror, Science Fiction, and Thriller.

Larry Fessenden
Executive
Email: larry@glasseyepix.com
IMDb: imdb.com/name/nm0275244

Brent Kunkle
Executive
Email: brentkunkle@gmail.com
IMDb: imdb.com/name/nm2390962

Peter Phok
Executive
Email: peter@peterphok.com
IMDb: imdb.com/name/nm1490961

GLORY ROAD PRODUCTIONS

23638 Lyons Ave.
Suite #470
Newhall, CA 91321
Phone: 661-367-7545

Email: info@gloryroadproductions.com
Home Page: gloryroadproductions.com
Facebook: facebook.com/pages/Glory-Road-Productions/152847784771624?ref=br_tf

Does not accept any unsolicited material. Project types include Feature Films. Preferred genres include Action, Comedy, Drama, Family, Fantasy, and Horror.

Michael Reymann
President
IMDb: imdb.com/name/nm1478831

Erik Elseman
Executive Vice President
IMDb: imdb.com/name/nm4831920

Tara Bonacci
Producer
IMDb: imdb.com/name/nm1742721

Val Mancini
Director of Development
IMDb: imdb.com/name/nm4441689

GOFF-KELLAM PRODUCTIONS

8491 Sunset Blvd, Suite 1000
West Hollywood, CA 90069
Phone: 310-666-9082
Fax: 323-656-1002

Email: info@goffproductions.com
Home Page: goffproductions.com

Accepts query letter from unproduced, unrepresented writers via email. Project types include Feature Films. Preferred genres include Comedy, Drama, Myth, Non-Fiction, Romance, and Thriller. Established in 1998.

Gina Goff
Producer
IMDb: imdb.com/name/nm0324574

Laura Kellam
Producer
IMDb: imdb.com/name/nm0445496

GO GIRL MEDIA

3450 Cahuenga Blvd West #802
Los Angeles, CA 90068
Phone: 310-472-8910
Fax: 818-924-9369

Email: info@gogirlmedia.com
Home Page: gogirlmedia.com

Accepts query letter from unproduced, unrepresented writers via email. Project types include Feature Films and TV. Preferred genres include Animation, Comedy, Drama, Family, Non-Fiction, and Reality. Established in 2004.

Don Priess
Head of Production. Writer/Producer/Editor
IMDb: imdb.com/name/nm1043744

Susie Carter
Owner/Producer/Writer
Email: Susie@gogirlmedia.com
IMDb: imdb.com/name/nm0802053

GOLD CIRCLE FILMS

233 Wilshire Blvd, Suite 650
Santa Monica, CA 90401
Phone: 310-278-4800
Fax: 310-278-0885

Email: info@goldcirclefilms.com
Home Page: goldcirclefilms.com

Does not accept any unsolicited material. Project types include Feature Films. Preferred genres include Action,

Comedy, Drama, Family, Horror, Romance, Science Fiction, and Thriller. Established in 2000.

Rayne Roberts
Creative Executive
IMDb: imdb.com/name/nm2458963

Paul Brooks
President
IMDb: imdb.com/name/nm0112189

Brad Kessell
IMDb: imdb.com/name/nm1733186

GOLDCREST FILMS

65/66 Dean St
London W1D 4PL
United Kingdom
Phone: +44 207-437-8696
Fax: +44 207-437-4448

Email: info@goldcrestfilms.com
Home Page: goldcrestfilms.com

Does not accept any unsolicited material. Project types include Feature Films and TV. Preferred genres include Animation, Comedy, Drama, Non-Fiction, Reality, and Romance. Established in 1977.

Stephen Johnston
President
IMDb: imdb.com/name/nm1158125

GOLDENRING PRODUCTIONS

4804 Laurel Canyon Blvd
Room 570
Valley Village, CA 91607
Phone: 818-508-7425

Email: info@goldenringproductions.net
Home Page: goldenringproductions.net

Accepts query letter from unproduced, unrepresented writers via email. Project types include Feature Films and TV. Preferred genres include Animation, Comedy, Drama, Family, and Non-Fiction.

Jane Goldenring
President/Producer
IMDb: imdb.com/name/nm0325553

Jon King
Development
Email: jonnyfking@gmail.com

GOLDSMITH-THOMAS PRODUCTIONS

239 Central Park West, Suite 6A
New York, NY 10024
Phone: 212-243-4147
Fax: 212-799-2545

Accepts query letter from unproduced, unrepresented writers. Project types include Feature Films and TV. Preferred genres include Comedy, Drama, Family, Non-Fiction, and Romance.

Elaine Goldsmith-Thomas
President/Producer
IMDb: imdb.com/name/nm0326063
Assistant: Anabel Graff

GOOD HUMOR TELEVISION

9255 W Sunset Blvd #1040
West Hollywood, CA 90069
Phone: 310-205-7361
Fax: 310-550-7962

Accepts query letter from unproduced, unrepresented writers. Project types include TV. Preferred genres include Animation and Comedy.

Tom Werner
Owner/Executive Producer
IMDb: imdb.com/name/nm0921492

Mike Clements
President/Executive Producer
IMDb: imdb.com/name/nm2540547

GORILLA PICTURES

2000 W Olive Ave
Burbank, CA 91506
Phone: 818-848-2198
Fax: 818-848-2232

Email: info@gorillapictures.net
Home Page: gorillapictures.net

Does not accept any unsolicited material. Project types include Feature Films. Preferred genres include Action,

Animation, Crime, Drama, Family, Fantasy, Science Fiction, and Thriller. Established in 1999.

Bill Gottlieb
CEO
Email: bill.gottlieb@gorillapictures.net
IMDb: imdb.com/name/nm1539281

Don Wilson
Executive Vice-President of Development
Email: don.wilson@gorillapictures.net
IMDb: imdb.com/name/nm0933310

GOTHAM ENTERTAINMENT GROUP

85 John St Penthouse 1
New York City, NY 10038
Phone: 814-253-5151
Fax: (801) 439-6998

Los Angeles, CA

Email: newyork@gothamcity.com
Email: losangeles@gothamcity.com
Home Page: gothamentertainmentgroup.com

Accepts query letter from unproduced, unrepresented writers via email. Project types include Feature Films and TV. Preferred genres include Action, Comedy, Crime, Drama, Non-Fiction, Reality, Romance, Science Fiction, and Thriller.

Joel Roodman
Partner
Email: joel@gothamentertainmentgroup.com
IMDb: imdb.com/name/nm0740211

Eric Kopeloff
Partner
IMDb: imdb.com/name/nm0465740

GRACIE FILMS

10201 W. Pico Blvd., Bldg. 41/42 Los Angeles, CA 90064
Phone: 310-369-7222

Email: graciefilms@aol.com
Home Page: graciefilms.com

Does not accept any unsolicited material. Project types include Feature Films and TV. Preferred genres include Animation, Comedy, Drama, Family, Non-Fiction, and Romance.

James Brooks
Producer/Writer/Director
IMDb: imdb.com/name/nm0000985

Richard Sakai
President
IMDb: imdb.com/name/nm0757017

Julie Ansell
President (Motion Pictures)
IMDb: imdb.com/name/nm0030572

GRADE A ENTERTAINMENT

149 S Barrington Ave, Suite 719
Los Angeles, CA 90049
Phone: 310-358-8600
Fax: 310-919-2998

Email: development@gradeaent.com
Home Page: gradeaent.com

Accepts query letter from unproduced, unrepresented writers via email. Project types include Feature Films and TV. Preferred genres include Fantasy.

Andy Cohen
Producer/Manager
Email: andy@gradeaent.com
IMDb: imdb.com/name/nm2221597

GRAMMNET PRODUCTIONS

2461 Santa Monica Blvd #521
Santa Monica, CA 90404
Phone: 310-317-4231
Fax: 310-317-4260

Does not accept any unsolicited material. Project types include Feature Films, TV, and Theater. Preferred genres include Comedy, Drama, Family, Non-Fiction, and Reality.

Kelsey Grammar
Actor/Producer/CEO
IMDb: imdb.com/name/nm0001288
Assistant: Xochitl L. Olivas

Stella Bulochnikov
Executive
Phone: 310-255-5089
Assistant: Melissa Panzer, mpanzer@lionsgate.com

GRAND CANAL FILM WORKS

1187 Coast Village Rd
Montecito, CA 93108
Phone: 818-259-8237

11135 Magnolia, SU 160
North Hollywood, CA 91601

Does not accept any unsolicited material. Project types
include Feature Films, TV, and Theater. Preferred
genres include Non-Fiction and Reality.

Rick Brookwell
Partner
Email: RBrookwell@GrandCanalFW.com
IMDb: imdb.com/name/nm2162558

Craig Haffner
Partner
Email: CHaffner@GrandCanalFW.com
IMDb: imdb.com/name/nm0353121

GRAND PRODUCTIONS

16255 Venture Blvd, Suite 400
Encino, CA 91436
Phone: 818-981-1497
Fax: (818) 380-3006

Email: grandproductions@mac.com

Does not accept any unsolicited material. Project types
include Feature Films and TV. Preferred genres
include Comedy and Drama.

Gary Randall
President/Owner/Executive Producer
IMDb: imdb.com/name/nm0709592

Jennifer Stempel
Development Executive
IMDb: imdb.com/name/nm4009105

GRAN VIA PRODUCTIONS

1888 Century Park East
14th Floor
Los Angeles, CA 90067
Phone: 310-859-3060
Fax: 310-859-3066

Does not accept any unsolicited material. Project types
include Feature Films and TV. Preferred genres
include Comedy, Drama, Fantasy, and Science Fiction.

Mark Johnson
President/Producer
IMDb: imdb.com/name/nm0425741
Assistant: Emily Eckert (Story Editor)

Mark Ceryak
Creative Executive
IMDb: imdb.com/name/nm1641437

GRAY ANGEL PRODUCTIONS

69 Windward Ave
Venice, CA 90291
Phone: 310-581-0010
Fax: 310-396-0551

Accepts query letter from unproduced, unrepresented
writers. Project types include Feature Films.

Anjelica Huston
CEO/Producer
IMDb: imdb.com/name/nm0001378

Jaclyn Bashoff
President/Manager
IMDb: imdb.com/name/nm1902472

GRAZKA TAYLOR PRODUCTIONS

409 N Camden Dr, Suite 202
Beverly Hills, CA 90210
Phone: 310-246-1107

Home Page: grazkat.com

Does not accept any unsolicited material. Project types
include Feature Films and TV. Preferred genres
include Drama, Non-Fiction, Reality, and Romance.

Grazka Taylor
Producer
Email: grazka@grazkat.com
IMDb: imdb.com/name/nm0852429

GREASY ENTERTAINMENT

6345 Balboa Blvd
Building 4, Suite 375

Encino, CA 91316
Phone: 310-586-2300

Email: info@greasy.biz
Home Page: greasy.biz

Accepts query letter from unproduced, unrepresented writers via email. Project types include Feature Films and TV. Preferred genres include Action and Comedy.

Jon Heder
CFO/Actor/Executive
IMDb: imdb.com/name/nm1417647

Doug Heder
CFO/Executive

Dan Heder
Executive

GREENESTREET FILMS

430 W Broadway 2nd Floor
New York City, NY 10012
Phone: 212-609-9000
Fax: 212-609-9099

Email: general@gstreet.com
Home Page: greenestreetfilms.com

Accepts query letter from unproduced, unrepresented writers via email. Project types include Feature Films. Preferred genres include Comedy, Drama, Horror, Romance, and Thriller.

John M Penotti
President
IMDb: imdb.com/name/nm0006597

Matthew Honovic
Creative Executive
Email: http://www.imdb.com/name/
nm2416270/?ref_=fn_al_nm_1

GREEN HAT FILMS

4000 Warner Blvd
Building 66
Burbank, CA 91522
Phone: (818) 954-3210
Fax: (818) 954-3214

Does not accept any unsolicited material. Project types include Feature Films. Preferred genres include Comedy, Drama, Non-Fiction, and Thriller.

Todd Phillips
President/Director
IMDb: imdb.com/name/nm0680846
Assistant: Joseph Garner

Mark O'Connor
Director of Development

Diana Davis-Dyer
Executive Assistant

GREENTREES FILMS

854-A 5th St
Santa Monica, CA 90403
Phone: 310-899-1522
Fax: 310-496-2082

Email: info@greentreesfilms.com
Home Page: greentreesfilms.com

Accepts query letter from unproduced, unrepresented writers via email. Project types include Feature Films, TV, and Commercials. Preferred genres include Comedy, Drama, Non-Fiction, and Reality.

Jack Binder
Producer/President
IMDb: imdb.com/name/nm0082784

GRINDSTONE ENTERTAINMENT GROUP

2700 Colorado Ave
Suite 200
Santa Monica, CA 90404
Phone: 310-255-5761
Fax: 310-255-3766

Home Page: thegrindstone.net

Accepts query letter from produced or represented writers. Project types include Feature Films. Preferred genres include Action, Drama, Period, and Thriller.

Barry Brooker
President
Email: barry@thegrindstone.net
IMDb: imdb.com/name/nm1633269

Stan Wertlieb
Partner & Head of Acquisitions
Email: stanwertlieb@gmail.com
IMDb: imdb.com/name/nm0921627

Ryan Black
Director of Development
Email: ryan@thegrindstone.net
IMDb: imdb.com/name/nm3337383

Teresa Sabatine
Executive Assistant
Email: teresa@thegrindstone.net
IMDb: imdb.com/name/nm3466608

GRIZZLY ADAMS PRODUCTIONS

201 Five Cities Dr SPC 172, Pismo Beach
CA 93449
Phone: (877) 556-8536
Fax: (805) 556-0393

Home Page: grizzlyadams.com

Does not accept any unsolicited material. Project types include Feature Films and TV. Preferred genres include Documentary, Drama, Family, Non-Fiction, and Reality.

David W. Balsiger
Vice President
IMDb: imdb.com/name/nm1901322

GROSSO JACOBSON COMMUNICATIONS CORP.

767 Third Ave
New York, NY 10017

373 Front St East
Toronto, Ontario M5A 1G4
Canada

1801 Ave of the Stars, Suite 911
Los Angeles, CA 90067
Phone: 310-788-8900

Email: grossojacobson@grossojacobson.com

Accepts query letter from unproduced, unrepresented writers via email. Project types include Feature Films, TV, and Theater. Preferred genres include Comedy, Crime, Drama, Horror, Non-Fiction, Reality, and Thriller. Established in 1999.

Sonny Grosso
Executive Producer
Phone: 212-644-6909
IMDb: imdb.com/name/nm0343780

Keith Johnson
Sr. VP Development
Phone: 310-788-8900
IMDb: imdb.com/name/nm1702242

GROSS-WESTON PRODUCTIONS

10560 Wilshire Blvd, Suite 801
Los Angeles, CA 90024
Phone: 310-777-0010
Fax: 310-777-0016

Email: gross-weston@sbcglobal.net

Accepts scripts from produced or represented writers. Project types include Feature Films, TV, and Theater. Preferred genres include Action, Comedy, Drama, Family, Non-Fiction, Reality, Romance, Science Fiction, and Thriller.

Mary Gross
Executive Producer
IMDb: imdb.com/name/nm0343437

Ann Weston
Executive Producer
IMDb: imdb.com/name/nm0922912

GROUNDSWELL PRODUCTIONS

11925 Wilshire Blvd, Suite 310
Los Angeles, CA 90025
Phone: 310-385-7540
Fax: 310-385-7541

Email: info@groundswellfilms.com
Home Page: groundswellfilms.com

Does not accept any unsolicited material. Project types include Feature Films, TV, and Theater. Preferred genres include Action, Comedy, Crime, Drama, Horror, Non-Fiction, Romance, and Thriller. Established in 2006.

Janice Williams
Vice-President of Production
IMDb: imdb.com/name/nm1003921

Kelly Mullen
Vice-President
IMDb: imdb.com/name/nm4133402

GUARDIAN ENTERTAINMENT, LTD.

71 5th Ave
New York, NY 10003
Phone: 212-727-4729
Fax: 212-727-4713

Email: guardian@guardianltd.com
Home Page: guardianltd.com

Accepts query letter from unproduced, unrepresented writers via email. Project types include Feature Films, TV, and Commercials. Preferred genres include Drama, Horror, Non-Fiction, Reality, Science Fiction, and Thriller.

Richard Miller
CEO/Executive Producer
Email: rmiller@guardianltd.com

Anita Agair
Production Coordinator
Email: agair@guardianltd.com

GUNN FILMS

500 S Buena Vista St
Old Animation Building, Suite 3-A7
Burbank, CA 91521
Phone: 818-560-6156
Fax: 818-842-8394

Does not accept any unsolicited material. Project types include Feature Films and TV. Preferred genres include Action, Comedy, Drama, Family, Fantasy, Romance, Science Fiction, and Thriller. Established in 2001.

Andrew Gunn
Producer
Email: andrew.gunn@disney.com
IMDb: imdb.com/name/nm0348151

Ann Marie Sanderlin
President
IMDb: imdb.com/name/nm1196285
Assistant: Marc Brunswick
marc.brunswick@disney.com

GUY WALKS INTO A BAR

236 W 27th St #1000
New York, NY 10001
Phone: 212-941-1509

Email: info@guywalks.com
Home Page: guywalks.com

Does not accept any unsolicited material. Project types include Feature Films, TV, and Commercials. Preferred genres include Animation, Comedy, Family, Fantasy, Romance, and Science Fiction.

Todd Komarnicki
Partner/Producer
IMDb: imdb.com/name/nm0464548

Jonathan Coleman
Director of Development

H2O MOTION PITURES

111 E 10th St Suite 8
New York, NY 10003
Phone: 212-533-3923

PO Box 990
1000 AZ Amsterdam
The Netherlands
Phone: +44-207-240-5656
Fax: +44-207-240-5647

23 Denmark St
Third Floor
London WC2H 8NH
United Kingdom

317 Warren Rd
Toronto, Ontario, M5P 2M7
Canada
Phone: 416-484-6754
Fax: 416-484-9229

Email: h2o@h2omotionpictures.com
Home Page: h2omotionpictures.com

Accepts query letter from unproduced, unrepresented writers via email. Project types include Feature Films.

Andras Hamori
Producer
IMDb: imdb.com/name/nm0358877

HAMMER FILM PRODUCTIONS

52 Haymarket
London, United Kingdom,
SW1Y 4RP
Phone: +44 20 3002 9510

Email: info@hammerfilms.com
Home Page: hammerfilms.com

Does not accept any unsolicited material. Project types include Feature Films and TV. Preferred genres include Action, Comedy, Documentary, Drama, Horror, and Thriller. Established in 1934.

Marc Schipper
COO
IMDb: imdb.com/name/nm2649227

Simon Oakes
Co-Chairman & CEO
IMDb: imdb.com/name/nm2649227

HAND PICKED FILMS

2893 Sea Ridge Dr
Malibu, CA 90265
Phone: (310) 361-6832
Fax: (310) 456-1166

Email: info@handpickedfilms.net
Home Page: handpickedfilms.net

Does not accept any unsolicited material. Project types include Feature Films, TV, and Commercials. Preferred genres include Animation, Comedy, Detective, Drama, Horror, Non-Fiction, and Reality. Established in 2005.

Anthony Romano
Producer
IMDb: imdb.com/name/nm0738853

Michel Shane
IMDb: imdb.com/name/nm0788062

Darren VanCleave
Executive
IMDb: imdb.com/name/nm2168166

HANDSOME CHARLIE FILMS

1720-1/2 Whitley Ave
Los Angeles, CA 90028
Phone: 323-462-6013

Does not accept any unsolicited material. Project types include Feature Films. Preferred genres include Action, Comedy, Drama, Non-Fiction, and Romance.

Natalie Portman
President
IMDb: imdb.com/name/nm0000204

Kimberly Barton
Creative Executive

Annette Savitch
VP Development

HANNIBAL PICTURES

8265 Sunset Blvd, Suite 107
West Hollywood, CA 90046
Phone: 323-848-2945
Fax: 323-848-2946

Email: contactus@hannibalpictures.com
Home Page: hannibalpictures.com

Accepts query letter from unproduced, unrepresented writers via email. Project types include Feature Films. Preferred genres include Action, Comedy, Crime, Drama, Non-Fiction, Romance, Science Fiction, and Thriller. Established in 1999.

Richard Del Castro
Chairman/CEO/Producer
IMDb: imdb.com/name/nm0215502

Cam Canoon
Director of Development
IMDb: imdb.com/name/nm1359191

HAPPY MADISON PRODUCTIONS

10202 W Washington Blvd Judy Garland Building
Culver City, CA 90232
Phone: 310-244-3100
Fax: 310-244-3353

Home Page: adamsandler.com/happy-madison
IMDb: imdb.com/company/co0059609

Does not accept any unsolicited material. Project types include Feature Films, Short Films, and TV. Preferred genres include Action, Animation, Comedy, Drama, Fantasy, Romance, and Thriller. Established in 1999.

Adam Sandler
Partner
IMDb: imdb.com/name/nm0001191

Jack Giarraputo
Partner
IMDb: imdb.com/name/nm0316406
Assistant: Rachel Simmer

Heather Parry
Head of Film
IMDb: imdb.com/name/nm1009782

Doug Robinson
Head of Television
IMDb: imdb.com/name/nm2120562
Assistant: Brianna Riofrio

Judit Maull
Executive
IMDb: imdb.com/name/nm1263796

Billy Wee
Vice President of Television

HARPO FILMS, INC.

345 N Maple Dr, Suite 315
Beverly Hills, CA 90210
Phone: 310-278-5559

Does not accept any unsolicited material. Project types include Feature Films and TV. Preferred genres include Comedy, Drama, Fantasy, Horror, Non-Fiction, and Romance.

Oprah Winfrey
Chairman/CEO/Producer
IMDb: imdb.com/name/nm0001856

HARTSWOOD FILMS

3A Paradise Rd
Richmond
Surrey
TW9 1RX
Phone: +44 (0) 20-3668-3060
Fax: +44 (0) 20-3668-3050

Nations and Regions Office
17 Cathedral Rd
Cardiff
CF11 9HA
Phone: +44 (0)29-2023-3333
Fax: +44 (0)29-2022-5878

Email: films.tv@hartswoodfilms.co.uk
Home Page: hartswoodfilms.co.uk
IMDb: imdb.com/company/co0023675

Does not accept any unsolicited material. Project types include TV. Preferred genres include Comedy, Crime, Detective, Drama, Horror, and Thriller. Established in 1980.

Elaine Cameron
Head of Development
IMDb: imdb.com/name/nm0131569

Beryl Vertue
Chairman
IMDb: imdb.com/name/nm0895054

Debbie Vertue
General Manager
IMDb: imdb.com/name/nm0895055

Sue Vertue
Producer
IMDb: imdb.com/name/nm0895056

HASBRO, INC./HASBRO FILMS

Burbank
2950 N Hollywood Way Suite 100
Burbank, CA 91504
Phone: (818) 478-4320

Home Page: hasbro.com/?US

Accepts query letter from unproduced, unrepresented writers. Project types include Feature Films. Preferred genres include Action, Animation, Comedy, Family, Fantasy, Non-Fiction, and Science Fiction.

Daniel Persitz
Creative Executive
IMDb: imdb.com/name/nm1974626

HAXAN FILMS

PO Box 261370
Encino, CA 91426

USA
Fax: 310-888-4242

Home Page: haxan.com
IMDb: imdb.com/company/co0112898

Accepts query letter from unproduced, unrepresented writers. Project types include Feature Films and TV. Preferred genres include Comedy, Documentary, Drama, Horror, Science Fiction, and Thriller. Established in 2004.

David Saunder
APA Talent and Literary Agency
Phone: 310-888-4200

Robin Cowie
Producer
Email: rob@haxan.com
IMDb: imdb.com/name/nm0184770

Eduardo Sánchez
IMDb: imdb.com/name/nm0844896

Gregg Hale
Executive
IMDb: imdb.com/name/nm0354918

Andy Jenkins
IMDb: imdb.com/name/nm1075637

HAZY MILLS PRODUCTIONS

4024 Radford Ave
Building 7 - 2nd Floor
Studio City, CA 91604
Phone: 818-840-7568

Home Page: hazymills.com

Does not accept any unsolicited material. Project types include Feature Films and TV. Preferred genres include Comedy, Drama, Family, Horror, Non-Fiction, and Reality. Established in 2004.

Sean Hayes
IMDb: imdb.com/name/nm0005003
Assistant: Jessie Kalick

Kiel Elliott
Development Executive

HBO FILMS & MINISERIES

2500 Broadway, Suite 400
Santa Monica, CA 90404
Phone: 310-382-3000
Fax: 310-382-3552

Does not accept any unsolicited material. Project types include TV. Preferred genres include Comedy, Drama, Family, Non-Fiction, Romance, and Thriller.

Len Amato
President, Films
IMDb: imdb.com/name/nm0024163

Kary Antholis
President, HBO Miniseries
IMDb: imdb.com/name/nm0030794

HDNET FILMS

c/o Magnolia Pictures
49 W 27th St, 7th Fl
New York, NY 10001
USA
Phone: 212-924-6701
Fax: 212-924-6742

IMDb: imdb.com/company/co0094788

Accepts query letter from unproduced, unrepresented writers. Project types include Feature Films and TV. Preferred genres include Comedy, Crime, Documentary, Drama, Reality, Romance, Science Fiction, and Thriller.

HEAVY DUTY ENTERTAINMENT

6121 Sunset Blvd, Suite 103
Los Angeles, CA 90028
Phone: 323-209-3545
Fax: 323-653-1720

Email: info@heavydutyentertainment.com
Home Page: heavydutyentertainment.com

Does not accept any unsolicited material. Project types include Feature Films and TV. Preferred genres include Action, Comedy, Drama, Horror, and Science Fiction.

Jeff Balis
Producer
IMDb: imdb.com/name/nm0050276

Rhoades Rader
Producer
IMDb: imdb.com/name/nm0705476

HEEL AND TOE FILMS

2058 Broadway
Santa Monica, CA 90404
Phone: 310-264-1866
Fax: 310-264-1865

Does not accept any unsolicited material. Project types include Feature Films and TV. Preferred genres include Action, Drama, and Romance.

Paul Attanasio
Writer/Executive Producer
Email: paul.attanasio@fox.com
IMDb: imdb.com/name/nm0001921

Katie Jacobs
Executive Producer
Email: katie.jacobs@fox.com
IMDb: imdb.com/name/nm0414498

HEMISPHERE ENTERTAINMENT

20058 Ventura Blvd
#316
Woodland Hills, CA 91364
Phone: 818-888-2263
Fax: 818-888-3651

Home Page: hemisphereentertainment.com

Accepts query letter from unproduced, unrepresented writers. Project types include Feature Films. Preferred genres include Action, Crime, Drama, Family, Horror, Romance, and Thriller.

Ralph E. Portillo
President & CEO
IMDb: imdb.com/name/nm1589685

Jamie Elliot
COO & EVP
IMDb: imdb.com/name/nm0254242

Brad Wilson
VP of Development
IMDb: imdb.com/name/nm0933085

HENCEFORTH PICTURES

1411 Fifth St, Suite 200
Santa Monica, CA 90401
Phone: 424-832-5517
Fax: 424-832-5564

Does not accept any unsolicited material. Project types include Feature Films and TV. Preferred genres include Action, Crime, Drama, and Thriller.

William Monahan
Producer/Writer
IMDb: imdb.com/name/nm1184258

Justine Jones
Vice-President of Development
IMDb: imdb.com/name/nm3540960

HENDERSON PRODUCTIONS

4252 Riverside Dr
Burbank, CA 91505
Phone: 818-955-5702
Fax: (818) 955-7703

Does not accept any unsolicited material. Project types include Feature Films and Theater. Preferred genres include Comedy, Drama, Family, and Romance.

Garry Marshall
Producer/Writer/Director
IMDb: imdb.com/name/nm0005190

HEYDAY FILMS

4000 Warner Blvd
Building 81, Room 207
Burbank, CA 91522
Phone: 818-954-3004
Fax: 818-954-3017

Email: office@heydayfilms.com

Does not accept any unsolicited material. Project types include Feature Films and TV. Preferred genres include Action, Comedy, Crime, Drama, and Fantasy.

Jeffrey Clifford
President
IMDb: imdb.com/name/nm0166641
Assistant: Kate Phillips

David Heyman
Partner
IMDb: imdb.com/name/nm0382268
Assistant: Ollie Wiseman (011) 442078366333

HGTV

9721 Sherrill Blvd
Knoxville, TN 37932
Phone: 865-694-2700
Fax: 865-690-6595

Home Page: hgtv.com
IMDb: imdb.com/company/co0004908

Does not accept any unsolicited material. Project types include Feature Films and TV. Preferred genres include Documentary and Reality.

Burton Jablin
Executive Vice President

Freddy James
Senior Vice President of Program Development

Chris Moore
Vice President (Creative Director)

Steven Lerner
Vice President of Development

Courtney White
Vice President of Development

HIGH HORSE FILMS

100 Universal City Plaza
Building 2128, Suite E
Universal City, CA 91608
Phone: 323-939-8802
Fax: 323-939-8832

Accepts query letter from unproduced, unrepresented writers. Project types include Feature Films and TV. Preferred genres include Comedy, Drama, and Romance. Established in 1990.

William Petersen
Actor/Producer
IMDb: imdb.com/name/nm0676973

Cynthia Chvatal
Producer
IMDb: imdb.com/name/nm0161558

HIGH INTEGRITY PRODUCTIONS

11054 Ventura Blvd
Suite 324
Studio City, CA 91604 USA
Phone: 714 313 9606

Home Page: highintegrityproductions.com

Accepts query letter from unproduced, unrepresented writers. Project types include Feature Films. Preferred genres include Animation, Horror, Romance, and Thriller.

Dale Noble
President & CEO
Phone: 909-883-0417
Email: dale@highintegrityproductions.com
IMDb: imdb.com/name/nm2303672

HOLLYWOOD GANG PRODUCTIONS

4000 Warner Blvd
Building 139, Room 201
Burbank, CA 91522
Phone: 818-954-4999
Fax: 818-954-4448

Does not accept any unsolicited material. Project types include Feature Films. Preferred genres include Action, Drama, Fantasy, Science Fiction, and Thriller.

Gianni Nunnari
President/Producer
IMDb: imdb.com/name/nm0638089

HORIZON ENTERTAINMENT

1025 S Jefferson Parkway
New Orleans, LA 70125
Phone: 504-483-1177
Fax: 504-483-1173

Email: jsasst@horizonent.tv
Home Page: horizonent.tv
IMDb: imdb.com/company/co0225725

Accepts query letter from unproduced, unrepresented writers. Project types include Feature Films and TV. Preferred genres include Action, Comedy, Crime, Drama, Family, Reality, Romance, and Thriller. Established in 2000.

Tom Benson
Executive Producer
IMDb: imdb.com/name/nm3390271
Assistant: Brittany Leigh Holtsclaw

Jason Sciavicco
Executive Producer
IMDb: imdb.com/name/nm2217296

Dwayne Smalls
Production Manager
IMDb: imdb.com/name/nm2979692

Melissa Dembrun Sciavicco
Coordinating Producer
IMDb: imdb.com/name/nm2847926

HUGHES CAPITAL ENTERTAINMENT

22817 Ventura Blvd, Suite 471
Woodland Hills, CA 91364
Phone: 818-484-3205

Email: info@trihughes.com
Home Page: trihughes.com

Accepts scripts from produced or represented writers.
Project types include Feature Films. Preferred genres
include Action, Comedy, Drama, Family, and
Romance.

Jacob Clymore
Executive Assistant
Email: jc@trihughes.com

Patrick Hughes
President/Producer
IMDb: imdb.com/name/nm1449018

HUTCH PARKER ENTERTAINMENT

Santa Monica
204 Santa Monica Blvd Suite A
Santa Monica, CA 90401

Email: hutchparkerentertainment@gmail.com

Accepts scripts from produced or represented writers.
Project types include Feature Films. Preferred genres
include Romance and Thriller. Established in 2012.

Aaron Ensweiler
Vice-President
IMDb: imdb.com/name/nm3943221

Hutch Parker
Founder
IMDb: imdb.com/name/nm0404446

HYDE PARK ENTERTAINMENT

14958 Ventura Blvd Suite 100
Sherman Oaks, CA 91423
Phone: 818-783-6060
Fax: 818-783-6319

Email: contact@hydeparkentertainment.com
Home Page: hydeparkentertainment.com

Accepts scripts from unproduced, unrepresented
writers via email. Project types include Feature Films
and Commercials. Preferred genres include Action,
Comedy, Crime, Drama, Fantasy, Romance, Science
Fiction, and Thriller. Established in 1999.

Ashtok Amiraj
Chairman/CEO
IMDb: imdb.com/name/nm0002170

Mike Dougherty
Creative Executive

Marc Fiorentino
Development and Production Executive

HYPNOTIC

12233 W Olympic Blvd, Suite 255
Los Angeles, CA 90064
Phone: 310-806-6930
Fax: 310-806-6931

Does not accept any unsolicited material. Project types
include Feature Films and TV. Preferred genres
include Action, Comedy, Crime, Drama, Horror, and
Thriller.

Doug Liman
Vice Chairman/Producer
IMDb: imdb.com/name/nm0510731

Lindsay Sloane
Development Executive

ICON PRODUCTIONS

808 Wilshire Blvd, Suite 400
Santa Monica, CA 90401

Phone: 310-434-7300
Fax: 310-434-7377

Home Page: iconmovies.com

Does not accept any unsolicited material. Project types include Feature Films and TV. Preferred genres include Action, Comedy, Crime, Drama, Horror, Non-Fiction, Science Fiction, and Thriller.

Mel Gibson
Actor/Producer/Writer
IMDb: imdb.com/name/nm0000154

ILLUMINATION ENTERTAINMENT

2230 Broadway Ave
Santa Monica, CA 90404
Phone: 310-593-8800
Fax: 310-593-8850

Email: info@illuminationent.com
Home Page: illuminationentertainment.com
IMDb: imdb.com/company/co0221986

Does not accept any unsolicited material. Project types include Feature Films and Short Films. Preferred genres include Animation, Comedy, Drama, and Family. Established in 2010.

Christopher Meledandri
Chief Executive Officer
IMDb: imdb.com/name/nm0577560
Assistant: Rachel Feinberg and Katie Kirnan

Dana Krupinski
Director of Development
IMDb: imdb.com/name/nm2145735

Kit Giordano
Vice President of Development
IMDb: imdb.com/name/nm2109293
Assistant: Colleen McAllister

Brooke Breton
Production Executive
IMDb: imdb.com/name/nm0107868
Assistant: Jenna Anderson

IMAGE MOVERS

100 Universal City
Bungalow 5170

Los Angeles, CA 91608
Phone: 818-733-4000

Does not accept any unsolicited material. Project types include Feature Films and TV. Preferred genres include Action, Animation, Comedy, Drama, Family, Fantasy, Period, Romance, and Thriller.

Robert Zemeckis
Partner
IMDb: imdb.com/name/nm0000709

Steve Starkey
Partner
IMDb: imdb.com/name/nm0823330

Jack Rapke
Partner
IMDb: imdb.com/name/nm0710759

Jackie Levine
Executive Vice President

Jimmy Skodras
Development Executive

IMAGINE ENTERTAINMENT

9465 Wilshire Blvd
7th Floor
Beverly Hills, CA 90212
Phone: 310-858-2000
Fax: 310-858-2020

Home Page: imagine-entertainment.com

Does not accept any unsolicited material. Project types include Feature Films and TV. Preferred genres include Action, Animation, Comedy, Crime, Drama, Family, Fantasy, Horror, Non-Fiction, Romance, Science Fiction, and Thriller.

Ron Howard
Chairman/Director
IMDb: imdb.com/name/nm0000165

Erin Fredman
Creative Executive

IMPACT PICTURES

9200 W Sunset Blvd, Suite 800
West Hollywood, CA 90069
Phone: 310-247-1803

Accepts query letter from unproduced, unrepresented writers via email. Project types include Feature Films. Preferred genres include Action, Comedy, Crime, Drama, Fantasy, Horror, Romance, Science Fiction, and Thriller.

Paul Anderson
Producer/Writer
IMDb: imdb.com/name/nm0027271
Assistant: Sarah Crompton

Jeremy Bolt
Producer
IMDb: imdb.com/name/nm0093337

IMPRINT ENTERTAINMENT

100 Universal City Plaza
Bungalow 7125
Universal City, CA 91608
Phone: 818-733-5410
Fax: (f) (818) 733-4307

Email: info@imprint-ent.com
Home Page: imprint-ent.com

Does not accept any unsolicited material. Project types include Feature Films, TV, and Commercials. Preferred genres include Action, Comedy, Crime, Drama, Fantasy, Horror, Non-Fiction, Reality, Romance, and Thriller. Established in 2008.

Lee Arter
Creative Executive
Email: larter@imprint-ent.com

Michael Becker
Executive

IN CAHOOTS

4024 Radford Ave
Editorial Building 2, Suite 7
Studio City, CA 91604
Phone: 818-655-6482
Fax: 818-655-8472

Does not accept any unsolicited material. Project types include Feature Films and TV. Preferred genres include Comedy, Drama, and Thriller.

Ken Kwapis
IMDb: imdb.com/name/nm0477129

Reynolds Anderson
Creative Executive
IMDb: imdb.com/name/nm1568030

INCOGNITO PICTURES

16027 Ventura Blvd
Suite 650
Encino, CA 91436
Phone: 818-724-4727

Email: info@incognitopictures.com
Home Page: incognitopictures.com
Facebook: facebook.com/pages/Incognito-Pictures/167198753371256

Does not accept any unsolicited material. Project types include Feature Films. Preferred genres include Crime, Drama, and Thriller.

Jack Selby
Chairman
IMDb: imdb.com/name/nm3095212

Scott G. Stone
CEO
IMDb: imdb.com/name/nm1680597

Farnaz Fahid
VP of Production & Development
IMDb: imdb.com/name/nm1804747

Drew Ruselowski
Assistant
IMDb: imdb.com/name/nm4866933

INDIAN PAINTBRUSH

1660 Euclid St
Santa Monica, CA 90404
Phone: 310-566-0160
Fax: 310-566-0161

Email: info@indianpaintbrush.com
Home Page: indianpaintbrush.com

Does not accept any unsolicited material. Project types include Feature Films. Preferred genres include Action, Animation, Comedy, Drama, Family, Horror, Romance, Science Fiction, and Thriller.

Mark Roybal
President, Production
IMDb: imdb.com/name/nm0747287
Assistant: Sam Roston

INDICAN PRODUCTIONS

2565 Broadway, Suite 138
New York, NY 10025
Phone: 212-666-1500

Does not accept any unsolicited material. Project types include Feature Films. Preferred genres include Crime, Drama, and Non-Fiction.

Julia Ormond
Email: julia.ormond@fox.com
IMDb: imdb.com/name/nm0000566

INDIE GENIUS PRODUCTIONS

361 Stryker Ave
St. Paul, MN 55107
Phone: 646-596-0937

IMDb: imdb.com/company/co0097647

Accepts query letter from unproduced, unrepresented writers. Project types include Feature Films. Preferred genres include Documentary. Established in 2007.

Curt Johnson
Principal
Email: curt_johnson@indiegeniusprod.com

INDOMITABLE ENTERTAINMENT

225 Varick St
Ste 304
New York, NY 10014
Phone: 212-352-1071
Fax: 212-727-3860

1920 Main St, Suite A
Santa Monica, CA 90405
Phone: 310-664-8700
Fax: 310-664-8711

Email: info@indomitable.com
Home Page: indomitableentertainment.com
Facebook: facebook.com/pages/Indomitable-Entertainment/20750471594844

Accepts query letter from unproduced, unrepresented writers via email. Project types include Feature Films and TV. Preferred genres include Action, Comedy, Drama, and Thriller.

Dominic Ianno
Founder, CEO
IMDb: imdb.com/name/nm1746156

Robert Deege
Vice President of Business & Creative Affairs
IMDb: imdb.com/name/nm1830098

Chris Mirosevic
Director of Film Services
IMDb: imdb.com/name/nm1746156

Stuart Pollok
Executive Producer
IMDb: imdb.com/name/nm0689415

INDUSTRY ENTERTAINMENT

955 S Carrillo Dr, Suite 300
Los Angeles, CA 90048
Phone: 323-954-9000
Fax: 323-954-9009

Accepts scripts from produced or represented writers. Project types include Feature Films and TV. Preferred genres include Comedy, Drama, Family, Fantasy, Horror, Romance, and Thriller.

Keith Addis
Chairman
IMDb: imdb.com/name/nm0011688

INEFFABLE PICTURES

9247 Alden Dr
Beverly Hills, CA 90210
Phone: 424-653-1122

Email: info@ineffablepictures.com
Home Page: ineffablepictures.com
IMDb: imdb.com/company/co0343339

Does not accept any unsolicited material. Project types include Feature Films. Preferred genres include Action, Comedy, Drama, Fantasy, and Science Fiction. Established in 2010.

Raphael Kryszek
President
IMDb: o.imdb.com/name/nm1398360

Ross Putman
Creative Executive
IMDb: imdb.com/name/nm3819444

Jesse Israel
Executive
IMDb: imdb.com/name/nm2368220

INFERNO ENTERTAINMENT

1888 Century Park East, Suite 1540
Los Angeles, CA 90067
Phone: 310-598-2550
Fax: 310-598-2551

Home Page: inferno-entertainment.com

Does not accept any unsolicited material. Project types include Feature Films. Preferred genres include Action, Comedy, Crime, Drama, Family, Fantasy, Horror, Romance, Science Fiction, and Thriller.

Campbell McInnes
Production Development Executive
IMDb: imdb.com/name/nm0570577
Assistant: Roger Porter

D.J. Gugenheim
Vice President of Production
IMDb: imdb.com/name/nm1486759
Assistant: Aaron Himmel

INFINITUM NIHIL

Phone: 323-651-2034

Home Page: infinitumnihil.com

Does not accept any unsolicited material. Project types include Feature Films. Preferred genres include Action, Comedy, Family, Fantasy, Myth, and Romance.

Johnny Depp
Principal
IMDb: imdb.com/name/nm0000136

Christi Dembrowski
President
IMDb: imdb.com/name/nm0218259
Assistant: Dawn Sierra & Erik Schmudde

Margaret French Isaac
EVP of Production & Development
IMDb: imdb.com/name/nm0410504
Assistant: Brandon Zamel

Sam Sarkar
Vice President of Development
IMDb: imdb.com/name/nm0765274

Norman Todd
Director of Development
IMDb: imdb.com/name/nm0865249

Ben Tierney
Creative Executive
IMDb: imdb.com/name/nm1599606

Bobby DeLeon
Development Associate
IMDb: imdb.com/name/nm3765677

JJ Holiday
Creative Research
IMDb: imdb.com/name/nm0006545

INFORMANT MEDIA

10866 Wilshire Blvd
4th Floor, Suite 422
Los Angeles, CA 90024
Phone: 310-470-9309
Fax: 310-347-4497

Email: development@informantmedia.com
Home Page: informantmedia.com

Accepts query letter from unproduced, unrepresented writers via email. Project types include Feature Films and TV. Preferred genres include Action, Comedy, Drama, Fantasy, Romance, and Thriller.

Rick Bitzelberger
Development
Email: development@informantmedia.com

IN FRONT PRODUCTIONS

2000 Ave Of The Stars
Century City, CA 90067
Phone: 424-288-2000

Email: aelkin@caa.com
IMDb: imdb.com/company/co0077065

Project types include TV. Established in 1992.

Danny Jacobson
Manager
IMDb: imdb.com/name/nm0414816

INK FACTORY

73 Wells St
London W1T 3QG
UK
Phone: +44-20-7096-1698

Email: INFO@INKFACTORYFILMS.COM
Home Page: inkfactoryfilms.com

Does not accept any unsolicited material. Project types include Feature Films. Preferred genres include Action, Drama, and Thriller. Established in 2010.

Rhodri Thomas
Email: rhodri@inkonscreen.co.uk
IMDb: imdb.com/name/nm2905579

Stephen Cornwell
Writer/Producer/Founder
Phone: 310-721-5409
Email: steven@inkonscreen.co.uk
IMDb: imdb.com/name/nm4051169

INPHENATE

9701 Wilshire Blvd
10th Floor
Beverly Hills, CA 90212
Phone: 310-601-7117
Fax: 310-601-7110

Does not accept any unsolicited material. Project types include Feature Films and TV. Preferred genres include Comedy, Drama, Non-Fiction, and Reality.

Glenn Rigberg
Producer
IMDb: imdb.com/name/nm0726572

INTREPID PICTURES

1880 CENTURY PARK EAST, SUITE 900
LOS ANGELES, CA 90067
Phone: 310-566-5000

Email: info@intrepidpictures.com
Home Page: intrepidpictures.com

Does not accept any unsolicited material. Project types include Feature Films. Preferred genres include Action, Comedy, Horror, and Thriller. Established in 2004.

Marc D. Evans
Partner & Founder
IMDb: imdb.com/name/nm2162955

Trevor Macy
Partner & Founder
IMDb: imdb.com/name/nm1006167

Anil Kurian
Vice President of Development
IMDb: imdb.com/name/nm1993005
Assistant: James Banks

Melinda Nishioka
Coordinator
Email: melinda@intrepidpictures.com
IMDb: imdb.com/name/nm2325559

IRISH DREAMTIME

3000 W Olympic Blvd
Building 3, Suite 2332
Santa Monica, CA 90404
Phone: 310-449-4081

Email: info@irishdreamtime.com
Home Page: irishdreamtime.com

Does not accept any unsolicited material. Project types include Feature Films and TV. Preferred genres include Action, Comedy, Crime, Drama, Non-Fiction, Romance, and Thriller. Established in 1996.

Pierce Brosnan
Partner/Producer
IMDb: imdb.com/name/nm0000112

Beau St. Clair
Partner/Producer
IMDb: imdb.com/name/nm0820429

Keith Arnold
Head of Development
IMDb: imdb.com/name/nm2993265

IRON OCEAN FILMS

1317 Luanne Ave
Fullerton, CA 92831
Phone: 323-957-9706

Does not accept any unsolicited material. Project types include Feature Films. Preferred genres include Crime, Drama, and Thriller.

Jessica Biel
Principal
IMDb: imdb.com/name/nm0004754

Michelle Purple
Principal
IMDb: imdb.com/name/nm0321977

IRONWORKS PRODUCTION

517 W 35th St 2nd Floor
New York City, NY 10001
Phone: (212) 216-9780
Fax: (212) 239-9180

Email: ironworksproductions@pobox.com

Accepts query letter from unproduced, unrepresented writers via email. Project types include Feature Films and TV. Preferred genres include Comedy, Drama, Non-Fiction, Reality, Romance, and Thriller.

Bruce Weiss
President/Producer
IMDb: imdb.com/name/nm0918933

Isa Freeling
Executive Vice President of Development
IMDb: imdb.com/name/nm2303742

IRWIN ENTERTAINMENT

710 Seward St
Los Angeles, CA 90038
Phone: 323-468-0700
Fax: 323-464-1001

IMDb: imdb.com/company/co0193199

Does not accept any unsolicited material. Project types include Feature Films and TV. Preferred genres include Comedy and Reality.

John Irwin
President
Email: john@irwinentertainment.com
IMDb: imdb.com/name/nm1685815

ISH ENTERTAINMENT

104 W 27th St Second Floor
New York, NY 10001
Phone: 212-654-6445

Email: info@ish.tv
Home Page: ish.tv
IMDb: imdb.com/name/nm4851905

Does not accept any unsolicited material. Project types include Feature Films, Short Films, and TV. Preferred genres include Documentary and Reality. Established in 2008.

Michael Hirschorn
President
IMDb: imdb.com/name/nm1337695

Wendy Roth
Executive Vice President of Production
IMDb: imdb.com/name/nm0745046

Madison Merritt
Vice President of Development
IMDb: imdb.com/name/nm3117402

Chris Choun
Head of Production
IMDb: imdb.com/name/nm1780111

Melissa Cooper
Director of Development
IMDb: imdb.com/name/nm2435108

Michael Saffran
Executive
IMDb: imdb.com/name/nm5249575

Larissa Neal
Coordinator of Production

ITHACA PICTURES

8711 Bonner Dr
West Hollywood, CA 90048
Phone: 310-967-0112
Fax: 310-967-3053

Does not accept any unsolicited material. Project types include Feature Films. Preferred genres include Drama and Non-Fiction.

Michael Fitzgerald
Executive
IMDb: imdb.com/name/nm028033

Richard Romero
Producer
IMDb: imdb.com/name/nm2484143

JACKHOLE INDUSTRIES

6834 Hollywood Blvd
Los Angeles, CA 90028
Phone: 323-860-5900

Accepts query letter from produced or represented writers. Project types include TV. Preferred genres include Comedy and Reality.

Jimmy Kimmel
Partner
IMDb: imdb.com/name/nm0453994

Adam Carolla
Partner
IMDb: imdb.com/name/nm0004805

Daniel Kellison
Partner
IMDb: imdb.com/name/nm0446058

Doug DeLuca
Producer
IMDb: imdb.com/name/nm0217891

JAFFE/BRAUNSTEIN FILMS

12301 Wilshire Blvd Suite 110 Los Angeles, CA 90025
Phone: (310) 207-6600
Fax: (310) 207-6069

Accepts scripts from produced or represented writers. Project types include Feature Films and TV. Preferred genres include Comedy, Drama, Horror, Romance, Science Fiction, and Thriller.

Howard Braunstein
Owner/Executive Producer
IMDb: imdb.com/name/nm0105946

Michael Jaffe
Partner
IMDb: imdb.com/name/nm0415468
Assistant: Lynn Delaney

JANE STARTZ PRODUCTIONS

244 Fift h Ave, 11th Floor
New York, NY 10001
Phone: 212-545-8910
Fax: 212-545-8909

Accepts query letter from unproduced, unrepresented writers. Project types include Feature Films and TV. Preferred genres include Animation, Comedy, Drama, Family, Fantasy, Romance, and Thriller.

Jane Startz
President/Producer
IMDb: imdb.com/name/nm0823661

Carolyn Mao
Development Assistant
Email: cmao@janestartzproductions.com

Kane Lee
VP Development and Production
IMDb: imdb.com/name/nm1634508

JEAN DOUMANIAN PRODUCTIONS

595 Madison Ave Suite 2200
New York City, NY 10022
Phone: 212-486-2626
Fax: 212-688-6236

Accepts query letter from unproduced, unrepresented writers. Project types include Feature Films and TV. Preferred genres include Comedy, Drama, Horror, Non-Fiction, Period, Romance, and Thriller.

Jean Doumanian
Founder
IMDb: imdb.com/name/nm0235389

Patrick Daily
Vice President of Production & Development
IMDb: imdb.com/name/nm4794210

Saul Nathan-Kazis
Executive Assistant
IMDb: imdb.com/name/nm2651163

Kathryn Willingham
Assistant
IMDb: imdb.com/name/nm5187379

JEFF MORTON PRODUCTIONS

10201 W Pico Blvd Building 226
Los Angeles, CA 90035
Phone: 310-467-1123
Fax: 818-981-4152

Does not accept any unsolicited material. Project types include Feature Films and TV.

Jeff Morton
Producer
Email: scoutspence@mindspring.com
IMDb: imdb.com/name/nm0608005

JERRY BRUCKHEIMER FILMS & TELEVISION

1631 10th St
Santa Monica, CA 90404
Phone: 310-664-6260
Fax: 310-664-6261

Home Page: jbfilms.com
IMDb: imdb.com/company/co0217391

Accepts query letter from unproduced, unrepresented writers. Project types include Feature Films and TV. Preferred genres include Action, Comedy, Crime, Detective, Drama, Family, Fantasy, Horror, Myth, Non-Fiction, Reality, Science Fiction, and Thriller.

Jerry Bruckheimer
President/Chairman/CEO
IMDb: imdb.com/name/nm0000988

Ryan McKeithan
Manager, TV
IMDb: imdb.com/name/nm4915007

Jonathan Littman
President
IMDb: imdb.com/name/nm0514779

JERRY WEINTRAUB PRODUCTIONS

190 N Canon Dr, Suite 204
Beverly Hills, CA 90210

Phone: 310-273-8800
Fax: 310-273-8502

Does not accept any unsolicited material. Project types include Feature Films. Preferred genres include Action, Comedy, Crime, Drama, Family, Non-Fiction, Science Fiction, and Thriller.

Jerry Weintraub
Producer
Assistant: Kimberly Pinkstaff

Susan Ekins
Vice-President, Physical Production
Assistant: Betsy Dennis

JERSEY FILMS

PO Box 491246
Los Angeles, CA 90049
Phone: 310-550-3200
Fax: 310-550-3210

IMDb: imdb.com/company/co0010434

Accepts query letter from unproduced, unrepresented writers. Project types include Feature Films. Preferred genres include Action, Comedy, Drama, Non-Fiction, Romance, and Thriller.

Danny DeVito
Executive
IMDb: imdb.com/name/nm0000362

Nikki Grosso
Business Manager/Legal
Phone: 310-477-7704
IMDb: imdb.com/name/nm0343777

JET TONE PRODUCTIONS

21/F Park Commercial Centre
No. 180 Tung Lo Wan Rd
Hong Kong
China
Phone: 852-2336-1102
Fax: 852-2337-9849

Email: jettone@netvigator.com
Home Page: jettone.net

Accepts query letter from unproduced, unrepresented writers via email. Project types include Feature Films. Preferred genres include Action, Animation, Comedy,

Crime, Drama, Romance, Science Fiction, and Thriller.

Wong Kar-wai
Producer/Director
IMDb: imdb.com/name/nm0939182

JOEL SCHUMACHER PRODUCTIONS

10960 Wilshire Bvld. Suite 1900
Los Angeles, CA 90024
Phone: 310-472-7602
Fax: 310-270-4618

IMDb: imdb.com/company/co0094915

Does not accept any unsolicited material. Project types include Feature Films, TV, and Commercials. Preferred genres include Action, Comedy, Crime, Drama, Fantasy, Romance, Science Fiction, and Thriller.

Joel Schumacher
Executive/Owner
Phone: 310-472-7602
IMDb: imdb.com/name/nm0001708
Assistant: Jeff Feuerstein

Aaron Cooley
Producer
Phone: 818-260-6065
IMDb: imdb.com/name/nm0177583

JOHN CALLEY PRODUCTIONS

10202 W Washington Blvd
Crawford Building
Culver City, CA 90232
Phone: 310-244-7777
Fax: 310-244-4070

IMDb: imdb.com/company/co0125552

Does not accept any unsolicited material. Project types include Feature Films and TV. Preferred genres include Action, Comedy, Detective, Drama, Romance, and Thriller.

John Calley
Producer
Phone: 310-244-7777
IMDb: imdb.com/name/nm1886942

Lisa Medwid
Executive Vice-President
Phone: 310-244-7777
IMDb: imdb.com/name/nm1886942

JOHN GOLDWYN PRODUCTIONS

5555 Melrose Ave, Dressing Room. 112
Los Angeles, CA 90038
Phone: 323-956-5054
Fax: 323-862-0055

IMDb: imdb.com/company/co0177677

Does not accept any unsolicited material. Project types include Feature Films and TV. Preferred genres include Action, Comedy, Crime, Detective, Drama, Non-Fiction, and Thriller. Established in 1991.

John Goldwyn
President
IMDb: imdb.com/name/nm0326415
Assistant: Jasen Laks

Hilary Marx
Creative Executive
IMDb: imdb.com/name/nm1020576
Assistant: Rebecca Crow

Erin David
Creative Executive
IMDb: imdb.com/name/nm1716252
Assistant: Rebecca Crow

JOHN WELLS PRODUCTIONS

4000 Warner Blvd
Building 1
Burbank, CA 91522-0001
Phone: 818-954-1687
Fax: 818-954-3657

Email: jwppa@warnerbros.com
IMDb: imdb.com/company/co0037310

Accepts query letter from unproduced, unrepresented writers. Project types include Feature Films and TV. Preferred genres include Action, Comedy, Drama, Family, Horror, Romance, Science Fiction, and Thriller.

Claire Polstein
President (Features)
IMDb: imdb.com/name/nm0689856
Assistant: Tessie Groff

Andrew Stearn
President (Television)
IMDb: imdb.com/name/nm1048942
Assistant: Quinn Tivey quinn.tivey@jwprods.com

John Wells
Principal
IMDb: imdb.com/name/nm2187561
Assistant: Kristin Martini

Jinny Joung
Vice President (Television)
Assistant: Irene Lee irene.lee@jwprods.com

JON SHESTACK PRODUCTIONS

409 N Larchmont Blvd
Los Angeles, CA 90004
Phone: 323-468-1113
Fax: 323-468-1114

IMDb: imdb.com/company/co0168855

Does not accept any unsolicited material. Project types include Feature Films. Preferred genres include Animation, Comedy, Crime, Drama, Family, Fantasy, Romance, Science Fiction, and Thriller. Established in 2006.

Jonathan Shestack
Producer, President
IMDb: imdb.com/name/nm0792871

Ginny Brewer
Producer, Vice President, Development
IMDb: imdb.com/name/nm2555285

Jeremy Stein
Executive
IMDb: imdb.com/name/nm1867504

JOSEPHSON ENTERTAINMENT

1201 W 5th St Suite M-170 Los Angeles, CA 90017
Phone: (213) 534-3995

IMDb: imdb.com/company/co0046572

Does not accept any unsolicited material. Project types include Feature Films and TV. Preferred genres include Action, Animation, Comedy, Crime, Drama, Family, Fantasy, Horror, Romance, Science Fiction, Sociocultural, and Thriller.

Barry Josephson
Producer/Founder
IMDb: imdb.com/name/nm0430742
Assistant: Sean Bennett

Tia Maggini
VP (Television)
Assistant: Mekita Faiye
mekita.faiye@josephsonent.com

JUNCTION FILMS

9615 Brighton Way, Suite M110
Beverly Hills, CA 90210
Phone: 310-246-9799
Fax: 310-246-3824

IMDb: imdb.com/company/co0099841

Accepts query letter from unproduced, unrepresented writers. Preferred genres include Action, Comedy, Crime, Drama, Horror, Reality, Science Fiction, and Thriller. Established in 2001.

Brad Wyman
Producer
Phone: 310-246-9799
IMDb: imdb.com/name/nm0943829

Donald Kushner
Producer
IMDb: imdb.com/name/nm0476291

Alwyn Kushner
Producer
IMDb: imdb.com/name/nm1672379

JUNIPER PLACE PRODUCTIONS

4024 Radford Ave, Bungalow 1
Studio City, CA 91604
Phone: 818-655-5043
Fax: 818-655-8402

Accepts query letter from unproduced, unrepresented writers. Project types include TV. Preferred genres include Drama. Established in -77.

Jeffrey Kramer
President/Executive Producer
IMDb: imdb.com/name/nm0469552

John Tymus
Director of Development
IMDb: imdb.com/name/nm2002980

KAPITAL ENTERTAINMENT

8687 Melrose Ave
9th Floor
West Hollywood, CA 90069
Phone: 310-854-3221

Does not accept any unsolicited material. Project types include TV. Preferred genres include Comedy and Drama.

Aaron Kaplan
Principal
Email: akaplan@kapital-ent.com
IMDb: imdb.com/name/nm3483168

Cailey Buck
Director of Development

KAPLAN/PERRONE ENTERTAINMENT

280 S Beverly Dr, #513
Beverly Hills, CA 90212
Phone: 310-285-0116

Home Page: kaplanperrone.com
IMDb: imdb.com/company/co0094257

Accepts scripts from produced or represented writers. Project types include Feature Films and TV. Preferred genres include Action, Comedy, Drama, Romance, and Thriller.

Aaron Kaplan
Executive and Partner

Sean Perrone
Executive and Partner

Tobin Babst
Manager and Partner

Josh Goldenberg
Manager

Alex Lerner
Manager

KARZ ENTERTAINMENT

4000 Warner Blvd Building 138, Suite 1205
Burbank, CA 91522
Phone: 818-954-1698
Fax: 818 954 1700

Email: karzent@aol.com
IMDb: imdb.com/company/co0033868

Does not accept any unsolicited material. Project types include Feature Films and TV. Preferred genres include Action, Comedy, Crime, Documentary, Drama, Family, Fantasy, Horror, Romance, and Thriller. Established in 1998.

Mike Karz
President
IMDb: imdb.com/name/nm0440344

Josie Rosen
Executive Producer
IMDb: imdb.com/name/nm0741998

KASSEN BROTHERS PRODUCTIONS

141 W 28th St, Suite 301
New York, NY 10001
Phone: 212-244-2865
Fax: 212-244-2874

IMDb: imdb.com/company/co0183529

Accepts query letter from unproduced, unrepresented writers. Project types include TV. Preferred genres include Action, Comedy, Drama, and Non-Fiction.

Adam Kassen
Partner/Writer/Director
Phone: 212-244-2865
IMDb: imdb.com/name/nm0440859

KATALYST FILMS

6806 Lexington Ave
Los Angeles, CA 90038
Phone: 323-785-2700
Fax: 323-785-2715

Email: info@katalystfilms.com
Home Page: katalystfilms.com
IMDb: imdb.com/company/co0102320

Accepts scripts from unproduced, unrepresented writers. Project types include Feature Films and TV. Preferred genres include Action, Animation, Comedy, Crime, Drama, Reality, Romance, Science Fiction, and Thriller.

Ashton Kutcher
Actor/Executive Producer
IMDb: imdb.com/name/nm0005110

Jason Goldberg
Producer
IMDb: imdb.com/name/nm0325229

Brinton Lukens
Director of Development
IMDb: imdb.com/name/nm2483033

KENNEDY/MARSHALL COMPANY

619 Arizona Ave
Second Floor
Santa Monica, CA 90401
Phone: 310-656-8400
Fax: 310-656-8430

Home Page: kennedymarshall.com

Does not accept any unsolicited material. Project types include Feature Films and TV. Preferred genres include Action, Comedy, Detective, Drama, Family, Non-Fiction, Romance, Science Fiction, and Thriller.

Frank Marshall
Principal
IMDb: imdb.com/name/nm0550881
Assistant: Mary T. Radford

Grey Rembert
President of Production
IMDb: imdb.com/name/nm0718880

Robert D. Zotnowski
Head of Television Development

Kiri Hart
VP of Development

James Erskine
Development Assistant

KERNER ENTERTAINMENT COMPANY

1888 Century Park East
Suite 1005
Los Angeles, CA 90067
Phone: 310-815-5100
Fax: 310-815-5110

Does not accept any unsolicited material. Project types include Feature Films. Preferred genres include Action, Animation, Comedy, Drama, Family, and Fantasy.

Jordan Kerner
President
IMDb: imdb.com/name/nm0449549

Ben Haber
Vice President
IMDb: imdb.com/name/nm1852209

Lauren Waggoner
Executive Assistant
IMDb: imdb.com/name/nm3786942

KGB FILMS

5555 Melrose Ave, Lucy Bungalow 101
Los Angeles, CA 90038
Phone: 323-956-5000
Fax: 323-224-1876

Email: turbo@kgbfilms.com
Home Page: kgbfilms.com

Accepts query letter from unproduced, unrepresented writers via email. Project types include Feature Films, Short Films, and TV. Preferred genres include Comedy, Crime, Drama, Non-Fiction, and Romance. Established in 1994.

Rosser Goodman
Producer/Director
IMDb: imdb.com/name/nm0329223

Justin Hogan
Producer
IMDb: imdb.com/name/nm0389556

KICKSTART PRODUCTIONS

3212 Nebraska Ave
Santa Monica, CA 90404
Phone: 310-264-1757

Home Page: kickstartent.com
IMDb: imdb.com/company/co0163548

Does not accept any unsolicited material. Project types include Feature Films. Preferred genres include Action, Animation, Comedy, Family, and Science Fiction.

Loris Lunsford
Executive Producer
IMDb: imdb.com/name/nm0469603

Jason Netter
President
IMDb: imdb.com/name/nm0626697

Susan Norkin
Head of Production
IMDb: imdb.com/name/nm0635379

Samantha Olsson
Vice President of Development
IMDb: imdb.com/name/nm2427387

KILLER FILMS

18th East 16th St, 4th Floor
New York, NY 10003
Phone: 212-473-3950
Fax: 212-807-1456

Home Page: killerfilms.com
IMDb: imdb.com/company/co0030755

Accepts query letter from unproduced, unrepresented writers. Project types include Feature Films, Short Films, and TV. Preferred genres include Comedy, Crime, Drama, Family, Horror, Romance, and Thriller. Established in 1995.

Christine Vachon
Principal/Producer
IMDb: imdb.com/name/nm0882927
Assistant: Gabrielle Nadig

Pamela Koffler
Principal/Producer
IMDb: imdb.com/name/nm0463025
Assistant: Gabrielle Nadig

David Hinojosa
Production and Development Executive
IMDb: imdb.com/name/nm3065267
Assistant: Gabrielle Nadig

KIM AND JIM PRODUCTIONS

787 N. Palm Canyon Dr
Palm Springs, CA 92262
Phone: 760-289-5464

Email: info@kimandjimproductions.com
Home Page: kimandjimproductions.com

Accepts query letter from unproduced, unrepresented writers. Project types include Feature Films. Preferred genres include Action, Comedy, Drama, Fantasy, Horror, Romance, and Thriller.

Kim Waltrip
Vice Chairman
Email: assist@kimandjimproductions.com
IMDb: imdb.com/name/nm0910601

Jim Casey
Vice Chairman
Email: jim@kimandjimproductions
IMDb: imdb.com/name/nm2816633

KINETIC FILMWORKS

11018 Moorpark St Suite 114
Toluca Lake, CA 91602
Phone: 818-505-3347

Email: kineticfilmworks@aol.com
Home Page: kineticfilmworks.com
IMDb: imdb.com/company/co0224342

Accepts query letter from unproduced, unrepresented writers via email. Project types include Feature Films. Preferred genres include Horror. Established in 2013.

Gary Jones
Partner
IMDb: imdb.com/name/nm0428109

Jeffrey Miller
Partner
IMDb: imdb.com/name/nm0588577

KINTOP PICTURES

7955 W Third St
Los Angeles, CA 90048
Phone: 323-634-1570
Fax: 323-634-1575

Email: kintopfilm@aol.com

Accepts query letter from unproduced, unrepresented writers. Project types include Feature Films and TV. Preferred genres include Comedy, Documentary, Drama, Family, Horror, Romance, and Thriller.

Deepak Nayar
Founder
IMDb: imdb.com/name/nm0623235

KIPPSTER ENTERTAINMENT

420 W End Ave, Suite 1G
New York, NY 10024
Phone: 212-496-1200

IMDb: imdb.com/company/co0310346

Does not accept any unsolicited material. Project types include Feature Films and TV. Preferred genres include Drama and Non-Fiction.

Perri Kipperman
Producer, Partner
IMDb: imdb.com/name/nm1069530

David Sterns
Producer, Partner
IMDb: imdb.com/name/nm3992907

KOMUT ENTERTAINMENT

4000 Warner Blvd Building 140, Suite 201
Burbank, CA 91522
Phone: 818-954-7631

IMDb: imdb.com/company/co0028360

Accepts query letter from unproduced, unrepresented writers. Project types include TV. Preferred genres include Comedy, Drama, and Thriller.

David Kohan
Producer
IMDb: imdb.com/name/nm0463172
Assistant: Melissa Strauss
Melissa.Strauss@wbconsultant.com

Max Mutchnick
Producer
IMDb: imdb.com/name/nm0616083

Heather Hicks
Executive Assistant
IMDb: imdb.com/name/nm1337402

K/O PAPER PRODUCTS (ALSO KNOWN AS: KURTZMAN ORCI PAPER PRODUCTS)

100 Universal City Plaza
Building 5125
Universal City, CA 91608
Phone: 818-733-9645
Fax: 818-733-6988

IMDb: imdb.com/company/co0315120

Does not accept any unsolicited material. Project types include Feature Films and TV. Preferred genres include Action, Animation, Drama, Fantasy, and Science Fiction. Established in 1997.

Alex Kurtzman
Producer/Writer
IMDb: imdb.com/name/nm0476064

Roberto Orci
Producer/Writer
IMDb: imdb.com/name/nm0649460

KRANE MEDIA, LLC.

7932 Woodrow Wilson Dr
Los Angeles, CA 90046
Phone: 323-650-0942
Fax: 323-650-9132

Email: info@thekranecompany.com
Home Page: TheKraneCompany.com
IMDb: imdb.com/company/co0323526

Does not accept any unsolicited material. Project types include Feature Films and TV. Preferred genres include Action, Comedy, Crime, Drama, Romance, Science Fiction, and Thriller. Established in 1993.

Konni Corriere
Associate Producer
Email: konni@thekranecompany.com
IMDb: pro.imdb.com/name/nm0180955

Jonathan Krane
Chairman & CEO
IMDb: imdb.com/name/nm0006790

KRASNOFF FOSTER PRODUCTIONS

5555 Melrose Ave Marx Brothers Building, Suite 110
Los Angeles, CA 90038
Phone: (323) 956-4668

IMDb: imdb.com/company/co0174525

Accepts query letter from unproduced, unrepresented writers. Project types include Feature Films and TV. Preferred genres include Action, Comedy, Drama, Non-Fiction, and Romance.

Russ Krasnoff
President/Partner
Phone: 310-244-3282
IMDb: imdb.com/name/nm0469929
Assistant: Beth Maurer

Gary Foster
Partner
IMDb: imdb.com/name/nm0287811
Assistant: Haley Totten

LAKESHORE ENTERTAINMENT

9268 W Third St
Beverly Hills, CA 90210
Phone: 310-867-8000
Fax: 310-300-3015

Email: info@lakeshoreentertainment.com
Home Page: lakeshoreentertainment.com
IMDb: imdb.com/company/co0005323

Accepts query letter from produced or represented writers. Project types include Feature Films. Preferred genres include Action, Comedy, Crime, Drama, Fantasy, Horror, Romance, Science Fiction, and Thriller. Established in 1994.

Tom Rosenberg
Chairman/CEO
Phone: 310-867-8000
IMDb: imdb.com/name/nm0742347
Assistant: Tiffany Shinn

Robert McMinn
Senior Vice President of Development
Phone: 310-867-8000
IMDb: imdb.com/name/nm0573372

Richard Wright
Executive Vice President (Head, Development)
IMDb: imdb.com/name/nm0002999

LANDSCAPE ENTERTAINMENT

9465 Wilshire Blvd Suite 500 Beverly Hills, CA 90212
Phone: 310-248-6200
Fax: 310-248-6300

IMDb: imdb.com/company/co0070807

Accepts query letter from unproduced, unrepresented writers. Project types include Feature Films and TV. Preferred genres include Action, Animation, Comedy, Crime, Drama, Family, Non-Fiction, Science Fiction, and Thriller. Established in 2007.

Bob Cooper
Chairman/CEO
IMDb: imdb.com/name/nm0178341
Assistant: Sandy Shenkman

Tyler Mitchell
Head of Features
IMDb: imdb.com/name/nm1624685

LANGLEY PARK PRODUCTIONS

4000 Warner Blvd
Building 144
Burbank, CA 91522
Phone: 818-954-2930

Home Page: langleyparkpix.com
IMDb: imdb.com/company/co0297907

Does not accept any unsolicited material. Project types include Feature Films. Preferred genres include Action, Comedy, Crime, Drama, Romance, and Thriller.

Kevin McCormick
Producer
Phone: 818-954-2930
IMDb: imdb.com/name/nm0566557
Assistant: Shamika Pryce

Rory Koslow
Vice President
Phone: 818-954-2930
IMDb: imdb.com/name/nm1739372
Assistant: Kari Cooper

Aaron Schmidt
Creative Executive
Phone: 818-954-2930
Email: aaron.schmidt@langleyparkpix.com
IMDb: imdb.com/name/nm2087164

LARRIKIN ENTERTAINMENT

1801 Ave Of The Stars, Suite 921
Los Angeles, CA 90067
Phone: 310-461-3030

Home Page: larrikin-ent.com
IMDb: imdb.com/company/co0369620

Accepts scripts from produced or represented writers.
Project types include Feature Films.

David Jones
Executive/Producer/Partner
IMDb: imdb.com/name/nm1965869

Greg Coote
Email: linw@larrikin-ent.com
IMDb: imdb.com/name/nm0178505
Assistant: Wayne Lin

Robert Lundberg
Head, Development & Production
Email: rll@larrikin-ent.com
IMDb: imdb.com/name/nm2302909

LAUNCHPAD PRODUCTIONS

4335 Van Nuys Blvd Suite 339
Sherman Oaks, CA 91403
Phone: 818-788-4896

IMDb: imdb.com/company/co0164701

Accepts query letter from unproduced, unrepresented
writers via email. Project types include Feature Films.
Preferred genres include Comedy, Crime, Drama,
Horror, Period, Science Fiction, and Thriller.
Established in 2005.

David Higgins
Partner
IMDb: imdb.com/name/nm0383370

Angelique Higgins
President
Email: ahiggins@launchpadprods.com
IMDb: imdb.com/name/nm1583157

LAURA ZISKIN PRODUCTIONS

10202 W Washington Blvd
Astaire Building, Suite 1310
Culver City, CA 90232

Phone: 310-244-7373
Fax: 310-244-0073

IMDb: imdb.com/company/co0095403

Accepts query letter from unproduced, unrepresented
writers. Project types include Feature Films and TV.
Preferred genres include Action, Drama, Fantasy,
Romance, Science Fiction, and Thriller. Established in
1995.

Pamela Williams
President
IMDb: imdb.com/name/nm0931423

David Jacobson
Director of Development
IMDb: imdb.com/name/nm5138376

LAURENCE MARK PRODUCTIONS

10202 W Washington Blvd
Poitier Building
Culver City, CA 90232
Phone: 310-244-5239
Fax: 310-244-0055

IMDb: imdb.com/company/co0027956

Accepts query letter from unproduced, unrepresented
writers. Project types include Feature Films and TV.
Preferred genres include Action, Comedy, Drama,
Family, Fantasy, Horror, Romance, Science Fiction,
and Thriller.

Laurence Mark
President/Producer
Phone: 310-244-5239
IMDb: imdb.com/name/nm0548257

Tamara Chestna
Director of Development
Phone: 310-244-5239
IMDb: imdb.com/name/nm2309894

David Blackman
Senior Vice President
Phone: 310-244-5239
IMDb: imdb.com/name/nm1844320
Assistant: Peter Richman

LAVA BEAR FILMS

3201-B South La Cienega Blvd
Los Angeles, CA 90016
Phone: 310-815-9600

Home Page: lavabear.com
IMDb: imdb.com/company/co0296971

Does not accept any unsolicited material. Project types include Feature Films. Preferred genres include Action, Comedy, Crime, Drama, Family, Fantasy, Romance, Science Fiction, and Thriller. Established in 2011.

David Linde
Principle
Phone: 310-815-9603
Email: Dlinde@lavabear.com
IMDb: imdb.com/name/nm0511482
Assistant: Allison Warren

Tory Metzger
President of Production
Email: Tmetzger@lavabear.com
IMDb: imdb.com/name/nm0582762
Assistant: Jon Frye

Zachary Studin
Vice-President of Production
Email: Zstudin@lavabear.com
IMDb: imdb.com/name/nm1713122
Assistant: Jake Thomas

LAWRENCE BENDER PRODUCTIONS

1015 Gayley Ave Suite 1017
Los Angeles, CA 90024
Phone: 323-951-4600
Fax: 323-951-4601

IMDb: imdb.com/company/co0093776

Accepts query letter from unproduced, unrepresented writers. Project types include Feature Films. Preferred genres include Action, Comedy, Crime, Drama, and Thriller.

Lawrence Bender
Partner
IMDb: imdb.com/name/nm0004744
Assistant: Vincent Gatewood

Janet Jeffries
Development
IMDb: imdb.com/name/nm0420377

Kevin Brown
Production
IMDb: imdb.com/name/nm0114019

LD ENTERTAINMENT

9000 Sunset Blvd
Suite 600
West Hollywood, CA 90069
Phone: 310-275-9600

Email: info@identertainment.com
Home Page: identertainment.com

Does not accept any unsolicited material. Project types include Feature Films. Preferred genres include Action, Comedy, Crime, Drama, Horror, and Thriller. Established in 2007.

Mickey Liddell
President
IMDb: imdb.com/name/nm0509176

David Dinerstein
President of Distribution
IMDb: imdb.com/name/nm2517209

Liz Berger
SVP of Publicity
IMDb: imdb.com/name/nm0074266

Jennifer Hilton Monroe
SVP of Production & Development
IMDb: imdb.com/name/nm0385268

Patrick Raymond
Director of Development
IMDb: imdb.com/name/nm4811895

LEE DANIELS ENTERTAINMENT

315 W 36th St Suite 1002
New York City, NY 10018
Phone: 212-334-8110
Fax: 212-334-8290

Email: info@leedanielsentertainment.com
Home Page: leedanielsentertainment.com
IMDb: imdb.com/company/co0048235

Accepts query letter from unproduced, unrepresented writers via email. Project types include Feature Films and TV. Preferred genres include Comedy, Crime, Drama, Period, Romance, and Thriller. Established in 2001.

Lee Daniels
Chief Executive Officer
IMDb: imdb.com/name/nm0200005
Assistant: Tito Crafts

Lisa Cortes
Senior Vice President of Production
IMDb: imdb.com/name/nm0181263

Doreen Oliver-Akinnuoye
Vice President of Development
IMDb: imdb.com/name/nm1403094

LEGENDARY PICTURES

4000 Warner Blvd
Building 76
Burbank, CA 91522
Phone: 818-954-3888
Fax: 818-954-3884

Home Page: legendarypictures.com
IMDb: imdb.com/company/co0159111

Does not accept any unsolicited material. Project types include Feature Films and TV. Preferred genres include Action, Comedy, Crime, Drama, Family, Fantasy, Non-Fiction, Romance, Science Fiction, and Thriller. Established in 2005.

Thomas Tull
Chairman/CEO
Phone: 818-954-3888
IMDb: imdb.com/name/nm2100078

Alex Hedlund
Creative Executive
Phone: 818-954-3888
IMDb: imdb.com/name/nm2906163

Lauren Ruggiero
Director of Development
Phone: 818-954-3888
IMDb: imdb.com/name/nm4549739

Alex Garcia
Senior Vice President of Creative Affairs
IMDb: imdb.com/name/nm1247503

Jillan Share Zaks
Vice President (Creative Affairs)
Email: jillian.zaks@legendarypictures.com
IMDb: imdb.com/name/nm2949271

Jennifer Preston Bosari
Creative Executive
Email: jpreston@legendary.com

LESLIE IWERKS PRODUCTIONS

1322 2nd St Suite 35
Santa Monica, 90401 CA
Phone: 310-458-0490
Fax: 310-458-7212

Email: info@leslieiwerks.com
Home Page: leslieiwerks.com/new
IMDb: imdb.com/company/co0188417

Does not accept any unsolicited material. Project types include Feature Films, Short Films, and TV. Preferred genres include Documentary. Established in 2006.

Leslie Iwerks
President
Email: leslie@leslieiwerks.com
IMDb: imdb.com/name/nm0412649

Jane Kelly Kosek
Producer
IMDb: imdb.com/name/nm1165704

Michael Tang
Co-Producer
IMDb: imdb.com/name/nm4046664

LIAISON FILMS

44 Rue Des Acacias
Paris 75017
France
Phone: +33-1-55-37-28-28
Fax: +33-1-55-37-98-44

Email: contact@liasonfilms.com
Home Page: liasonfilms.com
IMDb: imdb.com/company/co0120310

Does not accept any unsolicited material. Project types include Feature Films. Preferred genres include Action, Crime, Drama, and Thriller.

Stephane Sperry
President
Email: stephane.sperry@liasonfilms.com
IMDb: imdb.com/name/nm0818373

LIGHTSTORM ENTERTAINMENT

919 Santa Monica Blvd
Santa Monica, CA 90401
Phone: 310-656-6100
Fax: 310-656-6102

Does not accept any unsolicited material. Project types include Feature Films. Preferred genres include Action, Crime, Drama, Family, Fantasy, Horror, Romance, Science Fiction, and Thriller.

James Cameron
CEO
IMDb: imdb.com/name/nm0000116

Jon Landau
COO
IMDb: imdb.com/name/nm0484457

Rae Sanchini
Partner
IMDb: imdb.com/name/nm0761093

Geoff Burdick
Head of Post Production

LIKELY STORY

150 W 22nd St, 9th Floor
New York, NY 10011
Phone: 917-484-8931

Email: info@likely-story.com
Home Page: likely-story.com
IMDb: imdb.com/company/co0190175

Does not accept any unsolicited material. Project types include Feature Films.

Anthony Bregman
Producer/Founder
Phone: 917-484-8931
Email: info@likely-story.com
IMDb: imdb.com/name/nm0106835

Stefanie Azpiazu
VP, Production & Development
Phone: 917-484-8931
Email: info@likely-story.com
IMDb: imdb.com/name/nm1282412

LIN PICTURES

4000 Warner Blvd. Bldg 143
Burbank, CA 91522
Phone: 818-954-6759
Fax: 818-954-2329

Home Page: linpictures.com

Does not accept any unsolicited material. Project types include Feature Films and TV. Preferred genres include Action, Comedy, Crime, Drama, Family, Fantasy, Romance, Science Fiction, and Thriller.

Dan Lin
CEO
IMDb: imdb.com/name/nm1469853
Assistant: Ryan Halprin

Jon SIll
SVP of Production
IMDb: imdb.com/name/nm1698314
Assistant: Ryan Halprin

Jennifer Gwartz
Head of Television
IMDb: imdb.com/name/nm0350311
Assistant: Jeremy Katz

Seanne Winslow Wehrenfennig
Head of Development
IMDb: imdb.com/name/nm2253990

Mark Bauch
Creative Executive
IMDb: imdb.com/name/nm3113076

LIONSGATE

2700 Colorado Ave, Suite 200
Santa Monica, CA 90404

Phone: 310-449-9200
Fax: 310-255-3870

Email: general-inquiries@lgf.com
Home Page: lionsgate.com

Accepts query letter from unproduced, unrepresented writers via email. Project types include Feature Films and TV. Preferred genres include Action, Comedy, Crime, Drama, Family, Fantasy, Horror, Non-Fiction, Romance, Science Fiction, and Thriller. Established in 1997.

Jon Feltheimer
Co-Chairman/CEO
Phone: 310-449-9200
Email: jfeltheimer@lionsgate.com
IMDb: imdb.com/name/nm1410838

Matthew Janzen
Director of Development
Phone: 310-449-9200
IMDb: imdb.com/name/nm0418432

Jina Jones
Director of Development
IMDb: imdb.com/name/nm1061205

LIQUID THEORY

6725 Sunset Blvd Ste 240
Los Angeles, CA 90028
Phone: 323-460-5658
Fax: 323-460-4814

Home Page: liquid-theory.com
IMDb: imdb.com/company/co0113186

Accepts query letter from produced or represented writers. Project types include Feature Films and TV. Preferred genres include Animation, Comedy, Documentary, Drama, Horror, Reality, Romance, Science Fiction, and Thriller. Established in 2001.

Matt Lambert
Development Coordinator
Email: matt@liquid-theory.com
IMDb: imdb.com/name/nm1479457

Austin Reading
President
IMDb: imdb.com/name/nm1474879

Julie Reading
President
IMDb: imdb.com/name/nm1474880

LITTLE ENGINE

500 S Buena Vista St
Animation Building 3F-6
Burbank, CA 91521
Phone: 818-560-4670
Fax: 818-560-4014

Home Page: littleenginefilms.com
IMDb: imdb.com/company/co0014340

Accepts query letter from unproduced, unrepresented writers. Project types include Feature Films and TV. Preferred genres include Comedy, Crime, Drama, Non-Fiction, Reality, and Romance.

Gina Matthews
Partner/Producer
IMDb: imdb.com/name/nm0560033

Mitchell Gutman
Director of Development
IMDb: imdb.com/name/nm1393767

Grant Scharbo
Partner/Producer
IMDb: imdb.com/name/nm0770090

LLEJU PRODUCTIONS

3050 Post Oak Blvd.,
Suite 460
Houston, Texas 77056
Phone: 866-579-6444
Fax: 713-583-2214

Email: info@lleju.com
Home Page: lleju.com/index.html
IMDb: imdb.com/company/co0250136

Accepts query letter from unproduced, unrepresented writers. Project types include Feature Films. Preferred genres include Action, Comedy, Crime, Drama, Horror, and Thriller. Established in 2008.

Bill Perkins
Executive
IMDb: imdb.com/name/nm2645116

Keith Perkins
IMDb: imdb.com/name/nm1344801

Cooper Richey
IMDb: imdb.com/name/nm3295785

LONDINE PRODUCTIONS

1626 N. Wilcox Ave.
Ste. 480
Hollywood, CA 90028
Fax: 310-822-9025

IMDb: imdb.com/company/co0183894

Accepts query letter from unproduced, unrepresented writers via email. Project types include Feature Films and TV. Preferred genres include Comedy, Drama, and Thriller. Established in 1988.

Cassius Weathersby
President
Email: cassiusii@aol.com
IMDb: imdb.com/name/nm0915780

Joshua Weathersby
Vice President
IMDb: imdb.com/name/nm1500833

Nadine Weathersby
Vice President
IMDb: imdb.com/name/nm2325321

LUCASFILM LTD.

5858 Lucas Valley Rd
Nicasio, CA 94946
Phone: 415-662-1800

Home Page: lucasfilm.com
IMDb: imdb.com/company/co0071326

Does not accept any unsolicited material. Project types include Feature Films. Preferred genres include Action, Fantasy, and Science Fiction.

George Lucas
Co-Chairman
IMDb: imdb.com/name/nm0000184

Kathleen Kennedy
Co-Chairman
IMDb: imdb.com/name/nm0005086

David Anderman
General Councel
IMDb: imdb.com/name/nm2763931

LUCKY CROW FILMS

4335 Van Nuys Blvd.
Suite 355
Sherman Oaks, CA 91403
Phone: 818-783-7529
Fax: 818-783-7594

Email: info@indieproducer.net
Home Page: indieproducer.net
IMDb: imdb.com/company/co0102838

Accepts query letter from unproduced, unrepresented writers via email. Project types include Feature Films and TV. Preferred genres include Documentary and Drama. Established in 2004.

Kerry David
President
IMDb: imdb.com/name/nm0202968

Jon Gunn
President
IMDb: imdb.com/name/nm0348197

LYNDA OBST PRODUCTIONS

10202 W Washington Blvd
Astaire Building, Suite 1000
Culver City, CA 90232
Phone: 310-244-6122
Fax: 310-244-0092

Home Page: lyndaobst.com
IMDb: imdb.com/company/co0071668

Does not accept any unsolicited material. Project types include Feature Films and TV. Preferred genres include Action, Comedy, Crime, Drama, Family, Fantasy, Romance, and Thriller.

Lynda Obst
Vice President of Production
IMDb: imdb.com/name/nm0643553

Rachel Abarbanell
Vice President of Production
IMDb: imdb.com/name/nm1561964

MAD CHANCE PRODUCTIONS

4000 Warner Blvd
Building 81, Room 208
Burbank, CA 91522
Phone: 818-954-3500
Fax: 818-954-3586

IMDb: imdb.com/company/co0034487

Does not accept any unsolicited material. Project types include Feature Films. Preferred genres include Action, Comedy, Drama, Family, Fantasy, Romance, Science Fiction, and Thriller.

Andrew Lazar
Producer
IMDb: imdb.com/name/nm0493662
Assistant: Wynn Wygal

Miri Yoon
Executive
IMDb: imdb.com/name/nm1186661

MAD HATTER ENTERTAINMENT

9229 Sunset Blvd, Suite 225
West Hollywood, CA 90069
Phone: 310-860-0441

Home Page: madhatterentertainment.com
IMDb: imdb.com/company/co0266260

Accepts scripts from unproduced, unrepresented writers. Project types include Feature Films and TV. Preferred genres include Action, Animation, Comedy, Crime, Drama, Family, Fantasy, Horror, Myth, Science Fiction, and Thriller.

Michael Connolly
Founder/Manager/Producer
Email: mike@madhatterentertainment.com
IMDb: imdb.com/name/nm0175326
Assistant: Kyle Smeehuyzen (Development Assistant)

MAD HORSE FILMS

16000 Ventura Blvd, Suite 900
Encino, CA 91436
Phone: 310-571-8048

Email: queries@madhorsefilms.com
Home Page: madhorsefilms.com

Facebook: facebook.com/mad.horse.films
IMDb: imdb.com/company/co0382776

Accepts query letter from unproduced, unrepresented writers via email. Project types include Feature Films. Preferred genres include Action, Horror, Science Fiction, and Thriller.

John Swetnam
Principal
IMDb: imdb.com/name/nm4291727

Alexandru Celea
Vice President of Production
IMDb: imdb.com/name/nm5088556

MADHOUSE ENTERTAINMENT

10390 Santa Monica Blvd Suite 110
Los Angeles, CA 90025
Phone: 310-587-2200
Fax: 323-782-0491

Email: query@madhouseent.net
Home Page: madhouseent.net
IMDb: imdb.com/company/co0202761

Does not accept any unsolicited material. Project types include Feature Films and TV. Preferred genres include Action, Comedy, Crime, Drama, Romance, Science Fiction, and Thriller. Established in 2010.

Robyn Meisinger
Principal
IMDb: imdb.com/name/nm1159733

Adam Kolbrenner
Principal
IMDb: imdb.com/name/nm2221807

Ryan Cunningham
Manager
IMDb: imdb.com/name/nm1400515

Chris Cook
Manager
IMDb: imdb.com/name/nm2303601

MADRIK MULTIMEDIA

Los Angeles Center Studios
1201 W Fift h St, Suite F222

Los Angeles, CA 90017
Phone: 213-596-5180

Email: info@madrik.com
Home Page: madrik.com

Accepts query letter from unproduced, unrepresented writers. Project types include Feature Films, TV, and Commercials. Preferred genres include Comedy and Romance.

Chris Adams
Founder
Email: chris@madrik.com
IMDb: imdb.com/name/nm1886228

MAGNET RELEASING

115 W 27th St
Seventh Floor
New York City, NY 10001
Phone: 212-924-6701
Fax: 212-924-6742

Home Page: magnetreleasing.com
Facebook: facebook.com/magnetreleasing

Does not accept any unsolicited material. Project types include Feature Films. Preferred genres include Action, Comedy, Crime, Family, Fantasy, Horror, Myth, Romance, Science Fiction, and Thriller.

Mark Cuban
Executive
IMDb: imdb.com/name/nm1171860

Todd Wagner
Executive
IMDb: imdb.com/name/nm0906136

MALPASO PRODUCTIONS

4000 Warner Blvd
Building 81
Burbank, CA 91522-0811
Phone: 818-954-3367
Fax: 818-954-4803

IMDb: imdb.com/company/co0010258

Does not accept any unsolicited material. Project types include Feature Films. Preferred genres include Crime, Drama, Fantasy, Non-Fiction, Romance, and Thriller. Established in 1967.

Clint Eastwood
Producer/Actor/Director
IMDb: imdb.com/name/nm0000142

Robert Lorenz
Partner/Producer
IMDb: imdb.com/name/nm0520749
Assistant: Jessica Meier
jessica.meier@wbconsultant.com

MANDALAY PICTURES

4751 Wilshire Blvd, 3rd Floor
Los Angeles, CA 90010
Phone: 323-549-4300
Fax: 323-549-9832

Email: info@mandalay.com
Home Page: mandalay.com
IMDb: imdb.com/company/co0013922

Accepts query letter from produced or represented writers. Project types include Feature Films. Preferred genres include Action, Comedy, Drama, Family, Horror, Romance, and Thriller. Established in 1995.

Joey De La Rosa
Creative Executive
Phone: 323-549-4300

Peter Guber
Chairman/CEO
IMDb: imdb.com/name/nm0345542

Adam Stone
Vice-President of Development
IMDb: imdb.com/name/nm2625826
Assistant: Jessica Smith

MANDALAY TELEVISION

4751 Wilshire Blvd, 3rd Floor
Los Angeles, CA 90010
Phone: 323-549-4300
Fax: 323-549-9832

Email: info@mandalay.com
Home Page: mandalay.com
IMDb: imdb.com/company/co0018094

Does not accept any unsolicited material. Project types include TV. Preferred genres include Action, Comedy, Drama, Period, Romance, and Thriller.

Paul Schaeffer
Vice Chairman/COO
Phone: 323-549-4300
IMDb: imdb.com/name/nm2325215

MANDATE PICTURES

2700 Colorado Ave, Suite 501
Santa Monica, CA 90404
Phone: 310-360-1441
Fax: 310-360-1447

Email: info@mandatepictures.com
Home Page: mandatepictures.com
IMDb: imdb.com/company/co0142446

Accepts query letter from unproduced, unrepresented writers via email. Project types include Feature Films. Preferred genres include Comedy, Crime, Drama, Fantasy, Horror, Romance, Science Fiction, and Thriller. Established in 2003.

Nathan Kahane
President
Phone: 310-255-5700
IMDb: imdb.com/name/nm1144042

Nicole Brown
Executive Vice-President, Production
Phone: 310-255-5710
Email: nbrown@mandatepictures.com
IMDb: imdb.com/name/nm0114352

Aaron Ensweiler
Creative Executive
Phone: 310-255-5721
Email: aensweiler@mandatepictures.com
IMDb: imdb.com/name/nm3943221

MANDEVILLE FILMS

500 S Buena Vista St
Animation Building, 2G
Burbank, CA 91521-1783
Phone: (818) 560-7662
Fax: (818) 842-2937

Home Page: mandfilms.com
IMDb: imdb.com/company/co0064942

Accepts query letter from unproduced, unrepresented writers. Project types include Feature Films and TV.

Preferred genres include Action, Drama, Family, and Romance. Established in 1994.

David Hoberman
Partner
IMDb: imdb.com/name/nm0387674
Assistant: Derek Steiner

Laura Cray
Creative Executive
Phone: 818-560-4332
IMDb: imdb.com/name/nm1733050
Assistant: Liz Bassin

Todd Lieberman
Partner
IMDb: imdb.com/name/nm0509414
Assistant: Jacqueline Lesko

MANDY FILMS

9201 Wilshire Blvd, Suite 206
Beverly Hills, CA 90210
Phone: 310-246-0500
Fax: 310-246-0350

IMDb: imdb.com/company/co0032786

Accepts query letter from unproduced, unrepresented writers. Project types include Feature Films and TV. Preferred genres include Action, Comedy, Drama, Fantasy, Science Fiction, and Thriller.

Leonard Goldberg
President
IMDb: imdb.com/name/nm0325252

Amanda Goldberg
Vice-President of Development/Production
IMDb: imdb.com/name/nm0325144

MANGUSTA PRODUCTIONS

145 6th Ave
Suite #6E
New York, NY 10013
Phone: 212-463-9503

Email: info@mangustaproductions.com
Home Page: mangustaproductions.com

Project types include Feature Films. Preferred genres include Comedy, Documentary, Drama, and Romance.

Giancarlo Canavesio
Founder & President
IMDb: imdb.com/name/nm2184875

Sol Tryon
Producer
IMDb: imdb.com/name/nm0874501

Shannon McCoy Cohn
Producer
IMDb: imdb.com/name/nm3101571

Blake Ashman
Principal
IMDb: imdb.com/name/nm0039137

MANIFEST FILM COMPANY

619 18th St
Santa Monica, CA 90402
Phone: 310-899-5554

Email: info@manifestfilms.com
Home Page: janetyang.com
IMDb: imdb.com/company/co0005048

Accepts query letter from unproduced, unrepresented writers. Project types include Feature Films. Preferred genres include Comedy, Crime, Drama, Period, and Thriller. Established in 1998.

Janet Yang
President
Email: janetyang2013@gmail.com
IMDb: imdb.com/name/nm0946003

MAPLE SHADE FILMS

4000 Warner Blvd
Building 138, Room 1103
Burbank, CA 91522
Phone: 818-954-3137

IMDb: imdb.com/company/co0100155

Accepts query letter from unproduced, unrepresented writers. Project types include Feature Films. Preferred genres include Action, Drama, Fantasy, and Thriller.

Ed McDonnell
President
IMDb: imdb.com/name/nm0568093

MARC PLATT PRODUCTIONS

100 Universal City Plaza, Bungalow 5163
Universal City, CA 91608
Phone: 818-777-8811
Fax: 818-866-6353

IMDb: imdb.com/company/co0093810

Accepts query letter from unproduced, unrepresented writers. Project types include Feature Films and TV. Preferred genres include Action, Comedy, Crime, Drama, Family, Fantasy, Horror, Romance, and Thriller.

Adam Siegel
President
Phone: 818-777-9544
IMDb: imdb.com/name/nm2132113

Jared LeBoff
Development
Phone: 818-777-9961
IMDb: imdb.com/name/nm1545176

Marc Platt
Producer
Phone: 818-777-1122
Email: platt@nbcuni.com
IMDb: imdb.com/name/nm0686887
Assistant: Joey Levy

MARK VICTOR PRODUCTIONS

2932 Wilshire Blvd, Suite 201
Santa Monica, CA 90403
Phone: 310-828-3339
Fax: 310-828-9588

Email: info@markvictorproductions.com
Home Page: markvictorproductions.com

Accepts query letter from unproduced, unrepresented writers via email. Project types include Feature Films and TV. Preferred genres include Action, Animation, Horror, Non-Fiction, Reality, and Thriller.

Mark Victor
Producer/Writer
Phone: 310-828-3339
Email: markvictorproductions@hotmail.com
IMDb: imdb.com/name/nm0896131

Sarah Johnson
Director of Development
Phone: 310-828-3339
IMDb: imdb.com/name/nm1154417

MARK YELLEN PRODUCTION

183 S Orange Dr
Los Angeles, CA 90036
Phone: 323-935-5525
Fax: 323-935-5755

Accepts query letter from unproduced, unrepresented writers via email. Project types include Feature Films, TV, and Commercials. Preferred genres include Action and Family. Established in 2003.

Mark Yellen
Producer
Phone: 323-935-5525
Email: mark@myfilmconsult.com
IMDb: imdb.com/name/nm0947390

MARTIN CHASE PRODUCTIONS

500 S Buena Vista St
Burbank, CA 91521
Phone: 818-560-3952
Fax: 818-560-5113

Does not accept any unsolicited material. Project types include Feature Films and TV. Preferred genres include Family. Established in 2000.

Debra Chase
President/Producer
Phone: 818-526-4252
IMDb: imdb.com/name/nm0153744

Gaylyn Fraiche
Executive Vice-President
Phone: 818-526-4252
IMDb: imdb.com/name/nm2325210

Josh Stewart
Executive Assistant
Phone: 818-526-4252

MARTY KATZ PRODUCTIONS

22337 Pacific Coast Highway #327
Malibu, CA 90265

Phone: 310-589-1560
Fax: 310-589-1565

Email: martykatzproductions@earthlink.net

Accepts query letter from unproduced, unrepresented writers via email. Project types include Feature Films. Preferred genres include Action, Comedy, Drama, and Romance. Established in 1996.

Marty Katz
Producer
Phone: 310-589-1560
Email: martykatzproductions@earthlink.net
IMDb: imdb.com/name/nm0441794

Campbell Katz
Vice-President, Productions & Development
Phone: 310-589-1560
Email: martykatzproductions@earthlink.net
IMDb: imdb.com/name/nm0441645

MARVISTA ENTERTAINMENT

10277 W. Olympic Blvd
3rd Floor
Los Angeles, CA 90067
US
Phone: 310-737-0950
Fax: 310-737-9115

Email: info@marvista.net
Home Page: marvista.net

Accepts query letter from unproduced, unrepresented writers via email. Project types include Feature Films and TV.

Fernando Szew
CEO
Phone: 310-737-0950
Email: fszew@marvista.net
IMDb: imdb.com/name/nm2280496

Matt Freeman
Vice-President of Production & Development
Phone: 310-737-0950
IMDb: pro.imdb.com/name/nm0293513

Robyn Snyder
Executive Vice-President of Development &
Production
Phone: 310-737-0950
Email: rsnyder@marvista.net
IMDb: imdb.com/name/nm2237557

MASIMEDIA

11620 Oxnard St
North Hollywood, California 91606
Phone: 818-358-4803

Email: submissions@masimedia.net
Home Page: masimedia.net
IMDb: imdb.com/company/co0155931

Accepts scripts from unproduced, unrepresented
writers via email. Project types include Feature Films
and TV. Preferred genres include Documentary and
Horror. Established in 2006.

Anthony Masi
President
IMDb: imdb.com/name/nm1502845

MASS HYSTERIA ENTERTAINMENT

8899 Beverly Blvd, Suite 710
Los Angeles, CA 90048
Phone: 310-285-7800
Fax: 310-285-7801

Email: info@masshysteriafilms.com
Home Page: masshysteriafilms.com

Accepts query letter from unproduced, unrepresented
writers via email. Project types include Feature Films
and TV.

Daniel Grodnik
President
Phone: 310-285-7800
Email: grodzilla@earthlink.net
IMDb: imdb.com/name/nm0342841

MATADOR PICTURES

20 Gloucester Place
London W1U 8HA
United Kingdom

Phone: +44 (0) 20 7009-9640
Fax: +44 (0) 20 7009-9641

Email: admin@matadorpictures.com
Home Page: matadorpictures.com

Accepts query letter from unproduced, unrepresented
writers via email. Project types include Feature Films.
Preferred genres include Action, Comedy, Drama, and
Romance. Established in 1999.

Nigel Thomas
Producer
Phone: +44 (0) 20-7009-9640
IMDb: imdb.com/name/nm0859302

Lucia Lopez
Development Producer
Phone: +44 (0) 20-7009-9640
IMDb: imdb.com/name/nm2389416

Orlando Cubit
Development Executive
Phone: +44 (0) 20-7009-9640
IMDb: imdb.com/name/nm4919747

MAVEN PICTURES

148 Spring St
Fourth Floor
New York, NY 10012
Phone: 212-725-3550
Fax: 646-442-7500

Does not accept any unsolicited material. Project types
include Feature Films. Preferred genres include Action,
Comedy, Drama, Romance, and Thriller.

Celine Rattray
Principal
IMDb: imdb.com/name/nm1488027

Trudie Styler
Principal
IMDb: imdb.com/name/nm0836548

Alex Francis
SVP of Production & Development
IMDb: imdb.com/name/nm2123360

Hardy Justice
SVP of Production & Development
IMDb: imdb.com/name/nm1155511

Anita Sumner
SVP of Creative Affairs
IMDb: imdb.com/name/nm0838856

Nic Marshall
Director of Operations
IMDb: imdb.com/name/nm2090942

Jenny Halper
Development Executive
IMDb: imdb.com/name/nm3794516

MAXIMUM FILMS & MANAGEMENT

33 W 17th St, 11th Floor
New York, NY 10011
Phone: 212-414-4801
Fax: 212-414-4803

Email: lauren@maximumfilmsny.com
Home Page: maximumfilmsny.com

Does not accept any unsolicited material. Project types include Feature Films, TV, and Theater.

Marcy Drogin
Producer/Manager
Phone: 212-414-4801
IMDb: imdb.com/name/nm1216320

MAYA ENTERTAINMENT GROUP

1201 W 5th St, Suite T210
Los Angeles, CA 90017
Phone: 213-542-4420
Fax: 213-534-3846

Email: info@maya-entertainment.com
Home Page: maya-entertainment.com

Accepts query letter from unproduced, unrepresented writers via email. Project types include Feature Films and TV. Preferred genres include Comedy, Drama, Non-Fiction, and Reality. Established in 2008.

Moctesuma Esparza
CEO/Chairman/Producer
Phone: 213-542-4420
IMDb: imdb.com/name/nm0260800

Christina Hirigoyen
Development Executive
Phone: 213-542-4420
IMDb: imdb.com/name/nm3491113

MAYHEM PICTURES

725 Arizona Ave, Suite 402
Santa Monica, CA 90401
Phone: 310-393-5005
Fax: 310-393-5017

Does not accept any unsolicited material. Project types include Feature Films and TV. Preferred genres include Comedy, Family, Non-Fiction, and Reality. Established in 2003.

Mark Ciardi
Producer
Phone: 310-393-5005
Email: mark@mayhempictures.com
IMDb: imdb.com/name/nm0161891

Brad Butler
Creative Executive
Phone: 310-393-5005
Email: brad@mayhempictures.com
IMDb: imdb.com/name/nm2744089

Victor Constantino
Sr. Vice-President of Production & Development
Phone: 310-393-5005
Email: victor@mayhempictures.com
IMDb: imdb.com/name/nm2028391

MBST ENTERTAINMENT

345 N Maple Dr, Suite 200
Beverly Hills, CA 90210
Phone: 310-385-1820
Fax: 310-385-1834

Accepts query letter from unproduced, unrepresented writers. Project types include Feature Films, TV, and Theater. Preferred genres include Action, Comedy, Drama, and Romance. Established in 2005.

Larry Brezner
Partner
Phone: 310-385-1820
IMDb: imdb.com/name/nm010836

Jonathan Brandstein
Partner
Phone: 310-385-1820
IMDb: imdb.com/name/nm0104844

MEDIA 8 ENTERTAINMENT

15260 Ventura Blvd, Suite 710
Sherman Oaks, CA 91403
Phone: 818-325-8000
Fax: 818-325-8020

Email: info@media8ent.com
Home Page: media8ent.com

Does not accept any unsolicited material. Project types include Feature Films and TV. Preferred genres include Action, Comedy, Drama, and Romance. Established in 1993.

Stewart Hall
President
Phone: 818-826-8000
Email: info@media8ent.com
IMDb: imdb.com/name/nm1279593

MEDIA RIGHTS CAPITAL

1800 Century Park East/ 10th Floor
Los Angeles, CA 90067
Phone: 310-786-1600
Fax: 310-786-1601

Email: info@mrclp.com
Home Page: mrcstudios.com

Does not accept any unsolicited material. Project types include Feature Films and TV. Preferred genres include Animation, Comedy, Drama, Romance, and Thriller.

Asif Satchu
Co-CEO
Email: www.imdb.com/name/nm2640007
Assistant: Maggie Settli

Modi Wiczyk
Co-CEO
IMDb: imdb.com/name/nm1582943
Assistant: Maggie Settli

Brye Adler
Vice President, Production

Charlie Goldstein
Vice President, Television Production
IMDb: imdb.com/name/nm0326177

Joe Hipps
Vice President, Television Production & Creative Affairs

Alex Jackson
Creative Executive

Whitney Timmons
Director, Television

MEDIA TALENT GROUP

9200 Sunset Blvd, Suite 550
West Hollywood, CA 90069
Phone: 310-275-7900
Fax: 310-275-7910

Accepts query letter from unproduced, unrepresented writers. Project types include Feature Films and TV. Established in 2009.

Geyer Kosinski
Chairman/CEO
Phone: 310-275-7900
IMDb: imdb.com/name/nm0467083

Chris Davey
Producer/Manager
Phone: 310-275-7900
IMDb: imdb.com/name/nm1312702

MEDUSA FILM

Via Aurelia Antica 422/424
Rome, Lazio 00165
Italy
Phone: +39-06-663-901
Fax: +39-06-66-39-04-50

Email: info.medusa@medusa.it
Home Page: medusa.it
IMDb: imdb.com/company/co0117688

Does not accept any unsolicited material. Project types include Feature Films. Preferred genres include Comedy, Crime, Documentary, Drama, Family, Horror, Romance, and Thriller. Established in 1916.

Faruk Alatan
Head of Foreign Acquisitions
IMDb: imdb.com/name/nm0016092

Giampaolo Letta
Vice Chairman and Managing Director
IMDb: imdb.com/name/nm2325586

Luciana Migliavacca
Head of Home Entertainment
IMDb: imdb.com/name/nm3096618

Pier Paolo Zerilli
International Creative
IMDb: imdb.com/name/nm1047259

MELEE ENTERTAINMENT

144 S Beverly Dr, Suite 402
Beverly Hills, CA 90212
Phone: 310-248-3931
Fax: 310-248-3921

Email: acquisitions@melee.com
Home Page: melee.com

Does not accept any unsolicited material. Project types include Feature Films. Established in 2003.

Bryan Turner
CEO
Phone: 310-248-3931
IMDb: imdb.com/name/nm0877440

Scott Aronson
COO
Phone: 310-248-3931
IMDb: imdb.com/name/nm1529615

Brittany Williams
Creative Executive
Phone: 310-248-3931
IMDb: imdb.com/name/nm2950356

MEL STUART PRODUCTIONS, INC.

204 S Beverly Dr, Suite 109
Beverly Hills, CA 90210
Phone: 310-550-5872
Fax: 310-550-5895

Email: info@melstuartproductions.com
Home Page: melstuartproductions.com

Accepts query letter from unproduced, unrepresented writers via email. Project types include Feature Films and TV. Preferred genres include Non-Fiction and Reality.

Mel Stuart
President
Phone: 310-550-5872
Email: info@melstuartproductions.com
IMDb: imdb.com/name/nm0835799

MERCHANT IVORY PRODUCTIONS

372 Old St, Office 150
London EC1V 9LT
United Kingdom
Phone: +44-207-657-3988

PO Box 338
New York, NY 10276
Phone: 212-582-8049
Fax: 212-706-8340

Email: contact@merchantivory.com
Home Page: merchantivory.com
Facebook: facebook.com/pages/Merchant-Ivory-Productions/105682432798518

Accepts query letter from unproduced, unrepresented writers via email. Project types include Feature Films and TV. Preferred genres include Drama, Non-Fiction, and Reality. Established in 1961.

James Ivory
President/Director
Phone: 212-582-8049
Email: contact@merchantivory.com
IMDb: imdb.com/name/nm0412465

Neil Jesuele
Director of Development
Phone: 212-582-8049
Email: njesuele@merchantivory.com
IMDb: imdb.com/name/nm3134373

Paul Bradley
Producer
Email: paul@merchantivory.co.uk
IMDb: imdb.com/name/nm0103364

Simon Oxley
Producer
Email: simon@merchantivory.co.uk
IMDb: imdb.com/name/nm1774746

MERV GRIFFIN ENTERTAINMENT

130 S El Camino Dr
Beverly Hills, CA 90212
Phone: 310-385-2700
Fax: 310-385-2728

Email: firstname_lastname@griffgroup.com
IMDb: imdb.com/company/co0093384

Does not accept any unsolicited material. Project types include Feature Films, Short Films, and TV. Preferred genres include Action, Comedy, Crime, Documentary, Drama, Non-Fiction, Period, Reality, Romance, and Thriller. Established in 1964.

Ron Ward
Vice Chairman
IMDb: imdb.com/name/nm2302243

Robert Pritchard
President
IMDb: imdb.com/name/nm2923017

Mike Eyre
Executive Vice President

Tony Griffin
Executive Film Development

METRO-GOLDWYN-MEYER (MGM)

245 N Beverly Dr
Beverly Hills, CA 90210
Phone: 310-449-3000

Home Page: mgm.com

Does not accept any unsolicited material. Project types include Feature Films. Preferred genres include Action, Comedy, Crime, Drama, Family, Horror, Myth, Romance, Science Fiction, and Thriller.

Gary Barber
Chairman & CEO
Phone: 310-449-3000
IMDb: imdb.com/name/nm0053388

Cassidy Lange
Vice President of Production
Phone: 310-449-3000
IMDb: imdb.com/name/nm3719738

Dene Stratton
CFO
Phone: 310-449-3000
IMDb: imdb.com/name/nm4682676

MICHAEL DE LUCA PRODUCTIONS

10202 W Washington Blvd
Astaire Building, Suite 3028
Culver City, CA 90232
Phone: 310-244-4990
Fax: 310-244-0449

Does not accept any unsolicited material. Project types include Feature Films. Preferred genres include Action, Comedy, Drama, and Thriller.

Michael De Luca
Producer
Phone: 310-244-4990
IMDb: imdb.com/name/nm0006894
Assistant: Kristen Detwiler

Josh Bratman
Development Executive
Phone: 310-244-4916
IMDb: imdb.com/name/nm2302300
Assistant: Sandy Yep

Alissa Phillips
Development
Phone: 310-244-4918
IMDb: imdb.com/name/nm1913014
Assistant: Bill Karesh

MICHAEL GRAIS PRODUCTIONS

321 S Beverly Dr, Suite M
Beverly Hills, CA 90210
Phone: 323-857-4510
Fax: 323-319-4002

Accepts query letter from unproduced, unrepresented writers via email. Project types include Feature Films and TV. Preferred genres include Horror and Thriller.

Michael Grais

Producer/Writer

Phone: 323-857-4510

Email: michaelgrais@yahoo.com

IMDb: imdb.com/name/nm0334457

MICHAEL TAYLOR PRODUCTIONS

2370 Bowmont Dr

Beverly Hills, CA 90210

Phone: 213-821-3113

Fax: 213-740-3395

Email: taycoprod@aol.com

Accepts query letter from unproduced, unrepresented writers via email. Project types include Feature Films and TV. Preferred genres include Non-Fiction and Reality.

Michael Taylor

Producer

Phone: 213-821-3113

IMDb: imdb.com/name/nm0852888

Assistant: Yolanda Rodriguez

MIDD KID PRODUCTIONS

10202 W Washington Blvd

Fred Astaire Building, Suite 2010

Culver City, CA 90232

Phone: 310-244-2688

Fax: 310-244-2603

Accepts query letter from unproduced, unrepresented writers. Project types include TV. Preferred genres include Crime, Detective, and Drama.

Shawn Ryan

Principal

Phone: 310-244-2688

IMDb: imdb.com/name/nm0752841

Assistant: Kent Rotherham

Marney Hochman

President of Development

Phone: 310-244-2688

IMDb: imdb.com/name/nm2701117

Assistant: Kent Rotherham

MIDNIGHT SUN PICTURES

10960 Wilshire Blvd, Suite 700

Los Angeles, CA 90024

Phone: 310-902-0431

Fax: 310-450-4988

Accepts query letter from produced or represented writers. Project types include Feature Films and TV. Preferred genres include Comedy, Drama, Horror, and Romance.

Renny Harlin

Producer/Director

Phone: 310-902-0431

IMDb: imdb.com/name/nm0001317

Nikki Stanghetti

Co-Producer

Phone: 310-902-0431

Email: nikki@midnightsunproductions.com

IMDb: imdb.com/name/nm2325595

MIKE LOBELL PRODUCTIONS

9477 Lloydcrest Dr

Beverly Hills, CA 90210

Phone: 323-822-2910

Fax: 310-205-2767

Accepts query letter from unproduced, unrepresented writers. Project types include Feature Films. Preferred genres include Action, Comedy, Drama, and Romance. Established in 1973.

Mike Lobell

Producer

Phone: 323-822-2910

IMDb: imdb.com/name/nm0516465

Assistant: JanetChiarabaglio

MILLAR/GOUGH INK

500 S Buena Vista St

Animation Building 1E16

Burbank, CA 91521

Phone: 818-560-4260

Fax: 818-560-4216

Accepts query letter from unproduced, unrepresented writers. Project types include Feature Films and TV. Preferred genres include Action, Drama, Family, and Science Fiction.

Miles Millar
Principal
Phone: 818-560-4260
IMDb: imdb.com/name/nm0587692
Assistant: Mal Stares

Alfred Gough
Principal
Phone: 818-560-4260
IMDb: imdb.com/name/nm0332184
Assistant: Mal Stares

MILLENNIUM FILMS

6423 Wilshire Blvd
Los Angeles, CA 90048
Phone: 310-388-6900
Fax: 310-388-6901

Email: info@millenniumfilms.com
Home Page: millenniumfilms.com

Accepts query letter from unproduced, unrepresented writers via email. Project types include Feature Films. Preferred genres include Action, Comedy, Detective, Drama, Fantasy, Non-Fiction, Science Fiction, and Thriller. Established in 1992.

Avi Lerner
Co-Founder
IMDb: imdb.com/name/nm0503592

Trevor Short
Co-Founder
IMDb: imdb.com/name/nm0795121

Boaz Davidson
Head of Development and Creative Affairs
IMDb: imdb.com/name/nm0203246

MIMRAN SCHUR PICTURES

2400 Broadway, Suite 550
Santa Monica, CA 90404
Phone: 310-526-5410
Fax: 310-526-5405

Email: info@mimranschurpictures.com
Home Page: mimranschurpictures.com

Accepts query letter from produced or represented writers. Project types include Feature Films. Preferred genres include Drama. Established in 2009.

Jordan Schur
Co-Chairman/CEO
Phone: 310-526-5410
IMDb: imdb.com/name/nm2028525

David Mimran
Co-Chairman
Phone: 310-526-5410
IMDb: imdb.com/name/nm3450764
Assistant: Caroline Haubold

Lauren Pettit
Creative Executive
Phone: 310-526-5410
IMDb: imdb.com/name/nm2335692

MIRADA

4235 Redwood Ave
Los Angeles, CA 90066
Phone: 424-216-7470

Home Page: mirada.com

Does not accept any unsolicited material. Project types include Feature Films, TV, and Theater. Preferred genres include Animation, Drama, Fantasy, and Myth. Established in 2010.

Guillermo del Toro
IMDb: imdb.com/name/nm0868219

Guillermo Navarro
IMDb: imdb.com/name/nm0622897

Javier Jimenez
IMDb: imdb.com/name/nm3901643

MIRANDA ENTERTAINMENT

7337 Pacific View Dr
Los Angeles, CA 90068
Phone: 323-874-3600
Fax: 323-851-5350

Does not accept any unsolicited material. Project types include Feature Films and TV. Preferred genres include Comedy, Horror, and Thriller.

Carsten Lorenz
Producer
Phone: 323-874-3600
Email: clorenz1@aol.com
IMDb: imdb.com/name/nm0520696

MISHER FILMS

12233 Olympic Blvd, Suite 354
Los Angeles, CA 90064
Phone: 310-405-7999
Fax: 310-405-7991

Home Page: misherfilms.com

Does not accept any unsolicited material. Project types include Feature Films and TV. Preferred genres include Action, Crime, and Drama.

Kevin Misher
Producer/Owner
Phone: 310-405-7999
Email: kevin.misher@misherfilms.com
IMDb: pro.imdb.com/name/nm0592746
Assistant: Sarah Ezrin

MOCKINGBIRD PICTURES

Los Angeles, CA

Email: info@mockingbirdpictures.com
Home Page: mockinbirdpictures.com

Accepts query letter from unproduced, unrepresented writers via email. Project types include Feature Films. Preferred genres include Drama.

Bonnie Curtis
Principal
IMDb: imdb.com/name/nm0193268

Julie Lynn
Principal
IMDb: imdb.com/name/nm0528724

Kelly Thomas
Executive Producer
IMDb: imdb.com/name/nm1684437

MODERNCINE

18 4th Place, Suite 2
Brooklyn, NY 11231

Email: info@moderncine.com
Home Page: http://www.moderncine.com/index.php
IMDb: imdb.com/company/co0100731

Does not accept any unsolicited material. Project types include Feature Films and Short Films. Preferred genres include Comedy, Crime, Horror, and Thriller.

Andrew van den Houten
CEO
IMDb: imdb.com/name/nm0886156

Robert Tonino
CFO
IMDb: imdb.com/name/nm1720736

MOJO FILMS

500 S Buena Vista St
Animation Building, Suite 1D 13
Burbank, CA 91521
Phone: 818-560-8370
Fax: 818-560-5045

Accepts query letter from unproduced, unrepresented writers. Project types include Feature Films and TV. Established in 2007.

Gary Fleder
President
Phone: 818-560-8370
IMDb: imdb.com/name/nm0001219
Assistant: Pamy Sue Anton

Mary-Beth Basile
Vice-President, Production & Development
Phone: 818-560-8370
IMDb: imdb.com/name/nm1039389
Assistant: Jay Ashenfelter

MOMENTUM ENTERTAINMENT GROUP

8687 Melrose Ave
8th Floor
Los Angeles, CA 90069

Accepts query letter from unproduced, unrepresented writers via email. Project types include TV and Commercials. Preferred genres include Action, Animation, Comedy, Crime, Detective, Drama, Family, Fantasy, Horror, Myth, Non-Fiction, Reality, Romance, Science Fiction, Sociocultural, and Thriller.

Nick Hamm
Head of Scripted Development
Email: nick.hamm@megww.com
IMDb: imdb.com/name/nm0358327

MONSTERFOOT PRODUCTIONS

3450 Cahuenga Blvd West
Loft 105
Los Angeles, CA 90068
Phone: 323-850-6116
Fax: 323-378-5232

Accepts query letter from unproduced, unrepresented writers. Project types include Feature Films and TV. Preferred genres include Non-Fiction and Reality.

Ahmet Zappa
CEO
Phone: 323-850-6116
IMDb: imdb.com/name/nm0953257

Andrew Kimble
Creative Executive
Phone: 323-850-6116
IMDb: imdb.com/name/nm1130966

Devon Schiff
Executive
Phone: 323-850-6116
IMDb: imdb.com/name/nm3825595

MONTAGE ENTERTAINMENT

2600 Foothill Blvd
Ste 201
La Crescenta, CA 91214
USA
Phone: 1 818 248 0070
Fax: 1 818 248 0071

Email: david@montageentertainment.com
Home Page: montageentertainment.com

Accepts query letter from unproduced, unrepresented writers via email. Project types include Feature Films and TV.

David Peters
Producer
Phone: 310-966-0222
Email: david@montageentertainment.com
IMDb: imdb.com/name/nm0007070

Bill Ewart
Producer
Phone: 310-966-0222
Email: bill@montageentertainment.com
IMDb: imdb.com/name/nm0263867

MONTONE/YORN (UNNAMED YORN PRODUCTION COMPANY)

2000 Ave of the Stars
3rd Floor North Tower
Los Angeles, CA 90067

Accepts query letter from unproduced, unrepresented writers. Preferred genres include Action, Comedy, Family, and Fantasy. Established in 2008.

Rick Yorn
Principal
IMDb: imdb.com/name/nm0948833

MOONSTONE ENTERTAINMENT

PO Box 7400
Studio City, CA 91614
Phone: 818-985-3003
Fax: 818-985-3009

Email: submissions@moonstonefilms.com
Home Page: moonstonefilms.com

Accepts query letter from unproduced, unrepresented writers via email. Project types include Feature Films. Established in 1992.

Shahar Stroh
Director, Development & Acquisitions
Phone: 818-985-3003
IMDb: imdb.com/name/nm2325576

MORGAN CREEK PRODUCTIONS

10351 Santa Monica Blvd, Suite 200
Los Angeles, CA 90025
Phone: 310-432-4848
Fax: 310-432-4844

Accepts query letter from unproduced, unrepresented writers. Project types include Feature Films. Established in 1988.

Ryan Jones
Director of Development
Phone: 310-432-4848
IMDb: imdb.com/name/nm2325121

Larry Katz
Senior Vice-President Development
Phone: 310-432-4848
IMDb: imdb.com/name/nm0441765

Jordan Okun
Creative Executive
Phone: 310-432-4848
IMDb: imdb.com/name/nm1442312

MORNINGSTAR ENTERTAINMENT

350 N Glenoaks Blvd, Suite 300
Burbank, CA 91502
Phone: 818-559-7255
Fax: 818-559-7251

Accepts query letter from unproduced, unrepresented writers via email. Project types include TV. Preferred genres include Non-Fiction and Reality. Established in 1980.

Christian Robinson
Director, Development
Phone: 818-559-7255
IMDb: imdb.com/name/nm2384297

MOSAIC/MOSAIC MEDIA GROUP

9200 W Sunset Blvd
10th Floor
Los Angeles, CA 90069
Phone: 310-786-4900
Fax: 310-777-2185

Accepts query letter from unproduced, unrepresented writers. Project types include Feature Films and TV. Preferred genres include Action, Comedy, Drama, Family, and Myth.

David Householter
President, Production
Phone: 310-786-4900
Email: dhouseholter@mosaicla.com
IMDb: imdb.com/name/nm0396720
Assistant: Brendan Clougherty

Mike Falbo
Vice-President Production & Development
Phone: 310-786-4900
Email: mfalbo@mosaicla.com
IMDb: imdb.com/name/nm3824648
Assistant: Mark Acomb

Jimmy Miller
CEO/Chairman/Producer
Phone: 310-786-4900
Email: jmiller@mosaicla.com
IMDb: imdb.com/name/nm0588612
Assistant: Alyx Carr

MOSHAG PRODUCTIONS

c/o Mark Mower
1531 Wellesley Ave
Los Angeles, CA 90025
Phone: 310-820-6760
Fax: 310-820-6960

Email: moshag@aol.com

Accepts query letter from unproduced, unrepresented writers via email. Project types include Feature Films and TV.

Mark Mower
Producer
Phone: 310-820-6760
IMDb: imdb.com/name/nm0610272

MOXIE PICTURES

5890 W Jefferson Blvd
Los Angeles, CA 90016
Phone: 310-857-1000
Fax: 310-857-1004

Home Page: moxiepictures.com
IMDb: imdb.com/company/co0119462

Does not accept any unsolicited material. Project types include Feature Films and TV. Preferred genres include Comedy, Documentary, Drama, Reality, and Romance. Established in 2005.

Robert Fernandez
Chief Executive Officer
IMDb: imdb.com/name/nm0273045

Dan Levinson
President
IMDb: imdb.com/name/nm1829495

Lizzie Schwartz
Vice President (Executive Producer)
IMDb: imdb.com/name/nm2594272

Katie Connell
Head of Production for New York
Phone: 212-807-6901

Dawn Laren
Managing Director

David Casey
Director (Creative/TV)

MRB PRODUCTIONS

PO Box 311 N. Robertson Blvd., #513 Beverly HIlls, ca 90211
Phone: 323-965-8881
Fax: 323-965-8882

Home Page: mrbproductions.com

Does not accept any unsolicited material. Project types include Feature Films and TV. Preferred genres include Comedy, Documentary, Drama, Romance, and Thriller.

Matthew Brady
Executive Producer
Email: matthew@mrbproductions.com
IMDb: imdb.com/name/nm0103683

Lori Huck
Director of Development

Brenda Bank
Producer
Email: brenda@mrbproductions.com
IMDb: imdb.com/name/nm1870773
Assistant: Erica Weiss

Yvette Lubinsky
Executive

Luke Watson
Head of Production
Email: luke@mrbproductions.com
IMDb: imdb.com/name/nm2362830

MR. MUDD

137 N Larchmont Blvd, #113
Los Angeles, CA 9004
Phone: 323-932-5656
Fax: 323-932-5666

Does not accept any unsolicited material. Project types include Feature Films. Preferred genres include Comedy, Drama, Family, and Romance. Established in 1998.

John Malkovich
Producer/Director
IMDb: imdb.com/name/nm0000518

Lianne Halfon
Producer
IMDb: imdb.com/name/nm0355147

Russell Smith
Producer
IMDb: imdb.com/name/nm0809833

MYRIAD PICTURES

3015 Main St, Suite 400
Santa Monica, CA 90405
Phone: 310-279-4000
Fax: 310-279-4001

Email: info@myriadpictures.com
Home Page: myriadpictures.com
IMDb: imdb.com/company/co0033226

Does not accept any unsolicited material. Project types include Feature Films. Preferred genres include Comedy, Drama, Fantasy, Horror, Non-Fiction, and Romance. Established in 1998.

Kirk D'Amico
CEO
IMDb: imdb.com/name/nm0195136

Ari Haas
Director, Production & Acquisitions
IMDb: imdb.com/name/nm0351907

Juliana Dacunha
Office Assistant
Email: myriadasst@gmail.com

NALA FILMS

2016 Broadway Place
Santa Monica, CA 90404
Phone: 310-264-2555

Email: info@nalafilms.com
Home Page: nalafilms.com

Does not accept any unsolicited material. Project types include Feature Films and TV. Preferred genres include Drama and Thriller.

Emilio Barroso
CEO
IMDb: imdb.com/name/nm1950898

Rudy Scalese
Vice-President of Development & Production
IMDb: imdb.com/name/nm0768800

Blair Richman
Creative Executive
IMDb: imdb.com/name/nm3923771

NANCY TENENBAUM FILMS

43 Lyons Plain Rd Weston, CT 06883
Phone: 203-221-6830
Fax: 203-221-6832

Email: ntfilms2@aol.com
IMDb: imdb.com/company/co0012648

Accepts query letter from unproduced, unrepresented writers via email. Project types include Feature Films. Preferred genres include Comedy and Drama. Established in 1996.

Meredith Hall
Director of Development

Nancy Tenenbaum
President
Assistant: Lyndsy Celestino

NBC PRODUCTIONS

3000 W Alameda Ave
Burbank, CA 91523-0001
USA
Phone: 818-840-4444

Home Page: nbcuni.com
IMDb: imdb.com/company/co0065874

Does not accept any unsolicited material. Project types include Feature Films and TV. Preferred genres include Action, Comedy, Crime, Documentary, Drama, Family, Fantasy, Horror, Non-Fiction, Romance, Science Fiction, and Thriller. Established in 1947.

NBC STUDIOS

3000 W Alameda Ave
Burbank, CA 91523-0001
USA
Phone: 818-526-7000

Home Page: nbcuni.com
IMDb: imdb.com/company/co0022762

Does not accept any unsolicited material. Project types include Feature Films and TV. Preferred genres include Action, Comedy, Crime, Detective, Documentary, Drama, Non-Fiction, and Thriller. Established in 1950.

NBCUNIVERSAL

30 Rockefeller Plaza
New York, NY 10112
Phone: 212-664-4444

Home Page: nbcumv.com/mediavillage

Project types include Feature Films and TV. Preferred genres include Comedy, Crime, Documentary, Drama, Period, Reality, and Thriller. Established in 2009.

Steve Burke
President
IMDb: imdb.com/name/nm4446434

Jon Dakss
Vice President of Product Development for Interactive Television

Josie Ventura
Vice President of Production

Dan Berkowitz
Manager of Product Development for Interactive
Television

Marci Klein
Executive Producer
IMDb: imdb.com/name/nm0458885

Jessica Franks
Development Executive

Pearlena Igbokwe
Executive Vice President of Drama Development
IMDb: imdb.com/name/nm2303684

NBC UNIVERSAL TELEVISION

100 Universal City Plaza Building 1320, Suite 2C
Universal City, CA 91608
Phone: 818-777-1000
Fax: 818-866-1430

Home Page: nbcuni.com
IMDb: imdb.com/company/co0129175

Does not accept any unsolicited material. Project types
include Feature Films and TV. Preferred genres
include Action, Animation, Comedy, Crime,
Detective, Documentary, Drama, Family, Fantasy,
Horror, Reality, Science Fiction, and Thriller.
Established in 1971.

Robert Greenblatt
Chairman
IMDb: imdb.com/name/nm0338612

Jennifer Nicholson-Salke
President
IMDb: imdb.com/name/nm2323622

Bela Bajaria
Executive Vice President
IMDb: imdb.com/name/nm2704347

Jerry DiCanio
Executive Vice President of Production Operations
IMDb: imdb.com/name/nm3034292

Russell Rothberg
Executive Vice President of Drama
IMDb: imdb.com/name/nm1160205

Fernando J. Hernandez
Senior Vice President of Alternative Development
IMDb: imdb.com/name/nm0379943

Tracey Pakosta
Senior Vice President of Comedy
IMDb: imdb.com/name/nm2770837

Erin Underhill
Senior Vice President of Drama
IMDb: imdb.com/name/nm2492623

Andrew Weil
Vice President of Comedy Development
IMDb: imdb.com/name/nm0917944

NECROPIA ENTERTAINMENT

9171 Wilshire Blvd, Suite 300
Beverly Hills, CA 9021
Phone: 323-865-0547

Does not accept any unsolicited material. Project types
include Feature Films. Preferred genres include Action,
Fantasy, Horror, Myth, and Science Fiction.

Guillermo de Toro
Director
IMDb: imdb.com/name/nm0868219

NEO ART & LOGIC

5225 Wilshire Blvd Ste. 501
Los Angeles, CA 90036
Phone: 323-451-2040

Email: aaron@neoartandlogic.com
Home Page: neoartandlogic.com
IMDb: imdb.com/company/co0038165

Accepts query letter from unproduced, unrepresented
writers via email. Project types include Feature Films
and TV. Preferred genres include Action, Animation,
Comedy, Documentary, Drama, Family, Fantasy,
Horror, Science Fiction, and Thriller. Established in
2000.

Keith Border
Principal
IMDb: imdb.com/name/nm0096176

Mike Leahy
Principal
IMDb: imdb.com/name/nm0494999

Joel Soisson
Principal
IMDb: imdb.com/name/nm0812373

Aaron Ockman
Vice President of Production
IMDb: imdb.com/name/nm1845744

Kirk Morri
Executive
IMDb: imdb.com/name/nm0606294

NEW AMSTERDAM ENTERTAINMENT

1133 Ave. Of The Americas
Ste. 1621 New York, NY 10036
Phone: 212-922-1930
Fax: 212-922-0674

Email: mail@newamsterdamnyc.com
Home Page: newamsterdamnyc.com
IMDb: imdb.com/company/co0010962

Does not accept any unsolicited material. Project types
include Feature Films and TV. Preferred genres
include Action, Documentary, Drama, Fantasy,
Horror, Science Fiction, and Thriller. Established in
1996.

Katherine Kolbert
Vice President of Acquisitions
IMDb: imdb.com/name/nm0463946

Michael Messina
Senior Vice President
IMDb: imdb.com/name/nm0582175

Sarah Reiner
Executive Assistant
IMDb: imdb.com/name/nm2200017

Richard Rubinstein
CEO
IMDb: imdb.com/name/nm0748283

NEW ARTISTS ALLIANCE

16633 Ventura Blvd, #1440
Encino, CA 91436
Phone: 1 818 784 8341

Email: info@newartistsalliance.com
Home Page: newartistsalliance.com

Accepts query letter from unproduced, unrepresented
writers via email. Project types include Feature Films.
Preferred genres include Action, Drama, Horror, and
Thriller. Established in 2003.

Gabe Cowan
Founder/Producer
Email: gabe@naafilms.com
IMDb: imdb.com/name/nm1410462

John Suits
Founder/Producer
Email: john@naafilms.com
IMDb: imdb.com/name/nm2986811

NEW CRIME PRODUCTIONS

1041 N Formosa Ave
Formosa Building, Room 219
West Hollywood, CA 90016
Phone: 323-850-2525

Email: newcrime@aol.com
Home Page: newcrime.com
IMDb: imdb.com/company/co0079035

Accepts query letter from unproduced, unrepresented
writers via email. Project types include Feature Films.
Preferred genres include Comedy, Drama, Romance,
and Thriller.

John Cusack
Executive
IMDb: imdb.com/name/nm0000131

Grace Loh
Executive
IMDb: imdb.com/name/nm0517808
Assistant: Judy Heinzen

NEW LINE CINEMA

116 N Robertson Blvd
Los Angeles, CA 90048

Phone: 310-854-5811
Fax: 310-854-1824

Home Page: warnerbros.com
IMDb: imdb.com/company/co0046718

Does not accept any unsolicited material. Project types include Feature Films and TV. Preferred genres include Action, Comedy, Crime, Documentary, Drama, Family, Fantasy, Non-Fiction, Period, Romance, Science Fiction, and Thriller. Established in 1967.

Toby Emmerich
President
IMDb: imdb.com/name/nm0256497
Assistant: Joshua Mack

Richard Brener
President of Production
IMDb: imdb.com/name/nm0107196
Assistant: Kristin Schmidt

Sam Brown
Senior Vice President of Development
IMDb: imdb.com/name/nm1354041
Assistant: Celia Khong

Michael Disco
Senior Vice President of Development
Assistant: Celia Khong

Walter Hamada
Senior Vice President of Production
IMDb: imdb.com/name/nm1023578
Assistant: Victoria Palmeri

Dave Neustadter
Production Executive
IMDb: imdb.com/name/nm2692520
Assistant: Victoria Palmeri

Andrea Johnston
Creative Executive

NEW REGENCY FILMS

10201 W Pico Blvd
Bldg 12
Los Angeles, CA 90035
Phone: 310-369-8300
Fax: 310-969-0470

Email: info@newregency.com
Home Page: newregency.com

Project types include Feature Films. Preferred genres include Action, Comedy, Crime, Drama, Family, Romance, and Science Fiction.

Arnon Milchan
Chairman
IMDb: imdb.com/name/nm0586969

Justin Lam
Creative Executive
IMDb: imdb.com/name/nm3528759

David Manpearl
Vice President of Production
IMDb: imdb.com/name/nm1818404

Mimi Tseng
CFO
IMDb: imdb.com/name/nm2303729

NEW SCHOOL MEDIA

9229 Sunset Blvd, Suite 301
West Hollywood, CA 90069
Phone: 310-858-2989
Fax: 310-858 1841

Accepts query letter from unproduced, unrepresented writers. Project types include Feature Films.

Brian Levy
Manager/CEO
IMDb: imdb.com/name/nm2546392

NEW WAVE ENTERTAINMENT

2660 W Olive Ave
Burbank, CA 91505
Phone: 818-295-5000
Fax: 818-295-5002

Home Page: nwe.com

Does not accept any unsolicited material. Project types include Feature Films, TV, and Commercials. Preferred genres include Action, Animation, Comedy, Crime, Detective, Drama, Family, Fantasy, Horror, Myth, Non-Fiction, Reality, Romance, Science Fiction, Sociocultural, and Thriller.

Paul Apel
CEO
Phone: 1 818 295 5000
IMDb: pro.imdb.com/name/nm1318269

Gregory Woertz
Executive Vice President
Phone: +1 818 295 5000
Email: gwoertz@nwe.com
IMDb: pro.imdb.com/name/nm0937343

NICK WECHSLER PRODUCTIONS

1437 7th St, Suite 250
Santa Monica, CA 90401
Phone: 310-309-5759
Fax: 310-309-5716

Email: info@nwprods.com
Home Page: nwprods.com

Does not accept any unsolicited material. Project types include Feature Films and TV. Preferred genres include Action, Animation, Comedy, Crime, Drama, Family, Fantasy, Horror, Science Fiction, and Thriller. Established in 2005.

Nick Wechsler
Producer/Chairman
Email: nick@nwprods.com
IMDb: imdb.com/name/nm0917059

Elizabeth Bradford
Director of Development
Email: lizzy@nwprods.com
IMDb: imdb.com/name/nm4504768

Felicity Aldridge
Creative Executive
Email: felicity@nwprods.com
IMDb: imdb.com/name/nm4504820

NIGHT & DAY PICTURES

5225 Wilshire Blvd, Suite 524
Los Angeles, CA 90036
Phone: 323-930-2212

Email: info@nightanddaypictures.com
Home Page: nightanddaypictures.com
IMDb: imdb.com/company/co0253348

Accepts query letter from unproduced, unrepresented writers via email. Project types include Feature Films.

Rachel Berk
Creative Executive
IMDb: imdb.com/company/co0157684

Michael Roiff
President
Email: michael@nightanddaypictures.com
IMDb: imdb.com/name/nm1988698

NINJA'S RUNNIN' WILD PRODUCTIONS

7024 Melrose Ave, Suite 420
Los Angeles, CA 90038
Phone: 323-937-6100

Accepts scripts from produced or represented writers. Project types include Feature Films.

Zac Effron
Actor/Producer
IMDb: imdb.com/name/nm1374980

Jason Barrett
Producer
IMDb: imdb.com/name/nm2249074

NORTH BY NORTHWEST ENTERTAINMENT

903 W Broadway
Spokane, WA 99201
Phone: 509-324-2949
Fax: 509-324-2959

Email: moviesales@nxnw.net
Home Page: nxnw.net

Does not accept any unsolicited material. Project types include Feature Films. Preferred genres include Thriller.

Rich Cowen
CEO
Phone: 509-324-2949
Email: rcowan@nxnw.net
IMDb: imdb.com/name/nm0184616

NOVA PICTURES

6496 Ivarene Ave.
Los Angeles, CA 90068

Phone: 323-462-5502
Fax: 323-463-8903

Email: pbarnett@novapictures.com
Home Page: novapictures.com

Does not accept any unsolicited material. Project types
include Feature Films.

Peter Barnett
Executive Producer
IMDb: imdb.com/name/nm0055963

NU IMAGE FILMS

6423 Wilshire Blvd
Los Angeles, CA 90048
Phone: 310-388-6900
Fax: 310-388-6901

Email: info@millenniumfilms.com
Home Page: millenniumfilms.com

Does not accept any unsolicited material. Preferred
genres include Action, Comedy, Drama, and Science
Fiction.

Christine Crow
Director of Development
Phone: 310-388-6900
IMDb: imdb.com/name/nm4579268

Boaz Davidson
President of Production
Phone: 310-388-6900
IMDb: imdb.com/name/nm0203246

Mark Gill
President
Phone: 310-388-6900
IMDb: imdb.com/name/nm1247584

Joan Mao
Director of Development
Phone: 310-388-6900
IMDb: imdb.com/name/nm2668002

John Thompson
Head of Production
Phone: 310-388-6900
IMDb: imdb.com/name/nm0860315

NUYORICAN PRODUCTIONS

1100 Glendon Ave, Suite 920
Los Angeles, CA 90024
Phone: 310-943-6600
Fax: 310-943-6609

Does not accept any unsolicited material. Project types
include Feature Films, TV, and Commercials.
Preferred genres include Action, Comedy, Drama,
Non-Fiction, and Reality.

Jennifer Lopez
Founder-Entertainer-Producer
IMDb: imdb.com/name/nm0000182

Brian Schornak
Executive Film & TV
Email: bsasst@jlopezent.com
IMDb: imdb.com/name/nm1935985

Simon Fields
Producer - Vice-President of Development
Email: sfasst@jlopezent.com
IMDb: imdb.com/name/nm0276353

O2 FILMES

Rua Baumann, 930
Vila Leopoldina
São Paulo, SP 05318-000
Brazil
Phone: +55 1138 39 94 00
Fax: +55 11 38 32 48 11

Email: faleconosco@o2filmes.com
Home Page: o2filmes.com

Does not accept any unsolicited material. Project types
include Feature Films. Preferred genres include
Documentary and Drama.

Hank Levine
President, Producer
Phone: +49-162-7040135
Email: hanklevine@mac.com
IMDb: imdb.com/name/nm0505810

ODD LOT ENTERTAINMENT

9601 Jefferson Blvd, Suite A
Culver City, CA 90232

Phone: 310-652-0999
Fax: 310-652-0718

Email: info@oddlotent.com
Home Page: oddlotent.com

Does not accept any unsolicited material. Project types include Feature Films. Preferred genres include Drama.

Gigi Pritzker
CEO
IMDb: imdb.com/name/nm0698133

Linda McDonough
Exec Vice-President, Production and Development
IMDb: imdb.com/name/nm1261078

OFFSPRING ENTERTAINMENT

8755 Colgate Ave
Los Angeles, CA 90048
Phone: 310-247-0019
Fax: 310-550-6908

Does not accept any unsolicited material. Project types include Feature Films. Preferred genres include Comedy, Drama, and Family.

Adam Shankman
Executive
IMDb: imdb.com/name/nm0788202

Jennifer Gibgot
Executive
IMDb: imdb.com/name/nm0316774

OLIVE BRIDGE ENTERTAINMENT

10202 W Washington Blvd
Culver City, CA 90232
Phone: 310-244-1269

Home Page: olivebridge.com
IMDb: imdb.com/company/co0219609

Does not accept any unsolicited material. Project types include Feature Films and TV. Preferred genres include Action, Comedy, Drama, Period, and Romance. Established in 2003.

Will Gluck
Principal
IMDb: imdb.com/name/nm0323239

Alicia Emmrich
Executive (Features)
IMDb: imdb.com/name/nm1445355

Jodi Hildebrand
Executive (Features)
IMDb: imdb.com/name/nm1637492

Richard Schwartz
Executive (Television)
IMDb: imdb.com/name/nm1108160

OLMOS PRODUCTIONS INC.

500 S Buena Vista St
Old Animation Building, Suite 1G
Burbank, CA 91521
Phone: 818-560-8651
Fax: 818-560-8655

Email: olmosonline@yahoo.com

Accepts query letter from unproduced, unrepresented writers via email. Project types include Feature Films, TV, and Commercials. Preferred genres include Comedy, Drama, Family, Non-Fiction, and Reality. Established in 1980.

Edward Olmos
President
IMDb: imdb.com/name/nm0001579

OLYMPUS PICTURES

2901 Ocean Park Blvd, Suite 217
Santa Monica, CA 90405
Phone: 310-452-3335
Fax: 310-452-0108

Email: getinfo@olympuspics.com
Home Page: olympuspics.com

Accepts query letter from unproduced, unrepresented writers via email. Project types include Feature Films. Established in 2007.

Leslie Urdang
President, Producer
IMDb: imdb.com/name/nm0881811

Mandy Beckner
Creative Executive
Email: rrdecter@olympuspics.com

OMBRA FILMS

12444 Ventura Blvd, Suite 103
Studio City, CA 91604
Phone: 818-509-0552

Email: info@ombrafilms.com
Home Page: ombrafilms.com

Accepts query letter from unproduced, unrepresented writers via email. Project types include Feature Films and TV. Preferred genres include Fantasy, Horror, and Thriller. Established in 2011.

Jaume Serra
Producer
IMDb: imdb.com/name/nm1429471

Juan Sola
Producer
IMDb: imdb.com/name/nm4928159

O.N.C.

11150 Santa Monica Blvd, Suite 450
Los Angeles, CA 90025
Phone: 310-477-0670
Fax: 310-477-7710

Home Page: oncentertainment.com

Does not accept any unsolicited material. Project types include Feature Films. Preferred genres include Action, Comedy, Crime, Family, Romance, and Thriller.

Michael Nathanson
Producer
Email: michaelnathanson@oncentertainment.com
IMDb: imdb.com/name/nm0622296
Assistant: Robyn Altman

ONE RACE FILMS

9100 Wilshire Blvd
East Tower, Suite 535
Beverly Hills, CA 90212
Phone: 310-401-6880
Fax: 310-401-6890

Email: info@oneracefilms.com
Home Page: oneracefilms.com

Accepts query letter from unproduced, unrepresented writers via email. Project types include Feature Films

and TV. Preferred genres include Action, Crime, Drama, Science Fiction, and Thriller. Established in 1995.

Vin Diesel
Actor/Writer/Producer
IMDb: imdb.com/name/nm0004874

Samantha Vincent
Producer/Partner
Email: samantha@oneracefilms.com
IMDb: imdb.com/name/nm2176972

Thyrale Thai
Marketing and New Media
Email: thyrale@oneracefilms.com
IMDb: imdb.com/name/nm1394166

OOPS DOUGHNUTS PRODUCTIONS

500 S Buena Vista St
Old Animation Building, Room 2F8
Burbank, CA 91521
Phone: 323-936-9811
Fax: 818 560 6185

IMDb: imdb.com/company/co0248742

Accepts query letter from unproduced, unrepresented writers. Project types include Feature Films, TV, and Commercials.

Andy Fickman
Director/Producer
IMDb: imdb.com/name/nm0275698
Assistant: Whitney Engstrom

Betsy Sullenger
Producer
IMDb: imdb.com/name/nm0998095

OPEN CITY FILMS

55 Liberty St
New York, NY 10005
USA
Phone: 212-255-0500

Email: oc@opencityfilms.com
Home Page: opencityfilms.com

Accepts query letter from unproduced, unrepresented writers via email. Project types include Feature Films and TV. Preferred genres include Non-Fiction and Reality.

Jason Kilot
co-president, founder
IMDb: imdb.com/name/nm0459852

Joana Vicente
Co-President, Founder

OPEN ROAD FILMS

400 S Main St
Suite 306
Los Angeles, CA 90013
Phone: 323-353-0551

Home Page: openroadfilms.net
IMDb: imdb.com/company/co0178575

Does not accept any unsolicited material. Project types include Feature Films, Short Films, and TV. Preferred genres include Action, Crime, Documentary, and Drama. Established in 2002.

Mary Pat Betel
Producer

Denis Henry Hennelly
Principal
IMDb: imdb.com/name/nm0377203

Casey Suchan
Principal
IMDb: imdb.com/name/nm1093063

ORIGINAL FILM

11466 San Vicente Blvd
Los Angeles, CA 90049
Phone: 310-575-6950
Fax: 310-575-6990

Accepts query letter from unproduced, unrepresented writers. Project types include Feature Films. Preferred genres include Action, Comedy, and Drama.

Toby Ascher
Producer
IMDb: imdb.com/name/nm4457111

Jeni Mulein
Creative Executive
IMDb: imdb.com/name/nm2630667

Toby Jaffe
Producer
IMDb: imdb.com/name/nm0003993
Assistant: Hanna Ozer

Vivian Cannon
Television Executive
IMDb: imdb.com/name/nm0134279
Assistant: Ashley Deaton

Ori Marmur
Production Executive
IMDb: imdb.com/name/nm1506459
Assistant: Miguel Raya

ORIGINAL MEDIA

175 Varick St
7th Floor
New York, NY 10014
Phone: 212-683-3086
Fax: 212-683-3162

Home Page: originalmedia.com

Does not accept any unsolicited material. Project types include Feature Films and TV. Preferred genres include Comedy, Drama, Family, Romance, and Thriller.

Charlie Corwen
Founder & CEO
IMDb: imdb.com/name/nm1231965

Michael Saffran
COO/EVP Production & Development

Colleen Ocean Hall
SVP of Unscripted Development
IMDb: imdb.com/name/nm5066841

Patrick Moses
VP of Current Series

Jessica Matthews
VP of Scripted Development

Chelsey Throwbridge
VP of Post Productions & Operations
IMDb: imdb.com/name/nm2399791

OSCILLOSCOPE LABORATORIES

511 Canal St Suite 5E
New York City, NY 10013
Phone: 212-219-4029
Fax: 212-219-9538

Email: info@oscilloscope.net
Home Page: oscilloscope.net

Does not accept any unsolicited material. Project types include Feature Films. Preferred genres include Drama and Romance.

Dan Berger
Head of Productions & Acquisitions
IMDb: imdb.com/name/nm3088964

David Laub
Head of Distribution & Acquisitions
IMDb: imdb.com/name/nm3000864

Tom Sladek
Head of Home Entertainment

Amanda Lebow
Digital Sales
IMDb: imdb.com/name/nm4144904

Aaron Katz
Executive

O'TAYE PRODUCTIONS

12001 Ventura Place
#340
Studio City, CA 91604
USA
Phone: 1 818 232 8580
Fax: 1 818 232 8108

Accepts query letter from unproduced, unrepresented writers. Project types include TV.

Taye Diggs
Executive/partner
IMDb: imdb.com/name/nm0004875

Jennifer Bozell
Head of Development

OUTERBANKS ENTERTAINMENT

1149 N Gower St, #101
Los Angeles, CA 90038
Phone: 1 310 858 8711
Fax: 1 310 858 6947

Accepts query letter from unproduced, unrepresented writers via email. Project types include Feature Films and TV.

Kevin Williamson
President
Phone: 1 310 858 8711
Email: kevin@outerbanks-ent.com
IMDb: imdb.com/name/nm0932078

OUT OF THE BLUE...ENTERTAINMENT

c/o Sony Pictures Entertainment
10202 W Washington Blvd
Astaire Building, Suite 1200
Culver City, CA 90232-3195
Phone: 310-244-7811
Fax: 310-244-1539

Email: info@outoftheblueent.com
Home Page: outoftheblueent.com

Accepts query letter from unproduced, unrepresented writers via email. Project types include Feature Films and TV.

Sidney Ganis
Founder/Executive
IMDb: imdb.com/name/nm0304398

Marta Camps
Creative Executive
IMDb: imdb.com/name/nm2585482

Toby Conroy
Creative Executive
IMDb: imdb.com/name/nm1926762

OVERBROOK ENTERTAINMENT

450 N Roxbury Dr
4th Floor
Beverly Hills, CA 90210
Phone: 310-432-2400
Fax: 310-432-2401

Home Page: overbrookent.com

Accepts query letter from unproduced, unrepresented writers. Project types include Feature Films and TV. Established in 1998.

Will Smith
Producer/Partner, Actor
Phone: 310-432-2400
IMDb: imdb.com/name/nm0000226

Gary Glushon
Film Executive
Phone: 310-432-2400
IMDb: imdb.com/name/nm2237223

OVERNIGHT PRODUCTIONS

15 Mercer St, Suite 4
New York, NY 10013
Phone: 212-625-0530

Does not accept any unsolicited material. Project types include Feature Films. Established in 2008.

Rick Schwartz
Chairman/CEO
Phone: 212-625-0530
IMDb: imdb.com/name/nm0777408

Clara Kim
Head of Development and Production
Phone: 212-625-0530
IMDb: imdb.com/name/nm3247964

OWN: OPRAH WINFREY NETWORK

5700 Wilshire Blvd
Ste 120
Los Angeles, CA 90036
Phone: 323-602-5500

Home Page: oprah.com/own

Does not accept any unsolicited material. Preferred genres include Animation, Documentary, Family, and Reality.

Oprah Winfrey
CEO
IMDb: imdb.com/name/nm0001856

OZLA PICTURES, INC.

1800 Camino Palmero St
Los Angeles, CA 90046
Phone: 323-876-0180
Fax: 323-876-0189

Email: ozla@ozla.com
Home Page: ozla.com

Does not accept any unsolicited material. Project types include Feature Films and TV. Established in 1992.

Taka Ichise
Producer
Phone: 323-876-0180
IMDb: imdb.com/name/nm0406772
Assistant: Chiaki Yanagimoto

Erin Eggers
Development Vice-President
Phone: 323-876-0180
IMDb: imdb.com/name/nm0250929

PACIFICA INTERNATIONAL FILM & TV CORPORATION

PO Box 8329
Northridge, CA 91237
Phone: 818-831-0360
Fax: 818-831-0352

Email: pacifica@pacifica.la
Home Page: pacifica.la

Does not accept any unsolicited material.

Christine Iso
Executive Producer
IMDb: imdb.com/name/nm1259606

PACIFIC STANDARD

9720 Wilshire Blvd
4th Fl
Beverly Hills, CA 90212
Phone: 1 310 777 3119
Fax: 1 310 777 0150

IMDb: imdb.com/company/co0373561

Does not accept any unsolicited material. Project types include Feature Films. Established in 2012.

Reese Witherspoon
Actor/Producer/Partner
IMDb: imdb.com/name/nm0000702

Bruna Papandrea
Producer/Partner
IMDb: imdb.com/name/nm0660295

PALERMO PRODUCTIONS

c/o Twentieth Century Fox
10201 W Pico Blvd
Building 52, Room 103
Los Angeles, CA 90064
Phone: 310-369-1900

Accepts query letter from unproduced, unrepresented writers. Project types include Feature Films and TV.

John Palermo
Producer
Phone: 310-369-1911
IMDb: imdb.com/name/nm0657561
Assistant: Mike Belyea

PALMSTAR ENTERTAINMENT

14622 Ventura Blvd.
Suite 755
Sherman Oaks, CA 91403
Phone: 646-277-7356
Fax: 310-469-7855

Email: contact@palmstar.com
Home Page: palmstar.com
Facebook: facebook.com/PalmStarEntertainment

Does not accept any unsolicited material. Project types include Feature Films. Preferred genres include Action, Comedy, Drama, Family, Non-Fiction, Romance, and Thriller. Established in 2004.

Courtney Andrialis
Producer

Stephan Paternot
Chairman
IMDb: imdb.com/name/nm0665456

Kevin Scott Frakes
CEO
IMDb: imdb.com/name/nm0289694

Michael Bassick
Co-CEO

Josh Monkarsh
Producer
IMDb: imdb.com/name/nm1586268

PALOMAR PICTURES

PO Box 491986
Los Angeles, CA 90049
Phone: 310-440-3494

Email: ad@palomarpics.com

Does not accept any unsolicited material. Project types include Feature Films and TV. Established in 1992.

Joni Sighvatsson
CEO/Producer
Phone: 310-440-3494
IMDb: imdb.com/name/nm0797451

Aditya Ezhuthachan
Head of Development
Phone: 310-440-3494
IMDb: imdb.com/name/nm2149074

PANAY FILMS

500 S Buena Vista
Old Animation Bldg, Rm 3c-6
Burbank, CA 91521
Phone: 818-560-4265

Does not accept any unsolicited material. Project types include Feature Films. Preferred genres include Action, Comedy, Drama, and Fantasy.

Andrew Panay
Principal
IMDb: imdb.com/name/nm0659123
Assistant: Lukas Stuart-Fry

Adam Blum
Vice President (Production)
IMDb: imdb.com/name/nm3597471

Jared Iacino
Development Executive

Derrick Beyenka
Assistant

PANDEMONIUM

9777 Wilshire Blvd, Suite 700
Beverly Hills, CA 90212
Phone: 310-550-9900
Fax: 310-550-9910

Accepts query letter from unproduced, unrepresented writers via email. Project types include Feature Films.

Bill Mechanic
President/CEO
Phone: 310-550-9900
IMDb: imdb.com/name/nm0575312
Assistant: David Freedman

Suzanne Warren
Vice-President Production
Phone: 310-550-9900
IMDb: imdb.com/name/nm0913049

PANTHER FILMS

1888 Century Park East
14th Floor
Los Angeles, CA 90067
Phone: 424-202-6630
Fax: 310-887-1001

Does not accept any unsolicited material. Project types include Feature Films.

Brad Epstein
Producer/Owner
Phone: 424-202-6630
IMDb: imdb.com/name/nm0258431

Lindsay Culpepper
Phone: 424-202-6630
IMDb: imdb.com/name/nm0258431

PAPA JOE ENTERTAINMENT

14804 Greenleaf St
Sherman Oaks, CA 91403
Phone: 818-788-7608
Fax: 818-788-7612

Email: info@papjoefilms.com
Home Page: papjoefilms.com

Accepts query letter from unproduced, unrepresented writers via email. Project types include Feature Films and TV.

Joe Simpson
CEO
Phone: 818-788-7608
IMDb: imdb.com/name/nm1471425
Assistant: Heath Pliler

Erin Alexander
Vice-President Development & Production
Phone: 818-788-7608
IMDb: imdb.com/name/nm0018408
Assistant: Amelia Garrison

PAPER STREET FILMS

265 Canal St., Suite 212
New York, NY 10013
Phone: 646-524-6954
Fax: 646-417-6460

Email: info@paperstreetfilms.com
Home Page: paperstreetfilms.com
IMDb: imdb.com/company/co0222800

Does not accept any unsolicited material. Project types include Feature Films. Preferred genres include Comedy, Drama, Horror, and Thriller. Established in 2007.

Benji Kohn
Partner
IMDb: imdb.com/name/nm2803928

Chris Papavasilio
Partner
IMDb: imdb.com/name/nm2830113

Bingo Gubelmann
Partner
IMDb: imdb.com/name/nm1292502

Austin Stark
Partner
IMDb: imdb.com/name/nm0823133

Emily Buder
Creative Executive
IMDb: imdb.com/name/nm1692758

PARADIGM STUDIO

2701 2nd Ave North
Seattle, WA 98109

Phone: 206-282-2161
Fax: 206-283-6433

Email: info@paradigmstudio.com
Home Page: paradigmstudio.com

Accepts query letter from unproduced, unrepresented writers via email. Project types include Feature Films and TV.

John Comerford
President
Phone: 206-282-2161
IMDb: imdb.com/name/nm0173766

B Dahlia
Manager
Phone: 206-282-2161
IMDb: imdb.com/name/nm1148338

PARADOX ENTERTAINMENT

8484 Wilshire Blvd
Ste 870
Beverly Hills, CA 90211
Phone: 323-655-1700
Fax: 323-655-1720

Email: info@paradox entertainment.com
Home Page: paradoxentertainment.com

Does not accept any unsolicited material. Project types include Feature Films. Preferred genres include Action, Comedy, Drama, Fantasy, Romance, and Science Fiction.

Fredrik Malmberg
CEO & President
IMDb: imdb.com/name/nm1573406

Janet Sheppard
CFO
IMDb: imdb.com/name/nm5128822

Daniel Wagner
President of Production
IMDb: imdb.com/name/nm1016628

PARALLEL MEDIA

301 N Canon Dr, Suite 223
Beverly Hills, CA 90210
Phone: 310-858-3003
Fax: 310-858-3034

Email: info@parallelmediallc.com
Home Page: parallelmediafilms.com

Does not accept any unsolicited material. Project types include Feature Films. Established in 2006.

Tim O'Hair
Head of Production
Phone: 310-858-3003
IMDb: imdb.com/name/nm1943824

PARAMOUNT FILM GROUP

5555 Melrose Ave
Los Angeles, CA 90038
Phone: 323-956-5000

Home Page: paramount.com

Does not accept any unsolicited material. Project types include Feature Films.

Marc Evans
President of Production
IMDb: imdb.com/name/nm0263010

Ashley Brucks
Vice-President Creative Affairs
IMDb: imdb.com/name/nm2087318

Allison Small
Creative Executive
IMDb: imdb.com/name/nm1861333

PARAMOUNT PICTURES

5555 Melrose Ave
Los Angeles, CA 90038
Phone: 323-956-5000

Home Page: paramount.com

Does not accept any unsolicited material. Project types include Feature Films. Preferred genres include Action, Comedy, Crime, Drama, Family, Horror, Romance, Science Fiction, and Thriller.

Brad Grey
CEO
IMDb: imdb.com/name/nm0340522

Marc Evans
President/Production
IMDb: imdb.com/name/nm0263010

Mark Badagliacca
CFO
IMDb: imdb.com/name/nm3076670

PARIAH

9229 Sunset Blvd
Ste 208
West Hollywood, CA 90069
USA
Phone: 310-461-3460
Fax: 310-246-9622

Does not accept any unsolicited material. Project types include Feature Films and TV.

Gavin Polone
Owner
Phone: 310-461-3460
IMDb: imdb.com/name/nm0689780
Assistant: Stephen Iwanyk

Kathy Landsberg
Vice-President Physical Production
Phone: 310-461-3460
IMDb: imdb.com/name/nm0485130
Assistant: Ali Gordon-Goldstein

Lauren Pfeiffer
Director of Development
Phone: 310-461-3460
IMDb: pro.imdb.com/name/nm3604387

PARKER ENTERTAINMENT GROUP

8581 Santa Monica Blvd #261
West Hollywood, CA 90069
Phone: 323-400-6622
Fax: 323-400-6655

Email: cparker@parkerentgroup.com
Home Page: parkerentgroup.com

Accepts scripts from produced or represented writers. Project types include Feature Films. Established in 2008.

Christopher Parker
President
Email: cparker@parkerentgroup.com
IMDb: imdb.com/name/nm2034521

Gregory Parker
CEO
Phone: 323-400-6622
Email: gparker@parkerentgroup.com
IMDb: imdb.com/name/nm2027023

PARKES/MACDONALD PRODUCTIONS

1663 Euclid St
Santa Monica, CA 90404
Phone: 310-581-5990
Fax: 310 581 5999

Accepts query letter from unproduced, unrepresented writers. Project types include Feature Films and TV. Established in 2007.

Walter Parkes
Producer
Phone: 310-581-5990
IMDb: imdb.com/name/nm0662748

Laurie MacDonald
Producer
Phone: 310-581-5990
IMDb: imdb.com/name/nm0531827

PARKWAY PRODUCTIONS

7095 Hollywood Blvd, Suite 1009
Hollywood, CA 90028
Phone: 323-874-6207

Email: parkwayprods@aol.com

Accepts query letter from unproduced, unrepresented writers via email. Project types include Feature Films and TV.

Penny Marshall
Director/Producer
Phone: 323-874-6207
IMDb: imdb.com/name/nm0001508

PARTICIPANT MEDIA

331 Foothill Rd
3rd Floor
Beverly Hills, CA 90210
Phone: 310-550-5100
Fax: 310-550-5106

Email: info@participantproductions.com
Home Page: participantmedia.com

Does not accept any unsolicited material. Project types include Feature Films and TV. Preferred genres include Non-Fiction and Reality. Established in 2004.

Jonathan King
Executive Vice President of Production
Phone: 310-550-5100
IMDb: imdb.com/name/nm2622896

Erik Andreasen
Senior Director of Development, Narrative Films
Phone: 310-550-5100
IMDb: imdb.com/name/nm1849675

PARTIZAN ENTERTAINMENT

1545 Wilcox Ave Suite 200
Hollywood, CA 90028
Phone: 323-468-0123
Fax: 323-468-0129

Home Page: partizan.com
IMDb: Feature Films, Television

Does not accept any unsolicited material. Project types include Feature Films and TV. Preferred genres include Action, Animation, Comedy, Crime, Drama, Fantasy, Horror, Romance, Science Fiction, and Thriller. Established in 1991.

Sheila Stepanek
Executive Producer
Email: sstepanek@partizan.us
Assistant: Andrew Miller

Lori Stonebraker
Head of Production
Email: lstonebraker@partizan.us

Matt Tucker
Darkroom
Email: matt.tucker@partizan.com

Melissa Ross
West Coast Sales Rep
Email: melissa.ross@partizan.us

Li-Wei Chu
Head of Production & Development
Email: liwei.chu@partizan.us
Assistant: Jackson Sinder

PATHE PICTURES

6 Ramillies St
4th Floor
London W1F 7TY
United Kingdom
Phone: +44 207-462-4429
Fax: +44 207-631-3568

Email: reception.desk@pathe-uk.com
Home Page: pathe-uk.com

Accepts query letter from unproduced, unrepresented writers via email. Project types include Feature Films and TV. Preferred genres include Non-Fiction and Reality.

Mike Runagall
Senior Vice-President International Sales
Phone: +44 207-462-4429
IMDb: imdb.com/name/nm2553445

PATRIOT PICTURES

PO Box 46100
West Hollywood, CA 90046
Phone: 323-874-8850
Fax: 323-874-8851

Email: info@patriotpictures.com
Home Page: patriotpictures.com

Accepts query letter from unproduced, unrepresented writers via email. Project types include Feature Films and TV. Preferred genres include Non-Fiction and Reality.

Michael Mendelsohn
Chairman/CEO
Phone: 323-874-8850
IMDb: imdb.com/name/nm0578861

PCH FILM

3380 Motor Ave
Los Angeles, CA 90034
Phone: 310-841-5817

Home Page: pchfilms.com

Does not accept any unsolicited material. Project types include Feature Films. Preferred genres include Comedy and Romance.

Kayla Thorton
Development Manager
Phone: 310-841-5817
Email: kayla@pchfilm.com
IMDb: imdb.com/name/nm4267414

Jane Seymour
Producer
Phone: 310-841-5817
IMDb: imdb.com/name/nm0005412

PEACE ARCH ENTERTAINMENT GROUP INC.

4640 Admiralty Way, Suite 710
Marina del Rey, CA 90292
Phone: 310-776-7200
Fax: 310-823-7147

Email: info@peacearch.com
Home Page: peacearch.com

Does not accept any unsolicited material. Project types include Feature Films and TV. Established in 1986.

Sudhanshu Saria
Vice-President, Development
Phone: 310-776-7200
Email: ssaria@peacearch.com
IMDb: imdb.com/name/nm2738818

PEACE BY PEACE PRODUCTIONS

c/o Michael Katcher/CAA
2000 Ave of the Stars
Los Angeles, CA 90067
Phone: 323-552-1097

Email: peacebypeace1@mac.com

Accepts query letter from unproduced, unrepresented writers via email. Project types include Feature Films and TV.

Alyssa Milano
Producer
Phone: 323-552-1097
IMDb: imdb.com/name/nm0000192
Assistant: Kelly Kall

PEGGY RAJSKI PRODUCTIONS

918 Alandele Ave
Los Angeles, CA 90036
USA
Phone: 323 634 7020
Fax: 323 634 7021

Does not accept any unsolicited material. Project types include Feature Films and TV. Preferred genres include Non-Fiction and Reality.

Peggy Rajski
Producer
Phone: 323 634 7020
Email: rajskip@aol.com
IMDb: imdb.com/name/nm0707475

PERFECT STORM ENTERTAINMENT

1850 Industrial St, Penthouse
Los Angeles, CA 90021
Phone: 323-546-8886

Email: info@theperfectstorment.com

Does not accept any unsolicited material. Project types include Feature Films.

Justin Lin
Director
IMDb: imdb.com/name/nm0510912

Troy Poon
President
IMDb: imdb.com/name/nm1359290

PERMUT PRESENTATIONS

3535 Hayden Ave
4th Floor
Culver City, CA 90232
USA
Phone: 310-838-0100
Fax: 310-838-0105

Email: info@permutpres.com

Accepts query letter from unproduced, unrepresented writers. Project types include Feature Films and TV.

David Permut
Producer/President
Phone: 310-248-2792
IMDb: imdb.com/name/nm0674303

Chris Mangano
Development Executive
Phone: 310-248-2792
IMDb: imdb.com/name/nm2032016

PHOENIX PICTURES

10203 Santa Monica Blvd, Suite 400
Los Angeles, CA 90067
Phone: 424-298-2788
Fax: 424-298-2588

Email: info@phoenixpictures.com
Home Page: phoenixpictures.com

Accepts query letter from unproduced, unrepresented writers via email. Project types include Feature Films and TV.

Edward McGurn
Vice-President Production
Phone: 424-298-2788
IMDb: imdb.com/name/nm0570342

Douglas McKay
Vice-President Production
Phone: 424-298-2788
IMDb: imdb.com/name/nm1305822

Ali Toukan
Creative Executive
Phone: 424-298-2788
IMDb: imdb.com/name/nm4371255

PIERCE/WILLIAMS ENTERTAINMENT

1531 14th St
Santa Monica, CA 90404
Phone: 310-656-9440
Fax: 310-656-9441

Home Page: piercewilliams.com

Project types include Feature Films. Preferred genres include Drama, Horror, and Thriller.

Mark Williams
Executive Producer
IMDb: imdb.com/name/nm0931251

PILLER/SEGAN/SHEPHERD

7025 Santa Monica Blvd
Hollywood, CA 90038
Phone: 323-817-1100
Fax: 323-817-1131

Accepts query letter from unproduced, unrepresented writers. Project types include Feature Films and TV. Established in 2010.

Shawn Piller
Producer/Principal
Phone: 323-817-1100
IMDb: imdb.com/name/nm0683525

Lloyd Segan
Producer/Principal
Phone: 323-817-1100
IMDb: imdb.com/name/nm0781912

Scott Shepherd
Producer/Principal
Phone: 323-817-1100
IMDb: imdb.com/name/nm0791863

PINK SLIP PICTURES

1314 N. Coronado St.
Los Angeles, CA 90026
USA
Phone: 213-483-7100
Fax: 213-483-7200

Email: pinkslip@earthlink.net

Does not accept any unsolicited material. Project types include Feature Films and TV.

Max Wong
Producer
Phone: 213-483-7100
IMDb: imdb.com/name/nm0939246

Karen Firestone
Producer
Phone: 949-228-2354
Email: karenfirestone@hotmail.com
IMDb: imdb.com/name/nm0278652

PIPELINE ENTERTAINMENT

305 2nd Ave., Suite 302
New York, NY 10003
Phone: 212-372-7506

Home Page: pipeline-talent.com

Accepts query letter from unproduced, unrepresented writers. Project types include Feature Films and TV. Preferred genres include Action, Comedy, Crime, Drama, and Thriller.

Dan De Fillipo
Manager/Producer
Email: Dan@pipeline-talent.com
IMDb: imdb.com/name/nm2496568

Dave Marken
Manager/Producer
Email: Dave@pipeline-talent.com
IMDb: mdb.com/name/nm2441741

Patrick Wood
Manager/Producer
Email: Patrick@pipeline-talent.com
IMDb: imdb.com/name/nm3161377

Virginia Donovan
Director of Film Financing
Email: Virginia@pipeline-talent.com
IMDb: imdb.com/name/nm3270342

Katherine Brislin
Executive Assistant
Email: Katherine@pipeline-talent.com

PIXAR

1200 Park Ave
Emeryville, CA 94608
Phone: 510-922-3000
Fax: 510-922-3151

Email: publicity@pixar.com
Home Page: pixar.com
IMDb: imdb.com/company/co0017902

Does not accept any unsolicited material. Project types include Feature Films. Preferred genres include Animation, Comedy, Family, and Fantasy.

Ed Catmull
President
IMDb: imdb.com/name/nm0146216

John Lasseter
Cheif Creative Officer
IMDb: imdb.com/name/nm0005124

Jim Morris
Producer
IMDb: imdb.com/name/nm0606640

PLAN B ENTERTAINMENT

9150 Wilshire Blvd, Suite 350
Beverly Hills, CA 90210
Phone: 310-275-6135
Fax: 310-275-5234

Does not accept any unsolicited material. Project types include Feature Films and TV. Preferred genres include Action, Animation, Drama, Fantasy, and Myth. Established in 2004.

Brad Pitt
Principal/Actor
Phone: 310-275-6135
IMDb: imdb.com/name/nm0000093

Sarah Esberg
Creative Executive
Phone: 310-275-6135
IMDb: imdb.com/name/nm1209665

PLATFORM ENTERTAINMENT

128 Sierra St
El Segundo, CA 90425
Phone: 310-322-3737
Fax: 310-322-3729

Home Page: platformentertainment.com

Accepts query letter from unproduced, unrepresented writers. Project types include Feature Films. Established in 1998.

Daniel Levin
Producer
Phone: 310-322-3737
IMDb: imdb.com/name/nm0505575

Larry Gabriel
Producer
Phone: 310-322-3737
IMDb: imdb.com/name/nm0300181

Scott Sorrentino
Producer
Phone: 310-322-3737
IMDb: imdb.com/name/nm1391744

PLATINUM DUNES

631 Colorado Ave
Santa Monica, CA 90401
Phone: 310-319-6565
Fax: 310-319-6570

Does not accept any unsolicited material. Project types include Feature Films and TV. Established in 2001.

Michael Bay
Partner
Phone: 310-319-6565
IMDb: imdb.com/name/nm0000881

Sean Cummings
Assistant
Phone: 310-319-6565
IMDb: imdb.com/name/nm3594167

PLAYTONE PRODUCTIONS

PO Box 7340
Santa Monica, CA 90406
Phone: 310-394-5700
Fax: 310-394-4466

Home Page: playtone.com

Accepts query letter from unproduced, unrepresented writers. Project types include Feature Films and TV. Established in 1996.

Tom Hanks
Partner
Phone: 310-394-5700
IMDb: imdb.com/name/nm0000158

PLUM PICTURES

New York City, New York
Phone: 212-529-5820

IMDb: imdb.com/company/co0113146

Does not accept any unsolicited material. Project types include Feature Films. Preferred genres include Comedy and Drama. Established in 2003.

Joy Goodwin
Head of Development
Email: joy@pulmpic.com
IMDb: imdb.com/name/nm2205476

POLSKY FILMS

9220 Sunset Blvd., Suite 309
West Hollywood, CA 90069
Phone: 310-271-4300
Fax: 310-271-4301

Email: info@polskyfilms.com
Home Page: polskyfilms.com

Does not accept any unsolicited material. Project types include Feature Films. Preferred genres include Crime, Documentary, and Drama.

Alan Polsky
Producer
IMDb: imdb.com/name/nm2611223

Gabe Polsky
Producer
IMDb: imdb.com/name/nm2126907

Liam Satre-Meloy
Executive
IMDb: imdb.com/name/nm3176310

POLYMORPHIC PICTURES

4000 Warner Blvd
Building 81, Suite 212
Burbank, CA 91522
Phone: 818-954-3822

Does not accept any unsolicited material. Project types include Feature Films. Established in 2010.

Polly Johnsen
Producer/Principal
Phone: 818-954-3822
IMDb: imdb.com/name/nm1882593

PORCHLIGHT FILMS

94 Oxford St
Suite 31
Darlinghurst NSW 2010
Australia
Phone: 61-2-9326-9916
Fax: 61-2-9357-1479

Email: admin@porchlightfilms.com.au
Home Page: porchlightfilms.com.au

Project types include Feature Films and TV. Preferred genres include Comedy, Crime, Drama, Horror, and Thriller. Established in 1996.

Vincent Sheehan
Principal
Email: vincent@porchlightfilms.com.au
IMDb: imdb.com/name/nm0790636

Anita Sheehan
Principal
IMDb: mdb.com/name/nm1618460

Liz Watts
Principal
IMDb: imdb.com/name/nm0915192

PORTERGELLER ENTERTAINMENT

6352 De Longpre Ave
Los Angeles, CA 90028
Phone: 323-822-4400
Fax: 323-822-7270

Email: info@portergeller.com
Home Page: portergeller.com

Does not accept any unsolicited material. Project types include Feature Films and TV.

Aaron Geller
Producer
Phone: 323-822-4400
IMDb: imdb.com/name/nm1510467

Darryl Porter
Producer
Phone: 323-822-4400
IMDb: imdb.com/name/nm0692080

Michael Tyree
Producer
Phone: 323-822-4400
IMDb: imdb.com/name/nm2699784

POW! ENTERTAINMENT

9440 Santa Monica Blvd, Suite 620
Beverly Hills, CA 90210
Phone: 310-275-9933
Fax: 310-285-9955

Email: info@powentertainment.com
Home Page: powentertainment.com

Accepts query letter from unproduced, unrepresented writers via email. Project types include Feature Films and TV. Established in 2001.

Stan Lee
Chief Creative Offi cer
Phone: 310-275-9933
IMDb: imdb.com/name/nm0498278
Assistant: Mike Kelly

Ron Hawk
Chief Executive Assistant
Phone: 310-275-9933
IMDb: imdb.com/name/nm4078012

POWER UP

419 N Larchmont Blvd #283
Los Angeles, CA 90004
Phone: 323-463-3154
Fax: 323-467-6249

Email: info@powerupfilms.org
Home Page: powerupfilms.org

Accepts query letter from unproduced, unrepresented writers via email. Project types include Feature Films and TV. Established in 2000.

Stacy Codikow
Producer/Writer
Phone: 323-463-3154
IMDb: imdb.com/name/nm0168499

Lisa Thrasher
President, Film Production & Distribution
Phone: 323-463-3154
IMDb: imdb.com/name/nm1511212

PRACTICAL PICTURES

2211 Corinth Ave, Suite 303
Los Angeles, CA 90064
Phone: 310-405-7777
Fax: 310-405-7771

Does not accept any unsolicited material.

Jason Koffeman
Creative Executive
IMDb: imdb.com/name/nm1788896

PRANA STUDIOS

1145 N McCadden Place
Los Angeles, CA 90038
Phone: 323-645-6500
Fax: 323-645-6710

Email: info@pranastudios.com
Home Page: pranastudios.com

Project types include Feature Films. Preferred genres include Action, Animation, Comedy, Drama, Family, and Fantasy.

Samir Hoon
President

Kristin Dornig
Co-Creative Director & CEO
IMDb: imdb.com/name/nm0233921

Arish Fyzee
Creative Director
IMDb: imdb.com/name/nm0299564

Danielle Sterling
VP of Development
IMDb: imdb.com/name/nm1306678

Jason Lust
Executive VP of Feature Films & Content Development

PREFERRED CONTENT

6363 Wilshire Blvd, Suite 350
Los Angeles, CA 90048
Phone: 323-782-9193

Email: info@preferredcontent.net
Home Page: preferredcontent.net

Does not accept any unsolicited material. Project types include Feature Films. Preferred genres include Action.

Ross Dinerstein
Partner/Producer
IMDb: imdb.com/name/nm1895871

Kevin Iwashina
Partner/Producer
IMDb: imdb.com/name/nm2250990

Trace Sheehan
Head of Development
IMDb: imdb.com/name/nm2618717

PRETTY MATCHES PRODUCTIONS

1100 Ave of the Americas
G26, Suite 32
New York, NY 10036
Phone: 212-512-5755
Fax: 212-512-5716

IMDb: imdb.com/company/co0173730

Accepts query letter from unproduced, unrepresented writers. Project types include Feature Films and TV. Preferred genres include Comedy, Non-Fiction, Reality, and Romance.

Sarah Parker
President
IMDb: imdb.com/name/nm0000572

Alison Benson
Producer
IMDb: imdb.com/name/nm3929030
Assistant: Matt Nathanson

Benjamin Stark
Director, Development

PRETTY PICTURES

100 Universal City Plaza
Building 2352-A, 3rd Floor
Universal City, CA 91608
Phone: 818-733-0926
Fax: 818-866-0847

Does not accept any unsolicited material. Project types include Feature Films and TV. Preferred genres include Comedy, Drama, Non-Fiction, Romance, and Thriller.

Gail Mutrux
Producer

Tore Schmidt
Creative Executive

PRINCIPATO-YOUNG ENTERTAINMENT

9465 Wilshire Blvd, Suite 900
Beverly Hills, CA 90212
Phone: 310-274-4474
Fax: 310-274-4108

Accepts query letter from unproduced, unrepresented writers. Project types include Feature Films and TV. Preferred genres include Comedy.

Peter Principato
President
Phone: 310-274-4130
Assistant: Max Suchov

Susan Solomon
Manager
Phone: 310-274-4408

Tucker Voorhees
Manager
Phone: 310-432-5992

PROSPECT PARK

2049 Century Park East #2550
Century City, CA 90067
Phone: 310-746-4900
Fax: 310-746-4890

IMDb: imdb.com/company/co0276484

Accepts query letter from unproduced, unrepresented writers via email. Project types include Feature Films and TV. Preferred genres include Drama, Non-Fiction, and Reality.

Paul Frank
Executive Producer/Head, TV
IMDb: imdb.com/name/nm1899773

Jeff Kwatinetz
Executive Producer
IMDb: imdb.com/name/nm0477153

Laurie Ferneau
Director, Development, TV
IMDb: imdb.com/name/nm1017980

PROTOZOA

104 N 7th St
Brooklyn, NY 11211
Phone: 718-388-5280
Fax: 718-388-5425

Home Page: aronofsky.net

Does not accept any unsolicited material. Project types include Feature Films. Preferred genres include Action, Fantasy, Horror, Science Fiction, and Thriller.

Darren Aronofsky
Director/Producer/Writer/CEO
IMDb: imdb.com/name/nm0004716

Ali Mendes
Director Of Development
Email: ali@protozoa.com
IMDb: imdb.com/name/nm4070559

PURE GRASS FILMS LTD.

1st Floor, 16 Manette St
London, W1D 4AR

Email: info@puregrassfilms.com
Home Page: puregrassfilms.com

Accepts query letter from unproduced, unrepresented writers via email. Project types include Feature Films. Preferred genres include Action, Drama, Horror, Non-Fiction, Science Fiction, and Thriller.

Ben Grass
CEO/Producer
IMDb: imdb.com/name/nm2447240

QED INTERNATIONAL

1800 N Highland Ave, 5th Floor
Los Angeles, CA 90028
Phone: 323-785-7900
Fax: 323-785-7901

Email: info@qedintl.com
Home Page: qedintl.com

Accepts scripts from unproduced, unrepresented writers. Project types include Feature Films. Preferred genres include Action, Comedy, Crime, Drama, Fantasy, Horror, Myth, Romance, and Thriller. Established in 2005.

Bill Block
Founder/CEO
IMDb: imdb.com/name/nm1088848

QUADRANT PICTURES

9229 Sunset Blvd, Suite 225
West Hollywood, CA 90069
Phone: 424-244-1860

Email: assistant@quadrantpictures.com
Home Page: quadrantpictures.com

Accepts query letter from unproduced, unrepresented writers via email. Project types include Feature Films and TV. Preferred genres include Action, Drama, Family, Horror, Science Fiction, and Thriller. Established in 2011.

Doug Davison
President/Producer
IMDb: imdb.com/name/nm0205713

John Schwartz
Producer
IMDb: imdb.com/name/nm1862748

RABBITBANDINI PRODUCTIONS

3500 W Olive Ave
Ste 1470
Burbank, CA 91505
Phone: 818-953-7510

Home Page: rabbitbandinifilms.com

Does not accept any unsolicited material. Project types include Feature Films. Preferred genres include Thriller.

James Franco
Executive Partner
IMDb: imdb.com/name/nm0290556

Richie Hill
Producer
Email: richiehill44@gmail.com
IMDb: imdb.com/name/nm2002081

Vince Jolivette
Executive Partner
Email: vince@rabbitbandini.com
IMDb: imdb.com/name/nm0006683

Miles Levy
Executive Partner
Email: miles@jameslevymanagement.com
IMDb: imdb.com/name/nm0506553

RADAR PICTURES

10900 Wilshire Blvd, Suite 1400
Los Angeles, CA 90024
Phone: 310-208-8525
Fax: 310-208-1764

Email: info@radarpictures.com
Home Page: radarpictures.com
IMDb: imdb.com/company/co0023815

Does not accept any unsolicited material. Project types include Feature Films. Preferred genres include Action and Drama.

Ted Field
Chairman
IMDb: imdb.com/name/nm0276059

Thomas Van Dell
Partner/Producer
IMDb: imdb.com/name/nm0886033

@RADICAL MEDIA

435 Hudson St, 6th Floor
New York, NY 10014
Phone: 212-461-1500
Fax: 212-462-1600

1630 12th St
Santa Monica, CA 90404
Phone: 310-664-4500
Fax: 310-664-4600

Email: info@radicalmedia.com
Home Page: radicalmedia.com
IMDb: imdb.com/company/co0029540

Does not accept any unsolicited material.

Justin WIlkes
President of Media & Entertainment
Email: wilkes@radicalmedia.com

Frank Scherma
President
Email: bina@radicalmedia.com

Jon Kamen
Chairman & CEO
Email: hammer@radicalmedia.com

Cathy Shannon
Executive Vice President
Email: shannon@radicalmedia.com

Bob Stein
Head of Production
Email: stein@radicalmedia.com

Sidney Beaumont
Executive Producer
Email: beaumont@radicalmedia.com

Adam Neuhaus
Senior Director & Development
Email: neuhaus@radicalmedia.com

Brent Eveleth
Group Creative Director
Email: eveleth@radicalmedia.com

RAINBOW FILM COMPANY/RAINBOW RELEASING

1301 Montanta Ave, Suite A
Santa Monica, CA 90403
Phone: 310-271-0202
Fax: 310-271-2753

Email: therainbowfilmco@aol.com

Accepts query letter from unproduced, unrepresented writers via email. Project types include Feature Films. Preferred genres include Comedy, Drama, Non-Fiction, and Romance.

Henry Jaglom
President

Sharon Kohn
Vice-President, Distribution

Lauren Beck
Development

RAINMAKER ENTERTAINMENT

200-2025 W Broadway
Vancouver, BC
Canada
V6J 1Z6
Phone: 604-714-2600
Fax: 604-714-2641

Home Page: rainmaker.com
IMDb: imdb.com/company/co0298750
Facebook: facebook.com/RainmakerEnt

Does not accept any unsolicited material. Project types include Feature Films and TV. Preferred genres include Animation, Family, and Fantasy.

Craig Graham
Executive Chairman & CEO

Michael Hefferon
President

Kimberly Dennison
Director of Development

Kylie Ellis
Director of Production

RAINMAKER FILMS INC.

4212 San Felipe St 399
Houston, TX 77027
Phone: 832-287-9372

Email: rainmaker.inc@gmail.com

Accepts query letter from unproduced, unrepresented writers via email. Project types include Feature Films. Preferred genres include Science Fiction.

Grant Gurthie
President - Executive Producer
IMDb: imdb.com/name/nm0349262

RAINSTORM ENTERTAINMENT, INC.

345 N Maple Dr, Suite 105
Beverly Hills, CA 90210
Phone: 818-269-3300
Fax: 310-496-0223

Email: info@rainstormentertainment.com
Home Page: rainstormentertainment.com

Accepts query letter from unproduced, unrepresented writers via email. Project types include Feature Films and TV. Preferred genres include Non-Fiction and Reality.

Alec Rossel
Development Executive
Phone: 818-269-3300
IMDb: imdb.com/name/nm1952377

RALPH WINTER PRODUCTIONS

10201 W Pico Blvd Building 6 suite 1
Los Angeles, CA 90035
Phone: 310-369-4723
Fax: 310-969-0727

Does not accept any unsolicited material. Project types include Feature Films. Preferred genres include Action and Comedy.

Ralph Winter
Founder/Producer
IMDb: imdb.com/name/nm0003515

Susana Zepeda
President
Email: susana.zepeda@fox.com
IMDb: imdb.com/name/nm0954978

RANDOM HOUSE FILMS

1745 Broadway
New York, NY 10019
Phone: 212-782-9000

Home Page: randomhouse.com

Accepts query letter from unproduced, unrepresented writers. Project types include Feature Films. Established in 2007.

Valerie Cates
Executive Story Editor
Phone: 212-782-9000
IMDb: imdb.com/name/nm1161200

Brady Emerson
Story Editor
Phone: 212-782-9000
IMDb: imdb.com/name/nm3031708

Christina Malach
Story Editor
Phone: 212-782-9000
IMDb: imdb.com/name/nm4090138

RAT ENTERTAINMENT

100 Universal City Plz
Bungalow 5196
Universal City, CA 91608
Phone: 818-733-4603
Fax: 818-733-4612

Accepts query letter from unproduced, unrepresented writers. Project types include Feature Films and TV. Preferred genres include Non-Fiction and Reality.

Brett Ratner
Director/Producer/Chairman
Phone: 818-733-4603
IMDb: imdb.com/name/nm0711840
Assistant: Anita S. Chang

John Cheng
Head of Feature Development
Phone: 818-733-4603
IMDb: imdb.com/name/nm1766738

Agustine Calderon
Creative Executive

Jay Stern
President
IMDb: imdb.com/name/nm0827731

RCR MEDIA GROUP

1169 Loma Linda Dr,
Beverly Hills, CA 90210
Phone: 310-273-3888
Fax: 310-273-2888

Email: info@rcrmg.com
Home Page: rcrmediagroup.com
Facebook: facebook.com/rcrmediagroup

Does not accept any unsolicited material. Project types include Feature Films. Preferred genres include Action, Comedy, Crime, Drama, Horror, Romance, Science Fiction, and Thriller.

Eliad Josephson
CEO
IMDb: imdb.com/name/nm4035615

Rui Costa Reis
Chairman
IMDb: imdb.com/name/nm3926066

Ricardo Costa Reis
Producer/Creative Executive
IMDb: imdb.com/name/nm4579160

RCR PICTURES

8840 Wilshire Blvd
Beverly Hills, CA 90211
Phone: 310-358-3234
Fax: 310-358-3109

Accepts query letter from unproduced, unrepresented writers. Project types include Feature Films. Preferred genres include Crime, Drama, Romance, and Science Fiction.

Robin Schorr
Producer
IMDb: imdb.com/name/nm0774908

RECORDED PICTURE COMPANY

24 Hanway St
London W1T 1UH
United Kingdom
Phone: +44 20-7636-2251
Fax: +44 20-7636-2261

Email: rpc@recordedpicture.com
Home Page: recordedpicture.com

Accepts scripts from produced or represented writers. Project types include Feature Films.

Jeremy Thomas
Producer/Chairman
Phone: +44 20 7636 2251
IMDb: imdb.com/name/nm0859016
Assistant: Karin Padgham

Alainee Kent
Senior Development Executive
Phone: +44 20 7636 2251
IMDb: imdb.com/name/nm1599134

Peter Watson
Managing Director
Phone: +44 20 7636 2251
IMDb: imdb.com/name/nm0914838

RED CROWN PRODUCTIONS

630 5th Ave, Suite 2505
New York, NY 10111
Phone: 212-355-9200
Fax: 212-719-7029

Email: info@redcrownproductions.com
Home Page: redcrownproductions.com

Does not accept any unsolicited material. Project types include Feature Films. Preferred genres include Comedy and Drama. Established in 2010.

Riva Marker
Head of Production & Development
Email: riva@redcrownproductions.com
IMDb: imdb.com/name/nm1889450

Alish Erman
Creative Executive
Email: alish@redcrownproductions.com
IMDb: imdb.com/name/nm2289542

Daniel Crown
Founder/Producer
Phone: 212-355-9200
Email: dcrown@crownnyc.com
IMDb: imdb.com/name/nm3259054

RED GIANT MEDIA

535 5th Ave, 5th Floor
New York, NY 10017
Phone: 212-989-7200
Fax: 212-937-3505

Email: info@redgiantmedia.com
Home Page: redgiantmedia.com

Does not accept any unsolicited material. Project types include Feature Films. Preferred genres include Science Fiction. Established in 2008.

Kevin Fox
Executive Producer/Writer

Isen Robbins
Producer

Aimee Schoof
Producer

RED GRANITE PICTURES

9255 Sunset Blvd, Suite 710
Los Angeles, CA 90069
Phone: 310-703-5800
Fax: 310-246-3849

IMDb: imdb.com/company/co0325207

Does not accept any unsolicited material. Project types include Feature Films. Preferred genres include Drama.

Riza Aziz
CEO
IMDb: imdb.com/name/nm4265383

Joe Gatta
President of Production
IMDb: imdb.com/name/nm2211910

RED HEN PRODUCTIONS

3607 W Magnolia
Ste. L
Burbank, CA 91505
Phone: 818-563-3600
Fax: 818-787-6637

Home Page: redhenprods.com

Accepts query letter from unproduced, unrepresented writers. Preferred genres include Drama and Thriller.

Stuart Gordon
Director/Writer/Producer
Phone: 818-563-3600
IMDb: imdb.com/name/nm0002340

RED HOUR FILMS

629 N La Brea Ave
Los Angeles, CA 90036
Phone: 323-602-5000
Fax: 323-602 5001

Home Page: redhourfilms.com

Does not accept any unsolicited material. Project types include Feature Films and TV. Preferred genres include Action, Comedy, Family, Fantasy, and Science Fiction.

Ben Stiller
Writer/Director/Producer
IMDb: imdb.com/name/nm0001774

Conor Welch
Director of Development
Email: conor@redhourfilms.com
IMDb: imdb.com/name/nm3137428

Robin Mabrito
Story Editor
Email: robin@redhourfilms.com
IMDb: imdb.com/name/nm3142663

RED OM FILMS, INC.

3000 Olympic Blvd
Building 3, Suite 2330
Santa Monica, CA 90404
Phone: 310-594-3467

Does not accept any unsolicited material. Project types include Feature Films and TV. Preferred genres include Action, Comedy, Drama, and Family.

Julia Roberts
Actress/Producer
IMDb: imdb.com/name/nm0000210

Lisa Gillian
Producer
IMDb: imdb.com/name/nm0731359

Philip Rose
Producer
IMDb: imdb.com/name/nm0741615

RED PLANET PICTURES

13 Doolittle Mill
Froghall Rd
Ampthill, Bedfordshire MK45 2ND
UK
Phone: +44 (0)1525 408 970
Fax: +44 (0)1525 408 971

Email: info@redplanetpictures.co.uk
Home Page: redplanetpictures.co.uk

Does not accept any unsolicited material. Project types include TV. Preferred genres include Crime and Drama.

Simon Winstone
Director of Development
Email: simonwinstone@redplanetpictures.co.uk
IMDb: imdb.com/name/nm0935654

RED WAGON ENTERTAINMENT

10202 W Washington Blvd
Hepburn Building West
Culver City, CA 90232-3195
Phone: 310-244-4466
Fax: 310-244-1480

Does not accept any unsolicited material. Project types include Feature Films and TV. Preferred genres include Animation, Drama, Fantasy, and Horror.

Douglas Wick
Producer
Phone: 310 244 4466
IMDb: imdb.com/name/nm0926824

Lucy Fisher
Producer
Phone: 310 244 4466
IMDb: imdb.com/name/nm0279651

Rachel Shane
Executive Vice-President
Phone: 310 244 4466
IMDb: imdb.com/name/nm1247594

REGENCY ENTERPRISES

10201 W Pico Blvd
Building 12
Los Angeles, CA 90035
Phone: 310-369-8300
Fax: 310-969-0470

Email: info@newregency.com
Home Page: newregency.com
IMDb: imdb.com/company/co0021592

Accepts query letter from unproduced, unrepresented writers via email. Project types include Feature Films.

Michelle Kroes
Director, Feature & Literary Development
IMDb: imdb.com/name/nm3129676

Ryan Horrigan
Director of Development
IMDb: imdb.com/name/nm1673839

REGENT ENTERTAINMENT

10940 Wilshire Blvd, Suite 1600
Los Angeles, CA 90024
Phone: 310-806-4290
Fax: 310 806 6351

Email: info@regententertainment.com
Home Page: regententertainment.com
IMDb: imdb.com/company/co0045895

Accepts query letter from unproduced, unrepresented writers via email. Project types include Feature Films and TV. Preferred genres include Action, Drama, Horror, and Science Fiction.

David Millbern
Director of Development
Phone: 310-806-4290
IMDb: imdb.com/name/nm0587778

Roxana Vatan
IMDb: imdb.com/name/nm2985872

REHAB ENTERTAINMENT

1416 N La Brea Ave
Hollywood, CA 90028
Phone: 323-645-6444
Fax: 323-645-6445

Email: info@rehabent.com
Home Page: rehabent.com

Accepts query letter from unproduced, unrepresented writers via email. Project types include Feature Films.

John Hyde
President

Brett Coker
Production Executive

REINER/GREISMAN

335 N Maple Dr, Suite 350
Beverly Hills, CA 90210
Phone: 310-285-2300
Fax: 310-285-2345

Accepts query letter from unproduced, unrepresented writers. Project types include Feature Films. Preferred genres include Comedy and Drama.

Rob Reiner
Director/Producer
Phone: 310-285-2328
IMDb: imdb.com/name/nm0001661
Assistant: Pam Jones

Alan Greisman
Producer
Phone: 310-205-2766

Pam Jones
Assistant to Rob Reiner
Phone: 310-285-2352

RELATIVITY MEDIA, LLC

9242 Beverly Blvd, Suite 300
Beverly Hills, CA 90210
Phone: 310-724-7700
Fax: 310-724-7701

Accepts query letter from produced or represented writers. Project types include Feature Films, TV, and Commercials. Preferred genres include Non-Fiction and Reality.

Jonathan Karsh
Sr. Vice-President, Creative Affairs

Julie Link
Sr. Vice-President, Development

RELEVANT ENTERTAINMENT GROUP

10323 Santa Monica Blvd
Ste 101
Los Angeles, CA 90025
Phone: 310-277-0853

Project types include Feature Films and TV. Preferred genres include Comedy.

REMEMBER DREAMING, LLC

8252 1/2 Santa Monica Blvd, Suite B
West Hollywood, CA 90046
Phone: 323-654-3333

Accepts query letter from unproduced, unrepresented writers. Project types include Feature Films and TV. Preferred genres include Non-Fiction and Reality.

Stan Spry
President

Courtney Brin
Director, Production & Development
Email: courtney@freefall-films.com

RENAISSANCE PICTURES

315 S Beverly Dr, Suite 216
Beverly Hills, CA 90210
Phone: 310-785-3900
Fax: 310-785-9176

Accepts query letter from unproduced, unrepresented writers. Project types include Feature Films and TV. Preferred genres include Action, Drama, Fantasy, and Horror.

Sam Raimi
Director/Executive Producer

J.R. Young
Producer, Creative Executive

RENART FILMS

135 Grand St.
3rd Floor
New York, NY 10013
Phone: 212-274-8224
Fax: 212-274-8229

Email: info@renartfilms.com
Home Page: renartfilms.com

Accepts query letter from produced or represented writers. Project types include Feature Films. Preferred genres include Comedy, Drama, and Romance.

Tim Duff
President
Email: tim@renartfilms.com
IMDb: imdb.com/name/nm2178779

TJ Federico
EVP of Production
Email: tj@renartfilms.com

Julie Christeas
EVP of Development & Production
Email: julie@renartfilms.com
IMDb: imdb.com/name/nm2184127

Dan Schechter
EVP of Development
Email: dan@renartfilms.com

Caroline Dillon
Creative Director
Email: caroline@renartfilms.com
IMDb: imdb.com/name/nm0226974

RENEE MISSEL PRODUCTIONS

2376 Adrian St, Suite A
Newbury Park, CA 91320
Phone: 310-463-0638
Fax: 805-669-4511

Email: fi lmtao@aol.com

Accepts query letter from unproduced, unrepresented writers via email. Project types include Feature Films. Established in 1983.

Renee Missel
Producer

Bridget Stone
Story Editor

RENEE VALENTE PRODUCTIONS

13547 Ventura Blvd, #195
Sherman Oaks, CA 91423
Phone: 310-472-5342

Email: valenteprod@aol.com

Accepts query letter from unproduced, unrepresented writers via email. Project types include Feature Films and TV.

Renee Valente
Executive Producer

RENEGADE ANIMATION, INC.

111 E Broadway, Suite 208
Glendale, CA 91205
Phone: 818-551-2351
Fax: 818-551-2350

Email: contactus@renegadeanimation.com
Home Page: renegadeanimation.com

Accepts query letter from unproduced, unrepresented writers via email. Project types include TV.

Ashley Postlewaite
Vice-President/Executive Producer

Darrell Van Citters
President/Direct

RENFIELD PRODUCTIONS

c/o Th e Lot
1041 N Formosa Ave
Writer's Building, Suite 321
West Hollywood, CA 90046
Phone: 323-850-3905
Fax: 323-850-3907

Email: development@renfieldproductions.com
Home Page: renfieldproductions.com

Accepts query letter from unproduced, unrepresented writers via email. Project types include TV. Preferred genres include Action, Animation, Comedy, Drama, Family, Horror, Non-Fiction, and Reality.

Joe Dante
Director/Producer
Phone: 323-850-3905
IMDb: imdb.com/name/nm0001102

T.L. Kittle
Director, Development
Phone: 323-850-3905
IMDb: imdb.com/name/nm1473622

Mark Alan
Development Executive
Phone: 323-850-3905
IMDb: imdb.com/name/nm1591345

REVEILLE, LLC/SHINE INTERNATIONAL

1741 Ivar Ave
Los Angeles, CA 90028
Phone: 323-790-8000
Fax: 323-790-8399

Does not accept any unsolicited material. Project types
include TV. Preferred genres include Non-Fiction and
Reality.

Todd Cohen
Vice-President, Domestic Scripted TV

Rob Cohen
Vice-President Creative Affairs

Carolyn Bernstein
Executive Vice-President, Scripted TV
IMDb: imdb.com/name/nm3009190

REVELATIONS ENTERTAINMENT

1221 Second St
4th Floor
Santa Monica, CA 90401
Phone: 310-394-3131
Fax: 310-394-3133

Email: info@revelationsent.com
Home Page: revelationsent.com

Does not accept any unsolicited material. Project types
include Feature Films and TV. Preferred genres
include Action, Detective, Drama, and Family.

Morgan Freeman
President/Actor/Producer
Phone: 310-394-3131
IMDb: imdb.com/name/nm0000151

Lori McCreary
CEO/Producer
Phone: 310-394-3131
IMDb: imdb.com/name/nm0566975

Tracy Mercer
Vice-President, Development
Phone: 310-394-3131
IMDb: imdb.com/name/nm0580312

REVOLUTION FILMS

9-A Dallington St
London EC1V 0BQ
UK
Phone: +44-20-7566-0700

Email: email@revolution-films.com
Home Page: revolution-films.com
IMDb: mdb.com/company/co0103733

Does not accept any unsolicited material. Project types
include Feature Films. Preferred genres include Action,
Comedy, Drama, Non-Fiction, Period, and Thriller.

Michael Winterbottom
Producer
IMDb: imdb.com/name/nm0935863

Andrew Eaton
Producer
IMDb: imdb.com/name/nm0247787

RHINO FILMS

10501 Wilshire Blvd, Suite 814
Los Angeles, CA 90024
Phone: 310-441-6557
Fax: 310-441-6584

Email: contact@rhinofilms.com
Home Page: rhinofilms.com

Accepts query letter from unproduced, unrepresented
writers via email. Project types include Feature Films.

Stephen Nemeth
CEO
Email: stephennemeth@rhinofi lms.com
IMDb: imdb.com/name/nm0625932

Betsy Stahl
Email: betsystahl@rhinofi lms.com
IMDb: imdb.com/name/nm0821439

RHOMBUS MEDIA

99 Spadina Ave
Ste 600
Toronto, ON M5V 3P8
Canada
Phone: 416-971-7856
Fax: 416-971-9647

Email: info@rhombusmedia.com
Home Page: rhombusmedia.com

Does not accept any unsolicited material. Project types include Feature Films. Preferred genres include Action, Comedy, Crime, Horror, Science Fiction, and Thriller.

Fraser Ash
Assosiate Producer
IMDb: imdb.com/name/nm4350218

Kevin Krikst
Assosiate Producer
IMDb: imdb.com/name/nm2844322

Larry Weistein
Co-Founder
IMDb: imdb.com/name/nm0918452

RHYTHM & HUES

2100 E Grand Ave
El Segundo, CA 90245
Phone: 310-448-7500
Fax: 310-448-7600

Email: webmaster@rhythm.com
Home Page: rhythm.com

Does not accept any unsolicited material. Project types include Feature Films. Preferred genres include Action, Comedy, Crime, Drama, Family, Fantasy, Romance, and Science Fiction.

Lee Burger
President
IMDb: imdb.com/name/nm0074260

Venecia Duran
Director of Development
IMDb: imdb.com/name/nm1330358

Heather Jennings
Production
IMDb: imdb.com/name/nm0997142

Pauline Ts'o
Vice President of Development
IMDb: imdb.com/name/nm1173396

RICE & BEANS PRODUCTIONS

30 N Raymond, Suite 605
Pasadena, CA 91103

Phone: 626-792-9171
Fax: 626-792-9171

Email: vin88@pacbell.net

Accepts query letter from unproduced, unrepresented writers via email. Project types include Feature Films and TV. Preferred genres include Comedy and Drama.

Vince Cheung
Writer/Producer
IMDb: imdb.com/name/nm0156588

Ben Montanio
Writer/Producer
IMDb: imdb.com/name/nm0598996

RICHE PRODUCTIONS

9336 W Washington Blvd
Above Stage 3 West, Room 305
Culver City, CA 90232
Phone: 310-202-4850

Accepts query letter from unproduced, unrepresented writers. Project types include Feature Films and TV. Preferred genres include Action and Family.

Alan Riche
Partner
Assistant: Adrienne Novelly

Peter Riche
Partner

RIVE GAUCHE TELEVISION

15442 Ventura Blvd.
Ste. 101
Sherman Oaks, CA 91403
Phone: 818-784-9912
Fax: 818-784-9916

Home Page: rgitv.com

Project types include Feature Films. Preferred genres include Documentary.

Mark Rafalowski
President of Production
IMDb: imdb.com/name/nm2883793

Jon Kramer
CEO
IMDb: imdb.com/name/nm2883855

RIVER ROAD ENTERTAINMENT

2000 Ave of the Stars, Suite 620-N
Los Angeles, CA 90067
Phone: 213-253-4610
Fax: 310-843-9551

Home Page: riverroadentertainment.com

Does not accept any unsolicited material. Project types include Feature Films and TV. Preferred genres include Comedy, Drama, Non-Fiction, and Reality.

Sarah Hammer
Head, Creative Affairs
IMDb: imdb.com/name/nm3741550

ROADSIDE ATTRACTIONS

7920 Sunset Blvd
Suite 402
Los Angeles, CA 90046
Phone: 323-882-8490
Fax: 323-882-8493

Email: info@roadsideattractions.com
Home Page: roadsideattractions.com

Accepts query letter from produced or represented writers. Project types include Feature Films. Preferred genres include Comedy, Drama, Horror, and Thriller.

Howard Cohen
Co-President
IMDb: imdb.com/name/nm1383518

Eric d'Arbeloff
Co-President
IMDb: imdb.com/name/nm0195396

Gail Blumenthal
SVP of Distribution
IMDb: imdb.com/name/nm0089812

Vita Lusty
Office Manager

ROBERT CORT PRODUCTIONS

1041 N Formosa Ave
Administration Building, Suite 196
West Hollywood, CA 90046
Phone: 323-850-2644
Fax: 323-850-2634

Accepts query letter from unproduced, unrepresented writers. Project types include Feature Films and TV. Preferred genres include Comedy and Drama.

Robert Cort
Producer
IMDb: imdb.com/name/nm0181202
Assistant: Maritza Berta

Eric Hetzel
Vice-President, Production
IMDb: imdb.com/name/nm0381796

ROBERT GREENWALD PRODUCTIONS

10510 Culver Blvd
Culver City, CA 90232-3400
Phone: 310-204-0404
Fax: 310-204-0174

Email: info@rgpinc.com
Home Page: rgpinc.com

Does not accept any unsolicited material. Project types include Feature Films and TV. Preferred genres include Comedy, Drama, and Non-Fiction.

Robert Greenwald
Producer/Director
IMDb: imdb.com/name/nm0339254

Philip Kleinbart
Producer/Executive Vice-President
IMDb: imdb.com/name/nm0459036

ROBERT LAWRENCE PRODUCTIONS

1810 14th St
Ste 102
Santa Monica, CA 90404
Phone: 1 310 399 2762

Accepts query letter from unproduced, unrepresented writers. Project types include Feature Films. Preferred genres include Action, Comedy, and Drama.

Robert Lawrence
President
IMDb: imdb.com/name/nm0492994

ROBERTS/DAVID FILMS, INC.

100 Universal City Plaza
Bldg. 1320
Universal City, CA 91608
Phone: 818-733-2143
Fax: 818-733-1551

Does not accept any unsolicited material. Project types include Feature Films and TV. Preferred genres include Comedy, Non-Fiction, and Reality.

Mark Roberts
Partner
Email: mark@robertsdavid.com

Lorena David
Partner
Email: lorena@robertsdavid.com

ROBERT SIMONDS COMPANY

10202 Washington Blvd
Stage 6, 7th Floor
Culver City, CA 90232
Phone: 310-244-5222
Fax: 310-244-0348

Home Page: rscfilms.com

Does not accept any unsolicited material. Project types include Feature Films. Preferred genres include Action, Comedy, Family, and Thriller. Established in 2012.

Robert Simonds
CEO
Email: rasst@rscfilms.com
IMDb: imdb.com/name/nm0800465
Assistant: Jennifer Jiang

ROCKLIN/FAUST

10390 Santa Monica Blvd, Suite 200
Los Angeles, CA 90025
Phone: 310-789-3066
Fax: 310-789-3060

Does not accept any unsolicited material. Project types include Feature Films and TV. Preferred genres

include Animation, Comedy, Drama, Non-Fiction, and Reality.

Blye Faust
Producer
IMDb: imdb.com/name/nm1421308

ROOM 101, INC.

9677 Charleville Blvd.
Beverly Hills 90212
Phone: 310 271 1130

Accepts query letter from unproduced, unrepresented writers. Project types include Feature Films and TV. Preferred genres include Crime, Drama, and Horror.

Steven Schneider
Producer
IMDb: imdb.com/name/nm2124081

ROOM 9 ENTERTAINMENT

9229 Sunset Blvd, Suite 505
West Hollywood, CA 90069
Phone: 310-651-2001
Fax: 310-651-2010

Email: info@room9entertainment.com
Home Page: room9entertainment.com

Does not accept any unsolicited material. Project types include Feature Films and TV. Preferred genres include Drama and Non-Fiction.

David Sacks
CEO
IMDb: imdb.com/name/nm1616294

Michael Newman
Partner, Co-President
IMDb: imdb.com/name/nm1616293

Daniel Brunt
Partner, Co-President
IMDb: imdb.com/name/nm1616292

ROSA ENTERTAINMENT

7288 Sunset Blvd, Suite 208
Los Angeles, CA 90046
Phone: 310-470-3506
Fax: 310-470-3509

Email: info@rosaentertainment.com
Home Page: rosaentertainment.com

Does not accept any unsolicited material. Project types include Feature Films and TV. Preferred genres include Comedy and Drama.

Sidney Sherman
Producer
Email: sidney@rosaentertainment.com
IMDb: imdb.com/name/nm0792587

ROSEROCK FILMS

4000 Warner Blvd
Building 81
Burbank, CA 91522
Phone: 818-954-7528

Does not accept any unsolicited material. Project types include Feature Films.

Hunt Lowry
Producer
IMDb: imdb.com/name/nm0523324

Patricia Reed
Director of Development
Phone: 818-954-7673
IMDb: imdb.com/name/nm0715623

ROTH FILMS

2900 W Olympic Blvd
Santa Monica, CA 90404
Phone: 310-255-7000

Accepts query letter from unproduced, unrepresented writers. Project types include Feature Films.

Joe Roth
Producer
IMDb: imdb.com/name/nm0005387

Palak Patel
President, Production
IMDb: imdb.com/name/nm2026983

ROUGH HOUSE

1722 Whitley Ave
Hollywood, CA 90028
Phone: 323-469-3161

Accepts scripts from produced or represented writers. Project types include Feature Films. Preferred genres include Drama and Romance.

David Green
Director/Writer/Producer
IMDb: imdb.com/name/nm0337773

ROUTE ONE FILMS

1041 N Formosa Ave
Santa Monica East #200
West Hollywood, CA 90046
Phone: 323-850-3855
Fax: 323-850-3866

Home Page: routeonefilms.com

Does not accept any unsolicited material. Project types include Feature Films.

Jay Stern
Founder/Partner/Producer
IMDb: imdb.com/name/nm0827731

Russell Levine
Founder/Partner/Producer
IMDb: imdb.com/name/nm4149902

Chip Diggins
Founder/Partner/Producer
IMDb: imdb.com/name/nm0226505

RUBICON ENTERTAINMENT

3406 Tareco Dr.
Los Angeles, CA 90068
Phone: 323-850-9200
Fax: 323-378-5584

Email: submissions@rubiconentertainment.com
Home Page: rubiconentertainment.com

Accepts query letter from unproduced, unrepresented writers via email. Project types include Feature Films. Preferred genres include Comedy and Drama.

RUNAWAY PRODUCTIONS

7336 Santa Monica Blvd.
Ste 751
West Hollywood, CA 90046
Phone: 310-801-0885

Email: lindapalmer@runawayproductions.tv
Home Page: runawayproductions.tv

Project types include Feature Films and TV. Preferred genres include Comedy.

Linda Palmer
Producer, Writer
IMDb: imdb.com/name/nm1881313

Todd Wade
Producer, Director
IMDb: imdb.com/name/nm0905520

RYAN MURPHY PRODUCTIONS

5555 Melrose Ave Modular Building, First Floor
Los Angeles, CA 90038
Phone: 323-956-2408
Fax: 323-862-2235

IMDb: imdb.com/company/co0156994

Does not accept any unsolicited material. Project types include Feature Films and TV. Preferred genres include Comedy, Documentary, Drama, Horror, Non-Fiction, Science Fiction, and Thriller. Established in 2008.

Ryan Murphy
Principal
IMDb: imdb.com/name/nm0614682

Dante Di Loreto
President
IMDb: imdb.com/name/nm0223994

SACRED DOGS ENTERTAINMENT LLC

311 N Robertson Blvd.
Ste. 249
Beverly Hills, CA 90211
Phone: 323-656-6900

Email: victory@sacreddogs.com
Home Page: sacreddogs.com

Project types include Feature Films. Preferred genres include Documentary.

Arden Brotman
Phone: 323-656-6900
IMDb: imdb.com/name/nm2231224

Victory Tischler-Blue
Owner
Phone: 323-656-6900
IMDb: imdb.com/name/nm0089548

SAFRAN COMPANY

8748 Holloway Dr
West Hollywood, CA 90069
Phone: 310-278-1450

Does not accept any unsolicited material. Project types include Feature Films and TV. Preferred genres include Comedy and Family. Established in 2006.

Peter Safran
Manager/Producer
IMDb: imdb.com/name/nm0755911

Tom Drumm
Manager
IMDb: imdb.com/name/nm1619641

SALTIRE ENTERTAINMENT

6352 De Longpre Ave
Los Angeles, CA 90028

IMDb: imdb.com/company/co0104114

Does not accept any unsolicited material. Project types include Feature Films. Preferred genres include Drama, Myth, and Science Fiction.

Stuart Pollok
Producer
IMDb: imdb.com/name/nm0689415

SALTY FEATURES

682 Ave of the Americas, Suite 3
New York, NY 10010
Phone: 212-924-1601
Fax: 212-924-2306

Email: info@saltyfeatures.com
Home Page: saltyfeatures.com

Accepts query letter from unproduced, unrepresented writers via email. Project types include Feature Films and TV. Preferred genres include Non-Fiction and Reality.

Yael Melamede
Producer
IMDb: imdb.com/name/nm0577336

Eva Kolodner
Co-Founder, Producer
IMDb: imdb.com/name/nm0464286

SALVATORE/ORNSTON PRODUCTIONS

5650 Camellia Ave
North Hollywood, CA 91601
Phone: 310-466-8980
Fax: 818-752-9321

Accepts query letter from produced or represented writers. Project types include Feature Films. Preferred genres include Action, Animation, Comedy, Crime, Drama, Romance, and Thriller.

Richard Salvatore
Executive
IMDb: imdb.com/name/nm0759363

David E. Ornston
Executive
IMDb: imdb.com/name/nm0650361

SAMUELSON PRODUCTIONS LIMITED

10401 Wyton Dr
Los Angeles, CA 90024-2527
Phone: 310-208-1000
Fax: 323-315-5188

Email: info@samuelson.la
Home Page: samuelson.la

Does not accept any unsolicited material. Project types include Feature Films and TV. Preferred genres include Action, Comedy, and Drama.

Peter Samuelson
Owner
IMDb: imdb.com/name/nm0006873
Assistant: Brian Casey

Saryl Hirsch
Controller
IMDb: imdb.com/name/nm1950244

Marc Samuelson
IMDb: imdb.com/name/nm0760555

Renato Celani
IMDb: imdb.com/name/nm1954607

Josie Law
IMDb: imdb.com/name/nm1656468

SANDBAR PICTURES

1145 N. McCadden Place
Hollywood, CA 90038
Phone: 323-337-1183
Fax: 323-337-1434

760 Market St, Suite 507
San Francisco, CA 94102
Phone: 415-398-0780
Fax: 415-398-1598

Email: info@sandbarpictures.net
Home Page: sandbarpictures.net
IMDb: imdb.com/company/co0171098

Does not accept any unsolicited material. Project types include Feature Films. Preferred genres include Drama, Horror, and Thriller.

Greg Little
Founder
IMDb: imdb.com/name/nm0514571

Lizzie Friedman
Founder
IMDb: imdb.com/name/nm0295288

SANDER/MOSES PRODUCTIONS, INC.

c/o Disney
500 S Buena Vista St
Animation Building 1 E 13
Burbank, CA 91521-1657
Phone: 818-560-4500
Fax: 818-860-6284

Email: info@sandermoses.com
Home Page: sandermoses.com

Accepts query letter from unproduced, unrepresented writers via email. Project types include Feature Films, TV, and Commercials. Preferred genres include Drama, Non-Fiction, and Reality.

Ian Sander
Executive Producer/Writer/Director
IMDb: imdb.com/name/nm0761401

Kim Moses
Executive Producer/Writer/Director
IMDb: imdb.com/name/nm0608593

SANITSKY COMPANY

9200 Sunset Blvd.
Los Angeles, CA 90069
Phone: 310-274-0120
Fax: 310-274-1455

Does not accept any unsolicited material. Project types include TV. Preferred genres include Drama.

Larry Sanitsky
President
IMDb: imdb.com/name/nm0762792

SCARLET FIRE ENTERTAINMENT

561 28th Ave
Venice, CA 90291
Phone: 310-302-1001
Fax: 310-302-1002

Does not accept any unsolicited material. Project types include Feature Films and TV. Preferred genres include Comedy.

Allen Loeb
Producer
Phone: 310-302-1001
IMDb: imdb.com/name/nm1615610

Steven Pearl
Producer
Phone: 310-302-1001
IMDb: imdb.com/name/nm0669093

SCORE PRODUCTIONS INC.

2401 Main St.
Santa Monica, CA 90405
Phone: 604-868-7377

Email: score@scoreproductions.com
Home Page: scoreproductions.com

Accepts query letter from produced or represented writers. Project types include Feature Films and TV. Preferred genres include Detective, Drama, Fantasy, and Science Fiction.

SCOTT FREE PRODUCTIONS

634 N La Peer Dr
Los Angeles, CA 90069
Phone: 310-659-1577
Fax: 310-659-1377

Does not accept any unsolicited material. Project types include Feature Films and TV. Preferred genres include Action, Animation, Crime, Detective, Drama, Non-Fiction, Reality, and Thriller.

Ridley Scott
Co-Chairman
IMDb: imdb.com/name/nm0000631
Assistant: Nancy Ryan

David Zucker
President, TV
IMDb: imdb.com/name/nm0001878
Assistant: Mark Pfeffer

Maresa Pullman
Director, Film Development

SCOTT RUDIN PRODUCTIONS

120 W 45th St
10th Floor
New York, NY 10036
Phone: 212-704-4600

Accepts query letter from unproduced, unrepresented writers. Project types include Feature Films. Established in 1993.

Scott Rudin
Producer
Phone: 212-704-4600
IMDb: imdb.com/name/nm0748784

Eli Bush
Executive
Phone: 212-704-4600
Email: eli@scottrudinprod.com
IMDb: imdb.com/name/nm4791912

Julie Oh
Executive
Phone: 212-704-4600
IMDb: imdb.com/name/nm4791935

SCOTT SANDERS PRODUCTIONS

500 S Buena Vista Dr
Animation Building 3C-1
Burbank, CA 91521
Phone: 818-560-6350
Fax: 818-560-3541

Home Page: scottsandersproductions.com

Accepts query letter from unproduced, unrepresented writers. Project types include Feature Films and TV.

Scott Sanders
President, CEO
IMDb: imdb.com/name/nm0761712
Assistant: Jaime Quiroz

Bryan Kalfus
Creative Executive, Film
IMDb: imdb.com/name/nm0435729

SCREEN DOOR ENTERTAINMENT

15223 Burbank Blvd.
Sherman Oaks, CA 91411
Phone: 818-781-5600
Fax: 818-781-5601

Email: info@sdetv.com
Home Page: sdetv.com

Accepts query letter from unproduced, unrepresented writers. Project types include TV. Preferred genres include Reality. Established in 2001.

M. Alessandra Ascoli
Director of Development & Programming
Email: generalinfo@sdetv.com
IMDb: imdb.com/name/nm0038529

Joel Rizor
President
IMDb: imdb.com/name/nm1381432

Dave Shikiar
Co-Executive Producer

SCREEN GEMS

10202 W Washington Blvd
Culver City, CA 90232
Phone: 310-244-4000
Fax: 310-244-2037

IMDb: imdb.com/company/co0010568

Does not accept any unsolicited material. Project types include Feature Films, Short Films, and TV. Preferred genres include Action, Comedy, Documentary, Drama, Fantasy, Horror, Reality, Romance, Science Fiction, and Thriller. Established in 1926.

Clint Culpepper
President
IMDb: imdb.com/name/nm0191695

Pamela Kunath
Executive Vice President (General Manager)
IMDb: imdb.com/name/nm2242666

Loren Schwartz
Executive Vice President (Marketing)
IMDb: imdb.com/name/nm2817219

Scott Strauss
Executive Vice President of Production
IMDb: imdb.com/name/nm0833873

James Lopez
Senior Vice President of Production
IMDb: imdb.com/name/nm5144603

Eric Paquette
Senior Vice President of Development
IMDb: imdb.com/name/nm1789841

Glenn Gainor
Head of Physical Production/ Senior Vice President
IMDb: imdb.com/name/nm0004636

Carol Smithson
Vice President of Business

SE8 GROUP

9560 Cedarbrook Dr
Beverly Hills, CA 90210
Phone: 310-285-6090
Fax: 310-285-6097

Accepts query letter from unproduced, unrepresented writers. Project types include Feature Films. Preferred genres include Drama and Thriller.

Gary Oldman
Actor/Producer
IMDb: imdb.com/name/nm0000198

Douglas Urbanski
Producer
IMDb: imdb.com/name/nm0881703

SECOND AND 10TH INC.

51 MacDougal St, Suite 383
New York, NY 10012
Phone: 347-882-4493

Does not accept any unsolicited material. Project types include Feature Films. Preferred genres include Drama.

Anne Carey
Producer
IMDb: imdb.com/name/nm0136904

Shani Geva
Creative Executive
IMDb: imdb.com/name/nm2802616

SEE FILM INC./LAGO FILM GMBH

6399 Wilshire Blvd, Suite 1002
Los Angeles, CA 90048
Phone: 310-653-7826

Email: lago@lagofilm.com
Home Page: lagofilm.com

Does not accept any unsolicited material. Project types include Feature Films. Preferred genres include Comedy, Drama, and Horror.

Marco Mehlitz
Producer

Luane Gauer
Project Manager

SEISMIC PICTURES

8899 Beverly Blvd, Suite 810
Los Angeles, CA 90048
Phone: 213-245-1180

Email: info@seismicpictures.com
Home Page: seismicpictures.com

Does not accept any unsolicited material. Project types include Feature Films and TV. Preferred genres include Comedy, Drama, Non-Fiction, and Reality.

Robert Schwartz
Producer/President
IMDb: imdb.com/name/nm0777412

SENART FILMS

555 W 25th St, 4th Floor
New York, NY 10001
Phone: 212-406-9610
Fax: 212-406-9581

Email: info@senartfilms.com
Home Page: senartfilms.com

Does not accept any unsolicited material. Project types include Feature Films and TV. Preferred genres include Drama, Non-Fiction, and Reality.

Robert May
Producer
IMDb: imdb.com/name/nm1254338

SERAPHIM FILMS

c/o Sheryl Petersen/APA
405 S Beverly Dr
Beverly Hills, CA 90212
Phone: 310-888-4200 or 310-246-0050

Email: assistant@seraphimfilms.com
Home Page: seraphimfilms.com

Accepts query letter from unproduced, unrepresented writers via email. Project types include Feature Films. Preferred genres include Animation, Drama, Fantasy, and Horror.

Clive Barker
President

Joe Daley
Executive Vice-President, Produ

Anthony DiBlasi
Writer/Director

SERENDIPITY POINT FILMS

9 Price St
Toronto, ON M4W 1Z1
Canada
Phone: 416-960-0300
Fax: 416-960-8656

Home Page: serendipitypoint.com

Does not accept any unsolicited material. Project types include Feature Films and TV. Preferred genres include Action, Comedy, Drama, and Thriller.

Robert Lantos
Producer
Assistant: Cherri Campbell

Wendy Saffer
Head, Publicity & Marketing

SERENDIPITY PRODUCTIONS, INC.

15260 Ventura Blvd, Suite 1040
Sherman Oaks, CA 91403
Phone: 818-789-3035
Fax: 818-235-0150

Does not accept any unsolicited material. Project types include Feature Films and TV. Preferred genres include Drama, Horror, and Non-Fiction.

Daniel Heffner
Producer/Principal
Email: danheffner@earthlink.net
IMDb: imdb.com/name/nm0004527

Ketura Kestin
Email: keturak@gmail.com
IMDb: imdb.com/name/nm3109585

SEVEN ARTS PICTURES

8439 Sunset Blvd 4th Floor
Los Angeles, CA 90069
Phone: 323-372-3080
Fax: 323-372-3088

Email: info@7artspictures.com
Home Page: 7artspictures.com

Does not accept any unsolicited material. Project types include Feature Films. Preferred genres include Comedy, Drama, Science Fiction, and Thriller.

Peter Hoffman
CEO
IMDb: imdb.com/name/nm0389056
Assistant: Linda Silverthorn

Susan Hoffman
Producer
IMDb: imdb.com/name/nm1624597

SHADOWCATCHER ENTERTAINMENT

4701 SW Admiral Way
Box 32
Seattle, WA 98116
Phone: 206-328-6266
Fax: 206-447-1462

Email: kate@shadowcatcherent.com
Home Page: shadowcatcherent.com

Accepts query letter from unproduced, unrepresented writers via email. Project types include Feature Films, TV, and Theater. Preferred genres include Animation, Comedy, Drama, Non-Fiction, and Reality.

David Skinner
Executive Producer
Assistant: Kate Wickstrom

Tom Gorai
Producer

Robin Gurland
Producer

SHAFTESBURY FILMS

163 Queen St East Suite 100
Toronto, ON, Canada, M5A 1S1
Phone: 416-363-1411
Fax: 416-363-1428

4370 Tujunga Ave Suite 300
Studio City, CA 91604
Phone: 818-505-3361

Home Page: shaftesbury.ca

Does not accept any unsolicited material. Project types include Feature Films and TV. Preferred genres include Action, Animation, Comedy, Drama, Family, Romance, and Thriller. Established in 1987.

Christina Jennings
Chairman & CEO
Email: cjennings@shaftesbury.ca
IMDb: imdb.com/name/nm0421126

Jan Peter Meyboon
Senior Vice President, Production
Email: pmeyboom@shaftesbury.ca
IMDb: imdb.com/name/nm0582978

Adam Haight
Senior Vice President, Scripted Content
Email: ahaight@shaftesbury.ca

Suzanne French
Vice President, Children's & Family
Email: sfrench@shaftesbury.ca
IMDb: imdb.com/name/nm0294220

Julie Lacey
Vice President, Creative Affairs
Email: jlacey@shaftesbury.ca
IMDb: imdb.com/name/nm0479936

SHAUN CASSIDY PRODUCTIONS

500 S Buena Vista St
Old Animation Building
Burbank, CA 91521-1844
Phone: 818-560-6320

Accepts query letter from unproduced, unrepresented writers. Project types include TV. Preferred genres include Comedy and Drama.

Shaun Cassidy
Producer/Writer
Assistant: Dan Williams

SHEEP NOIR FILMS

438 W 17th Ave
Vancouver, BC V5Y 2A2
Fax: 604-762-8933

Email: info@sheepnoir.com
Home Page: sheepnoir.com

Does not accept any unsolicited material. Project types include Feature Films and TV. Preferred genres include Drama.

Wendy Hyman
Producer
IMDb: imdb.com/name/nm0405207

Nathaniel Geary
Writer/Director
IMDb: imdb.com/name/nm0311303

Marc Stephenson
Producer
Phone: 604-762-8933
Email: marc@sheepnoir.com

SHOE MONEY PRODUCTIONS

10202 W Washington Blvd
Poitier Building, Suite 3100
Culver City, CA 90232
Phone: 310-244-6188

Email: shoemoneyproductions@mac.com

Accepts query letter from unproduced, unrepresented writers via email. Project types include Feature Films and TV. Preferred genres include Drama.

Thomas Schlamme
Executive Producer/Director
IMDb: imdb.com/name/nm0772095

SHONDALAND

4151 Prospect Ave
4th Fl
Los Angeles, CA 90027
Phone: 323-671-4650

Does not accept any unsolicited material. Project types include Feature Films and TV. Preferred genres include Comedy and Drama.

Shonda Rhimes
Writer/Producer

Betsy Beers
Producer

Rachel Eggebeen
Development Executive

SHORELINE ENTERTAINMENT, INC.

1875 Century Park East, Suite 600
Los Angeles, CA 90067
Phone: 310-551-2060
Fax: 310-201-0729

Email: info@shorelineentertainment.com
Home Page: shorelineentertainment.com

Does not accept any unsolicited material. Project types include Feature Films and TV. Preferred genres include Drama, Horror, Non-Fiction, Reality, Science Fiction, and Thriller.

Morris Ruskin
CEO/Producer
Assistant: Timothy Tahir

Sam Eigen
Executive Vice-President
Assistant: Erin Schroeder

Brandon Paine
Director, Acquisitions

SHOWTIME NETWORKS

10880 Wilshire Blvd
Ste 1600
Los Angeles, CA 90024
Phone: 310-234-5200

Home Page: sho.com

Does not accept any unsolicited material. Project types include Feature Films and TV. Preferred genres include Action, Animation, Comedy, Crime, Detective, Drama, Family, Fantasy, Horror, Myth, Non-Fiction, Romance, Science Fiction, and Thriller.

Matthew Blank
Chairman, CEO
IMDb: imdb.com/name/nm2303194

Joan Boorstein
Vice President of Creative Affairs
IMDb: imdb.com/name/nm1140886

Tim Delaney
Production Operations
IMDb: imdb.com/name/nm2303906

Christina Spade
CFO
IMDb: imdb.com/name/nm5268270

SID & MARTY KROFFT PICTURES CORP.

4024 Radford Ave
Building 5, Suite 102

Studio City, CA 91604
Phone: 818-655-5314
Fax: 818-655-8235

Email: smkroft@aol.com

Accepts query letter from unproduced, unrepresented writers via email. Project types include Feature Films and TV. Preferred genres include Animation, Comedy, and Family.

Marty Krofft
President
Email: marty@krofft pictures.com
Assistant: Christine Bedolla

Sid Krofft
Executive Vice-President
Assistant: Bill Tracy

SIDNEY KIMMEL ENTERTAINMENT

9460 Wilshire Blvd., Suite 500
Beverly Hills, CA 90212
Phone: 310-777-8818
Fax: 310-777-8892

Email: reception@skefilms.com
Home Page: skefilms.com

Does not accept any unsolicited material. Project types include Feature Films. Preferred genres include Comedy, Crime, Drama, and Romance. Established in 2004.

Sidney Kimmel
CEO/Chairman
IMDb: imdb.com/name/nm0454004

Matt Berenson
President
IMDb: imdb.com/name/nm0073554

Jim Tauber
COO/President
IMDb: imdb.com/name/nm0851433

Mark Mikutowicz
Vice President (Production)
IMDb: imdb.com/name/nm2963870

SIERRA/AFFINITY

9378 Wilshire Blvd.
Suite 210
Beverly Hills, CA 90212
Phone: 424-253-1060
Fax: 424-653-1977

Email: info@sierra-affinity.com
Home Page: sierra-affinity.com

Does not accept any unsolicited material. Project types include Feature Films. Preferred genres include Action, Comedy, Crime, Detective, Drama, Fantasy, Horror, Romance, Science Fiction, and Thriller.

Nicholas Meyer
CEO
IMDb: imdb.com/name/nm0583293
Assistant: Pip Ngo

Kelly McCormick
SVP of Production & Development
IMDb: imdb.com/name/nm0566555

Jen Gorton
Creative Executive
IMDb: imdb.com/name/nm4224815

Ben Kuller
Executive Assistant

Hillary Taylor
Assitant
Email: hillary@sierra-affinity.com
IMDb: imdb.com/name/nm4751305

SIGNATURE PICTURES

8285 W Sunset Blvd, Suite 7
West Hollywood, CA 90046
Phone: 323-848-9005
Fax: 323-848-9305

Email: james@signaturepictures.com
Home Page: signaturepictures.com

Does not accept any unsolicited material. Project types include Feature Films. Preferred genres include Action, Drama, Non-Fiction, Romance, and Thriller.

Moshe Diamant
Producer

Illana Diamant
Producer

James Portolese
Production Executive

SIKELIA PRODUCTIONS

110 W 57th St
5th Floor
New York, NY 10019
Phone: 212-906-8800
Fax: 212-906-8891

Does not accept any unsolicited material. Project types include Feature Films. Preferred genres include Action, Crime, Drama, Romance, and Thriller.

Martin Scorsese
Director/Producer
IMDb: imdb.com/name/nm0000217

Emma Koskoff
President of Production
IMDb: imdb.com/name/nm0863374

Margaret Bodde
Producer

Lisa Frechette
Assistant

SILLY ROBIN PRODUCTIONS

30 Slope Dr
Short Hills, NJ 07078
Phone: 310-487-8234
Fax: 973-376-7639

Email: ribz99@aol.com
Home Page: alanzweibel.com

Accepts query letter from unproduced, unrepresented writers via email. Project types include Feature Films, TV, and Theater. Preferred genres include Comedy and Drama.

Alan Zweibel
Writer/Producer/Director

John Robertson
Director of Development

SILVER DREAM PRODUCTIONS

3452 E Foothill Blvd, Suite 620
Pasadena, CA 91107
Phone: 626-799-3880
Fax: 626-799-5363

Email: luoyan@silverdreamprods.com
Home Page: silverdreamprods.com

Accepts query letter from unproduced, unrepresented writers via email. Project types include Feature Films. Preferred genres include Drama and Myth.

Luo Yan
Actress/Producer
Assistant: Diana Chin

SILVER NITRATE

12268 Ventura Blvd
Studio City, CA 91604
Phone: 818-762-9559
Fax: 818-762-9177

Does not accept any unsolicited material. Project types include Feature Films. Preferred genres include Animation, Comedy, Drama, and Science Fiction.

Ash Shah
Producer
Email: ash@silvernitrate.net

SILVER PICTURES

4000 Warner Blvd
Building 90
Burbank, CA 91522
Phone: 818-954-4490
Fax: 818-954-3237

Accepts query letter from unproduced, unrepresented writers. Project types include Feature Films and TV. Preferred genres include Action, Animation, Drama, Family, Non-Fiction, Reality, Science Fiction, and Thriller.

Joel Silver
Chairman

Alex Heineman
Sr. Vice-President, Production

Sarah Meyer
Director of Development

SILVERS/KOSTER PRODUCTIONS, LLC

353 S Reeves Dr, Penthouse
Beverly Hills, CA 90212
Phone: 310-551-5245
Fax: 310-284-5797

Email: skfi lmco@aol.com
Home Page: silvers-koster.com

Accepts query letter from unproduced, unrepresented writers via email. Project types include Feature Films, TV, and Commercials. Preferred genres include Non-Fiction and Reality.

Iren Koster
President

Karen Corcoran
Vice-President, Development

Tracey Silvers
Chairman

SIMON SAYS ENTERTAINMENT

12 Desbrosses St
New York, NY 10013
Phone: 917-797-9704

Email: info@simonsaysentertainment.net
Home Page: simonsaysentertainment.net

Accepts scripts from unproduced, unrepresented writers. Project types include Feature Films. Preferred genres include Crime, Drama, and Romance.

Ron Simons
Principal
IMDb: imdb.com/name/nm1839399

April Yvette Thompson
Producing Associate
IMDb: imdb.com/name/nm1690743

Nora Duffy
COO

SIMON WEST PRODUCTIONS

3450 Cahuenga Blvd West
Building 510
Los Angeles, CA 90068
Phone: 323-845-0821
Fax: 323-845-4582

Email: submissions@simonwestproductions.com
Home Page: simonwestproductions.com

Accepts query letter from unproduced, unrepresented writers. Project types include Feature Films and TV. Preferred genres include Action, Drama, and Science Fiction.

Simon West
Director/Producer

Jib Polhemus
President, Production

SIMSIE FILMS LLC/MEDIA SAVANT

2934 1/2 Beverly Glen Circle
Suite 264
Los Angeles, CA 90077

Email: simsiefilms@mac.com

Accepts query letter from unproduced, unrepresented writers. Project types include Feature Films. Preferred genres include Comedy and Drama.

Gwen Field
Partner
IMDb: imdb.com/name/nm0275947

SINGE CELL PICTURES

PO Box 69691
West Hollywood, CA 90069
USA
Phone: 310-360-7600
Fax: 310-360-7011

Accepts query letter from unproduced, unrepresented writers. Project types include Feature Films and TV. Preferred genres include Comedy and Drama.

Michael Stipe
Producer

Sandy Stern
Producer

SINOVOI ENTERTAINMENT

1317 N San Fernando Blvd, Suite 395
Burbank, CA 91504
Phone: 818-562-6404
Fax: 818-567-0104

Email: maxwell@sinovoientertainment.com
Home Page: sinovoientertainment.com

Accepts query letter from unproduced, unrepresented writers via email. Project types include Feature Films. Preferred genres include Comedy, Drama, and Horror.

Maxwell Sinovoi
Producer

Kimberly Estrada
Vice President of Development

SKETCH FILMS

Does not accept any unsolicited material. Project types include Feature Films. Preferred genres include Action, Fantasy, Horror, Myth, and Science Fiction.

David Bernardi
President
Email: d.bernardi@sbcglobal.net
IMDb: imdb.com/name/nm2050171

Len Wiseman
IMDb: imdb.com/name/nm0936482

SKYDANCE PRODUCTIONS

5555 Melrose Ave
Dean Martin Building
Hollywood, CA 90038
Phone: 323-956-9900
Fax: 323-956-9901

Email: info@skydance.com
Home Page: skydance.com

Accepts scripts from produced or represented writers. Project types include Feature Films and TV. Preferred genres include Action, Comedy, Drama, Family, Fantasy, Myth, Science Fiction, and Thriller.

David Ellison
President
IMDb: imdb.com/name/nm1911103
Assistant: Bill Bost

Dana Goldberg
President of Production
IMDb: imdb.com/name/nm1602154
Assistant: Matt Grimm

Matthew Milam
Vice-President Production
IMDb: imdb.com/name/nm1297784
Assistant: Kyle Hebenstreit

Shannon Gregory
Creative Executive
IMDb: imdb.com/name/nm4087474
Assistant: Kyle Hebenstreit

Michelle Beress
Office Manager
IMDb: imdb.com/name/nm2234266

SKYLARK ENTERTAINMENT, INC.

12405 Venice Blvd, Suite 237
Los Angeles, CA 90066
Phone: 310-390-2659

Home Page: skylark.net

Does not accept any unsolicited material. Project types
include Feature Films and TV. Preferred genres
include Comedy, Drama, and Non-Fiction.

Jacobus Rose
President/Producer

SKY NETWORKS

9220 Sunset Blvd, Suite 230
West Hollywood, CA 90069
Phone: 310-860-2740
Fax: 310-860-2471

Home Page: sky.com

Accepts query letter from unproduced, unrepresented
writers. Project types include TV. Preferred genres
include Action and Science Fiction.

Rebecca Siegal
Sr. Vice-President

SMART ENTERTAINMENT

9595 Wilshire Blvd, Suite 900
Beverly Hills, CA 90212
Phone: 310-205-6090
Fax: 310-205-6093

Email: assistant@smartentertainment.com
Home Page: smartentertainment.com

Accepts query letter from unproduced, unrepresented
writers via email. Project types include Feature Films
and TV. Preferred genres include Comedy, Horror,
Non-Fiction, Reality, and Thriller.

John Jacobs
President
Email: john@smartentertainment.com

Zac Unterman
VP,Director, Development
Email: zac@smartentertainment.com

SMASH MEDIA, INC.

1208 Georgina Ave
Santa Monica, CA 90402
Phone: 310-395-0058
Fax: 310-395-8850

Email: info@smashmediafilms.com
Home Page: smashmediafilms.com

Accepts query letter from unproduced, unrepresented
writers via email. Project types include Feature Films
and TV. Preferred genres include Comedy, Drama,
and Science Fiction.

Harry Winer
President
Email: harry.winer@smashmediafi lms.com

Shelley Hack
Vice-President, Development
Email: shelley.hack@smashmediafi lms.com

Susan Winer
Vice-President, Business Affairs
Email: susan.winer@smashmediafi lms.com

SMOKEHOUSE PICTURES

12001 Ventura Pl., Suite 200
Studio City, CA 91604

Phone: 818-432-0330
Fax: 818-432-0337

IMDb: imdb.com/company/co0184096

Does not accept any unsolicited material. Project types include Feature Films. Preferred genres include Comedy, Drama, and Thriller.

George Clooney
Partner
IMDb: imdb.com/name/nm0000123

Grant Heslov
Partner
IMDb: imdb.com/name/nm0381416
Assistant: Tara Oslin

Katie Murphy
Creative Executive
IMDb: imdb.com/name/nm3682023

SNEAK PREVIEW ENTERTAINMENT

6705 Sunset Blvd
2nd Floor
Hollywood, CA 90028
Phone: 323-962-0295
Fax: 323-962-0372

Email: indiefilm@sneakpreviewentertain.com
Home Page: sneakpreviewentertain.com

Accepts query letter from unproduced, unrepresented writers via email. Project types include Feature Films. Established in 1991.

Steven Wolfe
Chairman/CEO/Producer
Phone: 323-962-0295
Email: sjwolfe@sneakpreviewentertain.com
IMDb: imdb.com/name/nm0938145

Chris Hazzard
Director of Development
Phone: 323-962-0295
Email: ch@sneakpe.com
IMDb: imdb.com/name/nm3302502

SOBINI FILMS

10203 Santa Monica Blvd
Los Angeles, CA 90067

Phone: 310-432-6900
Fax: 310-432-6939

Home Page: sobini.com
IMDb: imdb.com/company/co0086773

Does not accept any unsolicited material. Project types include Feature Films. Preferred genres include Comedy, Drama, Family, and Thriller.

Mark Amin
Producer/Chairman
IMDb: imdb.com/name/nm0024909

David Higgin
President/Producer
IMDb: imdb.com/name/nm0383371

Cami Winikoff
President
IMDb: imdb.com/name/nm0935121

SOCIAL CAPITAL FILMS

1617 Broadway, Suite A
Santa Monica, CA 90404
Phone: 310-401-6100
Fax: 310-401-6289

Email: info@socialcapitalfilms.com
Home Page: socialcapitalfilms.com

Does not accept any unsolicited material. Project types include Feature Films and TV. Preferred genres include Comedy, Drama, Family, Horror, Non-Fiction, Reality, Science Fiction, and Thriller.

Martin Shore
Chairman/Producer

Andy Schefter
Head of Production

SOGNO PRODUCTIONS

PO Box 55476
Portland, OR 97238
Phone: 561-676-4696

Email: angaelica@gmail.com
Home Page: ANGAELICA.com

Accepts scripts from unproduced, unrepresented writers. Project types include Feature Films. Preferred genres include Action, Comedy, Documentary, Drama, Fantasy, Romance, and Thriller.

Breven Angaelica Warren
Producer
IMDb: imdb.com/name/nm1938686

Braman Ariana Warren
Executive
Email: sognoproductions@gmail.com
IMDb: imdb.com/name/nm2736980

SOLIPSIST FILMS

465 N Crescent Heights Blvd
Los Angeles, CA 90048
Phone: 323 272 3122
Fax: 323 375 1649

Email: info@solipsistfilms.com
Home Page: solipsistfilms.com

Accepts query letter from unproduced, unrepresented writers via email. Project types include Feature Films and TV. Preferred genres include Detective, Drama, Fantasy, Non-Fiction, Reality, and Thriller.

Stephen L'Heureux
Managing Director

S PICTURES, INC.

4420 Hayvenhurst Ave
Encino, CA 91436
Phone: 1 818 995 1585
Fax: 1 818 995 1677

Email: info@spictures.tv
Home Page: spictures.tv

Does not accept any unsolicited material. Project types include Feature Films and TV. Preferred genres include Comedy, Non-Fiction, Reality, and Science Fiction.

Chuck Simon
President/Producer
Phone: 818-995-1585
Email: chuck@Spictures.TV
IMDb: imdb.com/name/nm1247168

SPITFIRE PICTURES

9100 Wilshire Blvd
Beverly Hills, CA 90212
Phone: 310-300-9000
Fax: 310-300-9001

Home Page: spitfirepictures.com

Does not accept any unsolicited material. Project types include Feature Films. Preferred genres include Documentary, Drama, Romance, and Thriller. Established in 2003.

Nigel Sinclair
Principal
IMDb: imdb.com/name/nm0801691

Guy East
Principal
IMDb: imdb.com/name/nm0247524

Anna Bocchi
Creative Executive
IMDb: imdb.com/name/nm3070564

Ben Holden
Creative Executive
IMDb: imdb.com/name/nm1592118

SPYGLASS ENTERTAINMENT

245 N Beverly Dr
Beverly Hills, CA 90024
Phone: 310-443-5800
Fax: 310-443-5912

Home Page: spyglassentertainment.com

Does not accept any unsolicited material. Project types include Feature Films. Preferred genres include Action, Comedy, Drama, Family, Horror, Non-Fiction, and Thriller.

Gary Barber
Co-Chairman/Founder

Rebekah Rudd
Executive Vice-President, Post Production

STAGE 6 FILMS

10202 W Washington Blvd
Culver City, CA 90232

Phone: 310-244-4000
Fax: 310-244-2626

Home Page: sonypicturesworldwideacquisitions.com
IMDb: imdb.com/company/co0222021

Does not accept any unsolicited material. Project types include Feature Films. Preferred genres include Action, Animation, Comedy, Crime, Documentary, Drama, Family, Horror, Period, Romance, Science Fiction, and Thriller. Established in 2007.

ST. AMOS PRODUCTIONS

3480 Barham Blvd
Los Angeles, CA 90068
Phone: 323-850-9872

Email: st.amosproductions@earthlink.net

Accepts query letter from unproduced, unrepresented writers via email. Project types include Feature Films and TV. Preferred genres include Comedy, Drama, Non-Fiction, and Reality.

John Stamos
Producer/Actor

Marc Alexander
Producer/Writer/Development

STARRY NIGHT ENTERTAINMENT

1414 Ave of the Americas, 12th Floor
New York, NY 10019
Phone: 212-717-2750
Fax: 212-794-6150

Email: info@starrynightentertainment.com
Home Page: starrynightentertainment.com
IMDb: imdb.com/company/co0183209

Accepts query letter from unproduced, unrepresented writers via email. Project types include Feature Films, TV, Commercials, and Theater. Preferred genres include Comedy, Drama, Non-Fiction, and Reality.

Craig Saavedra
Partner (LA)
Email: cs@starrynightentertainment.com

Michael Shulman
Partner (NY)
Email: ms@starrynightentertainment.com

Ryan Meekins
Creative Executive (LA)

Neika Masoori
Development Executive
Email: nyasst@starrynightentertainment.com

STATE STREET PICTURES

8075 W 3rd St, Suite 306
Los Angeles, CA 90048
Phone: 323-556-2240
Fax: 323-556-2242

Home Page: statestreetpictures.com
IMDb: imdb.com/company/co0068765

Does not accept any unsolicited material. Project types include Feature Films and TV. Preferred genres include Comedy and Drama.

Robert Teitel
Producer
Assistant: Michael Flavin

George Tillman
Director
Assistant: Jason Veley

Stacy Glassgold
Creative Executive

STEAMROLLER PRODUCTIONS, INC.

100 Universal City Plaza #7151
Universal City, CA 91608
Phone: 818-733-4622
Fax: 818-733-4608

Email: steamrollerprod@aol.com

Accepts query letter from unproduced, unrepresented writers via email. Project types include Feature Films and TV. Preferred genres include Action, Crime, Detective, Non-Fiction, Reality, and Thriller.

Steven Seagal
CEO/Director/Writer/Producer/Actor
Assistant: Tracy Irvine

Binh Dang
Production Executive

STEFANIE EPSTEIN PRODUCTIONS

427 N Canon Dr, Suite 214
Beverly Hills, CA 90210
Phone: 310-385-0300
Fax: 310-385-0302

Email: billseprods@aol.com
IMDb: imdb.com/company/co0171458

Accepts query letter from unproduced, unrepresented writers via email. Project types include Feature Films and TV. Preferred genres include Comedy and Drama.

Stefanie Epstein
Producer

Bill Gienapp
Creative Executive

STEVEN BOCHCO PRODUCTIONS

3000 Olympic Blvd, Suite 1310
Santa Monica, CA 90404
Phone: 310-566-6900

Email: yr@bochcomedia.com
IMDb: imdb.com/company/co0085628

Accepts query letter from unproduced, unrepresented writers. Project types include TV. Preferred genres include Crime, Detective, and Drama.

Steven Bochco
Chairman/CEO

Craig Shenkler
CFO/Vice-President, Finance

Dayna Kalins
President

Yemaya Royce
Director of Media Relations

STOKELY CHAFFIN PRODUCTIONS

1456 Sunset Plaza Dr
Los Angeles, CA 90069
Phone: 310-657-4559

Accepts query letter from unproduced, unrepresented writers via email. Project types include Feature Films and TV. Preferred genres include Action, Comedy, Horror, Non-Fiction, and Thriller.

Stokely Chaffin
Producer

David Reed
Development Assistant

STONEBROOK ENTERTAINMENT

10061 Riverside Dr, Suite 813
Toluca Lake, CA 91602
Phone: 818-766-8797

Accepts query letter from unproduced, unrepresented writers via email. Project types include Feature Films and TV.

Danny Roth
Producer
Email: danny@stonebrookent.com

STONE & COMPANY ENTERTAINMENT

c/o Hollywood Center Studios
1040 N Las Palmas Ave, Building 1
Los Angeles, CA 90038
Phone: 323-960-2599
Fax: 323-960-2437

Email: info@stonetv.com
Home Page: stonetv.com/home.html
IMDb: imdb.com/company/co0173288

Accepts query letter from unproduced, unrepresented writers via email. Project types include TV. Preferred genres include Non-Fiction and Reality.

Scott Stone
Principal

David Weintraub
Vice-President, Series Development

Ben Parrish
Development Producer

STONE VILLAGE PICTURES

9200 W Sunset Blvd
Ste 520
West Hollywood, CA 90069
Phone: 310-402-5171
Fax: 310-402-5172

Home Page: stonevillagepictures.com

Does not accept any unsolicited material. Project types include Feature Films. Preferred genres include Drama, Romance, and Thriller.

Dylan Russell
Vice President of Production
IMDb: imdb.com/name/nm1928375

Scott Steindorff
Executive Producer
IMDb: imdb.com/name/nm1127589

STOREFRONT PICTURES

1112 Montana Ave
Santa Monica, CA 90403
Phone: 310-459-4235

Email: betty@storefrontpics.com
Home Page: storefrontpics.com

Does not accept any unsolicited material. Project types include Feature Films. Preferred genres include Comedy, Drama, Family, Fantasy, and Romance.

Susan Cartsonis
Producer
Assistant: Betty Davolo

Roz Weisberg
Vice-President/Producer

STORY AND FILM

2934 1/2 Beverly Glen Circle, Suite 195
Los Angeles, CA 90077
Phone: 310-480-8833

IMDb: imdb.com/company/co0120778

Accepts query letter from unproduced, unrepresented writers via email.

STORYLINE ENTERTAINMENT

8335 Sunset Blvd, Suite 207
West Hollywood, CA 90069
Phone: 323-337-9045
Fax: 323-210-7263

Email: info@storyline-entertainment.com
Home Page: storyline-entertainment.com
IMDb: imdb.com/company/co0091980

Does not accept any unsolicited material. Project types include Feature Films, TV, and Theater. Preferred genres include Comedy, Drama, Non-Fiction, Reality, and Romance.

Craig Zadan
Executive Producer
Phone: 323-337-9045
Email: craig@storyline-entertainment.com

Neil Meron
Executive Producer
Phone: 323-337-9046
Email: neil@storyline-entertainment.com

Mark Nicholson
Head, Development
Phone: 323-337-9047
Email: mark@storyline-entertainment.com

STRAIGHT UP FILMS

1514 17th St.
Suite 201
Santa Monica, CA 90404
Phone: 424-238-8470

Email: hello@straightupfilms.com
Home Page: straightupfilms.com

Does not accept any unsolicited material. Project types include Feature Films and TV. Preferred genres include Comedy, Crime, and Drama.

Marisa Polvino
Co-CEO/Producer
IMDb: imdb.com/name/nm0689909

Kate Cohen
Co-CEO/Producer
IMDb: imdb.com/name/nm3154628

Regency Boies
Muse/Producer
IMDb: imdb.com/name/nm3151361

Casey A. Carroll
Creative Executive
IMDb: imdb.com/name/nm3554230

STRIKE ENTERTAINMENT

3000 W Olympic Blvd
Building 5, Suite 1250
Santa Monica, CA 90404
Phone: 310-315-0550
Fax: 310-315-0560

Accepts query letter from unproduced, unrepresented writers via email. Project types include Feature Films. Preferred genres include Action, Comedy, Drama, Horror, Science Fiction, and Thriller. Established in 2002.

Marc Abraham
Producer
Assistant: Jamie Zakowski

Tom Bliss
Producer
Assistant: Mark Barclay

Eric Newman
Producer
Assistant: Jesse Rose Moore

Kristel Laiblin
Assistant: Nhu Tran

STUDIO CANAL

9250 Wilshire Blvd, Suite 210
Beverly Hills, CA 90212
Phone: 310-247-0994

Does not accept any unsolicited material. Project types include Feature Films and TV. Preferred genres include Comedy, Crime, Drama, Fantasy, Horror, Non-Fiction, Reality, Romance, and Thriller.

Ron Halpern
Executive Vice-President, Int'l Production & Special Projects

SUBMARINE ENTERTAINMENT

525 Broadway
Ste 601
New York, NY 10012
Phone: 212-625-1410
Fax: 212-625-9931

Email: info@submarine.com
Home Page: submarine.com

Accepts query letter from produced or represented writers. Project types include Feature Films. Preferred genres include Documentary and Drama.

Josh Braun
Co-Founder
Email: josh@submarine.com
IMDb: imdb.com/name/nm2248562

David Koh
Executive

Dan Braun
Co-Founder
Email: dan@submarine.com
IMDb: imdb.com/name/nm2250854

SUCH MUCH FILMS

Santa Monica, CA 90405

Email: info@suchmuchfilms.com
Home Page: suchmuchfilms.com

Accepts query letter from unproduced, unrepresented writers via email. Project types include Feature Films. Preferred genres include Documentary and Drama.

Judi Levine
Executive
IMDb: imdb.com/name/nm0505861

Ben Lewin
IMDb: imdb.com/name/nm0506802

SUMMIT ENTERTAINMENT

1630 Stewart St
Ste 120
Santa Monica, CA 90404
Phone: 310-309-8400
Fax: 310-828-4132

Home Page: summit-ent.com
IMDb: imdb.com/company/co0046206

Does not accept any unsolicited material. Project types include Feature Films. Preferred genres include Action, Comedy, Crime, Drama, Fantasy, Romance, Science Fiction, and Thriller.

Gillian Bohrer
Vice President of Production
Phone: 310-309-8400
IMDb: imdb.com/name/nm2023551

Merideth Milton
Senior Vice President of Production
Phone: 310-309-8400
IMDb: imdb.com/name/nm0590693

Rob Friedman
CEO
Phone: 310-309-8400
IMDb: imdb.com/name/nm2263981

Patrick Wachsberger
President
Phone: 310-309-8400
IMDb: imdb.com/name/nm0905163

SUNDIAL PICTURES

511 Sixth Ave., Suite 375
New York, NY 10011

Email: info@sundialpicturesllc.com
Home Page: sundial-pictures.com

Does not accept any unsolicited material. Project types include Feature Films. Preferred genres include Comedy, Documentary, Drama, and Thriller.

Stefan Norwicki
President
IMDb: imdb.com/name/nm3378356

Joey Carey
Partner
IMDb: imdb.com/name/nm2909903

Benjamin Weber
EVP Development
IMDb: imdb.com/name/nm3373548

SUNLIGHT PRODUCTIONS

854-A Fifth St
Santa Monica, CA 90403
Phone: 310-899-1522

Email: contactus@sunlightproductions.com
Home Page: mikebinder.net
IMDb: imdb.com/company/co0028319

Does not accept any unsolicited material. Project types include Feature Films and TV. Preferred genres include Comedy, Drama, and Non-Fiction.

Mike Binder
Writer/Director/Actor

Rachel Zimmerman
Producer
Email: Rachel@sunlightproductions.com

SUNSWEPT ENTERTAINMENT

10201 W Pico Blvd
Building 45
Los Angeles, CA 90064
Phone: 310-369-0878
Fax: 310-969-0726

IMDb: imdb.com/company/co0226011

Does not accept any unsolicited material. Project types include Feature Films. Preferred genres include Animation, Comedy, Family, Fantasy, and Romance. Established in 2004.

Karen Rosenfelt
President/Producer
Assistant: Caroline MacVicar

Emmy Castlen
Story Editor

Caroline MacVicar
Assistant

SUNTAUR ENTERTAINMENT

1581 N Crescent Heights Blvd
Los Angeles, CA 90046
Phone: 323-656-3800

Email: info@suntaurent.com
Home Page: suntaurent.com
IMDb: imdb.com/company/co0183461

Does not accept any unsolicited material. Project types include Feature Films and TV. Preferred genres include Comedy and Drama.

Paul Aaron
President/CEO
Assistant: Matt Blessing

Zac Sanford
Vice-President, Development
Assistant: Adam Morris

SUPERFINGER ENTERTAINMENT

c/o Chris Hart/UTA
9560 Wilshire Blvd
Beverly Hills, CA 90212
Phone: 310-385-6715

IMDb: imdb.com/company/co0181284

Accepts query letter from unproduced, unrepresented writers via email. Project types include Feature Films and TV. Preferred genres include Animation, Comedy, Non-Fiction, and Reality.

Dane Cook
President/Actor/Comedian

SWEET 180

141 W 28th St #300
NYC, NY 10001
Phone: 212-541-4443
Fax: 212-563-9655

Home Page: sweet180.com

Does not accept any unsolicited material. Project types include Feature Films and TV. Preferred genres include Comedy, Drama, Non-Fiction, Reality, and Romance.

Lillian LaSalle
Prseident/Manager/Producer
Email: lillian@sweet180.com

Catherine Clausi
Office Manager/Executive Assistant
Assistant: Lindsay Carlson

Nina Schreiber
Manager
Email: nina@sweet180.com

Rachel Maran
Assistant
Email: assistant@sweet180.com

TAGGART PRODUCTIONS

9000 W Sunset Blvd
Suite 1020
West Hollywood, CA 90069
Phone: 424-249-3350
Fax: 424-249-3972

Home Page: taggart-productions.com
Facebook: facebook.com/taggartproductions

Does not accept any unsolicited material. Project types include Feature Films. Preferred genres include Action, Comedy, Crime, Drama, and Thriller.

Michael Nardelli
President & CEO
IMDb: imdb.com/name/nm1660148

Jason Michael Berman
Producer
Email: jberman@taggart-productions.com
IMDb: imdb.com/name/nm4132650

Rob Nardelli
Producer
IMDb: imdb.com/name/nm4360108

Lindsey Reiman
Assistant
Email: lindsey@taggart-productions.com
IMDb: imdb.com/name/nm4701862

TAGLINE PICTURES

9250 Wilshire Blvd
Ground Floor
Beverly Hills, CA 90212
Phone: 310-595-1515
Fax: 310-595-1505

Email: info@taglinela.com
Home Page: taglinela.com

Does not accept any unsolicited material. Project types include TV. Preferred genres include Comedy and Drama.

Chris Henze
Partner/Owner

J.B. Roberts
Partner/Owner

William Mercer
Partner/Owner

Ron West
Parnter/Owner

Kelly Kulchak
President
Assistant: Tim Goessling

TAMARA ASSEYEV PRODUCTIONS

1187 Coast Village Rd.
Suite 134
Santa Barbara, CA 93108
Phone: 323-656-4731
Fax: 323-656-2211

Email: tamaraprod@aol.com

Accepts query letter from unproduced, unrepresented writers. Project types include TV. Preferred genres include Drama.

Tamara Asseyev
Producer
Assistant: Constance Mead

TAPESTRY FILMS, INC.

9328 Civic Center Dr, 2nd Floor
Beverly Hills, CA 90210
Phone: 310-275-1191
Fax: 310-275-1266

Does not accept any unsolicited material. Project types include Feature Films. Preferred genres include Action, Comedy, Family, Romance, and Thriller.

Peter Abrams
Producer/Partner
IMDb: imdb.com/name/nm0009222

Robert Levy
Producer/Partner
IMDb: imdb.com/name/nm0506597

Michael Schreiber
President
IMDb: imdb.com/name/nm2325100

Kat Blasband Page
VP Development
IMDb: imdb.com/name/nm2321097

TAURUS ENTERTAINMENT COMPANY

5555 Melrose Ave
Marx Brothers Building, Suite 103/104
Hollywood, CA 90038
Phone: 818-935-5157
Fax: 323-686-5379

Email: taurusentco@yahoo.com
Home Page: taurusec.com

Accepts query letter from unproduced, unrepresented writers via email. Project types include Feature Films and TV. Preferred genres include Action, Animation, Drama, and Family. Established in 1991.

James Dudelson
President/CEO
Email: jgdudelson@yahoo.com
IMDb: imdb.com/name/nm0240054

Robert Dudelson
President/COO
Email: rfdudelson@mac.com
IMDb: imdb.com/name/nm0240055

T&C PICTURES

3122 Santa Monica Blvd #200
Santa Monica, CA 90404
Phone: 310-828-1340
Fax: 310-828-1581

Email: info@tandcpictures.com

Accepts query letter from unproduced, unrepresented writers. Project types include Feature Films and TV. Preferred genres include Action, Comedy, Drama, Family, Non-Fiction, and Thriller.

Barry Rosenbush
Producer
IMDb: imdb.com/name/nm0742492

Bill Borden
Producer
Email: christine@tandcpictures.com
IMDb: imdb.com/name/nm0096115

Arata Matsushima
President/Producer
Phone: 310-828-7801
IMDb: imdb.com/name/nm2606503

TEAM DOWNEY

1311 Abbot Kinney
Venice, CA 90291
Phone: 310-450-5100

Does not accept any unsolicited material. Project types include Feature Films. Preferred genres include Action, Comedy, and Drama. Established in 2010.

Robert Downey
Producer
IMDb: imdb.com/name/nm0000375

Susan Downey
Producer
IMDb: imdb.com/name/nm1206265

David Gambino
President of Production
IMDb: imdb.com/name/nm1312724

TEAM G

1839 Blake Ave #5 Los Angeles, CA 90039
Phone: 213-915-8106
Fax: 323-843-9210

Email: info@teamgproductions.com
Home Page: teamgproductions.com

Project types include Feature Films. Preferred genres include Comedy, Drama, and Science Fiction.

Trey Hock
Producer/Partner
IMDb: imdb.com/name/nm2465366

Jett Steiger
Producer/Partner
IMDb: imdb.com/name/nm2532520

TEAM TODD

2900 W Olympic Blvd
Santa Monica, CA 91404
Phone: 310-255-7265
Fax: 310-255-7222

Accepts scripts from produced or represented writers. Project types include Feature Films. Preferred genres include Animation, Drama, Family, Myth, and Romance.

Suzanne Todd
Producer
IMDb: imdb.com/name/nm0865297

Julianna Hays
Creative Executive
IMDb: imdb.com/name/nm3057670

TEMPLE HILL PRODUCTIONS

9255 Sunset Blvd, Suite 801
Los Angeles, CA 90069
Phone: 310-270-4383
Fax: 310-270-4395

Home Page: templehillent.com

Does not accept any unsolicited material. Project types include Feature Films and TV. Preferred genres include Comedy, Drama, Family, Fantasy, and Thriller. Established in 2006.

Marty Bowen
Partner
IMDb: imdb.com/name/nm2125212

Wyck Godfrey
Partner
IMDb: imdb.com/name/nm0324041

Adam C. Londy
Director of Development
IMDb: imdb.com/name/nm2173131

Isaac Klausner
Director of Development
IMDb: imdb.com/name/nm2327099

Tracy Nyberg
Senior Vice President
IMDb: imdb.com/name/nm2427937

TERRA FIRMA FILMS

468 N Camden Dr, Suite 365T
Beverly Hills, CA 90210
Phone: 310-480-5676
Fax: 310-862-4717

Email: info@terrafirmafilms.com
Home Page: terrafirmafilms.com

Accepts query letter from unproduced, unrepresented writers via email. Project types include Feature Films.

Preferred genres include Action, Comedy, Drama, Family, and Romance. Established in 2003.

Adam Herz
Writer/Producer
Phone: 310-860-7480
Email: info@terrafi rmafi lms.com
IMDb: imdb.com/name/nm0381221

Gregory Lessans
Co-President
IMDb: imdb.com/name/nm0504298

Josh Shader
Co-President
IMDb: imdb.com/name/nm1003558

Gregory Lessans
Co-President
IMDb: imdb.com/name/nm0504298

THE AMERICAN FILM COMPANY

c/o Business Affairs, Inc.
2415 Main St, 2nd Floor
Santa Monica, CA 90405
Phone: 310-392-0777

Email: info@americanfilmco.com
Home Page: theamericanfilmcompany.com

Accepts query letter from unproduced, unrepresented writers via email. Project types include Feature Films. Preferred genres include Drama, Non-Fiction, Period, and Thriller. Established in 2008.

Brian Falk
President
Email: bfalk@americanfi lmco.com
IMDb: imdb.com/name/nm1803137

Alfred Levitt
COO
IMDb: imdb.com/name/nm4662708

Kurt Graver
Manager of Development
Email: kgraver@americanfilmco.com
IMDb: imdb.com/name/nm4621255

THE ASYLUM

72 E Palm Ave
Burbank, CA 91502
Phone: 323-850-1214
Fax: 818-260-9811

Email: theasylum@theasylum.cc
Home Page: theasylum.cc

Does not accept any unsolicited material. Project types include Feature Films. Preferred genres include Action, Fantasy, Horror, Science Fiction, and Thriller.

Micho Rutare
Director of Development
IMDb: imdb.com/name/nm3026436

Mark Quod
Post Production Supervisor
IMDb: imdb.com/name/nm0704517

Joseph Lawson
Supervisor
IMDb: imdb.com/name/nm1037472

THE AV CLUB

2629 Main St #211
Santa Monica, CA 90405
Phone: (310) 396-1165

Does not accept any unsolicited material. Project types include Feature Films. Preferred genres include Comedy, Drama, Non-Fiction, Romance, and Science Fiction.

Amy Robertson
Film and TV Producer
IMDb: imdb.com/name/nm1516144

THE BADHAM COMPANY

16830 Ventura Blvd, Suite 300
Encino, CA, 91436
Phone: 818-990-9495
Fax: 818-981-9163

Email: development@badhamcompany.com
Home Page: badhamcompany.com

Accepts scripts from produced or represented writers. Project types include Feature Films and TV. Preferred genres include Drama, Family, and Non-Fiction.

John Badham
Director/Producer
IMDb: imdb.com/name/nm0000824

THE BEDFORD FALLS COMPANY

409 Santa Monica Blvd
Penthouse
Santa Monica, CA 90401-2388
Phone: 310-394-5022
Fax: 310-394-2512

Does not accept any unsolicited material. Project types
include Feature Films. Preferred genres include Action
and Drama.

Troy Putney
Creative Executive
IMDb: imdb.com/name/nm1586726

THE BUREAU

18 Phipp St
2nd Floor
London - EC2A 4NU
United-Kingdom
Phone: +44-0-207-033-0555

Email: mail@thebureau.co.uk
Home Page: thebureau.co.uk

Does not accept any unsolicited material. Project types
include Feature Films. Preferred genres include
Comedy, Documentary, Drama, Romance, and
Thriller. Established in 2000.

Bertrand Faivre
Producer
IMDb: imdb.com/name/nm0265724

Soledad Gatti-Pascual
Founder & Manager
IMDb: imdb.com/name/nm0309806

Tristan Golighter
Producer

Valentina Brazzini
Development

Matthew de Braconier
Producer/Development

THE COLLETON COMPANY

20 Fifth Ave, Suite 13F
New York, NY 10011
Phone: 212-673-0916
Fax: 212-673-1172

Accepts scripts from produced or represented writers.
Project types include Feature Films and TV. Preferred
genres include Crime, Detective, Drama, Non-Fiction,
and Thriller.

Sara Colleton
IMDb: imdb.com/name/nm0171780

THE DONNERS' COMPANY

9465 Wilshire Blvd
Ste 420
Beverly Hills, CA 90212
Phone: 310-777-4600
Fax: 310-777-4610

Home Page: donnerscompany.com

Does not accept any unsolicited material. Project types
include Feature Films. Preferred genres include Action,
Fantasy, and Science Fiction.

Richard Donner
Producer
IMDb: imdb.com/name/nm0001149

THE GOLD COMPANY

499 N Canon Dr, Suite 306
Beverly Hills, CA 90210
Phone: 310-270-4653

Accepts query letter from unproduced, unrepresented
writers. Project types include Feature Films. Preferred
genres include Comedy.

Eric Gold
Chairman/Producer
IMDb: imdb.com/name/nm0324970

Jessica Green
VP Production
IMDb: imdb.com/name/nm2783652

Caryn Weingarten
Manager
IMDb: imdb.com/name/nm1086864

THE GOLDSTEIN COMPANY

1644 Courtney Ave
Los Angeles, CA 90046
Phone: 310-659-9511

Home Page: garywgoldstein.com

Accepts query letter from unproduced, unrepresented writers via email. Project types include Feature Films, TV, and Commercials. Preferred genres include Action, Comedy, Non-Fiction, Reality, Romance, and Thriller.

Gary Goldstein
Producer
Email: gary@garywgoldstein.com
IMDb: imdb.com/name/nm0326214

Sandra Tomita
Associate Producer
IMDb: imdb.com/name/nm0866739

Catherine Wachter
Development Associate

THE GOODMAN COMPANY

8491 Sunset Blvd, Suite 329
Los Angeles, CA 90069
Phone: 323-655-0719

Email: ilyssagoodman@sbcglobal.net

Accepts query letter from unproduced, unrepresented writers. Project types include Feature Films and TV. Preferred genres include Comedy, Drama, Family, Non-Fiction, and Reality.

Ilyssa Goodman
President/Producer
IMDb: imdb.com/name/nm1058415

THE GOTHAM GROUP

9255 Sunset Blvd, Suite 515
Los Angeles, CA 90069
Phone: 310-285-0001
Fax: 310-285-0077

Home Page: gotham-group.com

Does not accept any unsolicited material. Project types include Feature Films, TV, and Commercials. Preferred genres include Action, Animation, Comedy, Drama, Family, Fantasy, Non-Fiction, Reality, and Science Fiction.

Julie Kane-Ritsch
Manager/Producer
Email: jkr@gotham-group.com
IMDb: imdb.com/name/nm1415970

Peter McHugh
Manager/Producer
Email: peter@gotham-group.com

Ellen Goldsmith-Vein
CEO/Founder
Email: egv@gotham-group.com
IMDb: imdb.com/name/nm1650412

THE GREENBERG GROUP

2029 S Westgate Ave
Los Angeles, CA 90025

Email: info@greenberggroup.com
Home Page: greenberggroup.com

Accepts query letter from unproduced, unrepresented writers via email. Project types include Feature Films, TV, and Commercials. Preferred genres include Action, Non-Fiction, Reality, and Thriller.

Randy Greenberg
CEO, Executive Producer
Email: randy@greenberggroup.com
IMDb: imdb.com/name/nm2985843

THE GROUP ENTERTAINMENT

115 W 29th St #1102
New York, NY 10001
Phone: 212-868-5233
Fax: 212-504-3082

Email: info@thegroupentertainment.com
Home Page: thegroupentertainment.com

Does not accept any unsolicited material. Project types include Feature Films and TV. Preferred genres include Action, Comedy, Drama, Non-Fiction, Reality, and Romance.

Gil Holland
Partner/Producer
IMDb: imdb.com/name/nm0390693

Rebecca Atwood
Creative Executive
Email: rebecca@thegroupentertainment.com

Kyle Luker
Partner
Email: kyle@thegroupentertainment.com

Jill McGrath
Partner
Email: jill@thegroupentertainment.com

THE HALCYON COMPANY

8455 Beverly Blvd
Penthouse Suite
Los Angeles, CA 90048
Phone: 323-650-0222

Email: info@thehalcyoncompany.com
Home Page: thehalcyoncompany.com

Does not accept any unsolicited material. Project types include Feature Films. Preferred genres include Action, Science Fiction, and Thriller. Established in 2006.

James Middleton
Creative Development and Production
IMDb: imdb.com/name/nm2194360

Derek Anderson
Co-CEO
IMDb: imdb.com/name/nm2203770

Victor Kubicek
Co-CEO
IMDb: imdb.com/name/nm2127497

THE HAL LIEBERMAN COMPANY

8522 National Blvd, Suite 108
Culver City, CA 90232
Phone: 310-202-1929
Fax: 323-850-5132

Accepts query letter from unproduced, unrepresented writers via email. Project types include Feature Films. Preferred genres include Drama, Family, Fantasy, Horror, and Thriller.

Dan Scheinkman
Vice President

Hal Lieberman
Producer
IMDb: imdb.com/name/nm0509386

THE HATCHERY

2950 N Hollywood Way
3rd Floor
Burbank, CA 91505
Phone: 818-748-4507
Fax: 818-748-4615/Attn: Dan Angel

Email: dangel@thehatcheryllc.com
Home Page: thehatcheryllc.com

Does not accept any unsolicited material. Project types include Feature Films and TV. Preferred genres include Comedy, Family, Horror, and Science Fiction.

Dan Angel
CCO/Executive Producer
Email: dangel@thehatcheryllc.com
IMDb: imdb.com/name/nm0029445

THE HECHT COMPANY

3607 W Magnolia, Suite L
Burbank, CA 91505
Phone: 310-989-3467

Email: hechtco@aol.com

Accepts query letter from unproduced, unrepresented writers via email. Project types include Feature Films and TV. Preferred genres include Drama, Non-Fiction, Reality, and Thriller.

Duffy Hecht
Producer
IMDb: imdb.com/name/nm0372953

THE JIM HENSON COMPANY

1416 N La Brea Ave
Hollywood, CA 90028
Phone: 323-802-1500
Fax: 323-802-1825

Email: info@henson.com
Home Page: henson.com

Does not accept any unsolicited material. Project types include Feature Films, TV, Commercials, and Theater.

Preferred genres include Animation, Comedy, Family, Fantasy, Non-Fiction, Reality, and Science Fiction. Established in 1958.

Brian Henson
Chairman

Halle Stanford
Executive Vice-President, Children's TV

Jason Lust
Sr. Vice-President, Feature Films

Blanca Lista
Director of Development

Halle Stanford-Grossman
EVP Children's Television

THE LITTLEFIELD COMPANY

500 S Buena Vista St Animation Building, Suite 3D-2
Burbank, CA 91521
Phone: 818-560-2280
Fax: 818-560-3775

Does not accept any unsolicited material. Project types include TV. Preferred genres include Drama.

Warren Littlefield
Principal
Phone: 818-560-2280
IMDb: imdb.com/name/nm0514716
Assistant: Patricia Mann

Andrew Bourne
Senior Vice President of Development
Phone: 818-560-2280
IMDb: imdb.com/name/nm2044331
Assistant: Janelle Young

Jill Young
Development Executive

THE MARK GORDON COMPANY

12200 W Olympic Blvd, Suite 250
Los Angeles, CA 90064
Phone: 310-943-6401
Fax: 310-943-6402

Does not accept any unsolicited material. Project types include Feature Films and TV. Preferred genres include Action and Drama.

Mark Gordon
Principal/Producer
IMDb: imdb.com/name/nm0330428
Assistant: Lindsey Martin

Bryan Zuriff
Executive Vice-President, Film
IMDb: imdb.com/name/nm3050339
Assistant: Ivey Harden

Shara Senderoff
Vice-President New Media & Director, Film Development
IMDb: imdb.com/name/nm2994844

THE MAZUR/KAPLAN COMPANY

3204 Pearl St
Santa Monica, CA 90405
Phone: 310-450-5838

Email: info@mazurkaplan.com
Home Page: mazurkaplan.com

Does not accept any unsolicited material. Project types include Feature Films and TV. Preferred genres include Comedy, Family, Fantasy, Non-Fiction, Reality, Romance, and Thriller. Established in 2009.

Paula Mazur
Producer
Phone: 310-450-5838
IMDb: imdb.com/name/nm0563394

Kimi Armstrong Stein
Vice-President of Development
Email: kimi@mazurkaplan.com
IMDb: imdb.com/name/nm2148964

Sarah Carbiener
Creative Executive
Email: sarah@mazurkaplan.com
IMDb: imdb.com/name/nm3745774

Mitchell Kaplan
Producer
IMDb: imdb.com/name/nm3125086

THE MONTECITO PICTURE COMPANY

9465 Wilshire Blvd, Suite 920
Beverly Hills, CA 90212

Phone: 310-247-9880
Fax: 310-247-9498

Home Page: montecitopicturecompany.com

Accepts query letter from unproduced, unrepresented writers. Project types include Feature Films and TV. Preferred genres include Action, Comedy, Drama, Family, Non-Fiction, Period, and Thriller. Established in 2000.

Alex Plapinger
Vice-President of Development
Phone: 310-247-9880
IMDb: imdb.com/name/nm3292687

Ivan Reitman
Partner
IMDb: imdb.com/name/nm0718645
Assistant: Eric Reich

Tom Pollock
Partner
IMDb: imdb.com/name/nm0689696
Assistant: Krystee Morgan

Joe Medjuck
Partner
IMDb: imdb.com/name/nm0575817

THE PITT GROUP

9465 Wilshire Blvd, Suite 420
Beverly Hills, CA 90212
Phone: 310-246-4800
Fax: 310-275-9258

Accepts query letter from unproduced, unrepresented writers. Project types include Feature Films and TV. Preferred genres include Animation, Comedy, Crime, Detective, Drama, and Romance. Established in 2000.

Lou Pitt
President
Email: lpitt@pittgroup.com
IMDb: imdb.com/name/nm2229316

Jeremy Conrady
Creative Executive
Email: jconrady@pittgroup.com
IMDb: imdb.com/name/nm262042

THE RADMIN COMPANY

9201 Wilshire Blvd, Suite 102
Beverly Hills, CA 90210
Phone: 310-274-9515
Fax: 310-274-0739

Email: queries@radmincompany.com
Home Page: radmincompany.com

Accepts query letter from unproduced, unrepresented writers via email. Project types include Feature Films. Preferred genres include Comedy, Drama, and Romance. Established in 1993.

Linne Radmin
Producer

Libby Allen
Creative Executive

Isabel Shanahan
Creative Executive
Email: isabel@radmincompany.com

THE SHEPHARD/ROBIN COMPANY

c/o Raleigh Studios
5300 Melrose Ave, Suite 225E
Los Angeles, CA 90038
Phone: 323-871-4412
Fax: 323-871-4418

Does not accept any unsolicited material. Project types include TV. Preferred genres include Drama.

Greer Shephard
Executive Producer/Owner

Michael Robin
Executive Producer/Owner

THE STEVE TISCH COMPANY

10202 W Washington Blvd
Astaire Building, 3rd Floor
Culver City, CA 90232
Phone: 310-244-6612
Fax: 310-204-2713

Accepts query letter from unproduced, unrepresented writers. Project types include Feature Films. Preferred genres include Action, Comedy, Drama, and Thriller.

Steve Tisch
Chairman

Lacy Boughn
Director, Development
Phone: 310-244-6620
Email: lacy_boughn@spe.sony.com

THE TANNENBAUM COMPANY

c/o CBS Studios
4024 Radford Ave, Bungalow 16
Studio City, CA 91604
Phone: 818-655-7181
Fax: 818-655-7193

Does not accept any unsolicited material. Project types include Feature Films and TV. Preferred genres include Comedy, Drama, Non-Fiction, and Reality.

Eric Tannenbaum
Producer

Jason Wang
Creative Affairs

Kim Haswell-Tannenbaum
Producer

Nicholas Pietryga
Assistant

Amanda Tomasetti
Assistant

THE WALT DISNEY COMPANY

500 S Buena Vista St
Burbank, CA 91521
Phone: 818-560-1000
Fax: 818-560-2500

Home Page: disney.com

Does not accept any unsolicited material. Project types include TV. Preferred genres include Action, Animation, Comedy, Drama, Family, Fantasy, Myth, and Non-Fiction. Established in 1923.

Robert Iger
Chairman of the Board, CEO
Email: bob.iger@disney.com
IMDb: imdb.com/name/nm2250609

Rita Ferro
Executive Vice President

Mary Ann Hughes
Vice President
IMDb: imdb.com/name/nm3134377

THE WEINSTEIN COMPANY

New York Branch:
375 Greenwich St, Lobby A
New York, NY 10013-2376
Phone: 212-941-3800
Fax: 212-941-3949

Los Angeles Branch:
9100 Wilshire Blvd, Suite 700W
Beverly Hills, CA 90212
Phone: 424-204-4800

Email: info@weinsteinco.com
Home Page: weinsteinco.com

Does not accept any unsolicited material. Project types include Feature Films and TV. Preferred genres include Action, Animation, Comedy, Drama, Family, Myth, Non-Fiction, Romance, and Thriller. Established in 2005.

Harvey Weinstein
Co-Chairman
Assistant: Brendon Boyea

Barbara Schneeweiss
Vice President (Development & Production for TV & Film)

Collin Creighton
Vice President (Production & Development)

Bob Weinstein
Co-Chairman

THE WOLPER ORGANIZATION

4000 Warner Blvd.
Bldg. 14, Ste. 200
Burbank, CA 91504
Phone: 818-954-1421
Fax: 818-954-1593

Home Page: wolperorg.com

Does not accept any unsolicited material. Project types include Feature Films and TV. Preferred genres include Crime, Detective, and Drama. Established in 1987.

Mark Wolper
President/Executive Producer
IMDb: imdb.com/name/nm0938679

Kevin Nicklaus
Vice-President Development
IMDb: imdb.com/name/nm2102454

Sam Alexander
Director of Development
Email: Sam.Alexander@wbtvprod.com
IMDb: imdb.com/name/nm3303012

David L. Wolper
President/Executive Producer
IMDb: imdb.com/name/nm0938678

THE ZANUCK COMPANY

16 Beverly Park
Beverly Hills, CA 90210
Phone: 310-274-0261
Fax: 310-273-9217

Does not accept any unsolicited material. Project types include Feature Films and TV. Preferred genres include Action, Comedy, Crime, Drama, Family, Fantasy, Period, Romance, and Thriller. Established in 1988.

Harrison Zanuck
Producer
Phone: 310-274-5929

Richard Zanuck
Producer
Phone: 310-274-0261
IMDb: imdb.com/name/nm0005573

Lili Fini Zanuck
Producer/Director
Phone: 310-274-0209
IMDb: imdb.com/name/nm0005572
Assistant: Aubrie Artiano

Brenda Berrisford
Assistant

THOUSAND WORDS

110 S Fairfax Ave, Suite 370
Los Angeles, CA 90036
Phone: 323-936-4700
Fax: 323-936-4701

Email: info@thousand-words.com
Home Page: thousand-words.com

Accepts query letter from unproduced, unrepresented writers via email. Project types include Feature Films. Preferred genres include Animation, Drama, and Thriller. Established in 2000.

Jonah Smith
Co-President
Phone: 323-936-4700
Email: info@thousand-words.com
IMDb: imdb.com/name/nm0808819

Palmer West
Founder, Co-President
Phone: 323-936-4700
Email: info@thousand-words.com
IMDb: imdb.com/name/nm0922279

Michael Van Vliet
Creative Executive
Phone: 323-936-4700
Email: info@thousand-words.com
IMDb: imdb.com/name/nm2702900

Jesse Johnston
Director of Development

THREE STRANGE ANGELS, INC.

9050 W Washington Blvd
Culver City, CA 90232
Phone: 310-840-8213

Does not accept any unsolicited material. Project types include Feature Films. Preferred genres include Action, Comedy, and Fantasy.

Lindsay Doran
President, Producer
Phone: 310-840-8213
IMDb: imdb.com/name/nm0233386
Assistant: Natasha Khrolenko

THUNDERBIRD FILMS

401 - 533 Smithe St
Vancouver, BC V6B 6H1
Canada
Phone: +604-683-3555
Fax: +604-707-0378

Email: info@hunderbirdfilms.net
Home Page: thunderbirdfilms.net/s/Home.asp
IMDb: imdb.com/company/co0163158

Does not accept any unsolicited material. Project types include TV. Preferred genres include Comedy and Drama.

Tim Gamble
CEO
IMDb: imdb.com/name/nm0303817

Alex Raffe
Head of Production & Development
Email: alex@thunderbirdfilms.com
IMDb: imdb.com/name/nm0706244

Danielle Kreinik
Head of Development

THUNDER ROAD PICTURES

1411 5th St Suite 400
Santa Monica, CA 90401
Phone: 310-573-8885

Does not accept any unsolicited material. Project types include Feature Films and TV. Preferred genres include Action, Crime, Detective, Drama, Non-Fiction, and Thriller. Established in 2003.

Basil Iwanyk
Owner
IMDb: imdb.com/name/nm0412588

Kent Kubena
Sr. Vice-President, Development & Production/ Producer
IMDb: imdb.com/name/nm0473423
Assistant: Noah Winter

Erica Lee
Vice President- Development
IMDb: imdb.com/name/nm3102707
Assistant: Noah Winter

Peter Lawson
President
IMDb: imdb.com/name/nm4498662
Assistant: Taylor Zea

Kerri L. Anderson
Executive - Director of Television
IMDb: imdb.com/name/nm2563841

TIG PRODUCTIONS

4450 Lakeside Dr
Ste 225
Burbank, CA 91505
Phone: 818-260-8707

Does not accept any unsolicited material. Project types include Feature Films. Preferred genres include Drama and Romance.

Kevin Costner
Executive Partner
IMDb: imdb.com/name/nm0000126

TIM BURTON PRODUCTIONS

8033 Sunset Blvd, Suite 7500
West Hollywood, CA 90046
Phone: 310-300-1670
Fax: 310-300-1671

Home Page: timburton.com

Does not accept any unsolicited material. Project types include Feature Films. Preferred genres include Action, Family, and Fantasy. Established in 1989.

Tim Burton
Director/Producer
Phone: 310-300-1670
Email: kory.edwrds@timburton.com
IMDb: imdb.com/name/nm0000318
Assistant: Kory Edwards

Derek Frey
Executive/Producer
Email: derek@lazerfilm.com
IMDb: imdb.com/name/nm0294553

TOM WELLING PRODUCTIONS

4000 Warner Blvd
Building 146, Room 201

Burbank, CA 91522
Phone: 818-954-4012

Does not accept any unsolicited material. Project types include TV. Preferred genres include Drama. Established in 2010.

Tom Welling
Principal
Phone: 818-954-4012
IMDb: imdb.com/name/nm0919991

Amy Suh
Director of Development
Phone: 818-954-4012

Stephanie Levine
President
Phone: 818-954-4012

TONIK PRODUCTIONS

27 W 24th St. Suite 1108
New York, NY 10010
Phone: 212-532-6565
Fax: 212-532-6650

Email: info@tonikproductions.com
Home Page: http://www.tonikproductions.com/home
IMDb: imdb.com/company/co0078138

Accepts query letter from unproduced, unrepresented writers via email. Project types include Feature Films. Preferred genres include Comedy, Drama, Family, Fantasy, and Science Fiction.

Tonya Lewis Lee
Producer
IMDb: imdb.com/name/nm1416174

Nikki SIlver
Producer
IMDb: imdb.com/name/nm1012185

TOOL OF NORTH AMERICA

2210 Broadway
Santa Monica, CA 90404
Phone: 310-453-9244
Fax: 310-453-4185

50 W 17th St, 4th Floor
New York, NY 10011

Phone: 212-924-1100
Fax: 212-924-1156

Home Page: toolofna.com
Facebook: facebook.com/toolofna

Accepts query letter from unproduced, unrepresented writers via email. Project types include Feature Films, TV, and Commercials. Preferred genres include Drama, Horror, Non-Fiction, Reality, and Thriller.

Brian Latt
Managing Director
Email: brian@toolofna.com
IMDb: imdb.com/name/nm0490373

Oliver Fuselier
Executive Producer
Email: oliver@toolofna.com
IMDb: imdb.com/name/nm0299336

Dustin Callif
Email: dustin@toolofna.com
IMDb: imdb.com/name/nm2956668

Rio Dylan Hernandez
Head of Feature Film and TV Development

TORNELL PRODUCTIONS

80 Varick St, Suite 10C
New York, NY 10013
Phone: 212-625-2530
Fax: 212-625-2532

Accepts query letter from unproduced, unrepresented writers. Project types include Feature Films.

Lisa Tornell
Producer
Phone: 212-625-2530
IMDb: imdb.com/name/nm0868178

TOWER OF BABBLE ENTERTAINMENT

854 N Spaulding Ave
Los Angeles, CA 90046
Phone: 323-230-6128
Fax: 323-822-0312

Email: info@towerofb .com
Home Page: towerofb .com

Accepts query letter from unproduced, unrepresented writers via email. Project types include Feature Films and TV. Preferred genres include Comedy and Romance.

Jeff Wadlow
Writer/Director
Phone: 323-230-6128
Email: info@towerofb .com
IMDb: imdb.com/name/nm0905592

Beau Bauman
Writer/Producer
Phone: 323-230-6128
Email: info@towerofb .com
IMDb: imdb.com/name/nm0062149

TRANCAS INTERNATIONAL FILMS

2021 Pontius Ave
2nd Fl
Los Angeles, CA 90025
Phone: 310-477-6569
Fax: 310-477-7126

Email: info@trancasfilms.com
Home Page: trancasfilms.com

Does not accept any unsolicited material. Project types include Feature Films and TV. Preferred genres include Action, Comedy, Drama, Horror, and Thriller.

Malek Akkad
Chairman & CEO
IMDb: imdb.com/name/nm0015443

Louis Nader
Vice President of Production & Development
IMDb: imdb.com/name/nm0618868

Thomas Fleming
Assistant Director Digital & New Media

TRIBECA PRODUCTIONS

375 Greenwich St, 8th Floor
New York, NY 10013
Phone: 212-941-2400
Fax: 212-941-3939

Email: info@tribecafilm.com
Home Page: tribecafilm.com

Does not accept any unsolicited material. Project types include Feature Films and TV. Preferred genres include Action, Comedy, Crime, Drama, Fantasy, Non-Fiction, Period, Romance, and Thriller. Established in 1989.

Robert De Niro
Partner
Phone: 212-941-2400
IMDb: imdb.com/name/nm0000134

Berry Welsh
Director of Development
Phone: 212-941-2400
IMDb: imdb.com/name/nm2654730

Jane Rosenthal
Partner
Assistant: Gigi Graff

TRICOAST STUDIOS

11124 W Washington Blvd
Culver City, CA 90232
Phone: 310-458-7707
Fax: 310-204-2450

Email: tricoast@tricoast.com
Home Page: tricoast.com

Does not accept any unsolicited material. Project types include Feature Films and TV.

Tory Weisz
Vice-President Development, Producer
Phone: 310-458-7707
IMDb: imdb.com/name/nm3258419

TRICOR ENTERTAINMENT

1613 Chelsea Rd
San Marino, CA 91108
Phone: 626-282-5184
Fax: 626-282-5185

Email: ExecutiveOffices@TricorEntertainment.com
Home Page: TricorEntertainment.com

Does not accept any unsolicited material. Project types include Feature Films.

Craig Darian
Co-Chairman/CEO
Phone: 626-282-5184
IMDb: imdb.com/name/nm1545768

TRILOGY ENTERTAINMENT GROUP

627 S Plymouth Blvd The Studio
Los Angeles, CA 90005
Phone: 310-656-9733
Fax: 310-424-5816

Home Page: trilogyent.com

Does not accept any unsolicited material. Project types include Feature Films and TV. Preferred genres include Action, Comedy, Fantasy, Romance, and Thriller.

Pen Densham
Partner
Phone: 310-656-9733
IMDb: imdb.com/name/nm0219720

Alex Daltas
President, Production
Email: adaltas@trilogyent.com
IMDb: imdb.com/name/nm0198226

Nevin Densham
Creative Executive/Head, Development
Email: bfl am@trilogyent.com
IMDb: imdb.com/name/nm0219719

John Watson
Partner
IMDb: imdb.com/name/nm2302370

Howard Han
Consultant

TROIKA PICTURES

2019 S Westgate Ave
2nd Floor
Los Angeles, CA 90025
Phone: 310-696-2859

Email: troikapics@gmail.com
Home Page: troikapictures.com

Does not accept any unsolicited material. Project types include Feature Films. Preferred genres include Action, Crime, Fantasy, Romance, and Thriller.

Robert Stein
Co-CEO
Phone: 310-696-2859
IMDb: imdb.com/name/nm3355501

Michael Helfant
Co-CEO
Phone: 310-696-2859
IMDb: imdb.com/name/nm0375033

Bradley Gallo
Head of Production & Development
Phone: 310-696-2859
IMDb: imdb.com/name/nm0303010

TROMA ENTERTAINMENT

36-40 11th St
Long Island City, NY 11106
Phone: 718-391-0110
Fax: 718-391-0255

Email: troma1@gmail.com
Home Page: troma.com

Accepts scripts from unproduced, unrepresented writers. Project types include Feature Films. Preferred genres include Action, Drama, Fantasy, Horror, Science Fiction, Sociocultural, and Thriller.

Lloyd Kaufman
President
Email: lloyd@troma.com
IMDb: imdb.com/name/nm0442207

Michael Herz
Vice President
IMDb: imdb.com/name/nm0381230

TURTLEBACK PRODUCTIONS, INC.

11736 Gwynne Ln
Los Angeles, CA, CA 90077
Phone: 310-440-8587
Fax: 310-440-8903

Accepts query letter from unproduced, unrepresented writers. Project types include Feature Films and TV.

Preferred genres include Crime, Drama, Fantasy, and Thriller. Established in 1988.

Howard Meltzer
President/Executive Producer
Phone: 310-440-8587
IMDb: imdb.com/name/nm0578430

TV LAND
1515 Broadway 38th Floor
New York, NY 10036
Phone: 212-258-7500

Email: info@tvland.com
Home Page: tvland.com

Accepts query letter from unproduced, unrepresented writers via email. Project types include TV. Preferred genres include Comedy and Drama. Established in 1996.

Larry Jones
President
Phone: 212-846-6000
Email: larry.jones@tvland.com
IMDb: imdb.com/name/nm1511130

Scott Gregory
Vice President (Programming)

Bradley Gardner
Vice President (Development & Original Programming)

Rose Catherine Pinkney
Vice President (Development & Original Programming)
IMDb: imdb.com/name/nm0684384

Miranda Acevedo
Executive Assistant

TV ONE LLC
1010 Wayne Ave
Silver Spring, MD 20910
Phone: 301-755-0400

Home Page: tvoneonline.com

Accepts query letter from produced or represented writers. Project types include TV. Preferred genres include Comedy and Drama. Established in 2004.

Alfred Liggins
Chairman
Phone: 301-755-0400
Email: aliggins@tv-one.tv
IMDb: imdb.com/name/nm3447190

Toni Judkins
Senior Vice President (Original Programming)

Jubba Seyyid
Director (Programming & Production)

TV REPAIR
857 Castaic Place
Pacific Palisades, CA 90272
Phone: 310-459-3671
Fax: 310-459-4251

Email: davidjlatt@earthlink.net

Accepts query letter from unproduced, unrepresented writers via email. Project types include TV.

David Latt
Producer/Writer
Phone: 310-459-3671
Email: davidjlatt@earthlink.net
IMDb: imdb.com/name/nm0490374

TWENTIETH CENTURY FOX FILM
10201 W Pico Blvd
Los Angeles, CA 90035
Phone: 310-369-1000
Fax: 310-203-1558

Email: foxmovies@fox.com
Home Page: fox.com

Does not accept any unsolicited material. Project types include Feature Films and TV. Preferred genres include Action, Comedy, Crime, Detective, Drama, Family, Fantasy, Horror, Myth, Non-Fiction, Romance, and Thriller. Established in 1935.

Emma Watts
President (Production)

Kimberly Cooper
Executive Vice President (Feature Productions)

Ted Dodd
Senior Vice President (Creative Affairs)

David A Starke
Senior Vice President (Production)

Steve Freedman
Vice President (Feature Production)

TWENTIETH CENTURY FOX TELEVISION

10201 W Pico Blvd
Building 103, Room 5286
Los Angeles, CA 90035
Phone: 310-369-1000
Fax: 310-369-8726

Email: info@fox.com
Home Page: fox.com

Does not accept any unsolicited material. Project types include TV. Preferred genres include Comedy and Drama. Established in 1949.

Gary Newman
Chairman
Email: gary.newman@fox.com
IMDb: imdb.com/name/nm3050096

Dana Walden
Chairman

Jonathan Davis
Executive Vice President (Comedy Development & Animation)

Dana Honor
Senior Vice President (Comedy Development)

Lisa Katz
Senior Vice President (Drama Development)

Mark Ambrose
Director (Drama Development)

Jennifer Carreras
Director (Comedy Development)

TWENTIETH TELEVISION

2121 Ave of the Stars
17th Floor
Los Angeles, CA 90067
Phone: 310-369-1000

Email: info@fox.com
Home Page: fox.com

Does not accept any unsolicited material. Project types include TV. Preferred genres include Comedy and Drama. Established in 1992.

Greg Meidel
President, Twentieth Television
IMDb: imdb.com/name/nm2518163

Roger Ailes
Chairman

Stephen Brown
EVP Programming and Development

Deborah Norton
VP, Programming

TWINSTAR ENTERTAINMENT

4041 MacArthur Blvd, Suite 475
Newport Beach, CA 92660
Phone: 949-474-8600

Email: info@twinstarentertainment.com
Home Page: twinstarentertainment.com

Accepts scripts from unproduced, unrepresented writers. Project types include TV. Preferred genres include Animation, Comedy, Drama, and Family. Established in 2003.

Russell Werdin
CEO
Phone: 949-474-8600
Email: info@twinstarentertainment.com
IMDb: imdb.com/name/nm2232609

TWISTED PICTURES

901 N Highland Ave
Los Angeles, CA 90038
Phone: 323-850-3232
Fax: 323-850-0521

Accepts query letter from unproduced, unrepresented writers. Project types include Feature Films and TV. Preferred genres include Crime, Horror, and Thriller.

Michael J. Menchel
President

Mark Burg
Principal
IMDb: imdb.com/name/nm0121117
Assistant: James Cole

Oren Koules
Executive
IMDb: imdb.com/name/nm0467977
Assistant: James Cole

Carl Mazzocone
Executive
IMDb: imdb.com/name/nm0563604

TWO TON FILMS

375 Greenwich St
New York, NY 10013
Phone: 212-941-3863

Email: info@twotonfilms.com
Home Page: twotonfilms.com

Accepts query letter from unproduced, unrepresented writers via email. Project types include Feature Films and TV. Preferred genres include Action, Comedy, Drama, and Family.

Justin Zackham
Partner/Producer/Writer
Phone: 212-941-3863
Email: info@twotonfilms.com
IMDb: imdb.com/name/nm0951698

Clay Pecorin
Partner/Producer
Phone: 212-941-3863
Email: info@twotonfilms.com
IMDb: imdb.com/name/nm2668976

UFLAND PRODUCTIONS

963 Moraga Dr
Los Angeles, CA 90049
Phone: 310-476-4520
Fax: 310-476-4891

Email: ufland.productions@verizon.net

Does not accept any unsolicited material. Project types include Feature Films and TV. Preferred genres include Comedy, Drama, and Romance. Established in 1972.

Harry Ufland
Principal/Producer
Phone: 310-437-0805
IMDb: imdb.com/name/nm0880036

Mary Jane Ufland
Producer
IMDb: imdb.com/name/nm0880040

UNDERGROUND FILMS

447 S Highland Ave
Los Angeles, CA 90036
Phone: 323-930-2588
Fax: 323-930-2334

Email: submissions@undergroundfilms.net
Home Page: undergroundfilms.net

Accepts scripts from unproduced, unrepresented writers via email. Project types include TV. Preferred genres include Action, Animation, Comedy, Drama, Family, Fantasy, Horror, Myth, Non-Fiction, Romance, and Thriller. Established in 2003.

Trevor Engelson
Principal/Producer
Phone: 323-930-2569
Email: trevor@undergroundfilms.net
IMDb: imdb.com/name/nm0257333

Noah Rothman
Producer
Phone: 323-930-2588
Email: noah@undergroundfilms.net

Josh McGuire Turner
Producer
Phone: 323-930-2435
Email: josh@undergroundfilms.net

Evan Silverberg
Producer
Phone: 323-930-2588
Email: evan@undergroundfilms.net

Austin Bedell
Producer
Phone: 323-930-2588
Email: austin@undergroundfilms.net

Chris Dennis
Producer/Principal
Phone: 323-930-2588
Email: chris@undergroundfilms.net

UNIFIED PICTURES

19773 Bahama St
Northridge, CA 91324
Phone: 818-576-1006
Fax: 818-534-3347

Email: info@unifiedpictures.com
Home Page: unifiedpictures.com

Accepts query letter from unproduced, unrepresented writers. Project types include Feature Films. Preferred genres include Action, Comedy, Crime, Detective, Drama, Horror, and Thriller. Established in 2004.

Keith Kjarval
Founder/Producer
IMDb: imdb.com/name/nm1761309

Kurt Rauer
Founder/Producer
IMDb: imdb.com/name/nm0970009

Shaun Clapham
Creative Executive
Email: sclapham@unifi edpictures.com
IMDb: imdb.com/name/nm4111097

Steve Goldstein
President/Business Development
IMDb: imdb.com/name/nm2179640

Paul Michael Ruffman
Vice President/Business Development

UNION ENTERTAINMENT

9255 Sunset Blvd, Suite 528
West Hollywood, CA 90069
Phone: 310-274-7040
Fax: 310-274-1065

Email: info@unionent.com
Home Page: unionent.com
IMDb: imdb.com/company/co0183888

Does not accept any unsolicited material. Project types include Video Games. Preferred genres include Animation. Established in 2006.

Richard Leibowitz
President
Phone: 310-274-7040
Email: rich@unionent.com
IMDb: imdb.com/name/nm2325318
Assistant: Sarah Logie

Howard Bliss
Business Affairs
Email: howard@unionent.com
IMDb: imdb.com/name/nm2973051

UNIQUE FEATURES

116 N Robertson Blvd, Suite 909
Los Angeles, CA 90048
Phone: 310-492-8009
Fax: 310-492-8022

IMDb: imdb.com/company/co0242085

Does not accept any unsolicited material. Project types include Feature Films and TV. Established in 2008.

Mark Kaufman
Head, East Coast Production & Development
Phone: 212-649-4855
IMDb: imdb.com/name/nm0442212

Dylan Sellers
Head, West Coast Production & Development
Phone: 310-492-8009
IMDb: imdb.com/name/nm0783346

Michael Lynne
Executive - West Coast Branch
Phone: 310-492-8009
IMDb: imdb.com/name/nm1088153

UNIQUE FEATURES

888 7th Ave, 16th Floor
New York, NY 10106
Phone: 212-649-4980
Fax: 212-649-4999

IMDb: imdb.com/company/co0242085

Does not accept any unsolicited material. Project types include Feature Films and TV. Established in 2008.

Mark Kaufman
Head, East Coast Production & Development
Phone: 212-649-4855
IMDb: imdb.com/name/nm0442212

Dylan Sellers
Head, West Coast Production & Development
Phone: 310-492-8009
IMDb: imdb.com/name/nm0783346

Michael Lynne
Executive - West Coast Branch
Phone: 310-492-8009
IMDb: imdb.com/name/nm1088153

UNISON FILMS

790 Madison Ave
Suite 306
New York, NY 10065
Phone: 212-226-1200
Fax: 646-349-1738

Email: info@unisonfilms.com
Home Page: unisonfilms.com

Project types include Feature Films. Preferred genres include Comedy, Drama, and Romance. Established in 2004.

Emanuel Michael
Partner
IMDb: imdb.com/name/nm1639578

Cassandra Kulukundis
Partner
IMDb: imdb.com/name/nm0474697

Ryan Brooks
Executive Producer

Cliff Curtis
Producer

UNITED ARTISTS

245 N Beverly Dr
Beverly Hills, CA 90210
Phone: 310-449-3000
Fax: 310-586-8358

Home Page: unitedartists.com
IMDb: imdb.com/company/co0026841

Does not accept any unsolicited material. Project types include Feature Films and TV. Preferred genres include Action, Crime, and Drama. Established in 1919.

Tom Cruise
Producer
Phone: 310-449-3000
IMDb: imdb.com/name/nm0000129

Don Granger
President, Production
Phone: 310-449-3000
IMDb: imdb.com/name/nm1447370

Elliot Kleinberg
COO
Phone: 310-449-3000
IMDb: imdb.com/name/nm2552087

UNIVERSAL CABLE PRODUCTIONS

100 Universal City Plaza
Building 1440, 14th Floor
Universal City, CA 91608
Phone: 818-840-4444

Home Page: nbcumv.com
IMDb: imdb.com/company/co0242101

Accepts query letter from unproduced, unrepresented writers. Project types include TV. Preferred genres include Comedy and Drama. Established in 1997.

Bonnie Hammer
Chairman, NBCUniversal Cable Entertainment
Phone: 818-840-4444
IMDb: imdb.com/name/nm1045499

UNIVERSAL STUDIOS

100 Universal City Plaza
Universal City, CA 91608
Phone: 818-840-4444

Home Page: universalstudios.com
IMDb: imdb.com/company/co0000534

Accepts query letter from unproduced, unrepresented writers. Project types include Feature Films and TV. Preferred genres include Action, Animation, Comedy, Crime, Detective, Drama, Family, Fantasy, Horror,

Myth, Non-Fiction, Romance, Science Fiction, and Thriller. Established in 1912.

Ron Meyer
President & COO, Universal Studios & NBCUniversal
Phone: 818-840-4444
IMDb: imdb.com/name/nm0005228

UNIVERSAL TELEVISION (FORMERLY UNIVERSAL MEDIA STUDIOS)

100 Universal City Plaza
Building 1360, 3rd Floor
Universal City, CA 91608
Phone: 818-777-1000

Home Page: universalstudios.com
IMDb: imdb.com/company/co0096447

Accepts query letter from unproduced, unrepresented writers. Project types include TV. Preferred genres include Action, Animation, Comedy, Crime, Detective, Drama, Family, Fantasy, Myth, Non-Fiction, Romance, Science Fiction, and Thriller.

Bela Bajaria
Executive Vice-President, Universal Television
IMDb: imdb.com/name/nm0338612

UNSTOPPABLE

c/o Independent Talent Agency
76 Oxford St
London W1D 1BS
United Kingdom

Email: info@unstoppableentertainmentuk.com
Home Page: unstoppableentertainmentuk.com

Accepts scripts from unproduced, unrepresented writers. Project types include Feature Films. Preferred genres include Action, Comedy, Crime, Drama, Romance, Science Fiction, and Thriller. Established in 2007.

Noel Clarke
Actor/Writer/Producer
Email: noel@unstoppableentertainmentuk.com

UNTITLED ENTERTAINMENT

350 S Beverly Dr, Suite 200
Beverly Hills, CA 90212
Phone: 310-601-2100
Fax: 310-601-2344

IMDb: imdb.com/company/co0034249

Accepts query letter from unproduced, unrepresented writers. Project types include TV. Preferred genres include Comedy, Drama, Fantasy, Myth, Non-Fiction, and Romance.

Jason Weinberg
Partner
Phone: 310-601-2100
IMDb: imdb.com/name/nm4156256

UPLOAD FILMS

8522 National Blvd., #106
Culver City, CA 90232
Phone: 323-375-4270

Home Page: uploadfilms.com/index.php
IMDb: imdb.com/company/co0195173

Does not accept any unsolicited material. Project types include Feature Films. Preferred genres include Action, Detective, Drama, Horror, and Thriller. Established in 2006.

Nick Thurlow
Partner
Email: nick@uploadfilms.com
IMDb: imdb.com/name/nm2250917

Andrew Mann
Partner

John Portnoy
Partner
Email: jportnoy@uploadfilms.com
IMDb: imdb.com/name/nm0692471

UPPITV

c/o CBS Studios
4024 Radford Ave, Bungalow 9
Studio City, CA 91604
Phone: 818-655-5000

Does not accept any unsolicited material. Project types include TV. Preferred genres include Comedy and Drama.

Samuel Jackson
Principal
Phone: 818-655-5000
IMDb: imdb.com/name/nm0000168

USA NETWORK

30 Rockefeller Plaza
21st Floor
New York, NY 10112
Phone: 212-664-4444
Fax: 212-703-8582

IMDb: imdb.com/company/co0014957

Accepts query letter from unproduced, unrepresented writers via email. Project types include TV. Preferred genres include Comedy and Drama. Established in 1971.

Sally Whitehill
Director Of Development
Phone: 212-644-4444

VALHALLA MOTION PICTURES

3201 Cahuenga Blvd W
Los Angeles, CA 90068-1301
Phone: 323-850-3030
Fax: 323-850-3038

Email: vmp@valhallapix.com
Home Page: valhallapix.com

Does not accept any unsolicited material. Project types include Feature Films and TV. Preferred genres include Action, Drama, Fantasy, Horror, and Thriller.

Gale Hurd
CEO/Producer
Phone: 323-850-3030
Email: gah@valhallapix.com
IMDb: imdb.com/name/nm0005036

Kris Henigman
Director of Development
Email: vmp@valhallapix.com
IMDb: imdb.com/name/nm1898339

VANDERKLOOT FILM & TELEVISION

750 Ralph McGill Blvd N.E.
Atlanta, GA 30312
Phone: 404-221-0236
Fax: 404-221-1057

Email: bv@vanderkloot.com
Home Page: vanderkloot.com

Does not accept any unsolicited material. Project types include TV. Preferred genres include Action, Comedy, Drama, Family, and Non-Fiction. Established in 1976.

William VanDerKloot
President/Producer/Director
Phone: 404-221-0236
Email: william@vanderkloot.com
IMDb: imdb.com/name/nm0886281

Erin Grass
Director of Marketing
Email: erin@magiclantern.com
IMDb: imdb.com/name/nm3084570

VANGUARD FILMS/VANGUARD ANIMATION

8703 W Olympic Blvd
Los Angeles, CA 90035
Phone: 310-888-8020
Fax: 310-362-8685

Email: contact@vanguardanimation.com
Home Page: vanguardanimation.com

Does not accept any unsolicited material. Project types include Feature Films. Preferred genres include Animation. Established in 2004.

Robert Moreland
President Production & Development
Phone: 310-888-8020
IMDb: imdb.com/name/nm0603668

John Williams
Chairman & CEO
Phone: 310-888-8020
IMDb: imdb.com/name/nm0930964

VANGUARD PRODUCTIONS

12111 Beatrice St
Culver City, CA 90230

Phone: 310-306-4910
Fax: 310-306-1978

Email: info@vanguardproductions.biz
Home Page: vanguardproductions.biz

Accepts query letter from unproduced, unrepresented writers via email. Project types include TV. Preferred genres include Action, Comedy, Drama, Family, and Non-Fiction. Established in 1986.

Terence O'Keefe

Founder/Writer/Producer/Director
Phone: 310-306-4910
Email: terry@vanguardproductions.biz
IMDb: imdb.com/name/nm0641496

VANQUISH MOTION PICTURES

10 Universal City Plaza
NBC/Universal Building, 20th Floor
Universal City, CA 91608
Phone: 818-753-2319

Email: submissions@vanquishmotionpictures.com
Home Page: vanquishmotionpictures.com

Accepts query letter from unproduced, unrepresented writers via email. Project types include Feature Films and TV. Established in 2009.

Neetu Sharma

Creative Executive
Phone: 818-753-2319
Email: ns@vanquishmotionpictures.com
IMDb: imdb.com/name/nm3434485

Ryan Williams

Creative Executive
Phone: 818-753-2319
Email: rs@vanquishmotionpictures.com
IMDb: imdb.com/name/nm4426713

VARSITY PICTURES

1040 N Las Palmas Ave
Building 2, First Floor
Los Angeles, CA 90038
Phone: 310-601-1960
Fax: 310-601-1961

Accepts query letter from unproduced, unrepresented writers. Project types include Feature Films and TV. Established in 2007.

Meghann Collins

Film Development
Phone: 310-601-1960
IMDb: imdb.com/name/nm1937533

Shauna Phelan

Television Development
Phone: 310-601-1960
IMDb: imdb.com/name/nm1016912

Carter Hansen

Creative Executive
Phone: 310-601-1960
IMDb: imdb.com/name/nm3255715

VELOCITY PICTURES

4132 Woodcliff Rd
Sherman Oaks, CA 91403
Phone: 310-804-8554
Fax: 310-496-1329

Accepts query letter from unproduced, unrepresented writers. Preferred genres include Action, Drama, Non-Fiction, Romance, and Thriller. Established in 2006.

Ryan Johnson

Co-Founder
Phone: 310-804-8554
Email: ryanj@prettydangerousfilms.com
IMDb: imdb.com/name/nm1010198

Patrick Gallagher

Co-Founder
Phone: 310-804-8554
Email: pfgla@aol.com
IMDb: imdb.com/name/nm1725050

VERISIMILITUDE

225 W 13th St
New York, NY 10011
Phone: 212-989-1038
Fax: 212-989-1943

Email: info@verisimilitude.com
Home Page: verisimilitude.com

Accepts query letter from produced or represented writers. Project types include Feature Films. Preferred genres include Comedy, Drama, Romance, and Thriller.

Tyler Brodie

Partner
IMDb: mdb.com/name/nm0110921

Phaedon Papadopoulos

Creative Executive
IMDb: imdb.com/name/nm3011396

Hunter Gray

Partner
IMDb: imdb.com/name/nm0336683

Alex Orlovsky

Partner
IMDb: imdb.com/name/nm0650164

VERITE FILMS

15 Beaufort Rd
Toronto, ON M4E 1M6
Canada
Phone: 416 693 8245
Fax: 416 693 8252

Email: verite@veritefilms.ca
Home Page: veritefilms.ca

Accepts query letter from unproduced, unrepresented writers. Project types include TV. Preferred genres include Comedy, Drama, and Family. Established in 2004.

Virginia Thompson

Partner/President/Executive Producer
Phone: 306-585-1737
Email: virginia@veritefilms.ca
IMDb: imdb.com/name/nm1395111

VERTEBRA FILMS

1608 Vine St, Suite 503
Hollywood, CA 90028
Phone: 323-461-0021
Fax: 323-461-0031

Home Page: vertebrafilms.com

Accepts query letter from unproduced, unrepresented writers. Project types include Feature Films. Preferred

genres include Horror and Thriller. Established in 2010.

Mac Cappucino

IMDb: imdb.com/name/nm2225247

VERTIGO FILMS

The Big Room Studios 77 Fortess Rd
London, United Kingdom,
NW5 1AG
Phone: +44-0-20-7428-7555
Fax: +44-0-20-7485-9713

Email: mail@vertigofilms.com
Home Page: vertigofilms.com

Does not accept any unsolicited material. Project types include Feature Films. Preferred genres include Action, Comedy, Crime, Drama, Fantasy, Horror, Romance, Science Fiction, and Thriller. Established in 2002.

NIck Love

Principal
IMDb: imdb.com/name/nm0522393

James Richardson

Producer
IMDb: imdb.com/name/nm0724597

Allan Niblo

Producer
IMDb: imdb.com/name/nm0629242

Rupert Preston

Producer
IMDb: imdb.com/name/nm0696486

Jim Spencer

Producer
IMDb: imdb.com/name/nm2005794

VH1

2600 Colorado Ave
Santa Monica, CA 90404
Phone: 310 752 8000

Email: info@vh1.com
Home Page: vh1.com

Accepts query letter from unproduced, unrepresented writers. Project types include TV. Preferred genres include Comedy, Drama, Non-Fiction, and Romance. Established in 1986.

Van Toffler
President, MTVN Music, LOGO & Film
Phone: 212-846-8000
Email: van.toffler@vh1.com
IMDb: imdb.com/name/nm0865508

VIACOM INC.

1515 Broadway
New York, NY 10036
Phone: 212-258-6000

Home Page: viacom.com

Does not accept any unsolicited material. Project types include TV. Preferred genres include Comedy, Drama, and Non-Fiction. Established in 1971.

Philippe Dauman
President & CEO
Phone: 212-258-6000
Email: philippe.dauman@viacom.com
IMDb: imdb.com/name/nm2449184

VILLAGE ROADSHOW PICTURES

100 N Crescent Dr, Suite 323
Beverly Hills, CA 90210
Phone: 310-385-4300
Fax: 310-385-4301

Home Page: vreg.com/films

Does not accept any unsolicited material. Project types include Feature Films. Established in 1998.

Matt Skiena
Vice President of Production
Phone: 310-385-4300
Email: mskiena@vrpe.com
IMDb: imdb.com/name/nm3466832

Bruce Berman
Chairman/CEO
Phone: 310-385-4300
IMDb: imdb.com/name/nm0075732
Assistant: Suzy Figueroa

VINCENT NEWMAN ENTERTAINMENT

8840 Wilshire Blvd
3rd Floor
Los Angeles, CA 90211
Phone: 310-358-3050
Fax: 310-358-3289

Email: general@liveheart-vne.com

Accepts query letter from unproduced, unrepresented writers via email. Project types include TV. Preferred genres include Action, Comedy, Drama, Fantasy, Myth, and Thriller. Established in 2011.

Vincent Newman
Principal
Phone: 310-358-3050
Email: vincent@liveheart-vne.com
IMDb: imdb.com/name/nm0628304
Assistant: John Funk

VIN DI BONA PRODUCTIONS

12233 W Olympic Blvd, Suite 170
Los Angeles, CA 90064
Phone: 310-571-1875

Home Page: vdbp.com

Accepts query letter from unproduced, unrepresented writers. Project types include TV. Preferred genres include Comedy. Established in 1987.

Vin DiBona
Chairman
IMDb: imdb.com/name/nm0223688

Joanne Moore
President

Cara Di Bona
Vice President (Creative Affairs)
IMDb: imdb.com/name/nm0223685

VIRGIN PRODUCED

315 S Beverly Dr, Suite 506
Beverly Hills, CA 90212
Phone: 310-941-7300

Email: media@virginproduced.com
Home Page: virginproduced.com

Does not accept any unsolicited material. Project types include TV. Preferred genres include Action, Animation, Comedy, Drama, Fantasy, and Thriller. Established in 2010.

Jason Felts
CEO
Phone: 310-941-7300
Email: jfelts@virginproduced.com
IMDb: imdb.com/name/nm1479777

Rebecca Farrell
Director of Operations
IMDb: imdb.com/name/nm2761874

VOLTAGE PRODUCTIONS

662 N Crescent Heights Blvd
Los Angeles, CA 90048
Phone: 323-606-7630
Fax: 323-315-7115

Email: sales@voltagepictures.com
Home Page: voltagepictures.com

Accepts scripts from produced or represented writers. Project types include Feature Films. Preferred genres include Action, Animation, Drama, Fantasy, Non-Fiction, Romance, and Science Fiction. Established in 2011.

Nicolas Chartier
Email: nicolas@voltagepictures.com
IMDb: imdb.com/name/nm1291566

Craig Flores
President/Partner Voltage Productions
IMDb: imdb.com/name/nm1997836
Assistant: Edmond Guidry

Zev Foreman
Head of Development
IMDb: imdb.com/name/nm2303301

VON ZERNECK SERTNER FILMS

c/o HCVT
11444 W Olympic Blvd
11th Floor
Los Angeles, CA 90064
Phone: 310-652-3020

Email: vzs@vzsfilms.com
Home Page: vzsfilms.com
IMDb: imdb.com/company/co0094479

Does not accept any unsolicited material. Preferred genres include Crime, Detective, Drama, Non-Fiction, and Thriller. Established in 1987.

Frank Von Zerneck
Partner
Phone: 310-652-3020
Email: vonzerneck@gmail.com
IMDb: imdb.com/name/nm0903273

Robert M. Srtner
Partner
IMDb: imdb.com/name/nm0785750

VOX3 FILMS

315 Bleecker St #111
New York, NY 10014
Phone: 212-741-0406
Fax: 212-741-0424

Email: contact@vox3films.com
Home Page: vox3films.com
IMDb: imdb.com/company/co0146502

Does not accept any unsolicited material. Project types include TV. Preferred genres include Drama, Romance, and Thriller. Established in 2004.

Andrew Fierberg
Partner/Founder/Producer
Phone: 212-741-0406
Email: andrew.fi erberg@vox3fi lms.com
IMDb: imdb.com/name/nm0276404

Steven Shainberg
Partner
IMDb: imdb.com/name/nm078760

Christina Lurie
Partner
IMDb: imdb.com/name/nm1417371

VULCAN PRODUCTIONS

505 Fifth Ave. S., Suite 900
Seattle WA 98104
Phone: 206-342-2277

Email: production@vulcan.com
Home Page: vulcan.com
IMDb: imdb.com/company/co0042766

Accepts query letter from unproduced, unrepresented writers via email. Preferred genres include Action, Non-Fiction, and Thriller. Established in 1983.

Jody Allen
President
Phone: 206-342-2277
Email: jody@vulcan.com
IMDb: imdb.com/name/nm0666580

WALDEN MEDIA

1888 Century Park East
14th Floor
Los Angeles, CA 90067
Phone: 310-887-1000
Fax: 310-887-1001

Email: info@walden.com
Home Page: walden.com
IMDb: imdb.com/company/co0073388

Accepts query letter from unproduced, unrepresented writers via email. Project types include Feature Films. Established in 2001.

Evan Turner
Sr. Vice-President, Development & Production
Phone: 310-887-1000
IMDb: imdb.com/name/nm1602263

Amanda Palmer
Sr. Vice-President, Development & Production
Phone: 310-887-1000
IMDb: imdb.com/name/nm2198853

Eric Tovell
Creative Executive
Email: etovell@walden.com
Assistant: Carol Tang ctang@walden.com

WALKER/FITZGIBBON TV & FILM PRODUCTION

2399 Mt. Olympus
Los Angeles, CA 90046
Phone: 323-469-6800
Fax: 323-878-0600

Home Page: walkerfitzgibbon.com
IMDb: imdb.com/company/co0171571

Accepts query letter from unproduced, unrepresented writers via email. Project types include TV. Preferred genres include Animation, Comedy, Drama, and Non-Fiction. Established in 1996.

Mo Fitzgibbon
Principal, Executive Producer/Director
Phone: 323-469-6800
Email: mo@walkerfitzgibbon.com
IMDb: imdb.com/name/nm0280422

Robert W. Walker
Writer/Director (Executive)
IMDb: imdb.com/name/nm0908166

WALT BECKER PRODUCTIONS

8530 Wilshire Blvd.
Suite 550
Beverly Hills, CA 90212
USA
Phone: 323-871-8400
Fax: 323-871-2540

IMDb: imdb.com/company/co0236068

Does not accept any unsolicited material. Project types include TV.

Walt Becker
Director/Producer
IMDb: imdb.com/name/nm0065608

Kelly Hayes
Director of Development
IMDb: imdb.com/name/nm0971886

WARNER BROS. ANIMATION

411 N Hollywood Way
Burbank, CA 91505
Phone: 818-977-8700

Email: info@warnerbros.com
Home Page: warnerbros.com
IMDb: imdb.com/company/co0072876

Does not accept any unsolicited material. Project types include TV. Preferred genres include Animation. Established in 1930.

Sam Register
Executive Vice-President, Creative
Email: sam.register@warnerbros.com
IMDb: imdb.com/name/nm1882146

WARNER BROS. ENTERTAINMENT INC.

4000 Warner Blvd
Burbank, CA 91522-0001
Phone: 818-954-6000

Home Page: warnerbros.com

Does not accept any unsolicited material. Project types include TV. Preferred genres include Action, Animation, Comedy, Crime, Detective, Drama, Family, Fantasy, Myth, Non-Fiction, Romance, Science Fiction, and Thriller. Established in 1923.

Barry Meyer
Chairman/CEO
Email: barry.meyer@warnerbros.com
IMDb: imdb.com/name/nm0583028

WARNER BROS. HOME ENTERTAINMENT GROUP

4000 Warner Blvd
Burbank, CA 91522-0001
Phone: 818-954-6000

Email: info@warnerbros.com
Home Page: warnerbros.com
IMDb: imdb.com/company/co0200179

Does not accept any unsolicited material. Project types include Feature Films, Short Films, and TV. Preferred genres include Action, Animation, Comedy, Crime, Drama, Family, Fantasy, Horror, Myth, Non-Fiction, Romance, Science Fiction, and Thriller. Established in 2005.

Kevin Tsujihara
President
Email: kevin.tsujihara@warnerbros.com
IMDb: imdb.com/name/nm2493597

WARNER BROS. PICTURES

4000 Warner Blvd
Burbank, CA 91522-0001
Phone: 818-954-6000

Email: info@warnerbros.com
Home Page: warnerbros.com
IMDb: imdb.com/company/co0026840

Does not accept any unsolicited material. Project types include Feature Films. Preferred genres include Action, Animation, Comedy, Crime, Detective, Drama, Family, Fantasy, Myth, Non-Fiction, Romance, and Thriller. Established in 1923.

Jeff Robinov
President
Email: jeff.robinov@warnerbros.com
IMDb: imdb.com/name/nm0732268
Assistant: Carrie Frymer

Greg Silverman
President of Production
IMDb: imdb.com/name/nm0798909
Assistant: Cate Adams

Lynn Harris
Executive Vice President of Production
IMDb: imdb.com/name/nm0365036
Assistant: Alexandra Amin

Andrew Fischel
Creative Executive (Production Group)
Assistant: Stephanie Rosenthal

Racheline Benveniste
Creative Executive
IMDb: imdb.com/name/nm3367909
Assistant: Matthew Crespy

WARNER BROS. TELEVISION GROUP

4000 Warner Blvd
Burbank, CA 91522-0001
Phone: 818-954-6000

Email: info@warnerbros.com
Home Page: warnerbros.com
IMDb: imdb.com/company/co0253255

Does not accept any unsolicited material. Project types include Feature Films and TV. Preferred genres include Action, Animation, Comedy, Drama, Family, Fantasy, Myth, Non-Fiction, Romance, and Thriller. Established in 2005.

Bruce Rosenblum
President
Email: bruce.rosenblum@warnerbros.com
IMDb: imdb.com/name/nm2686463

WARNER HORIZON TELEVISION

4000 Warner Blvd
Burbank, CA 91522-0001
Phone: 818-954-6000

Email: info@warnerbros.com
Home Page: warnerbros.com
IMDb: mdb.com/company/co0183230

Does not accept any unsolicited material. Project types include TV. Preferred genres include Action, Animation, Comedy, Drama, Family, Fantasy, Myth, Non-Fiction, and Romance. Established in 1999.

Peter Roth
President
Phone: 818-954-6000
Email: peter.roth@warnerbros.com
IMDb: imdb.com/name/nm2325137

WARNER SISTERS PRODUCTIONS

PO Box 50104
Santa Barbara, CA 93150
Phone: 818-766-6952

Email: info@warnersisters.com
Home Page: warnersisters.com
IMDb: imdb.com/company/co0121034

Does not accept any unsolicited material. Project types include Feature Films and TV. Preferred genres include Non-Fiction. Established in 2003.

Cass Warner
CEO/President
IMDb: imdb.com/name/nm2064300

WARP FILMS

Spectrum House 32-34 Gordon House Rd
London, United Kingdom, NW5 1LP
Phone: (011) 442072848350
Fax: 011) 442072848360

Email: info@warpfilms.co.uk
Home Page: warp.net/films
IMDb: imdb.com/company/co0251927

Accepts query letter from unproduced, unrepresented writers via email. Project types include Feature Films. Preferred genres include Action, Comedy, Documentary, Drama, Horror, Non-Fiction, and Romance. Established in 2004.

Mark Herbert
Principal
IMDb: imdb.com/name/nm0378591

Peter Carlton
Head of Warp Films Europe
IMDb: imdb.com/name/nm1275058

WARP X

Electric Works
Digital Campus
Sheffield S1 2BJ
UK
Phone: +44-114-286-6280
Fax: +44-114-286-6283

Email: info@warpx.co.uk
Home Page: warpx.co.uk
IMDb: imdb.com/company/co0202028

Does not accept any unsolicited material. Project types include Feature Films. Preferred genres include Comedy, Crime, Documentary, Drama, Horror, and Thriller. Established in 2008.

Mary Burke
Producer
IMDb: imdb.com/name/nm1537339

Robin Gutch
Managing Director
IMDb: imdb.com/name/nm0349168

Mark Herbert
Producer
IMDb: imdb.com/name/nm0378591

Barry Ryan
Head of Production
IMDb: imdb.com/name/nm1419213

WARREN MILLER ENTERTAINMENT

5720 Flatiron Parkway
Boulder CO 80301
Phone: 303-253-6300
Fax: 303-253-6380

Email: info@warrenmillertv.com
Home Page: warrenmillertv.com
IMDb: imdb.com/company/co0040142

Accepts query letter from unproduced, unrepresented writers. Project types include Feature Films and TV. Preferred genres include Action, Non-Fiction, and Reality. Established in 1952.

Jeffrey Moore
Sr. Executive Producer
Email: jeffm@warrenmiller.com
IMDb: imdb.com/name/nm2545455

Ginger Sheehy
Manager of Development
IMDb: imdb.com/name/nm1200078

Warren Miller
Chief Executive Officer

Ginger Sheehy
Manager of Development
IMDb: imdb.com/name/nm1200078

WARRIOR POETS

76 Mercer St Fourth Floor
New York, NY 10012
Phone: 212-219-7617
Fax: 212-219-2920

Email: em@warrior-poets.com
Home Page: warrior-poets.com
IMDb: imdb.com/company/co0169151

Does not accept any unsolicited material. Project types include Feature Films and TV. Preferred genres include Drama and Non-Fiction. Established in 2005.

Morgan Spurlock
President/Producer
IMDb: imdb.com/name/nm1041597
Assistant: Emmanuel Moran

Jeremy Chilnick
Partner (Head of Production and Development)
IMDb: imdb.com/name/nm2505733
Assistant: Marjon Javadi

Ethan Goldman
Executive Vice President of Development
IMDb: imdb.com/name/nm1134121

WAYANS BROTHERS ENTERTAINMENT

8730 W Sunset Blvd, Suite 290
Los Angeles, CA 90069-2247
Phone: 323-930-6720
Fax: 424-202-3520

Email: thawkins@wayansbros.com
IMDb: imdb.com/company/co0001823

Does not accept any unsolicited material. Project types include TV. Preferred genres include Comedy, Crime, Family, and Horror. Established in 1980.

Keenan Wayans
Principal
IMDb: imdb.com/name/nm0005540

Rick Alvarez
Principal
IMDb: imdb.com/name/nm0023315

Marlon Wayans
Principal
IMDb: imdb.com/name/nm0005541
Assistant: Shane Miller

Shawn Wayans
Principal
IMDb: imdb.com/name/nm0915465

Mike Tiddes
Creative Executive

WAYFARE ENTERTAINMENT VENTURES LLC

435 W 19th St
4th Floor
New York, NY 10011
Phone: 212-989-2200

Email: info@wayfareentertainment.com
Home Page: wayfareentertainment.com
IMDb: imdb.com/company/co0239158

Does not accept any unsolicited material. Project types include Feature Films. Preferred genres include Action, Comedy, Drama, Family, Fantasy, Myth, Non-Fiction, Romance, Science Fiction, and Thriller. Established in 2008.

Ben Browning
Co-Founder & CEO
Email: info@wayfareentertainment.com
IMDb: imdb.com/name/nm1878845

Michael Maher
Co-Founder
IMDb: imdb.com/name/nm3052130

Sarah Shepard
Vice President (Development)
IMDb: imdb.com/name/nm2416896

Jeremy Kipp Walker
Head (Production)
IMDb: imdb.com/name/nm0907844

WEED ROAD PICTURES

4000 Warner Blvd
Building 81, Suite 115
Burbank, CA 91522
Phone: 818-954-3771
Fax: 818-954-3061

IMDb: imdb.com/company/co0093488

Does not accept any unsolicited material. Project types include Feature Films and TV. Preferred genres include Action, Animation, Drama, Family, Fantasy, Horror, Non-Fiction, Science Fiction, and Thriller. Established in 2004.

Akiva Goldsman
President/Producer
IMDb: imdb.com/name/nm0326040
Assistant: Bonnie Balmos

Nicki Cortese
Vice President (Film and Television)
IMDb: imdb.com/name/nm2492480
Assistant: Mike Pence

WEINSTOCK PRODUCTIONS

316 N Rossmore Ave
Los Angeles, CA 90004
Phone: 323-791-1500

IMDb: imdb.com/company/co0032259

Accepts query letter from unproduced, unrepresented writers. Project types include Feature Films. Preferred genres include Comedy, Crime, Drama, Family, and Thriller.

Charles Weinstock
Producer
IMDb: imdb.com/name/nm091848

WEINTRAUB/KUHN PRODUCTIONS

1351 Third St Promenade, Suite 206
Santa Monica, CA 90401
Phone: 310-458-3300
Fax: 310-458-3302

Email: fred@fredweintraub.com
Home Page: fredweintraub.com
IMDb: imdb.com/company/co0031680

Does not accept any unsolicited material. Project types include Feature Films and TV. Preferred genres include Action, Comedy, Drama, Family, Fantasy, Myth, Non-Fiction, Romance, Science Fiction, and Thriller. Established in 1976.

Fred Weintraub
President
Email: fred@fredweintraub.com
IMDb: imdb.com/name/nm0918518

Tom Kuhn
Producer
IMDb: imdb.com/name/nm0474166

Maxwell Meltzer
Business Affairs
IMDb: imdb.com/name/nm0578443

Jackie Weintraub
Vice President Of Development
IMDb: imdb.com/name/nm0918520

WELLER/GROSSMAN PRODUCTIONS

5200 Lankershim Blvd
5th Floor
North Hollywood, CA 91601
Phone: 818-755-4800

Email: contact@wellergrossman.com
Home Page: wellergrossman.com
IMDb: imdb.com/company/co0102774

Accepts scripts from produced or represented writers. Project types include TV. Preferred genres include Comedy, Drama, and Reality. Established in 1993.

Robb Weller
Partner/Executive Producer
Email: contact@wellergrossman.com
IMDb: imdb.com/name/nm0919888

Debbie Supnik
Director Of Development
IMDb: imdb.com/name/nm0839489

Gary Grossman
Partner
IMDb: imdb.com/name/nm0343646

WENDY FINERMAN PRODUCTIONS

144 S Beverly Dr, #304
Beverly Hills, CA 90212
Phone: 310-694-8088
Fax: 310-694-8088

Email: info@wendyfinermanproductions.com
Home Page: wendyfinermanproductions.com
IMDb: imdb.com/company/co0004317

Accepts query letter from unproduced, unrepresented writers via email. Project types include Feature Films and TV. Preferred genres include Comedy, Drama, Family, Fantasy, Period, and Romance.

Wendy Finerman
Producer
Email: wfinerman@wendyfinermanproductions.com
IMDb: imdb.com/name/nm0277704

Lisa Zupan
Vice-President
Email: lzupan@wendyfinermanproductions.com
IMDb: imdb.com/name/nm0958702

WESSLER ENTERTAINMNET

11661 San Vicente Blvd., Suite 609
Los Angeles, CA 90049

Accepts query letter from unproduced, unrepresented writers. Project types include Feature Films. Preferred genres include Comedy and Family.

Charles B. Wessler
President
IMDb: imdb.com/name/nm0921853

WE TV NETWORK

11 Penn Plaza
19th Floor
New York, NY 10001
Phone: 212-324-8500
Fax: 212-324-8595

Email: contactwe@wetv.com
Home Page: wetv.com
IMDb: imdb.com/company/co0340786

Does not accept any unsolicited material. Project types include TV. Preferred genres include Comedy, Family, and Reality. Established in 1997.

Laurence Gellert
SVP, Original Production and Development
IMDb: imdb.com/name/nm1557598

WHITEWATER FILMS

11264 La Grange Ave
Los Angeles, CA 90025
Phone: 310-575-5800
Fax: 310-575-5802

Email: info@whitewaterfilms.com
Home Page: whitewaterfilms.com
IMDb: imdb.com/company/co0109361

Does not accept any unsolicited material. Project types include Feature Films. Preferred genres include Comedy, Crime, Drama, Non-Fiction, Romance, and Thriller. Established in 2008.

Nick Morton
Producer
IMDb: imdb.com/name/nm1134288

Bert Kern
Producer
IMDb: imdb.com/name/nm2817387

Rick Rosenthal
President/Producer
IMDb: imdb.com/name/nm0742819

Trent Brion
Producer

WHYADUCK PRODUCTIONS INC.

4804 Laurel Canyon Blvd
PMB 502
North Hollywood, CA 91607-3765
Phone: (818) 980-5355

Email: info@duckprods.com
Home Page: duckprods.com
IMDb: imdb.com/company/co0034143

Does not accept any unsolicited material. Project types include Feature Films and TV. Preferred genres include Comedy, Drama, Non-Fiction, Romance, and Science Fiction. Established in 1981.

Robert Weide
Principal
Email: rbw@duckprods.com
IMDb: imdb.com/name/nm0004332

WIDEAWAKE INC.

Los Angeles
8752 Rangely Ave
Los Angeles, CA 90048
Phone: 310-652-9200

IMDb: imdb.com/company/co0145942

Does not accept any unsolicited material. Project types include Feature Films and TV. Preferred genres include Action, Comedy, Family, and Romance. Established in 2004.

Luke Greenfield
Writer/Director/Producer
IMDb: imdb.com/name/nm0339004

Jake Detharidge
Creative Executive
IMDb: imdb.com/name/nm4681516

WIGRAM PRODUCTIONS

4000 Warner Blvd
Building 81, Room 215
Burbank, CA 91522
Phone: 818-954-2412
Fax: 818-954-6538

IMDb: imdb.com/company/co0204562

Accepts query letter from unproduced, unrepresented writers. Project types include Feature Films. Preferred genres include Action, Comedy, Crime, Fantasy, Science Fiction, and Thriller. Established in 2006.

Lionel Wigram
Principal/Producer
IMDb: imdb.com/name/nm0927880
Assistant: Jeff Ludwig jeff.ludwig@wbconsultant.com

Peter Eskelsen
Vice-President
Email: peter.eskelsen@wbconsultant.com
IMDb: imdb.com/name/nm2367411

WILD AT HEART FILMS

868 W Knoll Dr, Suite 9
West Hollywood, CA 90069
Phone: 310-855-1538
Fax: 310-855-0177

Email: wildheartfilms@aol.com
Home Page: wildatheartfilms.us
IMDb: imdb.com/company/co0096528

Does not accept any unsolicited material. Preferred genres include Animation, Comedy, Drama, Family, Myth, Non-Fiction, and Romance. Established in 2000.

James Egan
CEO/Writer/Producer
Email: jamesegan@wildatheartfilms.us
IMDb: imdb.com/name/nm0250680

Boris Geiger
Business Affairs
IMDb: imdb.com/name/nm1788313

Jewell Sparks
Head of Development/Producer
IMDb: imdb.com/name/nm3876152

WILDBRAIN ENTERTAINMENT INC.

15000 Ventura Blvd
3rd Floor
Sherman Oaks, CA 91403
Phone: 818-290-7080

Email: info@wildbrain.com
Home Page: wildbrain.com
IMDb: imdb.com/company/co0077172

Accepts query letter from produced or represented writers. Project types include Feature Films, Short Films, and TV. Preferred genres include Animation, Comedy, Family, and Fantasy. Established in 1994.

Michael Polis
President
Email: mpolis@wildbrain.com
IMDb: imdb.com/name/nm1277040

Bob Higgins
Head of Creative
IMDb: imdb.com/name/nm0383338

Lisa Ullmann
Vice President of Development
IMDb: imdb.com/name/nm0880520

WILDWOOD ENTERPRISES, INC.

725 Arizona Ave, Suite 306
Santa Monica, CA 90401
Phone: 310-451-8050

IMDb: imdb.com/company/co0034515

Does not accept any unsolicited material. Project types include Feature Films, Short Films, and TV. Preferred genres include Comedy, Crime, Drama, Fantasy, Non-Fiction, Romance, and Thriller.

Robert Redford
Owner
IMDb: imdb.com/name/nm0000602

Bill Holderman
Development Executive
IMDb: imdb.com/name/nm2250139

WIND DANCER FILMS

315 S Beverly Dr, Suite 502
Beverly Hills, CA 90212

Phone: 310-601-2720
Fax: 310-601-2725

Home Page: winddancer.com
IMDb: imdb.com/company/co0028602

Does not accept any unsolicited material. Project types include Feature Films and TV. Preferred genres include Comedy, Crime, Drama, Fantasy, and Romance. Established in 1989.

Matt Williams
Principal
IMDb: imdb.com/name/nm0931285
Assistant: Jake Perron

David McFadzean
Principal
IMDb: imdb.com/name/nm05687
Assistant: David Caruso

Catherine Redfearn
Creative Executive
Email: Catherine_Redfearn@winddancer.com
IMDb: imdb.com/name/nm1976144

Judd Payne
IMDb: imdb.com/name/nm1450928

WINGNUT FILMS LTD.

PO Box 15 208
Miramar
Wellington 6003
New Zealand
Phone: +64-4-388-9939
Fax: +64-4-388-9449

Email: reception@wingnutfilms.co.nz
Home Page: wingnutfilms.co.nz
IMDb: imdb.com/company/co0046203

Does not accept any unsolicited material. Project types include Feature Films and TV. Preferred genres include Animation, Comedy, Crime, Family, Fantasy, Horror, Non-Fiction, Romance, Science Fiction, and Thriller.

Peter Jackson
Director/Producer
IMDb: imdb.com/name/nm0001392

Carolynne Cunningham
Producer
IMDb: imdb.com/name/nm0192254

WINKLER FILMS

190 N Canon Dr Suite 500 Penthouse
Beverly Hills, CA 90210
Phone: 310-858-5780
Fax: 310-858-5799

Email: winklerfilms@sbcglobal.net
Home Page: winklerfilms.com
IMDb: imdb.com/company/co0049390

Accepts query letter from unproduced, unrepresented writers. Project types include Feature Films and TV. Preferred genres include Action, Crime, Drama, and Romance.

Irwin Winkler
CEO
Phone: 310-858-5780
IMDb: imdb.com/name/nm0005563
Assistant: Selina Gomeau

Charles Winkler
Director/Producer
Phone: 310-858-5780
IMDb: imdb.com/name/nm0935203
Assistant: Jose Ruisanchez

David Winkler
Producer
Phone: 310-858-5780
IMDb: imdb.com/name/nm0935210

Jill Cutler
President
IMDb: imdb.com/name/nm1384594

WINSOME PRODUCTIONS

PO Box 2071
Santa Monica, CA 90406
Phone: 310-656-3300

Email: info@winsomeprods.com
Home Page: winsomeprods.com
IMDb: imdb.com/company/co0129854

Does not accept any unsolicited material. Project types include Feature Films and TV. Preferred genres include Action, Comedy, Drama, and Non-Fiction. Established in 1989.

A.D. Oppenheim
Producer/Writer/Director
Email: info@winsomeprods.com
IMDb: imdb.com/name/nm0649148

Daniel Oppenheim
VP
IMDb: imdb.com/name/nm0649151

WITT-THOMAS PRODUCTIONS

11901 Santa Monica Blvd, Suite 596
Los Angeles, CA 90025
Phone: 310-472-6004
Fax: 310-476-5015

Email: pwittproductions@aol.com
IMDb: imdb.com/company/co0083928

Does not accept any unsolicited material. Project types include Feature Films. Preferred genres include Action, Comedy, Crime, Drama, Period, and Romance. Established in 2010.

Paul Witt
Partner
Email: pwittproductions@aol.com
IMDb: imdb.com/name/nm0432625
Assistant: Ellen Benjamin

Tony Thomas
Partner
IMDb: imdb.com/name/nm0859597
Assistant: Marlene Fuentes

WOLF FILMS, INC.

100 Universal City Plaza #2252
Universal City, CA 91608-1085
Phone: 818-777-6969
Fax: 818-866-1446

IMDb: imdb.com/company/co0019598

Does not accept any unsolicited material. Project types include Feature Films, Short Films, and TV. Preferred genres include Drama and Non-Fiction.

Dick Wolf
CEO
IMDb: imdb.com/name/nm0937725

Danielle Gelber
Executive Producer
IMDb: imdb.com/name/nm1891764

Tony Ganz
Feature Development
IMDb: imdb.com/name/nm0304673

WOLFMILL ENTERTAINMENT

9027 Larke Ellen Circle
Los Angeles, CA 90035
Phone: 310-559-1622
Fax: 310-559-1623

Email: info@wolfmill.com
Home Page: wolfmill.com
IMDb: imdb.com/company/co0184078

Accepts query letter from unproduced, unrepresented writers via email. Project types include Feature Films and TV. Preferred genres include Animation. Established in 1997.

Marv Wolfman
Partner
Email: marv@wolfmill.com
IMDb: imdb.com/name/nm0938379

Craig Miller
Partner
Email: craig@wolfmill.com
IMDb: imdb.com/name/nm0003653

WOLFRAM PRODUCTIONS

2104 Pisani Place
Venice, CA 90291
Phone: 323-253-8185

Home Page: wolfromproductions.com

Accepts query letter from unproduced, unrepresented writers via email. Project types include Feature Films. Preferred genres include Family and Romance.

Dawn Wolfrom
Producer
Email: dawnwolfrom@wolfromproductions.com
IMDb: imdb.com/name/nm0938402

WONDERLAND SOUND AND VISION

8739 Sunset Blvd
West Hollywood, CA 90069
Phone: 310-659-4451
Fax: 310-659-4451

Home Page: wonderlandsoundandvision.com
IMDb: imdb.com/company/co0080859

Does not accept any unsolicited material. Project types include Feature Films and TV. Preferred genres include Action, Comedy, Crime, Drama, Horror, Non-Fiction, Romance, and Science Fiction. Established in 2000.

Mary Viola
President of Production (Features)
IMDb: imdb.com/name/nm0899193

Steven Bello
Creative Executive
IMDb: imdb.com/name/nm2086605

Peter Johnson
President of Production (Television)
IMDb: imdb.com/name/nm1928296

WONDERPHIL PRODUCTIONS

4712 Admiralty Way #324
Marina del Rey, CA. 90292
Phone: 310-482-1324

Home Page: wonderphil.biz

Accepts scripts from unproduced, unrepresented writers. Project types include Feature Films. Preferred genres include Action, Drama, Fantasy, Horror, Science Fiction, and Thriller.

Phil Gorn
CEO
Email: phil@wonderphil.biz

Sanders Robinson
President
Phone: 925-525-7583
Email: sandman@wonderphil.biz

WORKING TITLE FILMS

9720 Wilshire Blvd
4th Floor

Beverly Hills, CA 90212
Phone: 310-777-3100
Fax: 310-777-5243

Home Page: workingtitlefilms.com
IMDb: imdb.com/company/co0057311

Does not accept any unsolicited material. Project types include Feature Films, Short Films, and TV. Preferred genres include Action, Comedy, Crime, Drama, Family, Fantasy, Non-Fiction, Romance, Science Fiction, and Thriller. Established in 1983.

Amelia Granger
Literary Acquisitions Executive (United Kingdom)
Phone: +44 20 7307 3000
IMDb: imdb.com/name/nm0335028

Liza Chasin
President, Production (US)
Email: liza.chasin@workingtitlefilms.com
IMDb: imdb.com/name/nm0153877
Assistant: Johanna Byer

Michelle Wright
Head (Production)
IMDb: imdb.com/name/nm0942657

WORLD FILM SERVICES, INC

150 E 58th St
29th Floor
New York, NY 10155
Phone: 212-632-3456
Fax: 212-632-3457

IMDb: imdb.com/company/co0184077

Accepts query letter from unproduced, unrepresented writers. Project types include Feature Films and TV. Preferred genres include Action, Comedy, Crime, Drama, Family, Fantasy, Horror, Non-Fiction, Romance, Science Fiction, and Thriller.

John Heyman
CEO
IMDb: imdb.com/name/nm0382274

Dahlia Heyman
Creative Executive
IMDb: imdb.com/name/nm3101094

Pamela Osowski
Creative Executive
IMDb: imdb.com/name/nm1948494

WORLD OF WONDER PRODUCTIONS

6650 Hollywood Blvd, Suite 400
Hollywood, CA 90028
Phone: 323-603-6300
Fax: 323-603-6301

Email: support@worldofwonder.net
Home Page: worldofwonder.net
IMDb: imdb.com/company/co0093416

Does not accept any unsolicited material. Project types include Feature Films and TV. Preferred genres include Action, Comedy, Crime, Drama, Family, Non-Fiction, Period, and Reality. Established in 1990.

Fenton Bailey
Executive Producer/Co-Director
IMDb: imdb.com/name/nm0047259

Tom Campbell
Head (Development)
IMDb: imdb.com/name/nm1737859

Chris Skura
Head (Production)
IMDb: imdb.com/name/nm1048940

WORLDVIEW ENTERTAINMENT

1384 Broadway
25th Floor
New York, NY 10018
Phone: 212-431-3090
Fax: 212-431-0390

Email: info@worldviewent.com
Home Page: worldviewent.com

Does not accept any unsolicited material. Project types include Feature Films. Preferred genres include Action, Comedy, Documentary, Drama, and Romance. Established in 2007.

Christopher Woodrow
Chairman/CEO
IMDb: imdb.com/name/nm2002108

Sarah Johnson Redlich
Partner
IMDb: imdb.com/name/nm3164071

Amanda Bowers
Vice President/Production
IMDb: imdb.com/name/nm4112873

Maria Cestone
Co-Founder
IMDb: imdb.com/name/nm2906036

WORLDWIDE BIGGIES

545 W 45th St
5th Floor
New York, NY 10036
Phone: 646-442-1700
Fax: 646-557-0019

Email: info@wwbiggies.com
Home Page: wwbiggies.com
IMDb: imdb.com/company/co0173152

Does not accept any unsolicited material. Project types include Feature Films and TV. Preferred genres include Action, Animation, Comedy, Drama, Family, Fantasy, Non-Fiction, and Reality. Established in 2007.

Albie Hecht
CEO
IMDb: imdb.com/name/nm0372935

Kari Kim
VP Development
IMDb: imdb.com/name/nm2004613

Scott Webb
Chief Creative Officer
IMDb: imdb.com/name/nm1274591

WORLDWIDE PANTS INC.

1697 Broadway
New York, NY 10019
Phone: 212-975-5300
Fax: 212-975-4780

IMDb: imdb.com/company/co0066959

Does not accept any unsolicited material. Project types include Feature Films and TV. Preferred genres

include Action, Animation, Comedy, Drama, Non-Fiction, and Romance.

Rob Burnett
President/CEO
IMDb: imdb.com/name/nm0122427

David Letterman
Principal
IMDb: imdb.com/name/nm0001468

Tom Keaney
Executive
IMDb: imdb.com/name/nm3174758

WWE STUDIOS

12424 Wilshire Blvd, Suite 1400
Los Angeles, CA 90025
Phone: 310-481-9370
Fax: (310) 481-9369

Email: talent.marketing@wwe.com
Home Page: wwe.com
IMDb: imdb.com/company/co0242604

Does not accept any unsolicited material. Project types include Feature Films and TV. Preferred genres include Action, Comedy, Crime, Detective, Drama, Family, Horror, Non-Fiction, Science Fiction, and Thriller. Established in 2002.

Michael Luisi
President
IMDb: imdb.com/name/nm0525405

Richard Lowell
Director (Senior Director of Development)
IMDb: imdb.com/name/nm1144067
Assistant: Cherie Harris Cherie.harris@wwecorp.com

X FILME CREATIVE POOL

Kurfuerstenstrasse 57
10785 Berlin
Germany
Phone: 49-30-230-833-11
Fax: 49-30-230-833-22

Email: x-filme@x-filme.de
Home Page: x-filme.de
IMDb: imdb.com/company/co0055954

Does not accept any unsolicited material. Preferred genres include Action, Comedy, Drama, Family, and Romance. Established in 1994.

Stefan Arndt
Founder/Managing Partner/Producer
Email: stefan.arndt@x-filme.de
IMDb: imdb.com/name/nm0036155

Wolfgang Becker
Partner (Co-Founder)
IMDb: imdb.com/name/nm0065615

Dani Levy
Partner (Co-Founder)
IMDb: imdb.com/name/nm0506374

XINGU FILMS LTD.

12 Cleveland Row
St. James
London SW1A 1DH
United Kingdom
Phone: 44-20-7451-0600
Fax: 44-20-7451-0601

Email: mail@xingufilms.com
Home Page: xingufilms.com

Does not accept any unsolicited material. Project types include TV. Preferred genres include Action, Animation, Comedy, Crime, Detective, Drama, Family, Fantasy, Horror, Myth, Non-Fiction, Romance, Science Fiction, and Thriller. Established in 1993.

Trudie Styler
Chairman/Producer/Director
Email: trudie@xingufilms.com
IMDb: imdb.com/name/nm0836548

Alex Francis
Producer
IMDb: imdb.com/name/nm2123360

Anita Sumner
CEO and Co-Producer
IMDb: imdb.com/name/nm0838856

Kate Henderson
Executive (Script Development)

XIX ENTERTAINMENT

9000 W Sunset Blvd, Penthouse
West Hollywood, CA 90069
Phone: 310-746-1919
Fax: 310-746-1920

Email: info@xixentertainment.com
Home Page: xixentertainment.com

Does not accept any unsolicited material. Project types include Feature Films and TV. Preferred genres include Drama, Non-Fiction, Period, Reality, Romance, and Thriller. Established in 2010.

Robert Dodds
CEO
Email: robert.dodds@xixentertainment.com
IMDb: imdb.com/name/nm2142323

XYZ FILMS

4223 Glencoe Ave, Suite B119
Marina del Rey, CA 90292
Phone: 310-956-1550
Fax: 310-827-7690

Email: team@xyzfilms.com
Home Page: xyzfilms.com
IMDb: imdb.com/company/co0244345

Does not accept any unsolicited material. Project types include Feature Films. Preferred genres include Action, Comedy, Crime, Drama, Horror, Non-Fiction, Science Fiction, and Thriller.

Nate Bolotin
Partner
Email: nate@xyzfilms.com
IMDb: imdb.com/name/nm1924867

Todd Brown
Partner
Email: info@xyzfilms.com
IMDb: imdb.com/name/nm1458075

Kyle Franke
Head of Development
Phone: 310-359-9099
Email: kyle@xyzfilms.com
IMDb: imdb.com/name/nm3733941

YAHOO!

2400 Broadway
1st Floor
Santa Monica, CA 90404
Phone: 310-907-2700
Fax: 310-907-2701

Home Page: yahoo.com
IMDb: imdb.com/company/co0054481

Accepts query letter from unproduced, unrepresented writers. Project types include Short Films, TV, and Commercials. Preferred genres include Comedy, Family, Non-Fiction, and Reality. Established in 1995.

David Filo
Founder

Ryan Clifford
Senior Manager (Creative Services)

Jacqueline Reses
Executive VP (People and Development)

YARI FILM GROUP

10850 Wilshire Blvd
6th Floor
Los Angeles, CA 90024
Phone: 310-689-1450
Fax: 310-234-8975

Email: info@yarifilmgroup.com
Home Page: yarifilmgroup.com
IMDb: imdb.com/company/co0136740

Does not accept any unsolicited material. Project types include Feature Films and TV. Preferred genres include Action, Animation, Comedy, Crime, Drama, Family, Romance, and Thriller.

Bob Yari
President & CEO
Email: byari@yarifilmgroup.com
IMDb: imdb.com/name/nm0946441
Assistant: Julie Milstead

Ethen Adams
Director Of Development
IMDb: imdb.com/name/nm2319337

David Clark
VP (Television)
IMDb: imdb.com/name/nm1354046

YORK SQUARE PRODUCTIONS

17328 Ventura Blvd, Suite 370
Encino, CA 91316
Phone: 818-789-7372

Email: assistant@yorksquareproductions.com
Home Page: yorksquareproductions.com

Accepts query letter from unproduced, unrepresented writers via email. Project types include Feature Films. Preferred genres include Comedy and Drama.

Jonathan Mostow
Executive
IMDb: imdb.com/name/nm0609236
Assistant: Emily Somers

YORKTOWN PRODUCTIONS

18 Gloucester Ln
4th Floor
Toronto ON M4Y 1L5
Canada
Phone: 416-923-2787
Fax: 416-923-8580

IMDb: imdb.com/company/co0184088

Does not accept any unsolicited material. Project types include Feature Films, Short Films, and TV. Preferred genres include Action, Comedy, Drama, Family, Fantasy, Romance, and Science Fiction. Established in 1986.

Norman Jewison
Founder
Phone: 416-923-2787
IMDb: imdb.com/name/nm0422484

Michael Jewison
Producer
IMDb: imdb.com/name/nm0422483

YOUR FACE GOES HERE ENTERTAINMENT

1041 N Formosa Ave
Santa Monica Bldg W, #7

West Hollywood, CA 90046
Phone: 323-850-2433

Does not accept any unsolicited material. Project types include TV. Preferred genres include Drama, Fantasy, Horror, Romance, Science Fiction, and Thriller.

Alan Ball
Head Producer
Phone: 323-850-2433
IMDb: imdb.com/name/nm0050332

ZACHARY FEUER FILMS

9348 Civic Center Dr, 3rd Floor
Beverly Hills, CA 90210
Phone: 310-729-2110
Fax: 310-820-7535

Accepts query letter from unproduced, unrepresented writers. Project types include TV. Preferred genres include Action, Comedy, Drama, and Thriller.

Zachary Feuer
Producer
Phone: 310-729-2110
IMDb: imdb.com/name/nm0275400

ZAK PENN'S COMPANY

6240 W Third St, Suite 421
Los Angeles, CA 90036
Phone: (323) 939-1700
Fax: (323) 930-2339

IMDb: imdb.com/company/co0185423

Does not accept any unsolicited material. Project types include Feature Films and TV. Preferred genres include Comedy, Family, Fantasy, Non-Fiction, Science Fiction, and Thriller.

Zak Penn
Writer/Producer/Director
IMDb: imdb.com/name/nm0672015
Assistant: Hannah Rosner

Morgan Gross
Editorial Guru
IMDb: imdb.com/name/nm2092616

ZANUCK INDEPENDENT

1951 N Beverly Dr
Beverly Hills, CA 90210
Phone: (310) 274-7586
Fax: (310) 273-9217

IMDb: imdb.com/company/co0279611

Accepts query letter from unproduced, unrepresented writers. Project types include Feature Films. Preferred genres include Action, Comedy, Drama, and Thriller.

Dean Zanuck
Producer
IMDb: imdb.com/name/nm0953124

ZEMECKIS/NEMEROFF FILMS

264 S La Cienega Blvd, Suite 238
Beverly Hills, CA 90211
Phone: (310) 736-6586

Email: info@enfantsterriblesmovie.com
Home Page: enfantsterriblesmovie.com
IMDb: imdb.com/company/co0141237

Does not accept any unsolicited material. Project types include Feature Films. Preferred genres include Comedy and Drama.

Leslie Zemeckis
Producer
IMDb: imdb.com/name/nm0366667

Terry Nemeroff
Writer/Director/Producer
IMDb: imdb.com/name/nm0625892

ZENTROPA ENTERTAINMENT

Filmbyen 22
Hvidovre, Denmark, 2650
Phone: +45-36-86-87-88
Fax: +45-36-86-87-89

Email: receptionen@filmbyen.dk
Home Page: zentropa.dk
IMDb: imdb.com/company/co0136662

Accepts scripts from unproduced, unrepresented writers. Project types include Feature Films. Preferred genres include Action, Comedy, Crime, Drama,

Family, Fantasy, Horror, Non-Fiction, Romance, Science Fiction, and Thriller. Established in 1992.

Ib Tardini
Producer
Email: ib.tardini@filmbyen.com
IMDb: imdb.com/name/nm0850385

Lars von Trier
Managing Director (Co-Founder)
IMDb: imdb.com/name/nm0001885

Peter Aalbaek Jensen
Managing Director (Co-Founder)
IMDb: imdb.com/name/nm0421639

ZEPHYR FILMS

33 Percy St
London W1T 2DF
Phone: +44 207-255-3555
Fax: +44 207-255-3777

Email: info@zephyrfilms.co.uk
Home Page: zephyrfilms.co.uk

Accepts query letter from unproduced, unrepresented writers via email. Project types include Feature Films and TV. Preferred genres include Action, Animation, Comedy, Crime, Drama, Family, Fantasy, Horror, Romance, and Thriller.

Chris Curling
Producer
IMDb: imdb.com/name/nm0192770

Phil Robertson
Producer
IMDb: imdb.com/name/nm0731990

Luke Carey
Assistant Producer
IMDb: imdb.com/name/nm2294645

ZETA ENTERTAINMENT

3422 Rowena Ave
Los Angeles, CA 90027
Phone: (310) 595-0494

IMDb: imdb.com/company/co0037026

Does not accept any unsolicited material. Project types include Feature Films and TV. Preferred genres

include Action, Comedy, Crime, Drama, Family, Fantasy, Horror, and Thriller.

Zane Levitt
President
Email: zanewlevitt@gmail.com
IMDb: imdb.com/name/nm0506254

Lisa Jan Savy
Creative Executive
IMDb: imdb.com/name/nm2957586

ZIEGER PRODUCTIONS

Phone: 310-476-1679
Fax: 310-476-7928

IMDb: imdb.com/company/co0114742

Accepts query letter from unproduced, unrepresented writers.

Michele Zieger
Producer
IMDb: imdb.com/name/nm1024135

ZING PRODUCTIONS, INC.

220 S Van Ness Ave
Hollywood, CA 90004
Phone: (323) 466-9464

Home Page: zinghollywood.com

Does not accept any unsolicited material. Project types include Feature Films, Short Films, and TV. Preferred genres include Animation, Comedy, Drama, Family, Fantasy, Reality, and Romance.

Laura Black
Director Creative of Affairs
Email: laura@zinghollywood.com
IMDb: imdb.com/name/nm4549208

Rob Loos
President
IMDb: imdb.com/name/nm0519763

ZODIAK USA

520 Broadway Suite 500
Santa Monica, CA 90401
Phone: (310) 460-4490
Fax: (310) 460-4494

Email: contact@zodiakusa.com
Home Page: zodiakusa.com
IMDb: imdb.com/company/co0314564

Accepts query letter from unproduced, unrepresented writers via email. Project types include TV. Preferred genres include Animation, Comedy, Non-Fiction, Reality, and Romance.

Timothy Sullivan
Senior VP (Development)
Phone: (212) 488-1699
IMDb: imdb.com/name/nm2432438

Natalka Znak
CEO
IMDb: imdb.com/name/nm1273500

ZUCKER PRODUCTIONS

2401 Mandeville Canyon Rd
Los Angeles, CA 90049

Phone: 310-656-9202
Fax: 310-656-9220

IMDb: imdb.com/company/co0110404

Accepts query letter from unproduced, unrepresented writers. Project types include TV. Preferred genres include Comedy, Drama, Fantasy, Romance, and Thriller. Established in 1972.

Jerry Zucker
Producer
IMDb: imdb.com/name/nm0958387

Janet Zucker
Producer
IMDb: imdb.com/name/nm0958384

Farrell Ingle
Creative Executive
IMDb: imdb.com/name/nm3377346

Index by Company Name

Index of Company Websites

AGAMEMNON FILMS, INC., 35
agamemnon.com

AGILITY STUDIOS, 35
agilitystudios.com

AHIMSA MEDIA, 36
ahimsamedia.com

AKIL PRODUCTIONS, 36
akilproductions.com

ALCON ENTERTAINMENT, LLC, 37
alconent.com

ALDAMISA ENTERTAINMENT, 37
aldamisa.com

ALIANZA FILMS INTERNATIONAL LTD., 38
alianzafilms.com

A-LINE PICTURES, 38
a-linepictures.com

ALLAN MCKEOWN PRESENTS, 39
ampresents.tv

ALLENTOWN PRODUCTIONS, 39
allentownproductions.com

ALLIANCE FILMS, 39
alliancefilms.com

ALLOY ENTERTAINMENT, 39
alloyentertainment.com

ALOE ENTERTAINMENT, 39
aloeentertainment.com

AL ROKER PRODUCTIONS, 40
alrokerproductions.com

ALTA LOMA ENTERTAINMENT, 40
alta-loma.com

ALTURAS FILMS, 40
alturasfilms.com

A-MARK ENTERTAINMENT, 40
amarkentertainment.com

AMBASSADOR ENTERTAINMENT, 41
ambassadortv.com

AMBER ENTERTAINMENT, 41
amberentertainment.com

AMBUSH ENTERTAINMENT, 41
ambushentertainment.com

AMERICAN MOVING PICTURES, 41
americanmovingpictures.com

AMERICAN WORLD PICTURES, 42
americanworldpictures.com

AMERICAN ZOETROPE, 42
zoetrope.com

ANCHOR BAY FILMS, 43
anchorbayent.com

ANDREW LAUREN PRODUCTIONS, 43
andrewlaurenproductions.com

ANGELWORLD ENTERTAINMENT LTD., 43
angelworldentertainment.com

ANIMUS FILMS, 44
animusfilms.com

ANNAPURNA PICTURES, 44
annapurnapics.com

AN OLIVE BRANCH PRODUCTIONS, INC., 44
anolivebranchmedia.com

ANONYMOUS CONTENT, 45
anonymouscontent.com

ANTIDOTE FILMS, 45
antidotefilms.com

APPLESEED ENTERTAINMENT, 46
appleseedent.com

ARC LIGHT FILMS, 46
arclightfilms.com

ARENAS ENTERTAINMENT, 47
arenasgroup.com

ARGONAUT PICTURES, 47
argonautpictures.com

ARIESCOPE PICTURES, 47
ariescope.com

ARS NOVA, 47
arsnovaent.com

ARTFIRE FILMS, 48
artfirefilms.com

ARTICLE 19 FILMS, 48
article19films.com

ARTISTS PUBLIC DOMAIN, 48
artistspublicdomain.com

A. SMITH & COMPANY PRODUCTIONS, 48
asmithco.com

ASYLUM ENTERTAINMENT, 49
asylument.com

ATLAS MEDIA CORPORATION, 49
atlasmediacorp.com

AUTOMATIC PICTURES, 50
automaticpictures.net

Index by Contact Name

Savitch, Annette, 130
Savjani, Anish, 110
Saxon, Ed, 97
Sayler, Joeanna, 54
Scalese, Rudy, 173
Schaeffer, Paul, 159
Schamus, James, 112
Scharbo, Grant, 155
Schechter, Dan, 203
Schechter-Garcia, Ivana, 71
Schefter, Andy, 221
Scheinkman, Dan, 234
Scheinman, Andrew, 69
Scherma, Frank, 197
Schiff, Devon, 170
Schipper, Marc, 130
Schlamme, Thomas, 215
Schlessel, Peter, 109
Schmidt, Tore, 195
Schmidt, Aaron, 150
Schneeweiss, Barbara, 237
Schneider, Steven, 207
Schnider, Daniel, 82
Schoof, Aimee, 200
Schornak, Brian, 178
Schorr, Robin, 199
Schrader, Wes, 83
Schreiber, Nina, 228
Schreiber, Michael, 229
Schumacher, Joel, 144
Schur, Jordan, 168
Schwartz, Richard, 179
Schwartz, Robert, 213
Schwartz, Loren, 212
Schwartz, Rick, 183
Schwartz, Lizzie, 172
Schwartz, Paula Mae, 72
Schwartz, John, 196
Schwartz, Jonathan, 81
Schwartz, Roger, 72
Schwartz, Steve, 72
Schwarzman, Teddy, 59
Schwatz, Josh, 107
Sciavicco, Jason, 135
Scorsese, Martin, 217
Scott, Ridley, 211
Scott, Benjamin, 96
Scott, Nicholas, 29
Scott, Andy, 70
Seagal, Steven, 223
Segal, Peter, 66

Segan, Lloyd, 190
Seifert-Speck, Anna, 101
Selbert, Fred, 115
Selby, Jack, 137
Sellers, Dylan, 247
Sellers, Dylan, 246
Senderoff, Shara, 235
Serra, Jaume, 180
Sertner, Robert, 32
Seymour, Jane, 189
Seyyid, Jubba, 243
Shader, Josh, 231
Shaffner, Tyrrell, 117
Shah, Anand, 109
Shah, Ash, 218
Shainberg, Steven, 253
Shamberg, Michael, 93
Shanahan, Isabel, 236
Shane, Michel, 130
Shane, Rachel, 201
Shankman, Adam, 179
Shannon, Cathy, 197
Shapiro, James Emanuel, 93
Shapiro, Leonard, 96
Share Zaks, Jillan, 153
Sharma, Neetu, 250
Shaw, Tony, 68
Sheehan, Anita, 193
Sheehan, Vincent, 193
Sheehan, Trace, 194
Sheehy, Ginger, 257
Sheehy, Ginger, 257
Shenkler, Craig, 224
Shepard, Sarah, 258
Shephard, Greer, 236
Shepherd, Scott, 190
Shepherd, John, 81
Sheppard, Janet, 186
Sher, Stacey, 93
Sherman, Sidney, 208
Shestack, Jonathan, 145
Shetty, Pavun, 71
Shieh, Aimee, 111
Shikiar, Dave, 212
Shore, Martin, 221
Short, Trevor, 168
Shub, Alex, 69
Shukla, Ameet, 93
Shuler Donner, Lauren, 92
Shulman, Michael, 223
Shultz, Steve, 34

Index by Submission Policy

Accepts query letter from produced or represented writers

Accepts query letter from unproduced, unrepresented writers

Accepts query letter from unproduced, unrepresented writers via email

Accepts scripts from produced or represented writers

Accepts scripts from unproduced, unrepresented writers

Accepts scripts from unproduced, unrepresented writers via email

Does not accept any unsolicited material